MusicScapes of Scotland

Vignettes from pre-history to pandemic

by Edward Scott Pearlman

Front cover photo/design: Edward Pearlman, sunset in Skye (fiddler silhouette inspired by an album cover, see p. 214)

Back cover photos:

Upper photos, clockwise from lower left: Arthur Cormack, Simon Thoumire, Eddi Reader, Gordon Duncan (photo: David Harrold), Julie Fowlis, Capercaillie (photo: Leila Angus), Màiri Mhòr, Cilla Fisher & Artie Trezise (photo: John Young), Aly Bain & Phil Cunningham, Fiona Ritchie, Ian Green, Anna Massie (photo: Alistair Cassidy), Iain MacFarlane & Ingrid Henderson, Tony Cuffe, David Francis, Sandy Brechin (photo: Ró Ó hEadhra)

Lower photos, from left: Blazin' Fiddles, Celtic Connections Festival concert, Luxembourg Pipe Band (photo: Diane Neises)

Paddledoo Books ISBN 979-8-9852104-0-8
P.O. Box 15002, Portland ME 04112 USA

CONTENTS

Section Four: Instrumentalists (cont'd.)

Fiddle

Bagpipes

Accordion

Section Five: Regional Music

INTRODUCTION

Join me on a journey through a music and culture that is in some ways still uncharted territory. The chapters are arranged into eight sections so that you can enjoy reading cover to cover, but you may well prefer to dip into any chapter at random; each can stand on its own.

You'll learn about ancient songs and instruments, and new music on the verge of breaking out. We'll dig beneath the veneer of stereotypes and find the pulse that brings it all to life.

The music of Scotland is rich and varied, influential in western folk and classical music, and yet relatively little examined in its own right. The stories in this book will be your tour guide to many nooks and crannies of an amazing musical landscape.

Drawn from twenty-four years of columns and articles in *Scottish Life* magazine, each chapter focuses on one facet of Scottish music while offering a bird's eye view of the broader context. We'll examine a panorama of musical styles, songs in Gaelic, Scots, and English and music of the pipes, fiddle, harp and other instruments. We'll tune in to music of Scots music abroad, pay tribute to those who make it all happen, and glimpse the future of traditional music.

The vignettes you'll encounter in this book include research as well as personal experiences from listening, traveling, performing, and interviews of key personalities in Scottish music.

Scotland, being a part of the U.K., is often presumed to be a well-trodden path, but too many observers, including some academics, have viewed its culture as laboring in the shadows of England or Ireland. Meanwhile, the Scots themselves have never inclined toward self-promotion. As a result, many aspects of Scottish culture are well developed but not broadly appreciated or understood.

BBC Radio Scotland once established a program which was to cover the history of Scotland's music in 26 half-hour segments. Much to their surprise, they ended up airing more than four times as much material without exhausting their sources.

The music of Scotland appeals to all listeners, regardless of background. Once upon a time, this kind of music was considered "ethnic" music, of interest only to local communities and experts. Then people began to think of it as "roots" music, suitable primarily for those who have Scottish heritage. More recently, the term "world music" has come into vogue, underlining the awareness that quality music with a coherent cultural backbone can enrich all of us, regardless of origin.

Personally, I find Scottish music captivating thanks to its melodies, rhythms and cultural context. I never tire of hearing it or playing it, whether for listening or dancing. My family's connection to Scottish heritage has played only a small role in my journey as a fiddler, teacher, writer, judge, organizer and distributor.

If you have no Scottish heritage, how can you feel passionate about this music and culture? Perhaps the most amusing and thought-provoking answer can be found in an anecdote about Handel, the great German composer who lived in London. One day, after Handel had premiered a piece written in honor of an English military victory over the Prussians, an angry Londoner approached him and demanded to know how Handel, a Prussian, dared write music for the English king. Handel replied simply, "I, sir, am English by choice. You, sir, are English by accident."

We can all be "Scots by choice" to the degree that we value and learn from the beauty of Scottish music and culture. The Scots themselves, and those whose roots are Scottish, are entitled to go one step further: they can take pride in it. And hopefully, they will also make sure to keep it alive and well. Fortunately, signs are pointing in the right direction, as you will see in this book. Enjoy the journey!

– Edward Scott Pearlman
  Maine, USA, July 2021

Thank Yous

Special thanks to Neill Kennedy Ray, editor and publisher of *Scottish Life* magazine, and my wife Laura Scott, for carefully reading through my drafts over the years, and for their support and patience at deadline times!

About Dates

The publication date below each chapter title is irrelevant to many chapters, such as those discussing an 8,000 year old song, the first harp or bagpipes, an 18th century fiddler and his family, or the bands, events, and individuals that made today's vibrant music scene possible. The date can add a certain poignancy, though, when speaking of special moments at the time they took place – a musician's last concert, the first appearance of a now-famous band, the stirring opening of the Parliament.

It's good to keep in mind, as you read, that any mention of a "recent" or "upcoming" CD release or event is tied to the publication date of that chapter. Be sure to look up the latest news and discographies of any artists that interest you.

About The Author

Edward Scott Pearlman has played music since 1958 but has been immersed in Scottish music since 1979, when he began a career of playing Scottish fiddle for listening and dancing, including Scottish country, ceilidh, Highland, and Cape Breton step dance.

He wrote the music column for *Scottish Life* magazine from 1996 to 2020, has co-led music and walking tours of Scotland, distributed recordings from Scotland and Atlantic Canada to stores throughout the U.S., and created fiddle-online.com to allow people to learn and improve their fiddling through access to online materials and live online workshops by Ed and guest instructors.

Ed co-founded the Boston Scottish Fiddle Club in 1981 and directed it for 18 years, helping members on all instruments learn and play Scottish fiddle music. He worked with the Cape Breton community, hosted concerts and workshops by great fiddlers from Scotland and Cape Breton, and generally fostered a community of musicians and listeners. Events presented by Ed included regular workshops, sessions, tours, an annual Scottish Fiddle Rally (of which there is a Highlights CD), and the Celtic Festival at the Hatch Shell in Boston, featuring top Scottish, Irish, and Cape Breton musicians and dancers.

With his son, the innovative pianist Neil Pearlman, Ed has toured widely and made several albums (paddledoo.com). His daughter Lillie, an excellent fiddler, joined them to form a trio called HST (Highland Soles Trio), which performed in the U.S. and Scotland and made an EP.

Laura Scott, Ed's wife, is a creative and accomplished Highland dancer who has explored the artistry of Highland dance, Highland folk dance and Cape Breton stepdance for many decades. Together they have performed, directed theatrical shows, and hosted ceilidhs. Their family band Highland Soles (at least until their three children grew up!) presented traditional and original music and dance rooted in Scottish traditions. Their *Pine Street Collection* tunebook includes 40 years of music written by family members, particularly Ed, Neil and Lillie, with a story and audio for each tune.

Ed has taught fiddle extensively, both privately and in workshops, and organized, played and taught Scottish music at many camps, including Ohio Scottish Arts School, Pinewoods, Ashokan, Maine Fiddle Camp, Blazin' in Beauly, and Swannanoa. He composed and performed music for several plays, including Shakespeare's Macbeth (the "Scottish play"), and has served as a judge for many local and national Scottish fiddle competitions in the U.S. Ed has written well over 100 essays for a music teacher's site and a similar number for the fiddle-online.com blog, as well as articles for *Fiddler* magazine. In life beyond Scottish music, he also enjoys listening to and playing other styles of music, and has published several novels.

SECTION ONE
History and Culture

Stone of Scone – a
musical instrument?

18th century
Scottish dancers

Niel Gow

Dertha
(Lady Dorothea
Stewart-Murray)

Hector Macdonald

ABOUT SECTION ONE
History and Culture

Open a chapter and a new "musicscape" will unfold. It might be a broad vista stretching into the distant past, or a more focused snapshot of a musician or a concept. For example, what makes Scottish music sounds Scottish? Several masters of music and dance share their views.

Did you know a song exists that describes the Outer Hebrides as they were just after the Ice Age? Or that ancient Scots played rock music? (Literally – rock gongs discovered by musical archaeologists!)

How can such a vibrant culture be distilled into one CD? It can't, really, but we'll take a look at one CD that does a pretty good job.

Which came first, music or dance? It's a chicken and egg question, really, but it's worth getting to know the traditional dance music that keeps Scots fit and energetic.

The strathspey is unique to Scottish tradition and essential to much of its music, dance, and song, but what is it, exactly? Let's find out.

One of Scotland's legendary fiddlers and composers was the head of a great musical family. We'll get a taste of 18th century culture by visiting Niel Gow, whose patrons were the 3d, 4th, and 5th Dukes of Atholl. A few generations later, the eldest daughter of the 7th Duke became an avid collector of Scottish traditional music. She even snatched Scotland's oldest bagpipe manuscript out of a fire.

The national tragedy of a Victorian Scottish military hero's suicide was transformed within days into one of Scotland's most famous laments by J.S. Skinner. The story behind that tune colors and enriches the hearing or playing of that popular tune.

You have no doubt heard of "Celtic music" but how does Scottish music fit into that generic description?

Honing in on a musical treasure within the bigger picture, we'll learn about one Scottish family that has had a strong impact on traditional, classical and jazz music.

We'll wrap up this section the way the year ends, with a look at Christmas and children's music. Though the Scottish church's theology did not acknowledge Christmas until relatively recently, there are many Scottish tunes, songs and recordings that celebrate the season.

1 ~ Heart of Scottish
fall 2005

I'd played the tune countless times before, but this time it was for Highland dancing. "Get rid of that grace note!" she said. No grace note? I had thought the grace notes were part of what made it sound Scottish.

But no, she didn't want the tune to start "bim b-dee." She wanted "bim pow!" She was placing a kick on that second "syllable" of the music and didn't want it weakened by a grace note.

The heart of Scottish music, I was to learn, is not governed by fancy grace notes, bowings, or syncopations. Rather, these are decorations at the service of what truly makes Scottish music unique — the heartbeat, the timing, the way the music breathes.

Interestingly, all of the artists I interviewed for this column came to the same conclusion, in their own ways, even though they represent very different Scottish arts: piping, fiddling, and dancing.

Perhaps it's not surprising, then, that my greatest teacher in Scottish fiddling, unbeknownst to her, has probably been a Highland dancer — Laura Scott, my wife. Her knowledge, in turn, is a tribute to her dance teacher from Scotland, Vera Miller Patterson. Vera passed away this spring, bringing to a close a long career in which she not only inspired dance students with a lifelong appreciation for the artistry of Highland dancing, but also taught many pipers the art of playing for dancing. Vera proudly traced her family to the piping Mackinnons of Skye.

Ray Scott, a dance piper and pipe major in Virginia, recalls how Vera would work with him for an hour and a half at a time, teaching him how to find the right tunes for dancing, and how to play tunes so that they pump life into the dancer. "The embellishments can make a tune sparkle but should never make the tune lose its pulse," says Scott. Vera showed him how some strathspeys can lift a dancer off the floor while others push them down into it. That lift seems to come from the pulse of the tune and the holding of the right notes.

"In piping," says piping judge and former Toronto pipe major Reay MacKay, "you can't increase or decrease the volume, so the only way you can interpret a piece of music and make it sound good is by extending or shortening a note. And it's most important in Scottish music how long those notes are held. Particularly in strathspeys and particularly in 2/4 marches."

Exactly how long those notes are held is the magic of Scottish music. MacKay describes it as being "on the edge of the beat." It is comparable to the difference between feeling the pulse in your wrist versus clapping your hands. Good music has a pulse, not just a beat. After seeing a video of Laura Scott dance a Highland Fling, stretching each beat, MacKay recognized the effect immediately. "Pipers do this all the time," he says. "Exactly the same thing. And that's what gives them that nice lift out of strathspeys. Well, you do the same thing with the fiddle. You're playing on the edge of the beat all the time."

But perhaps "holding" a note is not the best description. "We didn't hold; we extended," says Hugh Bigney. Hugh, one of Vera Miller Patterson's most illustrious students, was the first American to win the adult World Championships in Highland dancing. A hold, Hugh points out, is static. What is really being done is to extend, to breathe out, to suspend until you can't suspend any more within that beat. Then comes a rebound action. This suspension and rebound is a powerful ingredient not only in the dancing but in all good Scottish music.

Laura echoes these ideas about holds, whether in dance or music, also speaking in terms of breathing out rather than merely holding a beat. "The impression is a breathless moment of lightness," she says, "but it is within the context of a very grounded beat. Without weight, lightness is flimsy. Without absolute connection to the pulse of a tune, extending or holding is meaningless."

The same could be said about the use of a violin bow; after all, playing a musical instrument is a physical activity not so far removed from dancing. Fiddler Alasdair Fraser puts it this way: "There are certain beautiful things that I love that attracted me to this music. There are ways of entering and leaving notes, ways of spending time during notes, that are very informed." He speaks of the midpoint of a strathspey, where there can be "a little holding back and letting go again, and that just sends a shiver down my spine if I hear a fiddle player do that — or if he puts in a little hold-back and release in a reel. It goes deep into me; I know this guy's done his homework, and it's speaking to me in a way that is profound."

Fraser loves to see people experiment with music but feels that at some point, every player who cares about Scottish music needs to do some "homework" and find out more about the wellspring, the source of the music, which gave birth to it and renews it. He worries that not enough people will try to understand this wellspring "and then it's up for redefining." The integrity and diversity of the music could be lost or diverted.

Where can we find the wellspring of it all? Bigney would say it is in the living tradition passed along from teacher to student, generation to generation. He views great teachers as bearers of hidden knowledge that is only available to those who are ready for it. We often only hear what we can understand. A good teacher may either repeat ideas until we grasp them, or withhold the information until we are ready to receive it.

Verbalizing the artistry of Scottish music and dance is extremely difficult, and raises a question as to whether anyone can learn these ideas from a book, or from a single workshop, or even a few lessons. Patterson taught dancing by singing, in much the same way many piping instructors teach by singing Canntaireachd — specific syllables that represent rhythms and melodic shapes. Laura even recalls her teacher, at 80 years old, telling her over the phone, "Don't forget, Laura—" and rather than use words, she sang a phrase of a tune to make her point.

Highland Games competitions seek to foster an ongoing appreciation for tradition and clearly provide an important means of promoting it. Yet for some, these events are primarily about techniques for winning. This, of course, raises the cultural concern that if too many technical winners become teachers, who will pass along the artistry at the heart of Scottish music and dance? Who will aim for the kind of artistry that inspires Laura Scott to regard Highland dancing as worthy of study and performance for many decades beyond the competitive years?

It is clearly not enough to read dancing or music books. A dance musician playing Scottish music as written might as well hand a CD to a dancer and say, "Here are your notes, now use them." The magic is in the interaction. As Bigney says, it is the uneven notes and holds of Scottish music that challenge the dancer (as well as the listener and other musicians) to hear the phrasing of a tune and understand its story. It's an unevenness much like the ba-boom of a heartbeat, or the breathing of a person feeling emotions.

I think back to the way my dancing wife revised my playing of that reel, or the way my playing of a tune shifted the movements she used when dancing to it, and it reminds me that the heart of Scottish music is in that interactive timing. Whether on pipes, fiddle, voice, or represented in the movement of a dancer, Scottish music challenges us to listen more carefully than we ever expected.

We can almost hear ancient voices, passing through the teachers around us, telling us, as Bigney put it, "the breath of music and the phrasing of the dance come from the same source."

2 ~ Scotland's Music 1: Overview
spring 2005

Scotland's music, like its people, is the product of millennia of history. The oldest known musical instrument in Scotland is a piece of a metal horn from about 2800 years ago, during the Bronze Age, when the Celts first settled in the land. Later Pictish stone carvings in Ross-shire reveal the earliest images of the triangular harp, which we call the Celtic harp. Its triangular shape allowed it to handle the pressure of many more strings than the rectangular lyre.

Songs no doubt predated these instruments. The Gaelic word for music, ceol, means bird song, and some old Gaelic songs sound much like bird calls, both in melody and in the sound of the syllables. There are old fiddle tunes, particularly noticeable in the oldest Shetland music, that sound very much like imitations of birds.

One song appears to be 8,000 years old. It survives as a poem written down in 1870 following what was called a recitation, though Gaelic poems were generally sung. The poem describes the Outer Hebrides as a single island, and speaks of nuts being gathered in South Uist. This was regarded as preposterous until recent scientists determined that after the last glaciers of the Ice Age, these islands were indeed joined together. Nuts have been uncovered beneath the peat, just above the glacial rock layer.

In recent years, much has been learned about the history of Scottish music, from the misty beginnings to the diverse and vibrant musical expression of the past few hundred years. Unfortunately, this information is mostly scattered in a variety of sources, with many gaps in our knowledge just waiting for someone to explore further. In addition, a number of useful surveys of the subject have gone out of print.

One such book was *Scotland's Music,* by John Purser, one of Scotland's foremost music historians. He is also a composer, conductor, playwright, and cellist, but is perhaps best known in Scotland as a broadcaster. It was Purser's award-winning BBC broadcast about the history of Scottish music that formed the basis for the book in 1992.

A perfect coffee-table book, *Scotland's Music* was large, readable, and full of musical samples, illustrations and color plates. Purser intends to revise and rewrite the book, and has already begun that work. [See the next chapter about the second edition.]

In the mean time, the double CD that accompanied the book is still available from Linn Records. It begins with 9th century bells and includes pre-Christian Gaelic songs which sound similar to what we think of today as traditional Scottish music. There are also a number of selections of church music on the CD. One of these was written in the 16th century by Robert Carver, whom Purser regards as Scotland's greatest composer. In this piece, entitled "O Bone Jesu", Carver manages to weave together 19 separate vocal lines into a complex and moving texture. It may have been written for the funeral of King James III, and could well have served James IV as a kind of penance, for he led the rebellion that resulted in the murder of his father.

Music and history are often intertwined. One selection on the CD is the tune originally played by the carillonneur at Edinburgh's St. Giles church in 1707, on the very day the Treaty of Union between England and Scotland was signed. The title made its own statement: "Why Should I Be So Sad On My Wedding Day?"

Although the radio broadcast and the book included a significant amount of interesting material on bagpipe music, traditional songs, songwriters such as Robert Burns, and instrumentalists, the CD focuses primarily on the classical. Most people do not associate classical music very closely with Scotland, and yet its classical tradition has been ongoing, and has at times fed into the robust traditional music as well.

Purser champions not only Renaissance composer Robert Carver, but also several other key Scottish classical composers. One is James Oswald, who lived through both Jacobite rebellions, published many volumes of

Scottish folk music and was a dancing master, but also wrote 96 violin sonatas, sometimes using Scottish folk melodies as themes. Robert Burns used several of his melodies for songs, and Oswald's masonic anthems may well have found their way to the ears of the most famous of masonic composers of his time, Mozart.

Another Scottish masonic composer (Grand Master Mason of both the Scottish and English lodges, no less) was Thomas Erskine, 6th Earl of Kelly. He was a Scottish fiddler at home but studied composition in Germany and wrote some fine orchestral works similar to his contemporary, Haydn. The Earl died in 1781 at the age of 49. A short, bright symphony of his can be heard on the double CD. In addition, a new CD of works by the Earl of Kelly is being released in spring 2005 by Linn Records.

John Thomson, who lived only to age 36, was a fine Scottish composer whose work was admired by a well-known friend of his on the continent, Felix Mendelssohn. Several works by composer Hamish MacCunn (1868-1916) are included on the Scotland's Music double CD, as well as a piece by the prominent Sir Alexander Campbell MacKenzie (1847-1935).

Author John Purser was classically trained but says he has picked up a love of Scottish traditional music, partly through his research for the radio show and book. In his work, he kept an open mind as he sought any and all music that had something to say about Scotland and its cultural history. He discovered that virtually all the music he came across was quite good.

Now living in Skye, he finds himself surrounded by the Gaelic language and music, and has come across much repertoire he didn't know about at the time of the radio show. Purser has also become something of a music archaeologist, investigating and reviving ancient instruments such as the carnyx, a horn of war from Roman times. His latest project is a biography of Scottish composer Erik Chisholm, who ended his days in Cape Town, South Africa in 1965. Chisholm wrote a number of exciting pieces which use the form and ornamentation of the bagpipe pibroch as a point of departure.

Purser says he is pleased with the book, *Scotland's Music,* and indeed won a literary award for it, but feels there is now a much fuller picture to paint, with more stories and more discoveries to reveal when the new edition comes out.

The radio show clearly changed Purser's life, inspired a number of musicians and researchers, and was a point of pride for many Scottish listeners. Originally, BBC had planned 26 thirty-minute historical segments. These were to be followed by one-hour radio concerts featuring, but not limited to, relevant Scottish music. The truth was, the planners of the show didn't think there would be enough Scottish music to fill the time!

The richness and diversity of Scotland's music surprised them. Not only was there enough music to go around, but John Purser ended up filling 30 ninety-minute programs with information and examples which proved not only educational but also entertaining and popular.

The music of Scotland is powerful, dramatic, and stirring; and as John Purser and BBC Scotland found out, the closer we examine it, the more facets we see. It lurks like a gem in the shadows, waiting to be polished.

3 ~ *Scotland's Music 2: Neolithic to WWI*
spring 2009

From ancient musical rock gongs to Robert Burns songs, from battle harps to burgeoning folk festivals, music has always been woven into Scottish life. The second edition of John Purser's book, *Scotland's Music*, based on a BBC radio series of the same name, provides a captivating overview of Scottish music through the ages.

The original book and radio series came out in 1992, and achieved unexpected popularity. At first, BBC had planned 26 half-hour radio segments, but the discovery of so much rich material pushed them to expand the show to 30 ninety-minute programs. Ratings soared, and the book won several prominent awards. The book sold out, and remained out of print for some time, though it clearly retained its appeal — at one point a used copy of it cost £200 on eBay!

Fortunately, the second edition is available for far less. This colorful 9x12 book is one-third longer than the original edition, with over 100 illustrations (a third of them in color), and over 250 musical examples, plus the bibliography and discography. While the original edition remains accurate, Purser says that a wealth of new material discovered, revived, or recorded since 1992 allowed for many new additions.

A new version of Purser's radio show aired throughout 2007 in 52 weekly shows, and audio clips can still be heard on BBC's website. A double-CD with audio tracks from the original edition is available for download from Linn Records, and Purser recommends using his discography and internet searches as well, since the quantity of good recordings of Scottish music is probably a hundredfold greater since the first book came out. In fact, many new performances were recorded specifically for the radio show, including world premieres of some Scottish compositions.

In contemplating the history of Scotland's music, Purser deliberately embraces both the classical and traditional music, noting that "they have been inseparable in our history and I hope they will remain so."

In the earliest times, the inhabitants of today's Scotland made music with natural stone whistles, modified bull horns, and rocks that emit a musical sound when hit the right way. One such rock sounds like the crying of a baby (especially at midnight on Halloween, according to neighborhood children!). It is said by some that the Stone of Destiny, upon which Scottish kings were crowned, was a rock gong which could be played at coronations.

The oldest evidence of Scotland's musical history has been found in these ancient instruments and in stone carvings, such as the world's first depictions of triangular harps by the Picts, whose extra strings may have led to the greater sophistication of medieval Scottish music as compared with that of the continent. Purser's "musical archaeology" has also found evidence in writings, illustrations, written music and recordings.

The folk tradition, passed from generation to generation, provides its own kind of documentation. The "folk process" can involve changes and improvisations, but family histories and historical songs were often kept rigorously consistent. One Gaelic pibroch song some 500 lines long was composed by an illiterate Gaelic forester who later found someone to write it down for him. A poem performed in 1870 described the Outer Hebrides as a single long island with a climate warm enough for the gathering of nuts. According to scientists, this description of the Outer Hebrides was once in fact true, but not since the end of the Ice Age! Was this song passed down through hundreds of generations? Who knows how many songs and melodies have been retained for centuries or even millennia?

Purser's book places the music of Scotland into its cultural context through the telling of many tales. We read about the early Celtic church and its independent ways and sophisticated music. The Hymn to St Magnus, for example, was ahead of its time for medieval church music. Magnus was a former pirate who helped his cousin run the church in

Orkney until he was murdered and later canonized (in itself a story and a half!). The hymn in his honor is full of musical thirds at a time when European church music was generally limited to fourths and fifths. (For those unfamiliar with musical intervals, you can hear a "third" if you hold down one white key on a piano, skip over the next white key, and hold down the third white key at the same time as the first. A "fourth" can be heard by holding down the fourth key along with the first key, and so on.)

We learn of harps being used at the Battle of Harlaw in 1411. Since the first mention of bagpipes in Scotland can be traced to 1508, it may be that harpers were the ones who played "Hei Tuti Tati" at the Battle of Bannockburn in 1314; the song's original words satirized the English. Brought by Scottish archers to France, "Hei Tuti Tati" was apparently played as Joan of Arc entered Orleans in 1429. More than three centuries later, Robert Burns used the same melody for his song "Scots Wha Hae."

In the 16th century, Mary Queen of Scots was greeted in Edinburgh by several hundred people playing fiddles and singing psalms. John Knox certainly appreciated the Scots psalms, which were new at the time, but was aghast at Mary's penchant for dancing, and coldly pleased at the brutal murder of the Queen's paramour, fiddler David Riccio.

The book contains many stories about Scottish composers, such as the 17th century musician Robert Carver. Purser compares the construction of Carver's music to sophisticated medieval church architecture. One of his pieces begins with two voices and grows into nineteen separate musical lines sung by a choir at the same time. So begins "O Bone Jesu", a motet written for the funeral of King James III. It was apparently commissioned by King James IV, who had led the rebellion that resulted in the murder of his father.

In the 18th century, orchestras from New York to St Petersburg performed classical Scottish compositions by Thomas Erskine, 6th Earl of Kelly (Kellie). In London, his "Maid of the Mill" served as the overture to a hit comedy, and may well have been heard by Mozart, who was visiting London with his family. Of course, Mozart was only 6 years old at the time, but probably absorbed every note of music he came across.

A few years later, in 1780, the Earl of Kelly's compositions are said to have heavily influenced the writing of a symphony by Johann Christian Bach.

Not long after that, we come across a groundbreaking musical project conducted by Robert Burns, who avidly collected traditional Scottish melodies for the six-volume *Scots Musical Museum*. Many of the melodies were preserved because Burns wrote words to them. Purser's book delights in many details about Burns and other aspects of the vibrant cultural scene of the Scottish Enlightenment.

The book explores Scottish music into the 20th century, from Harry Lauder to Glasgow rock music. On a personal note, John Purser describes the discovery of 20th century Scottish composer Cecil Coles as perhaps his most moving experience in making the radio show and writing the book. Penny Coles, Cecil's daughter, had been only a baby when her father was killed in World War I, and because the family split up after the war, the first she ever heard about her father was the dying words of her brother. Coles's music was, as Purser puts it, a "hair's breadth" away from being lost to history.

As he uncovered the story, Purser learned that Cecil Coles had written music at an early age, studied in Edinburgh, and won a scholarship to the London College of Music — but only because he read about the scholarship competition on a piece of newspaper that had been used to wrap a pair of shoes. Coles ended up writing many compositions, and during the war, he managed to attend gramophone concerts run by the medical officer. His last composition, "Behind the Lines," was found on his body in the battlefield. It was marked "Feb 4th 1918, In the Field." Thanks to his daughter Penny, the BBC, and Purser's radio show, some of Coles's music has now been published and recorded.

Scotland's Music embraces an epic panorama of Scottish music history, from the earliest stone age musicians to the latest folk and rock bands. Even a brief dip into this book will reveal the fertile ground that nourishes Scotland's vibrant musical culture.

4 ~ Rough Guide
fall 2003

Suppose your local newspaper allowed you a few paragraphs to describe your family tree. What to say? What to leave out? What impression would you want to give?

The family tree of Scottish music is complex, so a single CD purporting to represent — in just one hour — all its many branches, musicians, bands, songs, and tunes, is certainly ambitious, and likely to be misleading. Yet such a compilation CD can be great listening, and can serve as a convenient way to learn about Scottish music.

One recent introductory CD is the *Rough Guide to Scottish Music, Second Edition*. The complete Rough Guide CD collection spans nearly every type of music in the world, and includes two previous offerings of Scottish music, which are quite good: the First Edition, from 1996, and the *Rough Guide to Scottish Folk*.

The Second Edition of the *Rough Guide to Scottish Music* was released in spring 2003. A fine window on the music and a good listening experience, this album tells much about the state of Scottish music today.

The CD starts off with the Battlefield Band, at 30 years perhaps the oldest Scottish concert band. Guitar and fiddle usher us through a Gaelic song melody, accelerating gradually until the band breaks loose into a sunny reel on bagpipes. It is typical of the drama of Scottish music to begin on the slower side and then let go with upbeat tunes. Often this effect is accomplished using the sustained tension of the "strathspey," a uniquely Scottish rhythmic tune, followed up by joyous reels.

The second track of the album offers a beautiful complement to the breathless reels. Young Emily Smith, winner of the 2002 BBC Radio Scotland Young Musician Award, sings in a fresh, clear voice, about love, loss, retribution and grief. She sings the traditional words using her own original pleasant and compelling melody.

Next we move to a quiet instrumental selection performed by Finlay MacDonald. An exciting young piper, on this album he takes a moment away from his bagpipes to play a reflective air on the low whistle.

The Deaf Shepherd band follows with double bagpipes and double fiddles. Rooted in traditional music and instrumentation, this band has never dodged the challenge of presenting its music in fresh and energetic ways.

From Deaf Shepherd we move effortlessly into the sultry music of the popular world/Gaelic band, Capercaillie. The musky voice of Karen Matheson nurses the rhythmic syllables of Gaelic over a quiet rhythmic texture, then breaks into a stronger sound for the chorus, adding backup voices, accordion, fiddle, uilleann pipes, and hand percussion.

The album includes several other Gaelic songs. One is sung by Christine Primrose, of the Isle of Lewis, backed by harp and flute. A medley of Gaelic songs is also offered by the "Gaelic supergroup" Cliar, featuring the smooth voice of Arthur Cormack with singers Maggie MacDonald and Mary Ann Kennedy, backed by Bruce MacGregor on fiddle and the sparkling, syncopated harp playing of Ingrid Henderson.

Some compilation CDs can sound patched together, but each selection of this one flows well into the next. Credit for this is due to the compiler, Pete Heywood, who is well versed in Scottish music, being the editor of Scotland's folk music magazine, *Living Tradition*.

All the performances are contemporary except for one 1973 archive recording by the late Borders fiddler Bob Hobkirk, who passed away last year. He plays a bold, clear rendition of "Gow's Lament for the Death of His Second Wife," an 18th century air that is a cherished part of the Scottish fiddle repertoire. Hobkirk is quite expressive without overdoing the sentimentality.

Played once, the Gow air hardly lingers long enough to slow the album down. It is followed by a strathspey and two polka-type reels from Orkney, played by Jennifer and Hazel Wrigley. Their spacious playing has a relaxed feeling, almost more settled than the slow air on the previous track. The two tracks flow well together, presenting a traditional air, strathspey, and reel in the same key.

Unfortunately, this is the only strathspey on the album, even though the strathspey is at the heart of much of Scottish music. This may have been an unintended oversight by Heywood, whose personal experience emphasizes the song and ballad tradition. Although strathspeys are often used as song tunes ("Comin' Through the Rye" is a famous example), singers rarely convey the drama and drive of strathspeys and reels the way instrumentalists do.

But Heywood's experience led happily to the next selection, the deep, sonorous voice of Jack Beck, singing a classic love song, inviting a girl to a dance. He promises to dress her in finery and make her the "flower of them all," though he also hopes to "bless the bower where we spend the midnight hour." Beck's solo album is on Heywood's *Tradition Bearers* series, which preserves some of the best-respected contemporary folk singers of Scotland.

Though the album includes appearances by several bands, the spotlight is mostly on solo performers, reflecting Heywood's conviction that "the core tradition is more of a solo and personal art."

Robert Mathieson, pipe major of the world champion Shotts & Dykehead pipe band, is featured as a soloist, in a track taken from his album, *The Big Birl*. On that tour de force, Mathieson plays solo pipes accompanied in a completely different style on each track. The selection on the Rough Guide CD is lively and fun, played with a calypso sound, complete with steel drums.

The Boys of the Lough have presented Scottish and Irish music to concertgoers for many decades, and happily are represented here with a thoughtful, rich arrangement of two jigs, including the famous "Calliope House," written by the Boys' own Dave Richardson.

Heather Heywood, wife of Pete Heywood, is one of Scotland's best respected singers, particularly for her ballad singing. Together, the Heywoods have done much to share their expertise and love of Scottish song, a tradition sometimes overlooked by today's music industry. Here Heather sings the lilting song, "Logie o' Buchan."

One of the most unusual performances on the album features harmonica and guitar. Donald Black's harmonica sound is amazingly close to the Western Isles accordion sound of such players as Iain McLachlan. He plays pipe tunes on harmonica with unexpected clarity and emotion.

Two other fiddle tracks present very different sides of the tradition. One has a classical touch, with Pete Clark backed by a simple cello line on an air by 18th/19th century composer Nathaniel Gow. The other is the contemporary, hotter sound of Blazin' Fiddles. This band, based in the Highlands, presents five top solo fiddlers in various combinations and sometimes in rich harmony, with inventive guitar and piano backup.

No Scottish music CD would be complete without a traditional piper. This honor goes to the prizewinning piper, Pipe Sgt. Gordon Walker, who performs a brief air and a catchy hornpipe, without accompaniment.

The album's exploration of Scottish musical traditions is summed up in the final track, by the influential traditional singer, Alison McMorland. This song about the rowan tree seems to symbolize the strength of Scottish tradition, even as Scotland's vital musical community reinterprets its heritage again and again: "The rowan stands rockfast, strong and enduring, whatever the turn of the season may bring."

The family tree of Scottish music remains strong as it grows with new and sparkling individual performers. Difficult as it may be in the scope of a single recording, the new *Rough Guide to Scottish Music* manages admirably to offer an enjoyable and high-quality introduction to Scotland's musical traditions.

5 ~ Dance Music
summer 2016

Whether you're dancing, exercising, or cleaning the house, nothing will lift your spirits higher than Scottish dance music. For centuries it has served to get the blood going and the feet moving.

Back in the 18th century, music books such as the influential Gow Collection contained about 2/3 dance music and 1/3 listening music. Even some of the listening tunes were marked "Play slowly when not danced." Of the dance music, about 80% was presented in strathspey-reel (occasionally strathspey-jig) pairs. This indicates that most of the dancing in those days made use of the exciting tempo change from the slower, more intense strathspey into the quicker, more carefree reels. Still a hallmark of Scottish music, this transition is at the dramatic heart of bagpipe and fiddle competitions. Today's Scottish social dances rarely change tempos in that way, preferring to stay with one type of tune for each dance. Vestiges of the traditional strathspey-reel dance progression can be found primarily in solo and performance forms such as Cape Breton step or Highland, or in a fairly rare type of Scottish country dance called a "medley."

Although there are many types of Scottish social dancing, two are currently popular: ceilidh dancing and Scottish country dancing. Ceilidh dancing is the most common form within Scotland; the number of ceilidh bands outnumbers Scottish country dance bands by nearly four to one. Outside of Scotland, Scottish ceilidh dancing is little known except at festivals or Caledonian Societies. Most Scottish dance bands working outside of Scotland play for Scottish country dancing. This ballroom form of dance has been developed and promoted by the Royal Scottish Country

Dance Society (RSCDS) since the 1920s (the "Royal" was added in 1947). The RSCDS has about 300 branches in the U.K. and since opening its first overseas branch in Boston in 1950, has spread round the world with nearly 200 branches, primarily in continental Europe, the U.S., Canada, Australia and Japan.

Ceilidh dances are high-energy events, featuring round-the-room couples dances such as the Gay Gordons, Canadian Barn Dance, and Brittannia Two-Step. The Dashing White Sergeant makes use of two trios of dancers. The Eightsome Reel requires a quartet of couples, and Strip the Willow interweaves two long lines of dancers, with partner facing partner as the lead couple turns each other and everyone else down the line. One Strip the Willow included 1,914 dancers snaking down Princes Street in Edinburgh during Hogmanay celebrations over the New Year's holiday in 2000; it even made it into The Guinness Book of World Records.

At a ceilidh dance, the band plays lively marches, bouncy strathspeys, jigs and reels for as long as the dancers or musicians wish. At one dance I attended, the band went on long enough for some dancers to drop out for a cup of tea or something stronger and join back in again before it was over. Often a caller helps people through the dances or provides some instruction, as for example at the Edinburgh Ceilidh Club every Tuesday night. In some traditional village halls, dance bands may simply begin playing, and dancers will know what to do based on the tempo and type of tune.

East coast ceilidh bands are sometimes adventurous with their music. The Bella MacNabs, Robert Fish band, or the Sensational Jimi Shandrix Experience make use of some musicians who are also well-known concert performers. As long as the music is danceable and energetic, the dancers are excited to hear what they have to offer. Other bands are more traditional, such as those led by accordionist Bill Black or Gordon Pattullo.

The west Highland tradition of ceilidh music is a little more conservative but has plenty of energy, using pipe tunes and Gaelic repertoire. Bands led by "Ceilidh King" Fergie Macdonald, accordionist Bobby MacLeod, and Alasdair MacCuish come out of this tradition. One of my favorite bands from the Highlands is the Glenfinnan Ceilidh Band, which plays regularly at dances in the Glenfinnan House Hotel.

Scottish country dance music is much more demanding for its musicians than ceilidh dancing. The RSCDS has an extensive repertoire of dances, each with its own combination of geometric figures, and often a required tune for starting the dance. Musicians must adhere to strict tempos, and play between three and eight tunes of a specific length in a particular order. The discipline required for playing this kind of dance music limits the number of suitable musicians, many of whom specialize in this style. Some of Scotland's fifty Accordion and Fiddle Clubs host workshops to help hone the skills of dance band players.

Despite these challenges for musicians, Scottish country dance music is exuberant and irresistible for listeners and dancers alike. Good energy and a strong beat keep dancers moving all evening. The hallmark of a good Scottish country dance band is its "lift," an ability to lead strongly into the beats and often clip certain notes, providing both a strong beat and a light touch.

You can hear music for both ceilidh dancing and Scottish country dancing by listening to Robbie Shepherd's *Take the Floor* program on BBC Radio Scotland. It can be heard live or via online archives. Originally called simply *Scottish Dance Music* when it began in 1936, the show has featured Robbie Shepherd for over 30 years as Scotland's radio voice for dance music.

Shepherd often plays music by classic bands led by accordionists such as Sir Jimmy Shand and Jim Johnstone, or fiddlers Jim Cameron, Adam Rennie and Ian Powrie. Their bands usually comprised two accordions, fiddle, piano, bass, and drums, but sometimes included a clarinet or cornet. A CD called *Scottish Dance Band Greats* provides a nice sampling of top bands of the 1950s and 60s led by Andrew Rankine, Ian Powrie, Jim McLeod, and Jimmy Blair. Recorded live at dances during that era, the album has a clean, exciting sound. Another good compilation is *The Old Scottish Dance Bands vol 1 & 2*, which presents a different band on each track, recorded from the 1940s to the 1970s. Bandleaders on these two CDs include Jimmy Shand, Jim Johnstone, Ian Holmes, and Stan Hamilton.

Stan Hamilton was a well known Canadian pianist whose band, The Flying Scotsmen, was deservedly popular. Several of his long-term band members, including Bobby Brown and Bobby Frew, eventually formed their own successful RSCDS bands in Canada. All three of these musicians had originally immigrated from Scotland.

Piano is commonly used for both accompaniment and solo playing Scottish country dance classes and dances. One of the RSCDS's favorite pianists is Muriel Johnstone, whose recordings include solo albums as well as several with fiddler Alasdair Fraser.

In 1954, when pianist Stan Hamilton's band was unable to make it down from Canada to play at a dance in New Hampshire, a local accordion-led band called The White Cockade took up the challenge of becoming possibly the first U.S. band to play for Scottish country dancing. Other U.S. bands have followed, particularly since the 1970s, most of them fiddle-based, including Reel of Seven, Tullochgorum, Terpsichore, Boston Hospitality and Parcel of Rogues. Musicians from many parts of the world have learned the RSCDS style; for example, in recent years a number of RSCDS musicians from Japan have been invited to play for classes and dances at the RSCDS summer school in St Andrews, Scotland.

If you haven't tried ceilidh dancing or Scottish country dancing, you can easily find instruction at classes, dances, or nowadays, online. The basic moves are easy to learn.

But you don't even have to dance to enjoy Scottish dance music. It's simply energizing. Listen to it, and you'll bring its energy to anything you do, whether driving, washing dishes, or even reading a book about Scottish music!

6 ~ *Strathspeys*
fall 2018

At the heart of traditional Scottish music is the strathspey, a type of tune unique to Scotland. If you're not sure what a strathspey is, you're not alone. Even many professional musicians have a hard time describing strathspeys, and yet they are essential to Scottish music. They are common in songs, instrumental dance and listening music, and in bagpipe and fiddle competitions, where the march/strathspey/reel medley, or "MSR," is prevalent.

One of the most magical moments of Scottish traditional music is when a strathspey, with all its drive and tension, releases into an upbeat reel. Let's take a look at what this means and why it works so well. The question of why this is not found in other cultures will have to be left for others to explore.

The word is pronounced strath-SPEY because it means "valley of the River Spey," and the name of the river is emphasized. "Strath" is Gaelic for "valley," and there are many straths, such as Strathclyde (valley of the River Clyde), or Strathdon (valley of the River Don), with the second syllable always the strong one. The first use of the word "strathspey" in describing a tune appeared in mid-18th century publications of tunes by several fiddler/composers, including Angus Cumming, who lived in the Eastern Highlands. This is the area where the River Spey flows, east of Inverness, about halfway to Aberdeen. In the 18th century this was still a Gaelic-speaking area, and some say that the rhythms peculiar to strathspeys come from Gaelic language and song. However, there are also many Scots songs that have these rhythms as well, so it's difficult to be certain where they originated.

The hallmark of a strathspey song is its pattern of strong syllables or beats. Every other syllable is emphasized, as in "NOW'S the TIME, and

NOW'S the HOUR" (from "Scots Wha Hae"), or "GIN a BO-dy MEET a BO-dy" (from "Comin' Thro' the Rye" – note that "gin" is not the drink! It's Scots for "if" and is pronounced with a hard "g".). These are both Burns songs, and Robert Burns was especially tuned into musical rhythms when he wrote his lyrics. A quick way to get a feel for a strathspey is to tap your hand on a table twice per second, and match each of your taps to a strong syllable in these examples.

Each of these song excerpts feature four strong beats/syllables, a defining characteristic of strathspeys. In written music, these four strong beats are expressed as 4/4 time, a way of writing four beats per measure or bar (so called because measures are separated visually by vertical "bar lines").

Just for comparison, two types of tunes that are not strathspeys are jigs and reels. A jig rhythm divides each beat in three, as can be heard in the words "GO to the CAR," where there are three syllables before the second strong beat, "CAR," is spoken. A reel rhythm has four notes per beat, and can be heard in the words, "TAKE a little TRIP," which has four syllables before the strong syllable "TRIP" is pronounced.

Another type of song that is not a strathspey is a slow, romantic song such as "The Lea Rig." Every other syllable is emphasized in "I'll MEET thee ON the LEA...RIG" (the word "lea" is held twice as long as the others) but all the syllables are smooth and equal in time. In strathspeys, the syllables are always uneven, creating tension and drive even in the sweetest strathspey melody.

To understand the unevenness of the syllables in a strathspey, think of how boring it would be if we said or sang "Now's the time and now's the hour" with every syllable being equal to every other one. Instead, we sing "Now's...the time...and now's...the hour." This unevenness strengthens the beats and forces us to hear the four strong beats that define the strathspey for our ears and our dancing feet.

Why does this uneven rhythm strengthen those four beats? Imagine sitting in the audience of a darkened theater. A spotlight pops on, and an actor leaps into the light shouting "Ta-DAH!" But what if the actor leaped out and simply shouted "DAH!" It would be much weaker, and probably a bit confusing. Somehow the "Ta" before the "DA" prepares us for the "DA" and makes it much stronger than simply shouting "DAH!" Musicians will note that these uneven rhythms, also called "pointed" rhythms by pipers, or "dotted notes" by those aware of the written music, force us to hear four beats not only in a strathspey measure but also in other tunes, such as 4/4 hornpipes, though sometimes hornpipes are played in reel time, with two beats per measure, and without the dotted rhythms.

Strathspeys typically have two notes or syllables per beat, a long one followed by a short one leading to the next beat. Sometimes the short syllable is spoken on the beat, as when we pronounce the word "body" or "fiddle." In these words, the first syllable is the stronger one but also the shorter one. This short-long rhythm is called the "Scots snap" and is common in strathspeys, helping strengthen and drive the beats of the tune.

The moment when the tension of a strathspey is released into the following reel is so exciting that many dancers and listeners can hardly hold back an enthusiastic shout (or "heuk!") when they hear it. Reels sound quicker than strathspeys because they have more notes per beat, but they have only two strong beats per measure (properly written in 2/2 or "cut time"), and these two beats are often slightly slower than the strathspey beats, allowing dancers enough time to hop off the ground and land on the next beat.

More than half the tunes in one of the foremost collections of Scottish listening and dance music, the 18th century Gow Collection, are strathspey-reel pairs. Clearly, these pairings were intended as suggestions for musicians playing for dancers. They started with the strathspey, moved into the suggested reel in the same key, and then no doubt moved on from there to play other reels for the dancers to continue. The prevalence of these strathspey-reel pairs shows how important this combination of tunes has always been in Scottish music.

The most common folk dances gave couples a chance to "set," showing their rhythmic steps to each other while dancing in place, followed by a traveling step, where they dance round each other in a figure-of-eight pattern. This setting and traveling combination would be repeated again and again, beginning in strathspey time and then moving exuberantly into reel time.

Strathspeys are almost always followed by reels, though there are several exceptions. Strathspey songs are often sung on their own, and instrumental strathspeys are sometimes slowed down and played lyrically for listening. In the Gow Collection, some of these tunes were specifically marked "Play slowly when not danced." Highland dancers use strathspeys for the Fling, the Sword, and the Seann Truibhas, without moving into reels, though one of their main competition dances is the Strathspey and Reel. Scottish country dancers also dance strathspeys without switching to reels (though they have a dance called a "medley" which does exactly that). To add to the confusion, however, Scottish country dancers sometimes dance a strathspey step to song tunes that are not actually strathspeys but can be played at the correct tempo for their dance.

Recognizing and understanding more about strathspeys enriches the experience of Scottish music for listener, musician and dancer alike. Listen for them in songs, dance tunes, and especially when they take us into the delight of a joyous reel.

7 ~ *Niel Gow*
summer 2011

Our small group of travelers was fully prepared for all types of weather as we walked the Highland hills each day and enjoyed live Scottish music in the evenings. For most of our trip, though, we had beautiful weather, until we visited Niel Gow (he spelled "Niel" the Gaelic way). This legendary fiddler and composer lived in the hamlet of Inver, just across and up the River Tay from Dunkeld. The day we arrived in Dunkeld, we finally had to pull out our rain gear so we could enjoy walking, warm and dry, in the misty Scottish rain.

Since Niel Gow had been dead for 202 years when we got there, the best way to say hello to him was to visit his cottage in nearby Inver, stop by his grave in Dunkeld, and to view his portrait and even hear his fiddle played at Blair Castle.

The tunes of Gow and his sons are still central to Scottish traditional music. Several of his sons were fiddlers, composers and band leaders, most notably Nathaniel, who published the Gow Collection. This series of tune books contains many tunes by Niel and his sons, as well as hundreds of other tunes popular in Scotland in the late 18th and early 19th century. The Gow Collection has been republished in recent years, though not always in its original format. The original version grouped listening tunes together and paired up dance tunes for easier use by musicians. It also contained curious old notations about composers, dances, and how to play some of the tunes.

Probably the most famous composition of Niel Gow is his "Lament for the Death of His Second Wife." In 1805, after the death of Margaret Urquhart, Gow's wife of 37 years, grief stopped him from playing the fiddle at all. When his family and friends finally convinced him to pick it up again, the first thing he played was this beautiful Lament. There are many recordings of the tune; two of the most moving are by Alasdair Fraser (*Legacy of the Scottish Fiddle, Vol. 1*) and Hector MacAndrew (*Legend of the Scots Fiddle*).

Three dukes of Atholl gave Niel Gow their patronage, beginning in 1745, when he won a fiddle competition at the age of 18. The blind judge claimed he would always remember Gow's strong playing style. That year, Gow played for Bonnie Prince Charlie in Dunkeld, and briefly joined his march south before returning home.

Although Gow wrote tunes of all types, including marches, strathspeys, reels and jigs, his slow airs stand out. One of his saddest tunes is called "Farewell to Whisky," written in 1799 when the barley crop failed and whisky making was prohibited. Some fiddlers have transformed this tune into an upbeat march, but I like it best played slowly with its original pathos. A year later, the barley crop returned, and Gow wrote a chipper strathspey called "Whisky Welcome Back Again."

A few drams of that whisky might explain one of the more famous of many tales told about Gow and his sense of humor. While managing the long walk home after playing for a dance, someone stopped to offer him a ride. They felt sorry that he would have to walk such a long way. Staggering a bit, after no doubt having accepted a number of drams in honor of his fine playing, Gow turned down the offer, explaining that it wasn't the *length* of the road that troubled him; it was the *breadth* of it!

We did not walk the 50 miles or so from Dunkeld to Blair Castle, but Gow certainly did in his day. Home of the dukes of Atholl, Blair Castle is also home to Sir Henry Raeburn's portrait of Niel Gow playing his fiddle. It is wonderful to see the portrait, because although the image is not uncommon in books, the real painting reveals a depth and humanity in Gow's face that doesn't come through in the paper versions. Beneath the portrait sits a clear display case showcasing Gow's fiddle.

The dukes of Atholl were Murrays, and it is thanks to Evelyn Murray, who vouched for my playing and dedication to Scottish music, that I've been allowed to play Niel Gow's fiddle for small groups visiting the castle nearly every summer. Evelyn was a leader of Clan Murray, with close ties to the Atholl Estates.

When we arrive at the castle, I am usually given a chance to examine and tune the violin, and sometimes replace a gut string or two. Gut strings were the type used in baroque times, and to play the old violin, I brought a baroque bow of my own. The instrument has been well used, repaired several times over the years, and has a date inside of 1787.

Standing in front of bookcases of leather-bound tomes, a marble fireplace, and intricate wood paneling, I placed the bow on the strings and began "Niel Gow's Lamentation for James Moray Esq. of Abercarney," a beautiful slow air Gow wrote for a man who served as his "early and kind patron." It was stirring to play tunes such as that early one, or one of his last tunes, the lament for his second wife, on Gow's own violin — possibly the violin he wrote the lament on. As we discussed Gow's life and his connections to the dukes, the castle archivist brought out the ledger book with Gow's signature in it. It was a receipt of his £5 annual retainer as the duke's fiddler — more than was paid the head gardener!

We returned to the town of Dunkeld, and walked to Gow's home, a humble cottage in the nearby village of Inver. Along the river, we passed the tree where Gow apparently played while the Duke fished from the other bank. There are giant sycamores and live oaks in the area, and once in a while, a lone trout fisherman can be seen working his fly line in his section of the river.

Gow's cottage is currently occupied privately, but the owners, through previous arrangement, were able to let us peek in and get a sense of the place. On an outside wall is a plaque placed by the Duchess of Atholl in 1949, quoting from a poem by Robert Burns about Niel Gow:

> Nae fabled wizard's wand I trow,
> Had e'er the magic art o' Gow,
> When wi' a wave he draws his bow
> Across his wondrous fiddle!

Gow's death was mourned as a sign of changing times, coinciding with the construction of a stout bridge across the River Tay, for which Gow wrote his final tune.

Gow's original tombstone became so weathered that in 1987, a replacement was installed at the gravesite at Little Dunkeld Kirk. After viewing the grave, we headed off to see the original tombstone, stored at Dunkeld Cathedral, a breathtaking structure dating to 1260. Gow's stone can be viewed there in a glass case in the Chapter House museum, along with various monuments and memorials relating to the dukes of Atholl. Near the cathedral is the old marketplace, where we stopped to see the Dunkeld's official ell, displayed on the side of a building. This tool, shaped into a Y at both ends, had a 37-inch span, and kept merchants honest by regulating their measurement of wool cloth. No doubt Niel Gow's father, a plaid weaver, was quite familiar with that ell. He may also have known the old expression, "Gie 'im an inch an he'll tak an ell."

Not far from Gow's home lives a fiddler and violinist well steeped in the music of the Gows, Pete Clark, who was involved in raising money for the replacement grave stone. Each spring since 2004, he has directed a Niel Gow Festival featuring several days of concerts, workshops and illustrated lectures. Clark has several fiddle recordings played in the Northeast Scottish style, with his own classical tone and control. One of them was recorded in the ballroom of Blair Castle using Niel Gow's own fiddle. This album, unfortunately no longer available, was called *Even Now*, a reference to a famous, clever couplet, which appeared in *Scots* magazine five years after Gow's death:

> Time and Gow are even now,
> Gow beat time, now Time's beat Gow.

The music of Niel Gow and his sons can be heard today anywhere Scottish music is played, and on countless CDs. Perhaps Time hasn't beat Gow after all.

8 ~ Dertha
winter 2016-7

Lady Dorothea Stewart-Murray must have shrieked when Charles Macintosh tossed the bagpipe manuscript into the fire. It was 1909, and Lady Dorothea had come from Blair Castle to the little village of Inver, near Dunkeld, to pick up a potentially precious book for her large and growing collection of traditional Scottish music. She could not have realized at the time that this book would prove to be the oldest collection of bagpipe music in the British Isles.

Lady Dorothea, or Dertha, as she was known, was an avid collector of Scottish music books throughout her life. Born in 1866, she was required, as eldest daughter of the 7th Duke of Atholl, to spend time with her mother and other ladies in social activities, but managed to devote herself to music as much as possible. She liked to sing, probably played keyboard, and copied out Scottish melodies into manuscript books, one of them dating from when she was 18 years old.

Her younger sister, Lady Evelyn, was also a serious collector, with a passion for Gaelic music and literature. Evelyn's sizable collection is now split between the University of Edinburgh's School of Scottish Studies and the National Library of Scotland. Her parents, however, considered Evelyn's serious academic pursuits inappropriate for a lady of her standing. The resultant discord led to estrangement from her parents, a series of psychosomatic illnesses, and the end of her collecting career.

Somehow, Dertha avoided this fate, perhaps because she married an army officer (becoming Lady Dorothea Ruggles-Brise) and maintained a level of socially acceptable activity in addition to her music collecting. One publication she purchased was the Glen Collection of Scottish Dance Music, which was published in two volumes in 1891 and 1895, and contains nearly 300 tunes by fine Scottish composers, plus extensive biographies and notes. Dertha herself made over 200 notations in the book. She loved to discuss Scottish music, and far from being simply a collector, it was said that not only did she know all the tunes in her books, for many of them she could also trace their evolution from the original version to later variants. After her brother was killed in World War I, Dertha presented the Glen Collection to the National Library of Scotland in his memory.

Having sought out Scottish music books far and wide, she must have leaped at the chance to pick up a valuable manuscript from a local man. Inver was not far from Blair Castle and was part of the vast Atholl Estates. In fact, it had been home to the fiddler for the 2d, 3d and 4th Dukes of Atholl, Niel Gow, who had taught fiddle to Charles Macintosh's grandfather.

Macintosh said to Lady Dorothea, "I have an old torn book upstairs; it is of no use to anyone; you may have it if you like." But when she insisted on paying him for it, he dropped it into the fire, saying that if she wouldn't accept his gift, he would not allow her to purchase it. Dorothea frantically fished the manuscript out of the fireplace and accepted the gift graciously. Note: When a Highlander offers you a gift, best not to question it!

That book, a bit scorched but otherwise in good condition, was bequeathed along with the rest of Lady Dorothea's collection, to the public library in Perth after her death in 1938. This valuable resource of more than 600 music books and manuscripts is called the Atholl Collection (not to be confused with the single book of Scottish dance music called *The Athole Collection* from 1894). Spanning 300 years of Scottish music, the extensive musical collection is open to public use.

Unfortunately, the Atholl Collection is not as well known as it ought to be. It was not fully catalogued until 1999, when the late Dr Sheila Douglas, a Perth resident since 1960, published a book listing the collection's contents. Though very active locally as a Scots singer, collector and organizer of traditional folk music, Dr Douglas lived in Perth for 30 years before learning that her local library contained Dertha's treasure trove of Scottish music. The catalog is now out of print as a book, but can be viewed at the library and may become available in PDF form.

The Atholl Collection is managed by the local history officer at the A.K. Bell library, Dr. Nicola Cowmeadow. She herself is a historian of Scottish noblewomen, and a singer as well. She has presented talks and performances of songs by Lady Carolina Nairne (1766-1845), many of whose songs are included in Atholl Collection books. In her time, Lady Nairne considered her songs and poetry writing a "great secret," and published one book under a pseudonym. For this reason, perhaps, her name is not always associated with some of her best-known songs, such as "The Rowan Tree," "Land of the Leal," "Hundred Pipers," "Will Ye No Come Back Again?" and "Caller Herring."

The Atholl Collection contains major works of Scottish music, such as the Gow Collection, and many lesser known works, such as the 1662 Forbes Cantus, one of the earliest secular music books published in Scotland. Books by myriad 18th century composers include a fourteen-tune publication of compositions by Lady Magdelina Stirling, one of whose tunes, the "Perth Hunt," is very popular in Scottish and Irish pub sessions today, though few are aware of the composer. One obscure book I came across in the library is a publication by Nathaniel Gow of tunes written by "two ladies from the remote Highlands." Scottish women have been musicians and composers for a long time, but like the shy Lady Nairne, or the chastised Lady Evelyn Stewart-Murray, women were not encouraged to come forward into the spotlight.

A few researchers have made use of the Collection, including Dr David McGuinness from the University of Glasgow, who used some music from the Atholl Collection for his research projects. Some material has been digitized and made available in the HMS.Scot online library. Eric and Helen Allan of the Highland Music Trust have drawn upon the Atholl Collection to reset and publish old music books in high-quality editions. They have made available previously unknown or hard-to-find books by William Marshall, Robert Mackintosh, composers of the eastern Highlands, and others, as well as a series of free downloads of smaller publications, such as Lady Magdelina Stirling's book.

The scorched bagpipe manuscript that Lady Dorothea rescued from the fire is also available for reference at the library. Copied out carefully by William Dixon of Northumbria between 1733 and 1738, it had been assumed that the music was for Northumbrian bagpipes until piper Matt Seattle came to the A.K. Bell library to research the book. He reset and published the book in 1995 as *The Master Piper – Nine Notes that Shook the World*. Noticing that many of the tunes required the nine notes of the Scottish bagpipes, rather than the eight notes of the Northumbrian pipes, Seattle realized that this book represented a major contribution to the historic repertoire of music from the Scottish Borders.

In May 2015, two pipers and a bagpipe maker visited the library to have a look at the William Dixon manuscript and other music in the Atholl Collection. Since they brought their smallpipes with them, Dr Cowmeadow invited them to play music from the books, and library patrons were treated to an impromptu concert. A video, now online, shows one of the pipers playing from the Dixon book, along with an image of the page he is playing. Dr Cowmeadow hopes to plan more musical events in the library, possibly in conjunction with the Perthshire Platform Festival at the end of March.

No doubt Lady Dorothea Stewart-Murray would be gratified to know that people are making use of her life's work. The Atholl Collection sits quietly in the local history department of the A.K. Bell Library in Perth, and welcomes inquiries and any visitors who might like to make use of this great resource.

9 ~ *Hector the Hero*
spring 2019

On March 25, 1903, one of the heroes of Victorian Scotland, Hector Macdonald, known as "Fighting Mac," returned to his room from breakfast at a Paris hotel after reading headline articles about himself in a New York newspaper. He took out his pistol and ended his life. Two days later, the great fiddler and composer James Scott Skinner wrote one of his most famous and moving tunes, "Hector the Hero."

Raised in a small town near Dingwall, north of Inverness, Major-General Sir Hector Macdonald had risen quickly through the ranks of the British army, distinguishing himself with feats of daring, discipline and leadership in Afghanistan, Egypt, Sudan, India and South Africa. There were those who dubbed him the greatest Scottish soldier since William Wallace. Macdonald had been appointed aide-de-camp to both Queen Victoria and King Edward VII, and was feted throughout the UK, though his humble origins did not prepare him for the gushing plaudits of society. His high position in the army was made possible by the Cardwell Reforms of 1871, which allowed for promotion based on merit, and abolished the purchase of commissions in the army by well-off seekers of glory who were not always the most qualified of military leaders.

That morning at the Paris hotel, Macdonald was startled to see his photo in the international edition of the *New York Herald*, accompanied by a story about "grave accusations" of "immorality" against him. Macdonald, who was commander of British forces in Ceylon at the time, had been given an ultimatum in London by the commander-in-chief of the armed forces, Lord Roberts (whose life Macdonald had saved in combat in Afghanistan), to either leave the army or clear his name via court-martial. He was on his way to the court-martial when he made his fateful stop in Paris.

One of the shocks to society after Macdonald's death was that this military hero, who was accused of homosexuality, turned out to have a secret wife and son. The British military required commitment from its soldiers and forbade marriage with rare exceptions. Officers were allowed to be married, but Macdonald married in 1884, several years before he became an officer.

We now know that before Macdonald made his fateful journey to Paris, he paid a secret visit to his wife and 15-year-old son in Edinburgh. The first anyone learned of this marriage was after his death, when Lady Macdonald presented proof to the authorities so she could take charge of her husband's funeral arrangements. This certainly upended Macdonald's brother, who arrived in Paris to retrieve the body, only to find it already gone. It also shook up Scottish societies who then pressured Lady Macdonald to allow a public funeral with full honors. She refused, citing personal reasons and her husband's wishes. Perhaps in his last visit to her, he had indicated his intentions. We'll never know.

After three overnight journeys by ferry and two trains, Hector Macdonald's body arrived in Edinburgh for a private funeral at Dean Cemetery at 6am on Monday, March 30, 1903. By Lady Macdonald's strict orders, no military from Edinburgh Castle were permitted to attend. The following Sunday, however, some 30,000 mourners stood in line at the cemetery gates so they could pay their last respects to "Fighting Mac." Memorials were later built at the cemetery, as well as in Dingwall and Mulbuie.

Three months after his death, Macdonald was exonerated by a commission report stating that no evidence of a crime could be found, and blaming the scandal on "vulgar feelings of spite and jealousy in his rising to such a high rank of distinction in the British Army." Macdonald's high rank and lower class Scottish roots rankled the old guard. It did not help that he preferred to get to know local people during his command in Ceylon rather than spend his time with the upper class British officers.

Ironically, none of the behavior of which he was accused was a crime in Ceylon.

Channeling the feelings of the nation, James Scott Skinner's manuscript of "Hector the Hero" describes the tune as "The Coronach – all crying together." A coronach is a Gaelic keening song, usually improvised at a death, funeral, or wake. The first part of his tune, Skinner wrote, represented a "coronach sighing through the trees," and we can hear what he means when we listen to Skinner's own recording of the tune. He played the first part entirely on the A string, with harmonics and slides up and down the string expressing the feeling of heavy sighing. The second part of the tune moves into a mournful and poignant minor key.

Skinner's "Hector the Hero," has become a staple of Scottish music. It is a beautiful lament written in slow 6/8 time, which is something like a slow waltz, though a lament is rarely used as dance music. A prolific composer, fiddler, violinist, and dancing master, James Scott Skinner was a Victorian Scottish hero himself, attracting thousands to his concerts, and composing over 600 tunes, many of which are still central to Scottish traditional music. His funeral in 1927 attracted 40,000 mourners, including his friend Harry Lauder, walking behind the pipes of Pipe Major G.S. McLennan.

On the back of the manuscript for "Hector the Hero", Skinner urgently wrote, "Play in the Kirk on Sunday & get the Minister to announce, as this is a national Calamity – my eyes are full." He asked his publishers to make the tune available immediately, and managed to include it at the last minute in his magnum opus, *The Harp and Claymore,* which was published in 1904. The tune was marked "suitable for pipes – piano – violin."

My first rather unremarkable encounter with the "Hector the Hero" was merely on paper in *The Harp and Claymore.* It was when I heard the moving rendition by the great fiddler Buddy MacMaster from Cape Breton, Nova Scotia, that I realized what a great tune it is.

The tune took on yet more meaning for me when I learned that Buddy MacMaster chose to play "Hector the Hero" for the funeral of his mother.

I recently asked Buddy's niece, Andrea Beaton, in her own right a well-respected Cape Breton fiddler, what she knew about the tune. She wrote that "it's always been referred to as a funeral tune, as far back as I can remember. It's how I remember my elders talking about it and where I heard it played most often." The Cape Breton fiddlers have it right. Skinner wrote the tune as a lament, expressing the grief of a nation.

Skinner himself recorded "Hector the Hero" in 1905, 1910 and 1922. I'm not sure that most contemporary players of the tune know much of its origins, but it has nevertheless become popular for its beauty. It was recorded by the Bothy Band in Ireland in the 1970s, by Celtic Fiddle Festival (a trio of Irish, Scottish and Breton fiddlers), by Tommy Peoples, and by various pipe bands. The Scottish folk-rock band Wolfstone recorded it on fiddle, and the Transatlantic Sessions series features the tune as played by Aly Bain and Jenna Reid. Tony Cuffe and Tony McManus recorded solo guitar arrangements of the tune, and bands like The Munros turned it into an upbeat tune played on electric guitar.

There was hope for more information about Hector Macdonald during the centennial of his death in 2003, since military archive material held by the old India Office in London were classified for 100 years and then released. One researcher into Macdonald's life, Dr. Kenneth MacLeod of Ullapool, had left an extensive letter about his research with solicitors in Dingwall, and upon his death in Massachusetts in 1998, required the papers to be sealed until the centennial. Alas, in 2003, nothing new was revealed, or perhaps whatever was found was kept under wraps by someone for future release.

Without documentation, the story of Hector Macdonald remains a tragedy clothed in mystery. But thanks to James Scott Skinner, we have a beautiful tune to commemorate "Fighting Mac."

10 ~ *The Celtic Forest*
winter 2000-01

So you'd like to find a nice Celtic CD. You visit a store, open a catalog, or search the internet, and find Celtic Connections, Celtic Colours, Celtic Legacy, Celtic Odyssey, Celtic Circles, Celtic Woman, Celtic Dance, Celtic Soul, Celtic Spirit…

Yes, there are upwards of 600 CDs with the word "Celtic" in the title. Perhaps we can find a way through this forest of Celtic music if we start by fixing our sights on the albums with Scottish content.

First of all, where is this forest? Since the 18th century, the word Celtic (pronounced kel-tik unless you speak basketball) has referred to certain people and cultures of Ireland, Scotland, Wales, Cornwall, Isle of Man, Brittany (northwest France), and Galicia (northwest Spain), because of similarities in their languages. Most people use "Celtic" to refer to Ireland and Scotland, especially the Gaelic-speaking cultures. Most Americans just keep it simple and think Irish! For this reason, there are many albums marketed in the U.S. under the name Celtic that are actually straight Irish.

This is not the place to delve into the fuller story of the Celts, which can be complicated, if not fanciful. Some suggest that the Irish/Balkan sounds of the show "Riverdance" are pure Celtic because the Celtic tribes originated in the Balkans. I have a book from 1840 that goes much farther, and asserts that in Biblical times the Celts went by the names "Phoenicians" and "Canaanites", and that the Celtic language actually pre-dated Adam and Eve!

Less far-fetched but still romantic are those who associate things Celtic with mysterious Druidic spiritual wisdom, and attribute to the Celts a new-age aura. Many albums describing themselves as Celtic, primarily in the American market, serve up gentle new-age sounds in a sauce of Celtic-style melody. Narada, a new-age record label, got into Celtic music for this reason, but the quality and popularity of the music pushed the label towards a more authentic presentation of Celtic music, usually with worldbeat and progressive elements. Narada's *Celtic Legacy*, for instance, presents music from most of the Celtic lands, though it leans towards the gentle, quiet side. *Celtic Odyssey* focuses on Scottish and Irish musicians, including such Scots as Alasdair Fraser, Relativity, Capercaillie, and Sileas. *Celtic Dance* steers toward lively dance music performed by a number of contemporary Scottish and Irish bands.

Much of U.S. Celtic music is basically new-age, but there are exceptions, even among CDs with "Celtic" titles. *Celtic Circles* by Bonnie Rideout is an American album that offers traditional Scottish fiddling, although the title concept of circles of life may appeal to a new-age audience. The album focuses most on meditative material, where Rideout has time to use her tone, pathos, and bagpipe-like ornamentation to best advantage.

For those who prefer the gentler Celtic sounds, veteran Scottish musician and composer William Jackson has put together *Celtic Experience*, Volumes 1, 2, and 3. Drawing on his circle of top Scottish musicians, and including a few vocal selections, Jackson uses his considerable talents to arrange and perform popular Irish and Scottish melodies for quiet, entertaining listening. For more challenging works by William Jackson, try *Celtic Suites*, a re-release on a single CD of two of his enduring suites, "St. Mungo" and "The Wellpark". In both compositions, traditional Scottish musicians perform with the sound of a chamber ensemble.

Many albums use the title "Celtic" because they cross Celtic cultural borders. Foremost among these are recordings associated with Celtic festivals, events that seek to bring together the best in Celtic music. *Celtic Connections* is a recording from the first Celtic Connections Festival in Glasgow, drawn from albums by many of the world's best Celtic musicians of 1994: Altan, Aly Bain, Boys of the Lough, Alasdair Fraser, Dougie MacLean, Deanta, Old Blind Dogs, Wolfstone, Iron Horse, Ceolbeg and more.

Several albums are named after that festival, including *The Piping Concert at Celtic Connections*, a live recording showcasing music of the Highland pipes (Gordon Duncan and Dr. Angus MacDonald), Irish uilleann pipes (Paddy Keenan), Northumbrian smallpipes (Pauline Cato), and pipes of Brittany (Patrick Molard). One of the Festival's commissioned works can be heard on Simon Thoumire's "Celtic Connections Suite," in which a nine-piece band pays tribute to Scottish music with a varied mix of traditional, quiet, passionate, and urban-frenetic moods. The superstar Gaelic rock band, Runrig, recently released its *Live at Celtic Connections 2000* CD, recorded at a festival performance.

The Celtic Colours International Festival from Cape Breton, Nova Scotia has produced a great CD annually since 1997. *Celtic Ceilidh 2000* is the newest Celtic Colours Festival album, featuring the Barra MacNeils, Blazin' Fiddles, Sean McGuire, William Jackson, Jerry Holland, Buddy MacMaster and others, with four previously unreleased tracks. Other CDs in the series include Natalie MacMaster, the Chieftains, Sharon Shannon, Capercaillie, Llan de Cubel, Altan, and Alasdair Fraser, among others.

Some CDs with "Celtic" titles are samplers, showing off the fine musicians available from a particular record label. Perhaps most notable is the "Celtic Collections" series from the Greentrax label. The first six volumes of this series are *Songs of Scotland, Songs of Robert Burns, Ceilidh Band Music of Scotland, Bagpipes of Scotland, Fiddles of Scotland,* and *Celtic Sounds of Scotland*. This last title uses "Celtic Sounds" to refer to contemporary bands that are Scottish but draw upon musical ideas popular in the general Celtic scene today.

There are over two dozen recordings called Celtic Collections, but if you have a predilection for Scottish music, this Greentrax collection is special. Greentrax is one of Scotland's most respected labels, dedicated to Scottish culture, with a large selection of albums by contemporary bands and soloists, plus the valuable School of Scottish Studies recordings. One innovative band on Greentrax is Keltik Elektrik. Keltik Elektrik (besides helping you pronounce the word Celtic) is a creation of some of Edinburgh's top musicians, who play traditional Scottish music with a modern electric energy. Their first album was *Edinburgh Hogmanay Party*

Mix, and they have just produced their newest, *Keltik Elektrik 2* ("Just when you thought it was safe to sit down...!").

Another sampler is the double CD from the KRL (or Lochshore) label, entitled *New Celtic Dimensions*, which offers 2-1/2 hours of music from Scottish bands such as Old Blind Dogs, Iron Horse, Whistlebinkies, Anna Murray, and Irish groups Craobh Rua and Oige, among others. This sampler focuses on contemporary music, and does not draw from Monarch, KRL's excellent bagpipes label.

Green Linnet, the U.S.-based Celtic label, has a whole sublabel, Celtophile, devoted to samplers of well-known Irish and Scottish performers available from Green Linnet. This label is organized into 20 budget-priced thematic albums, including *Celtic Love Songs, Celtic Music Today, Piping Hot: A Celtic Bagpipe Collection* and more (not all entitled Celtic-something!). Some of the Scottish groups represented are Capercaillie, Wolfstone, Andy M. Stewart, Aly Bain, Tannahill Weavers, and Relativity.

Two of Green Linnet's Celtic-titled recordings are especially interesting because they are live recordings that cross Celtic boundaries: *Celtic Fiddle Festival* and its sequel, *Celtic Fiddle Festival Encore*. Neither is actually a festival, but rather a trio of fiddlers: Johnny Cunningham from Scotland, Kevin Burke from Ireland, and Christian LeMaitre from Brittany. Playing separately and together, they paint an exciting musical portrait of their various Celtic fiddle styles.

Now that you have a window on some of the CDs with the word "Celtic" in the title, you only have about 570 more to consider! As you blaze your trail through this dense and growing forest of recordings, look for the tall trees that have withstood the test of time. Sometimes, to reverse the old adage, it can be hard to see the trees for the forest.

11 ~ *Trad Meets Classical*
summer 1999

A traditional, untrained singer can give an unaffected, moving performance. But what if she goes off to a conservatory, gains classical technique, and comes home to sing her native songs? Wouldn't she still sing from the heart? Is her music now "classical"?

The richness of Scottish music embraces a vast range of native styles, from gutsy folk musicians to classically trained performers. Usually we associate traditional music with the folksier side of the music. But the so-called classical side deserves a good look and listen, for in Scotland, this music too has strong traditional roots.

When we listen to the soaring operatic voice of Kenneth McKellar or the technically dazzling playing of Alasdair Fraser, we are not listening to classical music, but to Scottish traditional music brilliantly performed.

In the history of Scottish music, wherever traditional and classical music have met, Scotland's traditional music has held its own. This inner strength has baffled many an observer. One 18th century writer explained that although Scottish music may not hold fast to the rules of classical composition, "it produces its intended effect in a superior degree" and therefore "it is the preferable music."

Perhaps this is why classical music never developed strongly in Scotland until the 20th century. The Scots, including the aristocracy, simply preferred their own music. They loved to sing, write, and play it, and patronized its performances and publications. In 1847, one writer issued an awkward and revealing apology for the fact that the Scots preferred traditional to classical music. He wrote, "It is to be feared that the beauty of the melodies is itself partly to be blamed for the indifference to higher music."

I'll never forget the Scotsman who led a group of young players offering traditional fiddle tunes, and yet felt the necessity to assure me that his musical group also plays some "good stuff," by which he meant music of Handel and Haydn. He might as well have apologized for enjoying the traditional at the expense of the "higher music."

There has been confusion among Scots themselves about the value of their own traditions, and yet, by and large, they prefer their own music. In recent years, the popular operatic tenor Kenneth McKellar used his talents to bring out the beauty of those melodies. Though he could sing nearly anything, the clarity, tone and passion of McKellar's voice are unmistakable when he sings Scottish songs. In quicker songs such as "Wee Cooper of Fife," or "The De'il's Awa'," you can feel his exuberance. His is classical technique at the service of Scottish music, rather than Scottish song dressed up as classical music.

The same could be said about Anne Lorne Gillies, who sings with a trained voice in both Gaelic and English. Some have criticized the "cleaning up" of Gaelic songs by classically trained musicians, but we must distinguish between those who feel a need to "dignify" folk music, versus those who use classical skills to express their musical ideas. Gillies' most recent album, *Oh My Land*, is a tribute to Gaelic song, and rings with sincerity.

Haydn, Beethoven, Mendelssohn and Bruch were among those who used Scottish melodies in their own works. One recording of Haydn's Scottish songs features Scottish folksinger Jean Redpath. Because her fine voice is not classically trained, this album brings out the folk origin of the songs, even as they blend in with Haydn's classical accompaniment. A similar balance of folk song within a classical arrangement can be found in Redpath's seven albums of Robert Burns' songs, set by composer Serge Hovey.

Scotland's great fiddler, Aly Bain, recently linked up with a contemporary Norwegian composer and the BT Scottish Ensemble to record *Follow the Moonstone*. This lush classical setting of Scandinavian, Shetland and Scottish fiddle tunes includes the 18th century strathspey,

"Beauty of the North,"and several J.S. Skinner tunes that work well in both traditional and classical settings.

It is difficult to find a Scottish musician or composer who did not incorporate traditional music into his work. Composer James Oswald (1711-1769) wrote classical pieces, often using Scottish melodies, but also created tunes that have been part of the traditional repertoire, including many fiddle tunes, and melodies for songs such as Burns's "Ae Fond Kiss." You can hear some of Oswald's compositions on *Airs for the Seasons*, an album performed by the Leda string trio.

Bach Meets Cape Breton, by baroque violinist and Cape Breton fiddler David Greenberg, is a unique comparison of classical and folk styles. It features Scottish melodies arranged by Oswald, William McGibbon, Alexander McGlashan, John Gow and other 18th century Scottish musicians. Shortly after this music was written, many Highlanders were forced to emigrate to Cape Breton, Nova Scotia, and brought with them these same tunes, which they played in traditional style. In some tracks, *Bach Meets Cape Breton* brilliantly crosses over from baroque to folk and back again, switching between harpsichord accompaniment and guitar.

Composer, guitarist and conductor Scott MacMillan wrote a series of lively and innovative classical arrangements of Scottish and Cape Breton tunes for an unusual octet, which recorded them on *Songs from the Cape*. This album showcases the strong pulse of four traditional Cape Breton musicians, combined with the colorful background of a string quartet.

Scottish traditional music certainly holds its own against other styles in Pipe Major Robert Mathieson's *The Big Birl*. Here, traditional solo bagpiping is backed by a variety of accompaniments, including a string quartet, calypso band, rock band, and easy listening atmospherics.

One of the more prolific composers of classically inspired pieces is William Jackson. His work includes the "Wellpark Suite," "St. Mungo," and "A Scottish Island," all of which have the flow of melodies and shifting moods that is characteristic of classical compositions. Yet these pieces rely heavily on Scottish traditional melodies and instrumentation. In a sense, he is using a classical framework to express Scottish musical ideas.

Jackson's latest classical/traditional effort is one we may hear lots more about, because it won a competition seeking a possible new national anthem for Scotland. His contribution is called "Land of Light," and is featured on a CD of the same name, along with a selection of other Jackson performances.

In 1991, BBC Radio budgeted 26 half-hour radio programs to explore the music of Scotland. Once the producers got involved in the project, they ended up with no fewer than 30 ninety-minute programs, without exhausting their material. Sometimes even the experts underestimate the rich diversity of Scotland's music. This groundbreaking program resulted in a wonderful book by John Purser, called *Scotland's Music*. (For more about the book, see Chapters 2 and 3.)

With the flourishing of Scottish recordings, we all now have the opportunity to take a better look and listen for ourselves. Whether you prefer traditional or classical, there is plenty of each from Scotland, and some refreshing combinations of both. Call it what you will, you'll know when you've found the "good stuff," for great music speaks to the heart.

12 ~ *The Stevensons*
fall 2006

"Not many families now have this sort of musical connection," remarked Ronald Stevenson about his duo with granddaughter Anna-Wendy. Their CD, *Gowd & Silver*, features Ronald on piano and Anna-Wendy on violin, and their collaboration highlights the accomplishments of a remarkable Scottish family, spanning three generations.

Now 78, Ronald Stevenson is a world-class pianist and composer. His 32-year-old granddaughter is a violinist and fiddler in Edinburgh. Their new CD contains Ronald's lyrical violin and piano arrangements of Scottish fiddle tunes by 18th century fiddlers MacIntosh, Gow, Marshall, and Fraser, as well as song melodies from Burns, Scots ballads, and Gaelic songs. There are also three original compositions on the recording. One was based on a poem by Ronald's old friend, the celebrated Scottish poet Hugh MacDiarmid; another was his first composition after moving to Edinburgh from England at age 24.

Raised by a Scots father and Welsh mother, Ronald's energy and genius for music were clear at an early age. His father sang traditional songs at home, and Ronald always combined his respect for traditional music with his passion for classical piano and composition. He was one of the earliest users, possibly even the coiner, of the term "world music," and maintained a correspondence with ethnomusicologist Percy Grainger.

Ronald Stevenson's output has been enormous, and is slowly being published, thanks to the efforts of the Ronald Stevenson Society. His monumental 80-minute piano piece, "Passacaglia on DSCH," was dedicated and presented to the great Russian composer Shostakovich in 1962 in Edinburgh. It includes musical references from many sources and intimations of hope for humanity, including a Scottish bagpipe pibroch, an homage to victims of the Holocaust, and a tribute to an emergent Africa. This last part may have triggered a raid by the apartheid South African government on the music department of Cape Town University after Stevenson premiered the piece there. He has written two piano concertos, a violin concerto commissioned by Yehudi Menuhin, hundreds of songs, and many works for piano, chamber groups, and orchestra. His latest oeuvre is the culmination of 50 years of work, a colossal piece combining two choirs, one of them singing in Gaelic, a symphony orchestra and a chamber ensemble.

A musical biography of Ronald Stevenson by Malcolm Macdonald was published in 1989 by the National Library of Scotland in time for his 60th birthday celebration, which included a 3-month exhibition of his works at the National Library and a concert sponsored by BBC. Stevenson's portrait hangs in the Scottish National Portrait Gallery.

The CD documenting the grandfather/granddaughter duo was the brainchild of Ronald's son, Gordon Stevenson, who is Anna-Wendy's father. Gordon is a violinmaker and repairer in Edinburgh, and enjoys playing fiddle, guitar and piano as well. In the late 1980s, Gordon created Eclectic Records, making available unique Scottish music, including early recordings of his sister Savourna, an amazing harper and composer.

Those who haven't heard Savourna Stevenson may find it difficult to imagine her versatility on the harp. She effortlessly plays jazz, traditional, and classical music, and has been a great innovator and teacher. The CD *Cutting the Chord* is a tour de force of her harp playing; other recordings include her compositions for folk, chamber, and orchestral ensembles. Her *Tusitala, Teller of Tales* CD is original music written for a BBC production about the tales of Robert Louis Stevenson.

Savourna has put out several more recent CDs on the Cooking Vinyl label, offering harp, song, string quartet and other intriguing musical explorations. Lately, she has devoted much work to composing orchestral works accompanying spoken stories for children, in the tradition of Prokofiev's *Peter and the Wolf*. In 2003, Savourna's *Misterstourworm* was performed by the Royal Scottish National Orchestra, with lively narration by Billy Boyd (Pippin from Lord of the Rings), relating an enchanting mythical tale of the creation of the Scottish islands. The *Glasgow Herald* called Savourna "a composer who is a national treasure."

The third child of Ronald's is Gerda Stevenson, a fine singer and actress. You may recall her from the movie *Braveheart,* where she played the mother of William Wallace's young wife. She has also been prominent in many Scottish stage, film and TV productions.

Anna-Wendy Stevenson is the youngest of the Stevenson family so far to make a mark on Scottish music. In addition to her CD with her grandfather, she has a self-titled CD on Eclectic Records with the pianist James Ross. This CD offers enjoyable Scottish fiddling, much of it at a moderate pace, ranging from old Gaelic melodies to contemporary tunes, including a few of her own.

Although Anna-Wendy's first exposure to music was classical, which she still enjoys, her father Gordon piqued her interest by taking her to performances by some of the fiddlers whose instruments he had repaired, such as Dougie MacLean and Charlie McKerron. She tried to copy the way fiddlers like Aly Bain and Alasdair Fraser brought Scottish music to life, and promptly got in trouble with her strict Strathspey & Reel Society, where certain grace notes were frowned upon and straitlaced bowings were required.

But her interest persisted. While involved in a graduate program in anthropology in Edinburgh, Anna-Wendy devoted nearly every night for two years playing in sessions at the pubs of Edinburgh, learning the art of Scottish fiddling first-hand. Soon she was gigging with groups, at ceilidhs, with the fiddle-led Bella McNab dance band, and touring internationally with the band Anam. Stints followed with the all-woman band Calluna, and her trio Fine Friday. Currently she plays with one of Edinburgh's most venerable folk ensembles, Jock Tamson's Bairns.

Like others in her family, Anna-Wendy has been drawn to composing, a development in traditional music which has been strongly encouraged by grants from the Scottish Arts Council and commissions from the Celtic Connections Festival. Anna-Wendy's new composition is called "My Edinburgh," combining recorded interviews of colorful Edinburgh personalities with live music by string quartet, bouzouki, mandolin, piano, saxophone and percussion – appropriately enough, a mix of anthropological research and musical performance.

One section of this composition, "New Haven Sunset," reveals a heartwarming tale about an Edinburgh neighborhood. The voice of Colin MacLennan tells of the old days when the sea came right up to New Haven Road, and on summer nights everyone would line up, the men on one side and the women on another. "And do you know what they were doing?" relates Colin's voice. "They were watching the sun go down."

The Stevenson family's crossover between classical and Scottish music recalls the activities of many other families in Scotland before them, such as the Gow family of the 18th century, whose father, the great fiddler and composer Niel Gow, sent his sons to study music in Edinburgh. The Gows played and composed both folk and classical music, and published influential fiddle tune books as well as important classical collections. One of their compositions, "John Gow's Compliments to the Minstrels of Scotland," can be heard on the *Gowd & Silver* CD.

Ronald Stevenson has been described as a universalist who rejects boundaries between people, and an artist who seeks beauty and melody. But these are not abstract goals. His family has not only shared his passion and genius for music, but has also dedicated much time to living with, working with, and performing for special needs children at the Steiner schools. It reminds us that working in the arts is not merely about self-expression but about communication, reaching out, sharing and uplifting others. Perhaps the *Glasgow Herald's* description of Savourna Stevenson could be applied to the entire family: they are for Scotland a "national treasure."

13 ~ *Children and Christmas*
winter 1998-9

It's Christmas eve at the magic hour of midnight, and kids old enough to know better lie secretly awake, straining their ears to be the first to *really* hear the thump on the roof or the tinkle of sleigh bells high in the sky. They will, no doubt, always remember their youthful hopes and noble effort.

For them, as for most of us, Christmas and children will always be tightly linked. So it seems appropriate to review together some of the key children's and Christmas albums coming out of the Scottish and Nova Scotian traditions. We'll start with the kids' music and then take a look at Christmas music for the grownups.

It would be hard to find any better children's music than Scotland's "Singing Kettle" series. Cilla Fisher, of the famous Scottish family of singers that includes Archie and Ray, teams up with Artie Trezise in an unbeatable duo, with top quality singing, unpretentious good spirit, and a wonderful way of including the listening child. This series is to Scotland what Sesame Street is to America, and American families who haven't tried these albums have a real treat in store for them.

One of the best recommendations I can give about the Singing Kettle series is that my kids never tire of hearing them; moreover, neither do I! Perhaps one reason for this is the quality of the music. Cilla Fisher and Artie Trezise have long been respected performers on the Scottish folk music scene. In fact, their 1979 folk album, *Cilla and Artie*, was recently re-released as the first in a "Classics of Scotland" series from Greentrax Recordings.

Christmas and children come together on the Singing Kettle tape *On Christmas Day*. This is part of a series of song tapes for various ages, including several themed albums with fun plots enlivening the banter between Cilla and Artie, like *Pirates!*, *Wild West Show*, and *World Tour*. (For more about the Singing Kettle, see Chapter 37.)

In the U.S., two children's recordings with a Scottish flavor have won the Parent's Choice Gold Award in recent years: Nancy and Jerry Bell's *Celtic Tales for Bedtime Kids* and Bonnie Rideout's *Gi'me Elbow Room*.

Celtic Tales for Bedtime Kids and the followup, *True Tree Tales with Celtic Roots*, feature the music and storytelling duo of Jerry Bell, of Edinburgh, and his American wife Nancy. High-energy and friendly, the Bells alternate musical selections with captivating and witty stories built upon traditional fairy tale plots, but with thoughtful, positive themes. For example, in one story, Sean the flute player is abducted by fairies, and ends up being offered three wishes by the fairy king. But the king, fed up at the way humans always wish for gold, decides to choose Sean's wishes himself! He gives the gift of time, the gift of appreciating the music within, and the gift of understanding the true value of things.

Fiddler Bonnie Rideout's *Gi'me Elbow Room* is full of singing, fiddling, poems and children's rhymes. Children and parents will enjoy many of the familiar tunes, songs and rhymes on this recording. Rideout also put out an instrumental album, *A Scottish Christmas*. Bagpiper Eric Rigler (of *Braveheart* and *Titanic* soundtrack fame) joins fiddle, guitar, hammer dulcimer and cello for a mostly quiet album, ranging in pace from slow to moderate. Including popular melodies as well as aptly titled traditional tunes, it's a nice antidote to holiday stress.

Fans of vocal music will enjoy Jean Redpath's Christmas tape, *Shout for Joy!* One of Scotland's finest folksingers, Jean sings solo on several selections, and is joined for much of the album by an a cappella chorus singing a rich program of Christmas songs, both traditional and gospel style.

One of the finest of Christmas/winter musical offerings is *Midwinter Night's Dream* by the Boys of the Lough, led by premier Scottish/Shetland fiddler Aly Bain. Available in Europe under the original title of *Da Day Dawn*, this album is nothing short of a musical masterpiece, with soulful songs, crisp and creative arrangements, and delightful tunes.

From Cape Breton, Nova Scotia, comes *Nollaig Chridheil*, a unique holiday potpourri of songs and stories in Gaelic and English, with musical selections by piper Barry Shears and Cape Breton fiddlers Buddy MacMaster and Winnie Chafe.

Straying into mainstream music, the Rankin Family sisters, Heather, Cookie and Raylene, pay glowing tribute to Christmas with their *Do You Hear...* album. They start off with a bold, golden oldie, "Rockin' Around the Christmas Tree," followed by solos and triple harmonies on songs ranging from an upbeat, jazzy "Let It Snow, Let It Snow, Let It Snow" to a heartfelt and pure rendition of "Ave Maria." Cape Breton fiddlers Natalie MacMaster, Howie MacDonald, and John Morris Rankin join this tour de force.

Pop song enthusiasts will love the powerful and emotional renditions of holiday songs by Cape Breton's famous singer Rita MacNeil, on her holiday album, *Joyful Sounds*.

Finally, for a new (or is it old?) twist to familiar songs, try singing your favorite Christmas carols in Gaelic! Rosemary MacCormack of B&R Heritage in Cape Breton offers a tape teaching the Gaelic words to such songs as "Angels We Have Heard on High," "Silent Night," "O Come All Ye Faithful," "We Wish You a Merry Christmas," and more. Like the potpourri album of music and stories mentioned above, this tape is entitled *Nollaig Chridheil*, which means Merry Christmas in Gaelic.

Nothing has the power to boost — or calm — your holidays as well as music. So to children at heart everywhere, Nollaig Chridheil, and much happy music!

SECTION TWO
Bands

Capercaillie

Unusual Suspects

Anna Massie

Blazin' Fiddles

ABOUT SECTION TWO
Bands

Singers and instrumentalists have formed bands for ages, to pool their talents to entertain listeners and incite dancers. There are loads of bands — groups of two or more musicians who rehearse and perform together — and many are mentioned throughout this book.

In this section we'll take a look at a selection of Scottish bands that developed as a result of the folk revival that began with folk clubs in the 1950s and accelerated in the 1970s with an exploration of Scotland's musical heritage by concert folk bands. Some of these bands have lasted many decades and inspired the formation of countless bands that followed in their path.

Groups building on the rich melodic and rhythmic tradition of Gaelic song developed a keen following far beyond their home areas as they incorporated musical ideas from world music that enhanced the natural sounds of Gaelic song.

We'll also learn about a big band, the Unusual Suspects, that is certainly unusual as it blends traditional, jazz, and original music in spellbinding and immersive performances.

Finally, we'll look at bands from the little considered point of view of accompanists, the musicians who provide the rhythmic and harmonic glue for every band.

(Note that various bands are discussed in many places in the book; for example, the band Old Blind Dogs from Aberdeenshire is the focus of Chapter 66.)

14 ~ Folk Bands
summer 1997

It is not hard to find in American folk music the mark of Scottish immigrants. Last year I attended a modern dance concert where I never expected to hear Scottish music, but as I watched the dancers interpret their "American Suite," one old Scottish tune after another came over the P.A. system, rounded out by one Irish and one clearly old-timey Southern tune. All these tunes have become an integral part of the American tradition.

The strong connection between Scottish and American folk music makes Scottish music familiar and accessible to the American ear. We are often unaware of this connection, however. Americans tend to view Celtic music as an Irish stew with spices from the British Isles.

Let us strain the Scottish music out of the generic Celtic soup for a moment, and savor it, know its flavor. By listening to bands you know to be Scottish, you will learn that despite their borrowing of Irish, rock, folk, world, jazz, or country sounds, they usually retain a distinctly Scottish flavor, sometimes quite deliberately.

Scottish folk music clubs in the 1970s spawned a number of bands whose members set about exploring their Scottish musical roots. Such bands as the Whistlebinkies, Ossian, Battlefield Band, the Tannahill Weavers, and Silly Wizard avoided electrified music, using traditional folk instruments such as harp, fiddle, bagpipes, whistle, flute, concertina, guitar, cittern and bodhran or other drum (but not a rock-style drum set). Their vocals tend to be folk songs and ballads.

Often the band members researched their music from old books or recordings. Their liner notes show an interest in sharing their findings about Scottish traditions. This was more than entertainment; it was a cultural movement.

One folk band that energetically explored a Scottish traditional sound was Ossian. After tiring of playing electric folk rock like the English band Steeleye Span, the founders of Ossian decided in the mid 1970s to go completely acoustic. They worked with traditional instruments and included a Gaelic singer in their original lineup, a fairly new idea at the time. Ossian performed as an acoustic band with a strong Scottish flavor for some 15 years of concert tours and seven albums.

A compilation album, *The Best of Ossian*, was released a few years ago, and offers great listening as well as a window on the band's development over the years. One of my personal favorites is called *Borders*. Their first album (self-titled) has just been reissued on CD, featuring singer Billy Ross. Most of their albums spotlight singer and guitarist Tony Cuffe, who first recorded with Ossian on their popular *Seal Song* album. Other albums included soundtracks or programmatic compositions by harper William Jackson. A number of former Ossian members have moved on to solo careers or joined other bands such as Tannahill Weavers, Easy Club and Battlefield Band.

Many of the "folk club" bands still tour widely. Their many recordings deserve a good listen; here are brief descriptions of some of them.

One of the longest-lived bands (over 25 years) is the Whistlebinkies. Sometimes described as the "Chieftains of Scotland," the Whistlebinkies have a coherent, professional sound centered around the pipes, harp and fiddle, with English and Gaelic vocals. Their most recent albums are *Inner Sound* and *A Wanton Fling*.

The Battlefield Band's entertaining and evocative music is well known through worldwide tours and 17 albums. Their motto "Forward with Scotland's Past" conveys their keen interest in playing traditional music in the light of contemporary ideas. *Threads* is one of Battlefield's latest recordings, and *Across the Borders* is a new live album featuring an eclectic mix of guests.

The Tannahill Weavers have, since the 1970s, focused on traditional music, especially pipe tunes and folk songs. They often use a driving beat, and their singing has a sea-shanty robustness. Their latest album is *Leaving St. Kilda*.

Silly Wizard was a great favorite for its astonishing virtuosity, humor, and fine ballad singing. Some of its former members are active solo performers, notably fiddler Johnny Cunningham, accordionist Phil Cunningham, and singer Andy M. Stewart.

There is a new generation of bands standing on the shoulders of these "folk club" bands. They have absorbed the sound and style of the older bands, and bring fresh energy to Scottish culture. These include Old Blind Dogs, with fine musicians and the rich voice of Ian F. Benzie; his love of singing is almost palpable (look for their U.S. tour this fall). Other great young traditional bands include Deaf Shepherd and Iron Horse. In other chapters, we will take a look at some Gaelic, rock, and experimental bands.

Scotland's unquenchable musical heritage is inspiring its young musicians to flower in many new directions. The folk club bands we've been discussing have helped replenish the wellspring, and bring its traditions to new places. The venerable Whistlebinkies, for instance, have performed with Yehudi Menuhin and John Cage. Perhaps they'll even play for a modern dance company some time. But surely that piece would be called a "Scottish Suite," even if played in America.

15 ~ Contemporary Gaelic Bands
winter 1997-98

Most natives of Cape Breton, Nova Scotia have heard the Gaelic spoken; indeed, many speak it themselves. They are descendants of the Highland Scots who fled a homeland turned hostile during the Clearances of 1780-1850.

During the new Celtic Colours Festival held in Cape Breton this fall, one of the biggest hits was Capercaillie, the contemporary Gaelic band from Scotland. Cape Bretoners both young and old seemed to glow with the pulsing rhythms of the modern Gaelic-based music. The old traditions are being revitalized with new sounds, and the bonds across the Atlantic remain. In the famous words of one Canadian Scot back in 1829: "The blood is strong."

Capercaillie is at the forefront of Scotland's Gaelic bands. With worldwide tours and some half a million albums in circulation, they are one of the hottest Celtic groups today. Since winning the 1985 Pan-Celtic Festival, they've produced nine albums, two of them this year: *To the Moon*, and *Beautiful Wasteland*.

Perhaps you heard them in the film *Rob Roy*. They have also made soundtracks for television films, including one about the Highland Clearances entitled *The Blood Is Strong*. A CD by that name has come out featuring Gaelic songs from this and two other TV films, plus a bit of the atmospheric music that has become a part of Capercaillie's sound, perhaps as a result of their film work.

Capercaillie's music is not easy to categorize. People call it "world music." But it comes from the heart of Scotland.

Their singer, Karen Matheson, learned Gaelic songs from her grandmother, a MacNeill of Barra, in the Western Isles. Charlie McKerron, from the Buchan coast in northeastern Scotland, was an award-winning traditional fiddler before joining the band in the 1980s. These two musicians (out of eight in the band) exemplify the kind of crossbreeding of Scottish musical roots that infuses Capercaillie with a fresh sound not easily reproduced outside of Scotland.

The east coast music can be found in the medleys of traditional fiddle tunes interspersed in Capercaillie's recordings, especially on earlier albums such as *Crosswinds* and *Sidewaulk*. The Gaelic music of the west is evident in the song repertoire, and perhaps also in the soft edge of the band's sound, which is neither folk nor new age nor rock, despite its mix of electric and acoustic instruments.

In fact, I would venture to say that the Gaelic music has shaped Capercaillie's worldbeat style. As I listen to their music, I no longer hear the African drums and Latin percussion as imports to a Scottish band; I hear those instruments and other world music idioms being used because they help express Gaelic musical ideas.

Here are three of the "nonwestern" rhythms you could listen for in the Gaelic songs. First, listen to the way they sometimes leave out beats or shorten a musical phrase. Try singing "Twinkle, twinkle little star" and leave out the word "sky." You'll sing "...like a diamond in the Twinkle, twinkle..." You've just dropped a beat. Gaelic waulking songs (rhythmic songs for working the cloth) may seem like they lose a beat when the verse is not the same length as the chorus, or when phrases are of different lengths. This is not common in English-language songs or in western music in general.

Now sing part of a song, take a big breath, and then continue from where you left off. You've added time to the song. If someone is playing along with you, they may get confused. But if you have musicians of the caliber of Capercaillie, they work with the extra beats and make something musical of it. Gaelic singers often add time with a breath, and Capercaillie has built this idea into their music.

Another Gaelic quality to listen for is strong syncopation, especially in the "mouth music" (songs for dancing). This is not merely jazzy; it is integral to the Gaelic language and its songs. Capercaillie backs up these song rhythms with two drummers (one with a regular drum set and one with hand-beaten drums and marraccas) and two strummers (electric bass and bouzouki/guitar). Even the accordion, fiddle and whistle often play rhythm in this band.

Many of these rhythmic ideas can also be heard in other Gaelic-based bands with varying styles. Interestingly, the English-language songs and instrumentals of these bands, including Capercaillie, are often more regular and predictable in their rhythms and styles than Gaelic selections by the same band.

Some of these other Gaelic bands include the popular folk rock band Runrig (see the next chapter), and the more traditional Tannas. A recording by Mouth Music, with American singer Talitha MacKenzie, offers some amazing worldbeat music based on the Gaelic. Capercaillie's Karen Matheson has a solo album entitled *The Dreaming Sea*, and Gaelic singer and bagpiper Anna Mhoireach and her band are worth a good listen on *Out of the Blue* and *Into Indigo*. Canadian Mary Jane Lamond dishes up Gaelic songs with an attitude on her new solo album, *Suas e!*. And Scottish/Brazilian Paul Mounsey mixes Gaelic singing with hip-hop and techno grooves in his brilliant *Nahoo* album and the new *NahooToo* with Flora MacNeil.

Of course, although rhythm is the heartbeat of music, there is more to these Gaelic bands than pure rhythm. There is also a great sensitivity to the depth and beauty of Gaelic and English-language songs, and to the moving commemoration of the Highland Clearances. You need not know a word of Gaelic to appreciate their albums or concerts.

Ten years after visiting Cape Breton on its first foreign tour, Capercaillie returned this fall to a warm reception. What to many Americans may seem eclectic worldbeat music was heard in Cape Breton as familiar old rhythms with a fresh young face, there where the blood is strong.

16 ~ *Celtic Rock*
spring 2000

In recent decades, the powerful melodies and rhythms of Scottish music have moved some musicians to shift traditional Celtic themes into a rock mode. Does the music lend itself to this? Are traditional musicians capitalizing on rock, or are rock musicians capitalizing on Celtic? Perhaps it's just a formula — play rock music, toss in some bagpipes, and voila — Celtic rock!

The truth is, the bagpipes are too difficult an instrument to "toss" into a band. A band that integrates the Highland pipes and pipe tunes into its repertoire has to know the music. And any piper worthy of playing those tunes in performance has spent a number of years immersed in Scottish music, quite apart from any rock experience.

America's hottest Celtic rock band, Seven Nations, uses two pipers, in addition to bass, electric guitar, vocals, keyboard and fiddle. The bandleader, Kirk MacLeod, spent some 15 years as both a songwriter and a piper before even starting the band. Formerly a successful competitive piper, he naturally made pipe tunes a regular part of the band's repertoire. Although Kirk does whip out the pipes a few times in each performance, Seven Nations also has a full-time piper in Scott Long, a Grade 1 piper from Nova Scotia.

Kirk's songs address personal relationships, typical of rock ballads, as well as historical themes such as the tragedy of the Highland Clearances or the Irish Potato Famine. He also sings traditional songs, like "Johnny Cope," arranged in rock format.

The band has been so popular at Highland Games that they got accustomed to wearing the kilt, whether at Games or other gigs. As their popularity has exploded, they've gone well beyond the Scottish circuit, and the kilts have come off, but the piping, pipe tunes, and Scottish themes are still integral to their music.

The Factory is Seven Nation's most recent album, with five previous recordings still popular. As of this writing, three will go out of print to make room for newer projects — a studio project called *Rain and Thunder*, and two live albums, *Road Kill Vol. 1* and *Vol. 2*.

The piper on the first five albums was Neil Anderson, whose improvisatory piping style has led him to form a new band of his own, called *Full Circle*, offering eclectic music ranging from traditional Scottish to rock to jazz. Neil's beebop bagpipes can be heard on the Seven Nations albums, his *Full Circle* album, and on a new release with the tongue-in-cheek title *Irish Music in America, Volume Two* (there was no Volume One!).

Another popular U.S.-based rock band that uses lots of bagpipes is Brother. Originally from Australia, which has strong Scottish cultural elements, the three Richardson brothers that formed the band, Hamish, Angus and Fergus, all play the Highland pipes. Their song lyrics are personal and have no ambition to relate to Scotland, but the instrumentals and song accompaniments include strong doses of pipes. Some songs are belted out against sustained triple bagpipes. Some are introduced with traditional or original pipe tunes.

Brother's *Exit from Screechville* starts off with the band's arrangement of a piobaireachd, which is the meditative classical music of the traditional Scottish bagpipes. The backup includes rolling percussion sounds reminiscent of pipe band drumming, but performed using native Australian drums. This track recalls the feel of the Scottish pipe band MacUmba, which blends Brazilian and Caribbean drumming with standard pipe band tunes.

Their recent album *Your Backyard* features two of the brothers (hence the band's name), while the third brother, who goes by the name of Bur, has gone on the road with his own one-man "Acoustic and Electric Celtic World Orchestra."

Being from Australia, Brother makes use of their native digeridoo, a cylindrical or conical wind instrument which can be up to ten feet long, and perfect for playing long drone notes. Brother mixes it with pipes for a unique effect. There is also a Canadian band that uses the digeridoo with great results – MacCrimmon's Revenge out of Nova Scotia. This band has an innovative and very listenable album called *The Ransom*, featuring some excellent piping.

Another Canadian Celtic rock band that has a powerful sound is Rawlins Cross. Originally from Newfoundland, and now based in Nova Scotia, this group includes bagpipes and blends in Scottish and Irish tunes with the rock songs. The lyrics and the energy are hard hitting, and less introspective than some rock bands. If you take away their rock songs, you are left with well-played traditional Celtic tunes, which the band put together in an all-instrumental album called *Celtic Instrumentals*. Apart from this album, Rawlins Cross has three other titles, *Living River, Reel 'n' Roll*, and the most recent, *Make It On Time*.

You may well enjoy the music of hard-hitting bands such as Kilt, and Mackeel, both from Cape Breton, Nova Scotia, and Great Big Sea out of Newfoundland. These groups are a little hard to classify clearly as Celtic rock, though their aggressive acoustic combination of traditional, original and pub songs are very popular.

And what of the Celtic rock back in Scotland? There are a quite a few bands that take traditional Scottish instrumentation, songs, and themes into the direction of rock music.

Runrig is Scotland's superstar rock band from the Highlands. In 27 years, they've had several songs on the British charts, and are viewed with the awe accorded a band like the Rolling Stones. Runrig's ability to perform traditional Gaelic songs in a folk rock format has been very exciting for Scots, particularly Gaelic speakers, who no longer had to look outside of their own home to find rock music.

Runrig's *Gaelic Collection* is a double CD compiling their best Gaelic songs from 1973 to 1998. Their newest studio album is *In Search of Angels* featuring their new singer, Bruce Guthro of Cape Breton. Many of the songs are personal poems like much rock music, but the traditional Gaelic songs are still there. Runrig's earlier albums, such as *Highland Connection*, *Recovery*, and *Heartland*, are full of songs about places, events, and people from Highland Gaelic culture.

Wolfstone is another Highland-based band that took well-known fiddle and pipe tunes and gave them a hard-hitting treatment. Most of Wolfstone's innovative and strongly Scottish-based rock music can be easily found on the Green Linnet label. With about eight albums to choose from, the easiest way to sample them might be via their compilation, *Pick of the Litter*. Blending the virtuoso fiddler Duncan Chisholm with songwriter Ivan Drever (this duo also has albums of their own) and Stuart Eaglesham, Wolfstone added rock drums, electric guitars, and some powerful piping.

A very popular rock-ish band out of Shetland is Rock Salt & Nails. The band's rock songs are blended with a lot of traditional fiddle tunes, which takes some of their music away from the typical rock sound. All three of their albums are great listening: *Waves, More & More*, and the new *Boxed*.

A new album by the Scottish band Alba Vinyl called *Follow That Camel* offers some old-fashioned rock mixed with traditional tunes. The CD's artwork tells the story of old and new, showing kilt, combat boots, leather pants and a 1960s photo of parents dancing while wearing silly hats.

As with all music, there is a continuum from one genre of music to the next, and some great Scottish bands, like Shooglenifty or Tartan Amoebas, use rock elements but can't be properly called rock bands. (Listen to them anyway!)

Call them what you will, a tour through today's Scottish-based rock bands will be a real ear opener.

17 ~ *Unusual Suspects*
spring 2006

Last October, in Edinburgh, I went to see the Unusual Suspects without suspecting how unusual they'd be. A few musical friends had encouraged me to come see their gig in Queens Hall, but I had no clue how big the band was, nor how astounding their music.

Twenty-two of Scotland's best musicians took the stage, including a number of traditional folk instruments — six fiddles, piano, bass, harp, drum set, hand drums, bouzouki, two accordions, and three pipers — plus two trumpets, sax and trombone. Four of these musicians were also singers; a guest singer was featured later in the show as well. Before we knew it, we were drawn into a most thrilling and infectious concert of Scottish traditional music, powered by the energy of big band jazz.

Codirector David Milligan, a jazz/folk pianist, says, "I don't really think of it as a crossover thing, or as having a strong jazz element." Milligan and his wife, harper and singer Corrina Hewat, arrange the music together and select the musicians with a view towards presenting Scottish music, as interpreted both by traditional musicians and accomplished jazzers. There are some bands who play jazz, rock, or classical music while making use of Scottish instruments or melodies. The Unusual Suspects go the opposite route, playing Scottish traditional music well, while making use of some jazz instruments and ideas.

It works brilliantly. "Our whole idea was to put people in playing their own music, so they could relax," said Milligan and Hewat. It is clear from watching the band that all the musicians are more than competent, quite comfortable with their music, and enjoy the challenge of playing with others of varied musical backgrounds.

In recent years, many fine Scottish musicians have been teasing out the intriguing syncopations of traditional music, and filling in the open harmonies of the old tunes with ear-opening, sometimes jazzy ideas. In some ways, then, the full bore sound of the horn and rhythm sections of the Unusual Suspects is just an extension of what's already been going on in Scottish traditional music.

Indeed, the thriving traditional music scene in Scotland is what makes such a project possible. Most of the big band's musicians perform with their own small bands, which are well known in their own right. All of these bands are well worth a listen. Milligan and Hewat work together under the name Bachue in addition to each having their own duos with others. Musicians in the Unusual Suspects band come from some of Scotland's top performing groups: Blazin' Fiddles, Deaf Shepherd, Shooglenifty, Fiddlers' Bid, Iron Horse, Keep It Up, Salsa Celtica, and Old Blind Dogs.

"The scene in Scotland does feel quite special," says Milligan. "For the last 10 years at least there has been this thing, in Edinburgh particularly, where lots of musicians of different genres hang out together." The result, he says, is an acceptance and appreciation of each other's music, and inevitably, innovation in the creation of new music.

This description of Milligan's musical scene recalls stories of 18th century Edinburgh, when professionals of all walks of life — professors, business people, scientists, architects, philosophers — hung out over bottles of claret wine, presenting and discussing their latest thoughts and projects. This broad-based interaction (now known as a "liberal arts education") resulted in many pivotal innovations that we take for granted today — a tale well told in Arthur Herman's fascinating book, *How The Scots Invented The Modern World*.

The Unusual Suspects began in 2003 at Glasgow's Celtic Connections Festival with 31 musicians working on only a day and a half of rehearsal. "They walked on stage knowing about 60-70% of what was going to happen!" Hewat remarked. But it was material they were all comfortable with, everyone had a great time, and the energy was electric. She said the two-hour show seemed to pass like five minutes.

In 2004, the group went on tour with 22 musicians, and recorded a live album capturing the tremendous energy of their show. Hewat and

Milligan mortgaged their house to finance the album, but were helped out with pressing and distribution of the CD by Foot Stompin' Music, an Edinburgh record label which has specialized in spotlighting and promoting new talent in Scottish traditional music.

The CD presents not only exciting, brash instrumentals, with lively fiddles, sparring bagpipes and saxophone, and dueling trumpets, but also tender songs and quiet melodies. Four of the band's musicians are fine singers: Corrina Hewat, Annie Grace, John Morran, and Emily Smith. Singer Karine Polwart was also included as a special guest.

Several years ago, Brian McNeill, a founding member of one of Scotland's longest-lived folk bands, Battlefield Band, described a time when "the Scottish folk club bands took for granted that what we were going to do was this gentler thing. Even when we what we were doing was quite powerful, like Battlefield Band, we felt obliged to mitigate our effect a wee bit, and somehow make it prettier." Brian found it refreshing when musicians from Cape Breton, Nova Scotia arrived in Scotland in the 1990s with "this burst of energy" that made him want to see Scots play their music for all it was worth, to stop holding back, and to "take no prisoners" when entertaining audiences.

The tour de force of a band like Unusual Suspects, built on home ground by high-energy native Scots, leaves no doubt that Scottish musicians are no longer holding back.

Ironically, Hewat and Milligan found that one part of the Cape Breton scene, though exciting and full of talent, was a touch more restrained than what they were doing at home in Scotland — a reversal of sorts from what Brian McNeill experienced some 15 years earlier. They noticed this difference in style when they performed at the 2004 Celtic Colours Festival. The Cape Breton version of the Unusual Suspects was directed by Hewat and Milligan plus Cape Bretoner Gordie Sampson. Since one of the guiding principles of the band is to make sure the musicians are doing what they do best, the inclusion of lots of Cape Breton musicians naturally changed the feel of the show. Hewat commented that Cape Breton show was "orientated more toward dance steps rather than the flashy, over the top" sound they produce in Scotland.

Regardless of the differences in style and tempo in Cape Breton, Milligan and Hewat felt they achieved the same exciting sound and energy, and they look forward to having the Unusual Suspects perform again at the upcoming Celtic Colours Festival in October 2006.

It can't be easy directing a 22-piece band, especially when the directors are among the artists. But David Milligan points out the joys of working with this group. Last fall, the band began its tour in Mull, getting up at 4am to catch a ferry, rehearsing all day, having a night in the pub to relax, and performing the next day on next to no sleep.

"But when they get on stage, everybody is totally on top of their game and gives 150% – this never ceases to amaze me. You can't help being blown away by this amazing collective energy and mutual respect."

Last fall, two days after the concert I saw, the Unusual Suspects performed at the World Music Expo, the first and only Scottish band to have done so. Perhaps they may get the chance to represent Scotland throughout the world.

On stage, Corrina Hewat quipped that the Unusual Suspects are what the Scottish National Orchestra should really look like. Given that the group comprises some of Scotland's best musicians, and makes a habit of presenting Scotland's music with no holds barred, the Suspects might as well plead guilty as charged.

18 ~ Accompanists
fall 2019

When listening to a live band, we always get to know at least one member of the band a bit, usually the singer or lead melody player, because they are the ones who most often talk to the audience. The accompanists are the band members most taken for granted. How do accompanists make an ensemble sound good? How do they approach the tunes and work with other musicians?

All accompanists focus on timing and rhythm, without which even the most beautiful notes make little musical sense. But there is much more to their interaction with music than we might think. Let's meet several excellent accompanists for Scottish music and find out their perspectives.

Anna Massie is the guitarist with Blazin' Fiddles, which features four fiddlers up front, and behind them, Anna on guitar and Angus Lyon on keyboards and accordion. "The way the band is," Anna says, "with the interaction between all of us, I like to think that from the audience it feels like a six-piece band, rather than a fiddle line that has accompaniment. It feels very much equal."

Like most accompanists, Anna has many irons in the fire, performing various gigs outside of her regular bands. She loves working with singers, though as she says, "it's their gig, and you're there very much as part of the backing." Sometimes a bass player or pianist is added, and that requires some adjustment to the role of the guitarist, to contribute to the overall sound. Lyrics make a difference as well, building the feel of a song's story. "The words influence chord choices, swells, approaches to rhythm."

Anna likes to look for what distinguishes a tune from others, such as a quirky rhythmic bend or syncopation of the melody, and to highlight that moment with special chords or rhythms. She makes full use of the guitar's ability to provide a bass line while chording and even sometimes weaving in a countermelody.

Anna Massie started guitar at age 7, inspired by her father, who played guitar, mandolin and tenor banjo throughout northern Scotland with the Lochinver Ceilidh Band. She is also a fine fiddler, and currently playing with the innovative fiddle quartet, Rant. In that band, her accompanist's ear – a good sense of rhythm, bass lines and inner voices – no doubt serve her well within the complicated arrangements of the quartet. Even her guitar playing, though, is more than accompaniment. In her regular duo with versatile accordionist Mairearad (pronounced MYret) Green, the interplay between melody, accompaniment, and musical texture is captivating, making it impossible to call either player the lead or accompanist.

Brian McAlpine is a brilliant pianist from Glasgow, as well as a busy composer, producer, and arranger. He plays with the band Session A9, and particularly appreciates the band's semicircular setup when it performs. "The difference is amazing," Brian says. "When you can see people's faces, you hear them better."

Brian likes to react to the other musicians, trying interesting harmonic and rhythmic ideas if the melody players are comfortable with them. Once the tune is established, he infuses the music with nuance and dynamics to create an overall arc to the performance. Rather than hit the listener with too many challenging ideas, Brian prefers to pace them so that there is a mix of new and familiar, and in this way he helps organize the listener's experience.

Accompaniment often involves managing relationships musically, sometimes reassuring a singer or instrumentalist with solid tempos and predictable chords, and sometimes engaging in a conversation of musical ideas. "I like reading people, trying to make them feel comfortable," says Brian.

Brian's first instrument was the organ, because his parents loved the organ. (They never wanted a piano because it reminded them of a coffin!) Eventually Brian went on to play piano and synth, mostly in pop and rock bands such as the Pearlfishers and Deacon Blue. It wasn't until age

20 that he got into Scottish traditional music, but these days that is almost exclusively what he plays. His first trad band was Iron Horse, which in the 1990s developed a blend of acoustic trad and contemporary sounds.

After contributing to well over 60 albums, and playing with many top fiddlers and singers, Brian McAlpine recently came out with his first solo album, called *Mutual Imagination Society*, an atmospheric soundscape mixing styles and representing his own sense of modern Scottish culture and tradition.

Ingrid Henderson is a virtuoso west coast harp player and pianist, a regular member of the Glenfinnan Ceilidh Band. She also accompanies various Gaelic singers and instrumentalists, playing both melody and backup. "I like sight lines in all music, even in the recording studio," she says. Seeing a singer taking a breath, or a fiddler placing the bow, helps pulls the music together.

Ingrid can't help hearing what chords might suit a tune, even as a listener. If the other musicians are comfortable with it, she'll try new harmonic and rhythms, and see what comes back at her, especially in live settings, such as ceilidh dances. Before a performance she likes to have a good grasp of the structure of a tune or song so as to help shape and present it.

Ingrid started piano with her grandmother at 6, and picked up the harp a year later. One significant experience for her was playing piano with the band Cliar, featuring three of Scotland's top Gaelic singers, plus fiddle and guitar; their 2003 album won Best Album of the Year at the Scots Trad Awards. Ingrid comes from a very musical family, her brothers and sisters having been members of a number of top Scottish bands, including Blazin' Fiddles, Battlefield Band, Mànran, and Breabach.

Among her many musical projects is a duo with her husband, the great west coast fiddler, Iain MacFarlane, one of the founding fiddlers of Blazin' Fiddles. Ingrid and Iain recently made an album together, called *The Cockerel and the Creel*, with Ingrid on piano and harp, and Iain playing a selection of classic traditional Scottish, particularly Highland tunes, with his articulate and expressive west coast style. Their skills and depth of musical knowledge, comfort with each other's musical style, and a shared sense of humor, makes for great listening.

Ingrid occasionally teaches harp and piano, but notes that there is not a lot of actual teaching of accompaniment. It seems to be a skill developed mostly in the context of ensembles and bands.

Curious about the notion that accompaniment is rarely taught, I asked my son Neil Pearlman, who regularly teaches piano accompaniment at Alasdair Fraser's fiddle camps, Maine Fiddle Camp and other venues in the US, Canada, and Galicia (the Celtic part of Spain). As a result, he has developed his own ideas about teaching accompaniment and inspiring new players. Neil confirmed that accompaniment is not often taught in Scotland and very little if at all in Cape Breton, Nova Scotia.

Neil is a full-time pianist with a variety of projects, including a duo album project with fiddler Kevin Henderson of Fiddlers' Bid and Session A9. Neil grew up immersed in Scottish and Cape Breton music and dance, and plays with Fàrsan, Katie McNally Trio, Soulsha, and Alba's Edge.

In teaching accompaniment, as well as in playing, Neil likes to focus on the rhythm, the groove, and build chords on the bass line of the music, partly due to the Cape Breton influence in his style. Echoing the sentiment of other accompanists, Neil says, "I play very differently depending on the player, to fit into the energy and spirit of what that person is going for." True collaboration, Neil points out, can require "conscious crafting, to break out of default lead/accompanist roles."

These "default" roles of lead and accompanist players are, as we can see from Anna, Brian, Ingrid, and Neil, not as clear-cut as we might think. An accompanist might build a musical platform so the melody can shine, or might goad the fiddler or singer into new musical responses. Anything could happen in the moment of recording, and certainly at a live show. We can always listen for the layers and complexities that enrich and enliven Scottish traditional music today.

SECTION THREE
Scottish Song

Màiri Mhòr

Arthur Cormack

Julie Fowlis

Eddi Reader

Harry Lauder

Cilla Fisher, Artie Trezise,
and the Singing Kettle

Photo: John Young

ABOUT SECTION THREE
Scottish Song

No musical expression is older than the voice. As we learned in Section One (p. 17), one Scottish song that came down to us in Gaelic appears to be about 8,000 years old!

We'll start this section with some insights into Gaelic songs, and then turn to Scottish songs written in the two other principal languages of Scotland, Scots and English. Note that there is an additional discussion of efforts to preserve Gaelic language and song in the chapter about the Celtic Colours Festival (pp. 319-321).

The Gaelic songs express values of a Highland culture quite different from that of the Scots and English speakers. Over the years there have been serious efforts to suppress Gaelic, but it has managed to stay alive; we'll do a little survey of some of the albums that can provide a good feel for the music. We'll also learn about the most common types of Gaelic song, and will meet several important singers who carry on the tradition.

The gentle singing voice of Arthur Cormack is a counterpoint to his frenetic schedule of promoting and fostering Gaelic music and culture.

Julie Fowlis is a star of the Scottish music scene even as she focuses exclusively on Gaelic song. Her one English language song was for a Disney movie, *Brave*.

Mary Ann Kennedy grew up in Glasgow, her mother an important Gaelic singer in her own right. Mary Ann has not only performed and written music, and explored Gaelic Glasgow, she has also worked in radio and connected Scottish and Irish Gaelic cultures as a program host.

Fiona Kennedy, a radio and TV personality who includes a variety of styles including American country, is not primarily a Gaelic singer but is comfortable with the Gaelic repertoire because her parents were two of the most famous Gaelic singers of their time. Even in Scots or English, her voice has a flavor of the Gaelic.

While Gaelic has managed to weather attempts to suppress it, there has also been a struggle to foster and maintain respect for Scots as a language. It is spoken by a large percentage of people in Scotland, and has been used in many Scots songs, including those of Robert Burns.

Many songs were preserved by the traveling folk of Aberdeenshire, who have been acknowledged and honored on several fascinating recordings.

Robert Burns's influence never fades, whether presented by a traditional singer such as Jean Redpath or the intriguing modern singer Eddi Reader. And discoveries never cease. The duo The Cast revived the original melody for Auld Lang Syne for mainstream appreciation.

Music hall singers such as Harry Lauder were some of the most popular singers of the 20th century. Though widely imitated, their original recordings reveal a freshness and originality worth a good listen.

The powerful messages of singer Ewan MacColl came from a unique life that shaped his music.

Some of the music which shapes us is children's music. Some of the most brilliant and popular children's music of Scotland came from the Singing Kettle, a project by the great folksingers Cilla Fisher and Artie Trezise. Cilla's brother Archie Fisher is a legendary singer and songwriter, and we'll have a chance to meet him as well.

Alan Reid performed with the Battlefield Band for many decades as a singer and instrumentalist. His story is long and colorful, and continues in the form of new projects.

This is by no means a complete list of great Scottish singers, but sets the stage for a better understanding of a rich vocal tradition.

SECTION 3a ~ SONGS IN GAELIC

19 ~ *First Experience of Gaelic Song*
fall 1996

My first experience of Gaelic singing in Scotland was magical and unexpected.

It was nearly 11:00pm. The sun was setting over the striking landscape and glistening waters at the Kyle of Lochalsh. Brimming with a day of gorgeous Highland glens and castles, my wife and I impulsively decided to drive onto the ferry to Skye, and take our chances finding a place to stay.

Across the sea to Skye we rode, determined to stop at the first payphone we could find, with our list of B&B phone numbers in hand. Near the ferry was an inn. Alas, not a coin in our pockets!

I walked in to ask for change — and immediately heard the siren call of music drawing me down the hallway. A Gaelic singer and a local fiddler were giving a slide show of the Western Isles. The singer was Catherine-Anne MacPhee of Barra, one of Scotland's finest Gaelic singers.

A year later, Catherine-Anne made the first of her three beautiful recordings of Gaelic singing, backed by some of Scotland's best musicians, members of the bands Ossian, Capercaillie, and Easy Club. In her latest album she sings the title role from the soundtrack of *Màiri Mhòr*, a TV production about a Gaelic woman ousted from her native Skye in the 19th century. Màiri Mhòr began writing her own songs at age 50, and her first song begins,

> I am weary of the speakers of English
> I long for some warmth and music

The warmth and music of Gaelic singing is accessible to us all. It took hold of me that lucky night on Skye. Never mind that I don't speak a word of Gaelic. Gaelic singing is some of the most enjoyable listening you could hope for — sweet, lilting music punctuated by powerful rhythms and haunting melodies.

It is one of the wellsprings of Scottish music. Many songs of Robert Burns, and tunes played on fiddle, pipes and harp, derive from Gaelic songs. Even some tunes and gospel songs found in the U.S. can be traced through Scottish immigrants to old Gaelic melodies. It is said that Dvorak's theme in the New World Symphony was inspired by the Gaelic song, McIntosh's Lament, heard by Dvorak while traveling in U.S.

No matter how strong the beat, or how plaintive the song, there is an effortless flow in the music and words of the Gaelic song. The descriptive songs can be sparkling and light-hearted, and the love songs or laments may be dark and haunting, sometimes with breathtaking twists in the melody. The songs for working the cloth (waulking songs) have a powerful rhythm, while the "mouth music" (puirt-a-beul) pulses with a dance beat. Yet overall, listening to an album of Gaelic singing is somehow a quieting experience.

One of my favorite albums of Gaelic songs is *Mairidh Gaol Is Ceol* by the "supergroup" Mac-Talla. This group includes three of the finest contemporary singers of the Western Isles: Arthur Cormack of Skye, and Christine Primrose and Eilidh MacKenzie, both of Lewis. Their soaring harmonies and heartfelt singing are captivating, with instrumental accompaniment on harp, cello and keyboards. Each of these singers also has at least one solo album, backed by musicians from the Battlefield Band.

While some seek to preserve traditions, others incorporate them into their own artistry. The result is often striking and creative. Runrig is a Gaelic band with a rock beat. Capercaillie, which appeared in the movie *Rob Roy*, offers beautiful Gaelic singing mixed with English-language songs and instrumentals. The Rankin Family of Cape Breton sings Gaelic songs with rich harmonies, and solo singers such as Mairi MacInnes make Gaelic a major part of their popular repertoire.

The older traditional recordings have an unmatched heart and soul despite the rough edges of untrained singers. The School of Scottish Studies offers a series of traditional albums available on Greentrax Recordings, including *Music from the Western Isles, Waulking Songs from Barra,* and *Gaelic Psalms from Lewis.*

Temple Records released several Gaelic albums, such the traditional but polished voice of Flora MacNeil of Barra, who helped revive Gaelic singing in Scotland after the war, and scholar, piper and singer Finlay MacNeill from Lewis.

The choices are growing. Listen also to Maeve MacKinnon of Skye, or the Glasgow Gaelic Music Association's choral music. There is no better way to appreciate Gaelic singing than by actually listening to it. It is one of Scotland's musical treasures.

By the way, we did find a B&B on Skye after 11pm, but do you think it was easy to tear myself away from the singing of Cathy-Anne MacPhee, just to make a few phone calls?

20 ~ *Gaelic is Alive, A Survey*
fall 2001

"It would have been better if Gaelic had died out quietly," said the young Scotswoman, as our conversation touched upon the tragedy of the Highland Clearances. This jarring, callous attitude, so casually embraced by a seemingly intelligent young Scot, may well sum up the difficulties faced regularly by Gaelic culture. One would think that the Gaelic co-founders of the nation of Scotland deserve better.

So many cultures have been damaged or destroyed to pave the way for something or somebody. In this case, it was the centuries-old Highland Gaelic culture that was dismantled and excised to make way for a woolen industry. We must learn from such events in order to avoid repeating the nightmares of history.

But if we want to appreciate and draw out some of the beauty and fresh perspectives of endangered cultures, we can do more than study their destruction; we can experience them, through their people, language, music, and other (hopefully living) traditions.

Scottish Gaelic culture is alive, fortunately, and one of its most beautiful and meaningful treasures is its song. A growing body of recordings now allows everyone to enjoy Gaelic song in its many guises, from raw traditional performances to folk, rock, and pop renditions.

Never mind if you don't understand Gaelic (half the time I can't make out the words of a lot of songs in English either!). The Gaelic melodies are unique, with rhythms rooted in the flow of the language. If you don't hear the songs in Gaelic, you miss out on the beauty of their melodies. The words and music are made for each other.

Even if you haven't listened specifically to Scottish Gaelic song, some of it will sound familiar, because it has served as a source for music of the pipes, fiddle, harp, and Scots song, not to mention the music of Irish bands such as the Bothy Band, Altan, and others. Some of the melodies can even be found in American gospel songs via the early Scottish immigrants to America. One Gaelic song, heard by composer Anton Dvorak during his trip to America, became a theme in his New World Symphony.

Let's take a look at some of the current Gaelic albums that provide a good feel for the music. The popular band Capercaillie provides some of the most accessible of Scottish Gaelic songs. Their most recent albums are *Nadurra, Dusk Till Dawn,* and *A Beautiful Wasteland,* which, like most of their CDs, contain sophisticated renditions of Gaelic songs, with worldbeat arrangements that accentuate the natural Gaelic rhythms. Capercaillie's *The Blood Is Strong* is packed with traditional Gaelic songs, being a soundtrack for the TV film of the same title. Now available on video as a trilogy, this film portrays the history of the Gaelic people, their dispersion to foreign lands, and modern efforts in Scotland to maintain Gaeldom. The golden voice of Capercaillie's singer, Karen Matheson, also shines on her captivating solo album, *The Dreaming Sea,* both in Gaelic and English.

Several other bands take Gaelic song into realms familiar to contemporary ears. The legendary Gaelic rock band, Runrig, has always struck an emotional chord for Scots with traditional and original Gaelic songs performed in a powerful folk rock style. Runrig's double-CD, *The Gaelic Collection,* highlights 25 years of the band's best Gaelic songs, with singer Donnie Munro.

The contemporary band Tannas has earned a place in the contemporary Celtic music scene with rhythmic grooves and evocative Gaelic ballads and fiddling. Their latest release, *Suilean Dubh (Dark Eyes),* is their finest. Another band with a modern sound is led by Gaelic singer and piper Anna Murray (Mhoireach in Gaelic). On her three albums, she is backed by a tight ensemble of musicians mixing traditional, folk, and rock sounds.

A number of accessible but traditional albums feature excellent Gaelic singers backed by their bands. The band Cliar, from Skye, showcases the smooth voice of Arthur Cormack, with top Highland musicians on vocals, harp, piano, fiddle, and guitar. Mackenzie is a trio of sisters, each well known for their Gaelic singing. Their album, *Camhanach (Dawn)*, makes use of triple vocal harmonies, fiddle, harp, cello and pipes. Singers from both these bands, Arthur Cormack and Eilidh Mackenzie, recorded together under the name Mac-Talla, with Lewis singer Christine Primrose, harper Alison Kinnaird and Runrig's keyboardist Blair Douglas. Their timeless, enjoyable album is called *Mairidh Gaeol is Ceol (Music and Song Will Endure)*.

As entertaining as the band sound may be, there is a quiet focus to solo Gaelic singing. One recent solo album is *Shore Street* by Billy Ross, who offers both Gaelic and poignant English language songs in a rich and relaxing voice. Billy played an important role in introducing Gaelic song to the Scottish folk clubs of the 1970s as the original singer with the group Ossian.

To get a handle on some of the great traditional Gaelic singers active today, listen to *Orain nan Gaidheal (The Song of the Gael)*. This CD was recorded at the 50th Edinburgh International Festival, where a series of seven concerts and a church service spotlighted Gaelic song and its culture. Most of the singers on the album come from the isles of Lewis and Barra, but several are from Skye, including Seamus and Kenna Campbell, and singer and folklorist Margaret Bennett.

From Lewis comes the warm voice of Ishbel MacAskill, Donnie Murdo MacLeod's deep and heartfelt singing, Mary Smith's rich voice, and Margaret Stewart, whose solo album, *Fhuair Mi Pog (I Got a Kiss)*, with piper Allan MacDonald, highlights the connections between Gaelic song and bagpipe traditions.

Barra singers on the *Orain nan Gaidheal* CD include Catherine-Anne MacPhee, whose clear singing voice enlivens three solo albums. The boisterous energy of Maeve MacKinnon is worth a listen; her solo album *Fo Smuain (Thoughtful)* is a little-known but rich treat to the ears, with several breathtaking songs. Legendary Barra singer Flora MacNeil is represented on the CD, as well as Roddy Campbell, whose solo album, *Tarruinn Anmoch (Late Cull)*, includes piping by his son Rory of Old Blind Dogs, and fiddling by his daughter Marianne of Deaf Shepherd.

Another excellent CD allowing you to hear a variety of singers is *Gaelic Women*, which offers new performances by many of the singers just mentioned, plus Capercaillie's Karen Matheson, Mairi MacInnes (her new solo work *Orosay* came out in August), Anna Murray, MacKenzie, and the trained but heartfelt voice of Anne Lorne Gillies. This CD includes all lyrics in both Gaelic and English.

Many Scottish Gaelic songs spread far from Scotland, partly a result of the Highland Clearances. An album called *Cape Breton's Gaelic Gold* offers a sampling of such singing from Nova Scotia. A traditional Cape Breton men's singing group can be heard on the album *A Tribute to the North Shore Gaelic Singers*. In recent years, the popular singer Mary Jane Lamond has performed Gaelic songs from Cape Breton in evocative, contemporary settings, on her CDs *Suas e! (Keep It Up!)* and *Lan Duil (Expectations)*. Her latest release, *Orain Ghaidhlig (Gaelic Songs)*, dwells compellingly on traditional material.

Those who are keen on authentic traditional recordings will enjoy the series of CDs from the School of Scottish Studies, with Gaelic psalms, waulking songs (for working the cloth), *Gaelic Bards & Minstrels*, and many more, including informative booklets, on the Greentrax label.

Perhaps this little survey and discussion will point you in the direction you like best, whether traditional or contemporary, solo or group music, so that you can sample the richness and beauty of Gaelic song. Thanks to the Gaelic speakers and singers who perform, organize, and record this music, we can all appreciate the unique melodies, rhythms and poetry that have been an essential ingredient of Gaelic culture. (And on a political note, we can tip our hat to the new Scottish Parliament for backing Gaelic education and culture in a way Westminster had little inclination to do.)

Perhaps even that young lady who hoped Gaelic would vanish may listen to some of this music and realize what she has been missing, and what the world would be missing if she'd had her way.

21 ~ *Varieties of Gaelic Song*
summer 2007

Some of the sweetest melodies in Scotland can be found in the Gaelic songs. Not only are they are beautiful in their own right, but they have also lent their melodies to music of the pipes, the fiddle, the songs of Burns, American country songs, even cowboy songs.

There is no need to understand Gaelic to enjoy the songs. They are easy on the ear, and yet full of emotion, rhythm, and variety. Just now I'm listening to young Jenna Cumming sing a Gaelic song about the isle of Scalpay, off the coast of Harris, from her album *Kintulavig*. The melody is quite familiar — it's the same one that was chosen by Robert Burns for his famous song, "A man's a man for a' that." The guitar accompaniment by Chaz Stewart uses supporting rhythms and chords that are intriguing and compelling; Brian McAlpine joins in later with a tasteful and inventive touch on the piano.

These songs seem to invite the creative accompaniment today's musicians are giving them. Just as pipe band drummers draw out of traditional Scottish tunes the most amazing rhythms, so do modern guitarists, pianists, and band arrangers draw out of the Gaelic songs some captivating and even unexpected moods and interpretations. This can be heard in many modern Gaelic song albums, but the creative use of contemporary styles is most obvious in Gaelic songs by popular bands such as Capercaillie, or the folk rock band, Runrig. Capercaillie's singer, Karen Matheson, can also be heard solo, as on her recent album, *Downriver*, which presents quiet and beautiful renditions of Gaelic songs from her childhood. Matheson's singing successes were recognized with an OBE from the Queen on New Year's Eve 2005.

In traditional Gaelic culture, poetry and music are one. Until recent decades, when several poets started writing in Gaelic for its own sake,

Gaelic poems have always been sung. There have been songs about land and sea, songs about love, mouth music for dancing, songs for working the cloth or rowing the boat, religious songs, and before the clan system broke down, there were songs in honor of clan events and chieftains.

One of the most haunting songs about nature is called "An Ataireachd Ard" (The Eternal Surge of the Sea). Listen to it on the CD *Essential Ishbel* by Ishbel MacAskill, or *Canan nan Gaidheal* by Cathy-Ann MacPhee. One of my favorite sea songs, about sailing through storms from Ireland, is also a love song, called "Mo thruaigh leir"; its breathtaking melody can be heard on Maeve Mackinnon's album, *Fo Smuain*.

The love songs are heart-rending, especially in laments such as "Griogal Cridhe" (Beloved Gregor), written by a woman for her husband, a MacGregor who was beheaded by Campbells. This song is on the *Essential Ishbel* album as well, and on Mac-Talla's *Mairidh Gaol Is Ceol*, an older album delightfully sung by Gaelic master singers Arthur Cormack, Eilidh MacKenzie and Christine Primrose. Another Gaelic love song, "Mo shuil ad dheidh" (My Eye Is After You), also called "My Lily", was written to lament Lily's decision to choose a wealthier suitor than the songwriter, but the happy ending is that once the song was sung, Lily changed her mind! A beautiful rendition of this song is on the album *Fama Clamosa*, with captivating rhythms and triple harmonies by the Mackenzie sisters, each sister a well-known singer in her own right.

Gaelic mouth music (puirt a beul) was often used for dancing, with tongue-twisting syllables, sometimes even nonsense syllables. It's a pleasure to hear a good singer enunciate cleanly all the syllables of a dance tune with a strong, rhythmic and simple but catchy melody. Many Gaelic song albums include at least one or two samples of mouth music. Being dance tunes, the mouth music melodies can often be found in the pipes and fiddle repertoires as well. One sampling of them can be heard on a new album, *Mara tha mo Chridhe* (As My Heart Is), by up-and-coming singer Julie Fowlis, who also plays pipes and is joined by fiddler John McCusker. This CD offers many enjoyable arrangements of Gaelic songs, and several instrumental tracks.

Working ("waulking") songs are very rhythmic, call-and-response songs used to keep a steady beat as women at a table work together to pound tweed cloth and tighten its weave. While these songs can be heard on a number of song albums, perhaps the most interesting is a new CD/DVD called *Bho Dhorn gu Dorn*, by Bannal (literally, "group of women"). Not only does the recording offer a full CD's worth of waulking songs, but if you turn it over, you have a DVD with a film made for BBC showing the women singing as they do the waulking, and speaking in Gaelic about the songs and the work, with English subtitles.

Religious Gaelic songs include pre-Christian as well as Christian songs. Listening to Gaelic psalm-singing is a unique experience. The song leader, called the precentor, keeps the congregation more or less together as they slowly chant the psalms. A recording of Gaelic psalms from Lewis is available in the Scottish Tradition Series from Greentrax Recordings.

A different religious sound can be found on the grandiose live recording of spiritual Gaelic music called *Lasair Dhe*, including massed Gaelic choirs (some 200 singers) with solo singers from the Gaelic "supergroup" Cliar (Arthur Cormack, Mary Ann Kennedy and Maggie Macdonald), and guest singers Kenna Campbell and Donnie Murdo MacLeod. This is on the Macmeanmna ("Imagination") label from Skye, which has a large selection of recordings by many of the best Gaelic singers.

With Gaelic on the rise in schools, cultural events, and recordings, it is natural that there is a growing number of young Gaelic singers. The National Mod competition and various local Mods have encouraged young singers for over 100 years to learn the songs seriously and compete for national honors in the Gaelic arts, while the "Fèisean" (pronounced fayshen) have offered festivals of instruction in Gaelic arts throughout Scotland.

Many of the singers mentioned above have been winners of the Gaelic Mod; some recent winners to look for are Jenna Cumming, Darren MacLean, and Gillebride MacMillan.

Two fairly new music awards have also drawn attention to Gaelic singers. The Scots Trad Music Awards includes a category for top Gaelic singer, most recently given to the smoky voice of Kathleen MacInnes, and in previous years to Julie Fowlis, Maggie MacInnes, and Ishbel MacAskill.

The BBC Radio Scotland Young Traditional Musician of the Year has also become a prestigious award, twice awarded to a Gaelic singer — once to the smooth voice of James Graham a few years back, and this year to Catriona Watt.

It is easy to get hooked on Scottish Gaelic songs and their lilting melodies, whether sung unaccompanied or in harmony with others, or with simple or intricate accompaniment. Not only are the melodies beautiful, but they are also somehow familiar, since the intonation and rhythms of the Gaelic language can be heard throughout the music of the pipes and fiddle. In fact, singer Margaret Stewart devoted two CDs to the deep historical link between pipe music and Gaelic song, with piper Allan MacDonald.

To gain a fuller, richer appreciation for what makes Scottish music Scottish, and simply to enjoy some heart-stirring music, listen to the compelling songs of the Scottish Gaelic tradition.

22 ~ *Arthur Cormack*
summer 2004

Maybe it's the beauty of his native Isle of Skye, or the emotional depths of Gaelic song, that gives singer Arthur Cormack his calm, unhurried manner. It certainly doesn't come from a relaxed schedule. Cormack single-handedly does so much for Gaelic song and culture that one of his associates suspects he's been cloned!

Arthur Cormack sings with ease, beauty and power, always a joy to the ears. Like a good meal, his sound is always nourishing, even when unaccompanied. There is purity in his voice, and obvious sincerity in his musical expression.

These qualities helped Arthur win Scotland's highest award for Gaelic singing at the age of 18 – a Gold Medal at the 1983 National Mod competition. As luck would have it, BBC radio's report on that competition was noticed by Robin Morton of Temple Records, who found himself unexpectedly captivated by Arthur's voice. Within the week, he offered Cormack a chance to make a recording.

The result was his first solo album, *Nuair Bha Mi Og* (When I Was Young). Simple and beautiful, some of the songs are unaccompanied, while others include one or more well-known accompanists on guitar, keyboards, harp, fiddle, or backup vocals.

A second solo recording followed, called *Ruith Na Gaoith* (Chasing the Wind), with more hypnotic singing and tasteful accompaniment. Arthur also worked with the group Mac-Talla, which included three Gaelic superstar singers: Cormack, Eilidh MacKenzie, and Christine Primrose. Their recording is quite varied and beautiful, entitled *Mairidh Gaol Is Ceol*.

But that's only a small part of the story. Arthur Cormack's inspired singing, plus his well-researched appreciation and understanding of the songs he sings, has led him down many other paths.

Cormack grew up with a Gaelic-speaking father and a non-Gaelic-speaking but musical mother. Gaelic was not spoken in the home, but Arthur and his sister began learning Gaelic songs early on. His first performance was at the local Mod when he was 8 years old. As a teenager he began seriously learning Gaelic in order to understand the songs, and seeing his interest, his father began speaking with him in Gaelic.

Their home was in Portree, which Arthur says was not very Gaelic at the time he grew up. But thanks to Gaelic regional education, says Cormack, "you can hear Gaelic on the streets of Portree, which you never ever heard when I was a kid." His own home is a Gaelic one. His wife, Shona, teaches Gaelic at Portree High School, and their three kids attend all-Gaelic schools.

Shona is also a Gaelic singer. In 1987, she and Arthur, along with a musician and photographer, toured with a multi-media show called "Skye — the Island." When they decided to record a tape to sell on the tour, a new record label was born. They named it "Macmeanmna," Gaelic for "imagination." This record label has grown to include some 25 significant titles, with Gold Medalists from the Gaelic Mod and various instrumentalists. The list includes female Gaelic singers Ishbel MacAskill, Maeve Mackinnon, and the gorgeous triple harmonies of the Mackenzie sisters; male singers Donnie Murdo MacLeod and Iain MacKay; the sonorous Highland fiddling of Bruce MacGregor; ceilidh band music; and *Lasair Dhe* (Flame of God), a performance featuring Gaelic psalms performed by various singers and choirs.

Perhaps the most significant band on the Macmeanmna label is Cliar (pronounced CLEAR). Featuring Arthur Cormack and two other Gaelic Mod Gold medallist singers, Mary Ann Kennedy and Maggie Macdonald, plus fiddle, guitar, harp and piano, Cliar has become something of a Gaelic supergroup, one of Scotland's finest bands. Cliar presents traditional Gaelic songs, some of them beautiful but little known, in fresh, contemporary arrangements. Their two albums, the self-titled *Cliar* and *Gun Tamh* (Restless), are a rich blend of solo and group songs, along with impeccable and exciting instrumentals. This spring, Cliar will join forces to tour with the Irish band Altan.

The Macmeanmna record label also maintains an informative website at www.gaelicmusic.com with all its albums and bios of all its artists. Running a record label and performing in one of Scotland's best bands might seem like a lot of work. But Arthur Cormack does not stop there.

In around 1985, he inherited the family clothing shop, and later started a music shop called "Eisd" (Gaelic for "listen"), both located in Portree. The Cormack family also runs the local post office and a bed and breakfast.

But Cormack's primary job is as Director of Fèisean nan Gàidheal. This arts organization manages the burgeoning phenomenon of "Fèisean" (pronounced "fayshen"), arts festivals which offer instruction in Gaelic music, language, drama and sports to kids aged 8-18, and some adults as well. Having started with a single event in Barra in 1981, the program now serves some 4,000 participants taught by 200 instructors in nearly 40 Fèisean, half of them in the Highland and Islands and the other half throughout the rest of Scotland. Some are week-long festivals; others present year-round programs in local communities. Supported by the Scottish Arts Council and the Highland Council, the Fèisean have had a strong impact on the high level of quality of music in Scotland by inspiring and training many fine musicians.

Yet another of Cormack's hats is his position as a member of the new governmental body, Bòrd na Gàidhlig, set up by the Scottish Executive to advise government ministers on Gaelic policy. With the help of this Gaelic Board, a new Gaelic Bill is being introduced in the parliament to help ensure support for Scotland's indigenous Gaelic culture and language.

Arthur also serves as chair of Aros, Ltd., which he set up with three others. Aros Centre is a venue in Portree for concerts, books, music, whisky, videos, and cinema, employing more than 20 staff members year round.

My presumption is that Arthur accomplishes all this for Gaelic music and culture within his waking hours, but it's hard to imagine! As I mentioned earlier, one associate has a hunch that Arthur has cloned himself. When he goes off to a Scottish Arts Council meeting in Edinburgh, he has a 5-hour drive each way from Portree. Sometimes he'll work all day on funding proposals for the Fèisean, and then go off at night to sing or be interviewed for television. In the meantime, he is running a record label, a music shop, a performing band, and a host of other projects and businesses.

As singer Mary Ann Kennedy puts it, Arthur Cormack is "without doubt the finest Gaelic singer of his generation" while also being "one of the single most influential figures in the Gaelic and Highland world today."

By rights, he should be pulling his hair out, and yet, take a look: Arthur stands calmly, hands in pockets, his voice pure and sincere as ever. If I were stranded on the proverbial desert island with one recording of Gaelic songs, I'd make sure it was one by Arthur Cormack.

23 ~ *Mary Ann Kennedy*
summer 2019

Outside of the Highlands and Islands, the largest concentration of Gaelic speakers in Scotland can be found in the Glasgow area. Singer Mary Ann Kennedy's new album, *Glaschu,* is a celebration of Gaelic Glasgow.

Glaschu is the original Gaelic name for the city, and means "the dear green place." And yet the artwork for the CD booklet suggests something more complex, using imagery of Clutha, ancient goddess of the River Clyde, and elements of the legend of St Mungo, Glasgow's patron saint. Mary Ann appears in a lacy outfit with gold lipstick, amid stonework in dark and mysterious lighting, her arms strewn with sea shells and wet sand, wearing jewelry both cheap and costly. Is this an image of Glasgow – mystical, magical, flashy, potent, gritty, sexy, and a touch sinister?

All of these notions are contained in the music and poetry of the album. Mary Ann's no-nonsense voice sings in clear and articulate tones, cutting through as needed, yet expressive and heartfelt in the slower songs. For the listener, knowledge of the Gaelic takes a back seat to the rhythmically compelling lilt of the songs, and the often sparse but perfectly matched backup, whether single guitar, backing chorus, string quartet, or soundscapes of city life.

Mary Ann Kennedy is well known in Scottish music as a Gaelic singer, broadcaster, composer, and producer. She has been an emcee for all the annual Scots Trad Music Awards ceremonies except the first one in 2003, when her band Cliar won Best Album. Cliar was a "supergroup" comprised of musicians who were all accomplished in their own right – Mary Ann plays some clàrsach (harp) but mostly sings in Gaelic with Arthur Cormack and the late Maggie Macdonald, joined by Blazin' Fiddles founder Bruce MacGregor, Ingrid Henderson on clàrsach and piano, and Chaz Stewart on guitar and bass.

Mary Ann's broadcasting career began in the mid 1990s, when she began working in the newsroom for BBC Radio Scotland in Inverness, reading the Gaelic news each day, and eventually running the newsroom. She credits that job with honing some of her performance skills, since editing and reading live news requires staying on one's toes at all times! She went on to host a world music radio program for BBC called *Mary Ann Kennedy's Global Gathering*, and one for BBC Radio 3 called *World on 3*. For some 25 years, she has worked with Irish Gaelic presenter Seán Ó hÉanaigh on *Sruth na Maoile*, a bilingual Irish-Scottish Gaelic music program, which brought together BBC Scotland and RTÉ Ireland Gaelic radio in a unique collaboration.

Mary Ann Kennedy's first exposure to music was the singing of her mother, the well-known Gaelic singer and teacher Kenna Campbell. Kenna sang solo and in groups, and was one of the founders of the Barra Fèis in 1981, which began a wave of successful week-long Fèisean throughout Scotland, particularly in the Highlands, teaching music, Gaelic language and song, and other Gaelic traditions. She was on the original faculty of the Scottish traditional music program at the Royal Conservatoire and taught there for many years, developing what is now a huge extended family of appreciative students. Kenna Campbell received an OBE in 2017 for services to Gaelic music, language and education.

Mary Ann studied classical piano and harp seriously, but ultimately focused on her Gaelic singing, and in the late 1980s won gold medals for singing at the National Gaelic Mòd.

Although she has worked as musician or producer on some 35 albums, her new album is only her second solo CD. The first was *An Dàn: Gaelic Songs for a Modern World,* a recording of all-original songs.

Most Gaelic song albums spotlight traditional material, and the singers love to sing about their home areas. Mary Ann's parents spent nearly their entire lives in Glasgow, and yet they don't think of Glasgow as their home area. As far as they are concerned, her father belongs to

Tiree, and her mother to Skye. Mary Ann has undertaken major projects about both her parents' home communities. In 2012 she developed a book and recording called *Fonn* (Gaelic for both "land" and "melody") about the music of her mother's family, the Campbells of Greepe. The book describes the family's cultural legacy on Skye and beyond, and shares 100 songs, many of which are included in the accompanying CD. Kennedy's exploration of the rich musical traditions of her father's tiny island of Tiree led to performances and a double CD called *The Tiree Songbook,* which won a Scots Trad music award for Community Project of the Year in 2017.

While an artist in residence at the Gaelic College in Skye a few years ago, she had an epiphany about Gaelic singers. "Gaels love singing about home, and it's usually their home island," she says. "And I realized that actually, home for me was Glasgow, so I should be singing about the city. I was curious to see what there was in terms of Gaelic songs, and Gaels – new arrivals to the city, but also born-and-breds like me. And it was a very rich theme. I've called it my home town love song."

Glaschu features Mary Ann's clear voice with thoughtful accompaniment lending richness and playful musicality. Many of the tracks include one of Kennedy's long-time musical partners, guitarist Finlay Wells, playing acoustic, electric and even blues guitar. Sprinkled in are several brief poems in both Gaelic and English by Derrick Thomson, read by actors, with city soundscapes lending color to the spoken words. Written between the late 1970s and the early 1990s, these poems described Glasgow at the times when Mary Ann was growing up in the south side of the city.

The album begins with an 1876 song by the famous Màiri Mhòr describing a shinty match on New Year's Day in Glasgow. Shinty is an ancient Gaelic sport using a stick and ball, related to hockey and lacrosse, and nearly the same as the Irish sport, hurling.

Other songs paint portraits of the 19th century Clutha ferries plying the River Clyde, a tribal clash between Irish immigrants, a Gael's experiences moving to the city for the first time, a description of a storm on the Broomilaw, and one about dancing among the statues of Georges Square.

Two of the songs were masterfully translated into Gaelic by Kenna Campbell. One was the inspiration for the album – "A Song for Glasgow," an old temperance song unflinchingly describing the city's social ills. "Mother Glasgow" was the other, originally written in English by singer Michael Marra, pointedly but gently reminding the city of its sectarian struggles.

The CD ends with a song by John MacFadyen from 1897, expressing the Gaelic community's embrace of its culture and its diaspora. We too will end with some of this song's words, as translated in the liner notes:

> No instrument, however finely-tuned
> Can wake my heart's joy
> Like a song from the lips of the young lasses;
>
> ...
>
> Our wellspring is the well of freshwater,
> Our elders' language, its elegant turn of phrase;
>
> ...
>
> No ocean can separate us
> And the goodwill of kinship binds us tight;
>
> ...
>
> Goodnight and bless you all.

24 ~ *Julie Fowlis*
spring 2014

When Scottish singer Julie Fowlis enthralled an American audience last fall with a program of Gaelic songs, it was striking that language posed no barrier. In fact, only one song in English was performed that night, and that was in the encore. Familiar to many, it was "Touch the Sky," which Fowlis recorded for the Grammy and Oscar-winning Disney movie, *Brave.* Its soaring melody touched the soul via Julie's beautiful voice.

But in the middle of the encore Julie disappeared, leaving the stage to the musicians. She then surprised the audience by sweeping back to center stage carrying her bagpipes for the first time that evening, and finishing the concert with a boisterous pipe tune.

Originally from North Uist in the Western Isles, Julie Fowlis is best known today as a Gaelic singer, but is also a fine piper, pennywhistle player, and oboist. She grew up surrounded by traditional music, competed as a singer in the Gaelic Mod, and like many of her friends, learned to play pipes. She was even on the verge of becoming a Highland dance teacher, but decided instead to commit her time to music.

While in college in the 1990s, the exciting traditional music scene in Glasgow gave her a chance to participate. This was a welcome release from the formality and intensity of studying classical oboe and English horn. After completing her B.A. in music at the University of Strathclyde, Fowlis cast her lot with traditional music. She joined Dochas, a band of young women from the Highlands and Islands, and together they flourished, with concerts, tours, and in 2002, a self-titled album.

Well worth a listen for its quality and variety, the Dochas CD features Julie Fowlis singing and playing whistle, pipes and oboe; Jenna Reid, now of Blazin' Fiddles, on fiddle, and other members on harp, accordion and piano. In 2004 the band added its only male musician, world champion bodhran player Martin O'Neill of Glasgow, and recorded a fine new album, *An Darna Umhail* (A Second Glance).

It was in Dochas that Julie Fowlis first became widely known as a Gaelic singer. Listen to her singing and you'll hear a voice of innocence and clarity, strong but gentle, never dark or brooding. She shares with us the sweet and passionate music of the Gaelic tradition. We hear waulking songs that inspire the working of the cloth; *puirt a beule* (mouth music) for dancers to step and leap; and lullabies, laments, and tales of woe or heroic deeds, which take us to another world. Rather than aiming songs at us with a commanding voice, Fowlis sings as if we were her community.

Taking off in new directions, Fowlis won "Best Gaelic Singer" at the Scots Traditional Music Awards in 2005 and 2007, the years of her first two solo CDs. Her first, *Mar a tha mo chridhe* (As My Heart Is), begins with several flowing songs, followed by a lively instrumental set with Julie on pennywhistle, and a selection of melodic songs that never get old. Great musicians joined her for this project, including John Doyle, Kris Drever, John McCusker, Iain MacDonald, and two members of the Irish band Danu – their lead singer, and Eamonn Doorley (Julie's future husband).

Her 2007 and 2009 CDs both won "Best Album of the Year" awards. The 2007 album, *Cuilidh,* spotlights songs from her native North Uist. The precision of her singing is a delight from the start, as we hear a set of lively *puirt a beule* songs. In this "mouth music," Fowlis's voice is like an instrument, articulating every syllable with an unmistakable beat. A beautiful love song follows, telling of a man's pain upon learning that his love was emigrating to Australia. A nice variety of songs is here accompanied by impeccable musicians, including members of the bands Capercaillie, Altan, Solas, and Nickel Creek.

Julie has had the privilege of singing several times with Transatlantic Sessions, most recently in 2013. This long-running series of TV shows, CDs, DVDs and tours brings together great Scottish and American musicians. Julie was particularly thrilled to have a chance to sing with James Taylor. "I lost the power of speech, I was so in awe of him!" she says.

Fowlis's 2009 CD, *Uam (From Me)*, features several musicians from the Transatlantic Sessions group, including Phil Cunningham on piano and accordion, box player Sharon Shannon, and dobro player Jerry Douglas. Piper Allan MacDonald plays on the album, in addition to Julie's regular touring musicians: fiddler Duncan Chisholm, guitarist Tony Byrne, and Julie's husband, Eamonn Doorley, on bouzouki.

On one track of the CD, Julie is joined by Scots singer Eddi Reader. Together, they present a Gaelic waulking song followed by an American Irish song, sung in both English and Gaelic. Eddi Reader gamely learned to sing some of the Gaelic lyrics for the recording, and blends well with Julie Fowlis, although the two women have quite distinct vocal styles.

Two tracks on *Uam* feature vocal duets with Mary Smith, a Gaelic singer from whom Fowlis has learned many songs. Originally from Lewis, Smith lived and traveled in Uist and Eriskay, meeting well respected singers and learning songs and stories of the Gaelic community. She was awarded an MBE in 1999 for her services to traditional music, and made a fine solo CD, *Sgiath Airgid (Silver Wings)*, backed by four other singers and an excellent studio band.

When Pixar Animation Studios was making the Disney film, *Brave*, they sought out one of Scotland's best young female singers for the soundtrack, and selected Julie Fowlis. They gave her free reign to choose her musicians for this exciting and demanding project, but there was certainly pressure to get it done on time. This was not only due to the filmmakers' schedule, but also because Julie was 8 months pregnant at the time.

In the past few years, Fowlis earned a Masters degree researching Gaelic culture and was awarded an honorary Doctorate in Music; she has also worked as Artist in Residence for an ambitious project to digitally archive Gaelic music. Her broadcast projects have included a BBC Radio Scotland program called "Fowlis and Folk," and narration for a BBC Alba TV documentary aired this past Christmas, celebrating the 30th anniversary of the Gaelic band Capercaillie. Despite the demands, Fowlis limits her busy schedule in order to enjoy and tend to her two small children.

Her newest CD, *Gach Sgeul (Every Story)*, features lush accompaniments and arrangements, and a new sound for Julie's voice. She finds that, since her previous CD, her voice has strengthened and matured as a result of becoming a mother.

Born in North Uist, surrounded by traditional music, a Gaelic-speaking mother and a Scots father from Pitlochry, Julie Fowlis never consciously chose to fly the flag of Gaelic culture; she just performs the music she knows and loves. But as she's become better known, she has taken up that flag to share the rich Gaelic tradition with the world, and possibly even help Gaeldom grow again after a long decline in native speakers. In 2008, she was appointed by the Scottish government to be the first official *Tosgaire an Gàidhlig,* or Ambassador for Gaelic.

With her crystalline voice and expressive musicianship, a new album out, and hopefully many more to come, Julie Fowlis is just getting warmed up, reaching across language barriers to a world that is delighted to enjoy the beauty of Gaelic song.

25 ~ *Fiona Kennedy*
fall 2017

One of the hidden treasures on YouTube is a video clip of the great Scottish singer, Calum Kennedy, singing a duet with his daughter Fiona, probably in the late 1970s. Calum's characteristically sweet and heartfelt delivery is perfectly matched by Fiona's voice. The clip is just long enough for us to hear the last verse of "The Crookit Bawbee":

An' ye are the laddie that gave me the penny,
The laddie I'll lo'e till the day that I dee;
Ye may cleed me wi' satin, an' mak' me a lady,
An' I will gang wi' ye to bonnie Glen Shee.

By the time of that video, Fiona Kennedy had already acted in movies and television series since her teens, and toured as the eldest of five daughters in the Kennedy family band. Since then, she has continued to entertain, with countless projects in Scotland and on American television. This fall, she is releasing a new solo CD we'll discuss in a moment.

Calum Kennedy and his wife, singer Anne Gillies, were household names in Scotland in the 1950s and 60s. In fact, when JFK was assassinated in 1963, many Scots feared at first that the headline "Kennedy Shot" referred to Calum! A native of the Isle of Lewis, Kennedy began his singing career after moving to Glasgow for work. There, he met Anne Gillies, and was embraced by her musical family. Anne won the 1952 gold medal for Gaelic singing at the Mod, the national competition promoting Gaelic culture, held annually since 1892. Anne's younger brother, Alasdair, won the gold medal five years later, and has only recently retired from two long, successful careers, as a singer and a dentist. Their mother Euphemia, originally from Skye, made sure to keep a welcoming

Highland home away from home, with broth on the stove, music, and a sociable dram at the ready.

Calum and Anne married in 1953, and sang together for many years. In 1955, Calum himself won the gold medal for Gaelic singing at the Mod, and moved into the international spotlight when he won the 1957 World Ballad Championship in Moscow, beating out 750 other singers with the Gaelic song, "O Mhairi E Mhairi." Singing mostly traditional songs in Gaelic, Scots, and English, Kennedy also wrote several popular songs such as "Lovely Stornaway."

The diction and tone of his voice, though not operatic, was polished as compared to the average folksinger. But it was the sincerity of his emotional singing that garnered him loving listeners in Scotland and beyond. Perhaps the intense emotion focused in his voice was what caused him to totally lose that voice for 18 months after his wife tragically passed away in 1974, due to complications from a routine surgery.

Calum recovered and sang again, but the family band was at an end. Though never quite rising to his previous peak, Calum continued singing until his death in 2006. Five years later, the Gaelic Mod instituted an annual Kennedy competition, a top-level contest limited exclusively to past winners of the Mod in Gaelic singing. In presenting the trophy to honor Calum and Anne Kennedy, their eldest daughter Fiona commented that "in many ways they were a golden couple, blessed with hauntingly beautiful voices which delighted and moved audiences at home and abroad."

Fiona Kennedy has gone on to delight and move audiences in her own right. She has headlined many projects, but particularly enjoys creative collaboration. She sang a Gaelic duo with Karen Matheson of Capercaillie for *Transatlantic Sessions*, a program which brings together American and Scottish musicians on television, live performance, CD and DVD. She produced a performance featuring herself and five other Scottish singers, called *Highland Heartbeat*, which is available on a CD but originally was a PBS TV show filmed in Glasgow. This show grew out of her relationship with American public television, where she hosted over 70 episodes of *Tartan TV*, a magazine-style program exploring stories about Scotland.

While hosting *Tartan TV*, Fiona came across a stirring exhibit at Ellis Island, sponsored by the National Museum of Scotland. Piles of kists, or chests, were on display, containing items that immigrants brought with them from Scotland on their harrowing journeys across the sea to America. Kennedy turned this experience into "The Kist," which was born as a song, then grew into a theatrical production which won a 5-star review at the Edinburgh Festival Fringe. It is an ongoing project drawing upon the kist and its contents as a metaphor for the cultural treasures immigrants from around the world keep close to them in their journeys.

Fiona's solo CDs offer contemporary and traditional material in English, Scots, and Gaelic, with a gentle folk-pop sound. Her 1995 album *Maiden Heaven* was produced by Phil Cunningham, and for her 2004 *Coming Home* album she was backed by top musicians from the traditional Scottish music scene.

Fiona's newest solo CD is called *Time to Fly*, evocative of the moment in life when a parent's children are launched and ready to take flight. Her older two children have followed their father in business careers, while her youngest, Sophie Kennedy Clark, is an award-winning actress. She plays the lead in the 2017 film *The First*, about silent movie star Mary Pickford and her pivotal role in the development of the Hollywood film industry.

It's also Fiona's "time to fly" creatively. She had a hand in writing half the songs on her new CD. The first song, "Down the Line," speaks of passing on the music to the next generation. She wrote it with the albums's guitarist and arranger, Calum MacColl. MacColl, like Fiona, grew up in a famous musical family, his father being singer and songwriter Ewan MacColl.

The only traditional Scottish song is a beautiful Gaelic/English version of "Christ Child Lullaby," by a 19th century Highland minister. Otherwise, the American influence in the CD's music is strong. Fiona wrote one song with Beth Nielsen Chapman, a 2016 inductee into the Nashville Songwriters Hall of Fame; two songs were collaborations with Marcus Hummon, a Grammy Award-winning country songwriter.

However, to my ears, the country music influence can't disguise the Scottish sound of Fiona's voice. The sound of American folksingers often draws upon an aggrieved or rebellious attitude, and country singers like to project an edge of toughness or underlying hurt. But Fiona Kennedy's voice is unfailingly sweet and lyrical, not so different from the voice in that YouTube clip of herself singing with her father Calum. It's a sweetness and sincerity of sound that I feel is traceable to the Gaelic song tradition. You can hear it in the sound of many Gaelic singers, and it is captivating.

One of the songs Kennedy cowrote for her CD came to her while volunteering in Africa for F.R.O.M Scotland (Famine Relief of Malawi). It's called "Weaver of Dreams," inspired by a description of Calum Kennedy in an old review he once showed Fiona, and incorporates thoughts about the life of opera singer Maria Callas.

Fiona is a major supporter of F.R.O.M Scotland as well as other community-oriented projects. For 30 years, she has helped VSA, the Volunteer Service Agency of Aberdeen. She's particularly enthused about their "Sing, Sing, Sing" program, in which hundreds of ordinary workers learn, rehearse and perform songs for a contest, raising huge sums to benefit mental health patients.

Fiona Kennedy's tireless engagements include an O.B.E. awarded by the Queen, services as one of Aberdeenshire's Deputy Lord-Lieutenants, appearances on TV, film, musical theater, at the G8 Summit and in performance for all the NATO ambassadors in Brussels. And yet, she maintains her roots in family, Gaelic song, the songs of Robert Burns, and community service.

The list of her achievements is long and getting longer. "I don't ever stop, I don't ever intend to stop," Fiona says. "Music is a great driving force, that thread woven from my birth. It connects in every way with every thing."

SECTION 3b ~ SONGS IN SCOTS AND ENGLISH

26 ~ *Appreciating Robert Burns*
winter 1999-2000

Some people think that Scots can never quite agree on anything, but it's not true. One thing all Scots (and lots of non-Scots) share is a respect and appreciation for Robert Burns. Don't tell me you don't agree!

The poems and songs of Burns inspire a feeling which crosses all ages and walks of life. Each January 25, the poet's birthday is celebrated round the world with Burns Suppers, concerts and readings. Some enjoy stories of his flair for love, others his love of nature, or his satire of the high and mighty. But everyone loves the music he chose and the flow of his songs.

Burns did not actually make up tunes for his songs; he selected them from the rich musical soup of Scots and Gaelic cultures that surrounded him. He preserved many beautiful Scottish melodies, which his unfailing ear nabbed and pinned to paper by writing verses to them.

The heart of music is its rhythm and phrasing, and anyone who can write words to fit music as naturally as Burns has the soul of a great musician. In his own words, "Until I am complete master of a tune, in my own singing, ... I can never compose for it."

Sometimes he used tunes from older songs and wrote new verses, as in "The Soldier's Return," or he mixed old and new words, as in "Auld Lang Syne." Sometimes he took a contemporary fiddle tune and made it into a new song, as in "My Love is a Red Red Rose" and "Of All the Airts the Wind Can Blaw."

While Burns songs, and the tunes they made famous, can be found everywhere in Scottish music, there are some recordings devoted specifically to Burns.

Amid the flurry of Burns activity during the 1996 bicentennial of the poet's death, one of the most notable projects to emerge was Linn Records' *Complete Songs of Robert Burns*, a projected 12-CD series, produced at a rate of two per year. This series gathers a glittering array of the top professional folk musicians in Scotland today, many of whom are working in well-known bands such as Battlefield Band, Tannahill Weavers, Capercaillie, Ossian, Old Blind Dogs, Deaf Shepherd, Ceolbeg, Seelyhoo, and Tabache. The bands themselves are not included in these recordings, just players from them; each song is arranged by a different singer and his or her fellow musicians. In future this series will serve as a who's who of Scottish folk music in the 1990s.

Despite the broad variety of performers, the high quality of the music is fairly even throughout. Heartfelt or upbeat renditions of the songs are dressed in the energetic garb of traditional folk instruments: fiddle, guitar, whistle, accordion and concertina. Each CD offers from 20 to 30 songs.

One of the singers featured on the series is Rod Paterson, who has his own Burns album, entitled *Songs from the Bottom Drawer*, on the Greentrax label. No voice can quite match his open, rich, unaffected warmth.

Rod is also included on an REL recording entitled Pride and Passion, along with singers Carol Laula and George Drennan. This dramatic presentation of Burns songs crosses over between folk and classical sounds, with a chamber ensemble arranged by folk cellist Ron Shaw.

Also crossing the folk/classical boundaries is the Burns series by Jean Redpath. Originally intended to cover all Burns songs in 20 LPs/cassettes, the series ended after seven (now condensed onto three CDs) because of the death of composer Serge Hovey. Redpath's clear voice and Hovey's creative and evocative arrangements make for a unique and enjoyable listening experience.

Home alone on January 25th? If you miss the classic sounds of a Burns supper, or if you want to see what one is like without getting tickets, you can pick up Lismor's *Burns Supper*. This double CD gives you all the humorous speeches, the live sound of dinner guests clinking glasses and reacting to the show, good old Andy Stewart belting out the "Address to the Haggis" and "Tam O' Shanter," plus some accordion (John Carmichael band), pipes (Iain MacFadyen), fiddle (Ian Powrie), and songs (Kenneth McKellar and Isobel Buchanan).

Several other albums in Lismor's Burns series include *The Words* (readings), *The Music* (easy listening by the Gaelforce Orchestra), and *The Songs*. This last has such a breadth of styles that it will doubtless have something for everyone. It is a testimony to the universal affection Scots have for Burns. Unfortunately, there are so many different styles that it may well include something you won't like! Included are operatic singers Peter Morrison and Moira Anderson, the Scottish Philharmonic Singers, folksinger Jean Redpath, Tony Cuffe with the folk band Ossian, sentimental favorite Alex Beaton, and the rock style of Dalriada.

Just as Dalriada's rock ballad style brings Burns to new audiences with fresh emotion, so do Scottish performers of all ages embrace Burns for his timeless sentiments and compelling melodies. Fans of the Celtic concert band Silly Wizard, who loved being wowed by virtuosos Johnny and Phil Cunningham, also sank into the ballads (including Burns songs) sung by the band's singer, Andy M. Stewart. Stewart's romantic voice could stir any listener with his album *Andy M. Stewart Sings the Songs of Robert Burns*.

If like most Scots you love to wallow in sentimental songs, you'll enjoy the well-balanced mix of Lochshore's *Tribute to Robert Burns*, featuring the emotional pop singing of Valerie Dunbar, the clear, trained voices of Peter Mallan and Anne Lorne Gillies, and the upbeat singing of the Clydesiders.

Spotlighting Burns's love songs, Gillian Bowman starts off her *Toasting the Lassies* album with "Green Grow the Rashes O." This well-known song sports a line most apt for this album: "the sweetest hours that e'er I spent were spent among the lassies, o!" Bowman's clear folk voice is accompanied quietly by harper Wendy Stewart, along with guitar, fiddle and flute.

For heartfelt, fun singing, you can't do better than Alastair McDonald's *Honest Poverty* (the title is from the poem "A Man's A Man for A' That"). A fine entertainer, McDonald has a smile in his voice, enjoyable musical arrangements, and diction that lets you understand every word.

One group of Burns songs that usually gets left out of the "complete" collections are the songs we're not supposed to know about – the bawdy ones. Iona Records put them out on the album *The Merry Muses*, complete with a red "Parental Guidance" sticker (probably more to attract attention than to warn parents!). Songs such as "Ye Jovial Boys Who Loved the Joys" and "Nine Inch Will Please a Lady" are set to very nice music, and well sung. In fact, the music is not raucous or particularly rowdy. It's the lyrics that include the occasional four-letter word and the colorful subject matter. And yet this is still the work of a great poet: frank, sincere, and meaningful. I'd have to side with my great-uncle, the judge who decided to allow the publication of Henry Miller's books, and pronounce this verdict: these dirty songs have socially redeeming value!

Last but certainly not least, we'll take in the sounds of Scotland's masterful tenor, Kenneth McKellar. His *To Robert Burns: A Tribute* shows McKellar in his element. Backed by piano and a chamber ensemble for which he arranged and directed the music, McKellar's operatic voice lays bare his love of these songs with great energy but no heaviness, and a certain simplicity throughout, as if the songs sing themselves.

In his liner notes, Kenneth McKellar speaks for everyone when he writes that his arrangements "reflect all my feelings for Robert Burns, my love for the melodies he chose, for the words he wrote, and for the privilege of getting to know him better with every passing year." I think we can all agree with that.

27 ~ Burns's Homecoming
fall 2009

This year's Homecoming in Scotland 2009 was built around the 250th birthday of Scotland's national songwriter, Robert Burns. His actual birthday, January 25, was the focal point for many exhibits, discussions and celebrations, including a world-wide Burns Supper which connected over 3,600 Burns Night suppers around the world. Throughout the year, there continue to be many Burns events, as well as longer-term projects such as the construction of a new Robert Burns Birthplace Museum.

Did I say "Scotland's national songwriter"? Maybe I should have said "poet" or "bard". After all, literature classes around the world, including in Scotland, teach Burns as a great poet, not a songwriter. Yet a majority of his work was conceived as lyrics for songs, not as poetry later to be set to music. The music was uppermost in Burns's mind as he wrote many of his poems. "Until I am complete master of a tune, in my own singing," said Burns, "I can never compose [words] for it." As a result, his words seem to fit effortlessly with their melodies.

"Music is the language of nature," wrote Burns, "and poetry, particularly songs, are always more or less localised… this is the reason why so many of our Scots airs have outlived their original and perhaps many subsequent sets of verses."

The evidence over the past 200 years is that the songs and poems of Burns rise above being "localised." Even though he uses the Scots language, as when he speaks to a "wee, sleekit, cow'rin, tim'rous beastie", his keen thoughts turn to more general reflections. While pondering the destruction of a mouse hole in Ayrshire, he concludes famously that "the best-laid schemes o' mice an' men gang aft agley." Thoughts about "hamely fare" and "yon birkie, ca'd a lord" lead to the uplifting conclusion that "it's coming yet for a' that, that Man to Man, the world o'er, shall brothers be for a' that."

It was a fateful meeting in Edinburgh that gave Burns the opportunity to direct the world's attention to the richness of the music and song of Scotland, including his own work.

Escaping a dire situation in 1786, involving two women newly pregnant and a desperate attempt to raise money by locally publishing some of his poems, Burns arrived in Edinburgh to unexpectedly become the toast of society. He was the poor farmer revealed as genius. Robert Louis Stevenson wrote of Burns's arrival in Edinburgh that "such a revolution is not to be found in literary history." One of the few poems Burns wrote during that trip was "Address to a Haggis", and I sometimes wonder if Edinburgh society made him feel like the "Rustic, haggis-fed" who trumped the fancy foreigners with his "honest, sonsie face."

While in Edinburgh, Burns met James Johnson, who invited him to work on the *Scots Musical Museum*. Originally intended as a two-volume collection of the best of Scottish, Irish and English songs, the project ended up, with the energetic help of Robert Burns, as a six-volume collection of some 600 Scottish songs, with music printed for each song. More than 200 of the songs were written by Burns himself.

Of his work on collecting songs, Burns wrote, "I have been absolutely crazed about it, collecting old stanzas, and every information remaining respecting their origin, authors, etc." He compiled much of this information into notes about many of the songs. In one note, he comments that "I have paid more attention to every description of Scots songs than perhaps anybody living has done."

Many of these notes reveal fascinating perspectives about the songs and Scottish culture. About the song "Bed of Sweet Roses," he writes that "this song, as far as I know, for the first time appears here in print. When I was a boy it was a very popular song in Ayrshire." The song "There's Nae Luck About the House," Burns writes, is "one of the most beautiful songs in the Scots, or in any other language." Wherever possible, he comments on the origin of both music and words, including older versions where he found them: "This song is by Dr Blacklock; and I believe, but am not quite certain, that the air is his too." Burns discovered that "The Lass of Livington" had an original set of verses which "have a very great deal of poetic merit but are not quite ladies' reading." About "The Flowers of Edinburgh," he writes that its title "has no manner of connection with the present verses, so I suspect there has been an older set of words, of which the title is all that remains."

In writing about the songs, Burns also reveals much about his own life and views. "I would always take it as a compliment to have it said, that my heart ran before my head," he writes while discussing a song. Sometimes we'd like to know more, of course. Here's what he says about one of his own songs: "The tune is by Oswald. The song alludes to a part of my private history, which it is of no consequence to the world to know."

Probably the best representation of Burns songs is Linn Records' landmark *Complete Songs of Robert Burns*. Begun at the bicentennial of his death in 1996, and completed in 2003, this 12-volume series of CDs captures all 365 of the songs identified with Burns. A treasury of music and song that we could only wish was available in every public library, this series gave us, for the first time in history, a chance to hear any and all of Burns's songs. Over 100 of Scotland's best contemporary musicians were involved, including well-known soloists and members of popular bands such as Battlefield Band, The Cast, The Corries, Deaf Shepherd, Malinky, and Old Blind Dogs, interpreting the music in straightforward and spirited renditions that must have set Burns to smiling in his grave.

Jean Redpath toured for years as a leading exponent of Burns songs, and made two series of recordings of his songs. One series features whimsical arrangements by classical composer Serge Hovey, and the other series offers more traditional folksong arrangements, with straightforward voice and guitar.

Recordings of Burns by singer Kenneth McKellar, with his operatic voice and orchestral accompaniment, may not fit the image of the ploughman poet, but might well have pleased the Robert Burns who enjoyed being the toast of Edinburgh society in 1787. McKellar's sincerity shines through his gifted and trained voice and his emotional arrangements.

Several compilations of earlier recorded songs have been released in time for Homecoming 2009, and a number of recent recordings have sought a new take on the traditional music. Eddi Reader's free-spirited renditions of Burns songs is a refreshing, beautifully sung album with excellent accompanying musicians. Rod Paterson's clear and expressive voice can be heard on his Burns CD entitled *Songs from the Bottom Drawer*. A new Ayrshire group called Borealis offers Burns songs mixed with influences from classical music, blues, jazz and folk. There's even a dance party album that cranks Burns songs up to the third degree, called *Burn It Up! - Red Hot Rabbie Burns Dance Tracks*.

This wild variety of styles for performing Burns songs reveals the continuing broad appeal of Burns's keenly observed poetry, set to evocative music. Some might feel there is a correct way to present Burns songs, but I'm not sure Burns would have agreed. Time and again, he revealed a desire, reflected often in the Scottish experience, for acceptance and appreciation, and a passion for ignoring class distinctions. Burns embraced everyone as people and celebrated nature for embracing us all.

And for this reason, perhaps, the Homecoming to Burns's Scotland is really a welcome "home" to all.

28 ~ *Keeping Scots Alive*
summer 2000

Last year marked a curious paradox of Scottish culture. On the one hand, all Scotland celebrated the 250th birthday of Robert Burns, Scotland's world-renowned poet and songwriter, who wrote much of his work in Scots, the language of his native Ayrshire. On the other hand, support for many Scots language and song projects faltered as funding was cut during that same celebratory year.

It appears that while enthusiasts happily pay tribute to Scots as the language of Burns, many also view Scots as the language *of his time*. And yet, today, about one out of three Scottish schoolchildren speak Scots on a daily basis. The Scottish government's educational guidelines "advocate the inclusion of Scots in the school curriculum where appropriate," and although there is some impressive work in that direction, the inclusion of Scots in schools appears to be half-hearted.

Some organizations and individuals are working to preserve and develop the vitality of Scots. Among these are Itchie Coo for schoolchildren and teachers, with its Scots books, poems, games, and its Itchie-Cool website for kids; the Traditional Music and Song Association (TMSA), sponsoring festivals, workshops, sessions, and competitions since 1966; Springthyme Records, with over 35 years of recordings devoted mostly to Scots songs; and the School of Scottish Studies, which has researched the subject for decades, and has recordings available on the Scottish Tradition Series released by Greentrax Recordings.

The Scottish government officially supports Scots in concept, having stated to the European community that it "recognises, respects and celebrates the Scots language as an integral part of our cultural heritage." (UK Report to the Council of Europe, 2007)

But there are cultural barriers. One such barrier is implied in the government's assurance that it "recognises and respects Scots as a distinct language, and does not consider the use of Scots to be an indication of poor competence in English." Perhaps foremost among the cultural problems is that Scots is often viewed as the language of peasants. Robert Burns was celebrated in Edinburgh despite being a poor farmer. In fact, his status as a peasant made his genius especially exciting to Edinburgh society. But Burns was a special case, of course. If Scots speakers today are perceived by themselves and others as lower class because of their language, how many can rely on genius as a ticket to respect?

At least one kind of genius among Scots speakers, however, is widely respected: Scots culture, particularly its songs. The artistry of Robert Burns in using Scots for his songs and poems is internationally recognized for its quality. The artistry of countless other Scots songwriters, singers, and poets is also easy to respect and enjoy, and is a source of pride for Scotland. (For a discussion of the richness of the Scots song repertoire, see Chapter 29.)

It is this powerful connection between Scots language and music that is being nurtured by such organizations as Scotland's Traditional Music and Song Association (TMSA). One of TMSA's directors, John Morran, is a Scots singer in his own right, having performed for many years with Deaf Shepherd, a long-lived and innovative traditional band. The band has put out three fine albums over the past fifteen years and is working on a new one. Morran hails originally from a small town in Ayrshire where Scots is spoken regularly, and freely acknowledges that even into his 20s he shared the common prejudices against his own language. "A lack of understanding of grammar, history and European languages," says Morran, "has left the lowland Scots with the regard that their own tongue is slang English."

But like many others in recent years, Morran has come to strongly appreciate the history and significance of Scots as a language in its own right. Morran speaks for many Scots speakers when he refers to the impact of the most famous of Scots songwriters, Robert Burns. "His significance to people like me is huge. It gives me ownership of my language and lends gravitas to what I do."

One of Morran's projects through the TMSA is to push for increased funding for Scots song and language projects. He has thoroughly researched the situation, and although he finds the current lack of support for Scots very sobering, there are rays of hope. At workshops where he taught Burns songs, he has found kids wholeheartedly taking to the songs written in the same Scots they speak themselves. He has noticed more people speaking in Scots, including some in governmental positions. Studies have shown that in some areas, such as Aberdeenshire, many kids do not regard Scots as merely slang English, but as their own language.

Although the TMSA promotes Scots song and has worked to promote Scots culture, it is a national organization with broad interests. Based in Edinburgh, with some 900 members and ten branches throughout Scotland, TMSA last year sponsored nearly 250 events for over 17,000 participants, and helps affiliated groups promote their events. Each January, it publishes an annual calendar of traditional music events taking place throughout the year in Scotland, and runs community-based festivals each year in Keith, Kirriemuir, and Auchtermuchty. Since 2004, it has put together a national tour of the winners of the BBC Radio Scotland Young Traditional Musician of the Year Award, recording an annual CDs of these young artists on the TMSA's own label. For the Homecoming Year, TMSA organized traditional music sessions in cooperation with venues throughout Scotland.

Veteran Scottish musicians support TMSA's efforts to promote Scotland's traditional music, by lending their names as official patrons and performing at fundraising concerts. These artists include folklorist and Gaelic singer Margaret Bennett, fiddler Aly Bain, accordionist and composer Phil Cunningham, popular folksinger and actress Barbara Dickson, and Scots singer Sheena Wellington.

But with mostly volunteer help and a small paid staff, the TMSA can only do so much as it seeks to nurture Scots song and push for support. There is no knight in shining armor fighting for the Scots culture, but there are many groups and individuals who may yet pull together and gain traction on behalf of the language of not only Robert Burns but of many of today's lowland Scots.

Some take heart from the way that Gaelic culture has managed, through years of hard work and persistence, to develop respect and vitality through Gaelic schools and a growing movement of cultural Fèisean promoting Gaelic music, language, sports and crafts. In 2006, Gaelic achieved acceptance as an official language of Scotland alongside English (see Chapter 22 for a profile of Arthur Cormack, arguably Gaeldom's knight in shining armor).

The Scottish government has now established a Scots Language Working Group. It remains to be seen what the mosaic of efforts by the government, arts organizations, teachers, performers and writers can do for Scots language and culture, but their hopes were summed up by former culture minister Michael Russell, who stated last October that securing "a successful way forward for the Scots language" would be "a fantastic legacy of the Year of Homecoming" that "would make Burns himself proud."

29 ~ *Richness of Scots Song*
summer 2000

Her rich voice filled every note with a passion so plain that no one could listen unaffected. Her songs told old stories that felt urgent, and yet she sang each word as if she had all the time in the world.

Such was Jeannie Robertson of Aberdeenshire, "one of the angels of folk song that have kept the tradition alive and burning across time," as folklorist Alan Lomax described her.

Plucked from ordinary lives and set down in the new folk festivals and clubs of the 1950s, Jeannie and other singers like her inspired a generation of post-war Scots to re-evaluate and explore their own native traditions. The cultural ripple effect of their singing upon modern Scottish music is remarkable.

CDs are now available that include Jeannie and other key Aberdeenshire singers, among them Jane Turriff, Jock Duncan, Jimmy MacBeath, Sheila MacGregor, Lizzie Higgins, Margaret Stewart, John Strachan, and Willie Scott. All can be heard on the Scottish Tradition series made available by the University of Edinburgh's School of Scottish Studies on the Greentrax label, and on the Alan Lomax Collection CDs recently released by Rounder Records.

Jeannie Robertson's solo CD, *Queen of the Heather*, part of the Alan Lomax series, offers many previously unreleased songs, plus brief interviews revealing some of Jeannie's thoughts about the songs. Jane Turriff has a solo album as well, drawn from archival recordings and aptly called *Singin is Ma Life*, while Jock Duncan recently recorded his first album, *Ye Shine Whar Ye Stan!*, at the age of 70, full of spirit and accompanied by his famous piping son, Gordon Duncan, along with Brian

McNeill and Peter Shepheard. Both Turriff's and Duncan's albums are on Springthyme Records, a label devoted to traditional Scots music.

The northeast of Scotland is a treasure trove of songs. Some 1/3 of the ballads collected and catalogued by Francis Child originated in this area, and variants of these songs have spread throughout Britain and America. One of the largest folksong collections in the world is the Greig-Duncan Collection – over 3,000 songs found in Aberdeenshire by Gavin Greig and James Duncan at the beginning of the 20th century. At the time, nobody dreamed there could be so many songs in that area. As Lomax later noted, "the Scots have the liveliest folk tradition of the British Isles," and the northeast of Scotland figures as one of the richest of regional cultures.

The School of Scottish Studies series includes an album of *Bothy Ballads* (songs from the farmworkers of Aberdeenshire and Fife), and an album of *The Muckle Sangs* (narrative ballads) from northeast Scotland, both of which present many of the traditional singers mentioned above.

In addition to Jeannie Robertson's album, the Alan Lomax Collection includes four other CDs featuring music of Scotland: the *World Library of Folk and Primitive Music Vol. 3*, which highlights the first recorded survey of Scottish music (1951); two volumes of Child ballads in *Classic Ballads of Britain and Ireland*; and *Songs of Seduction*, which presents the more ribald folk songs.

Although the School of Scottish Studies series and the Lomax Collection are all digitally remastered from the original tape recordings to ensure reasonable sound quality, they are intended as documentation of a living tradition rather than as entertaining listening. Some of the singers are captivating, but others are unfortunately past their prime, and were recorded because of their repertoire or their renown.

A more listenable introduction to traditional songs can be found in *Folk Songs of Northeast Scotland*, an album recorded live at the 1995 Edinburgh International Festival. This album includes older singers such as Jane Turriff and Jock Duncan, and the classic singers Sheila Stewart, Elizabeth Stewart, and Norman Kennedy. There's a song from Hamish Henderson, who developed the School of Scottish Studies and brought many traditional singers to light. Contemporary favorites Isla St. Clair,

Sheena Wellington, Aileen Carr, Gordeanna McCulloch, and several other solo and group songs round out the album.

One stumbling block in listening to the songs of Aberdeenshire is the strong Scots accent, called Lallans (as in "Lowlands") or Doric. It can frustrate English-speakers to listen to songs that seem to be in English but, because of the Scots words and accent, are sometimes just beyond understanding. Yet the melodies and the lilting voices are worth hearing in and of themselves, and with a little practice, it's not too difficult to understand most of the lyrics as well.

Isla St. Clair is one singer who was directly inspired by the great traditional singers performing in the Aberdeen Folk Club during the 1960s. A few years ago she was featured on a BBC television program filmed live in a village hall. Two resulting CDs, *Tatties and Herrin': The Land*, and *Tatties and Herrin': The Sea* are educational and entertaining, alternating traditional songs with descriptions of life in northeast Scotland. She has gone on recently to sing the soundtrack for *When the Pipers Play*, celebrating the legend of the bagpipes in Britain and America.

Though music of the Scottish northeast is not widely known, it is increasingly available. A new record label, Sleepytoon Records, has made several albums by the traditional northeast singing group, The Gaugers, as well as a bothy song collection. Ross Records has a new compilation of greatest hits from a popular annual Aberdeenshire concert series called *The Auld Meal Mill 1982-1999*, including singers Robert Lovie, John Mearns and Ina Miller, along with some fine northeast-style fiddling, dance band music and whistle playing.

If you become familiar with the songs kept alive by the old traditional singers, you'll hear them crop up in many contexts in Scottish music today, whether performed by modern Celtic bands, popular entertainers, or urban folksingers. For example, the popular band Old Blind Dogs, originally based in Aberdeen, has included in its recordings quite a few old ballads and bothy songs, such as "The Bonnie Bonnie Banks of Fordie," "Cruel Sister," "Battle of Harlaw," "Mormond Braes," "Barnyards of Delgaty," and "Gin I Were Where Gadie Rins," all with innovative, contemporary arrangements.

A new and promising series of traditional recordings is currently being produced by the editors of *Living Tradition*, Scotland's folk music magazine. It is called the "Tradition Bearers" series to emphasize the notion that each generation produces singers with the talent and desire to immerse themselves in the tradition and become sources for the generation to follow. The first two albums of the series came out this year, featuring Bob Blair and Jimmy Hutchison in relaxed, enjoyable performances.

It would be difficult to list the many contemporary singers in Scotland today who draw upon the great song traditions of Aberdeenshire. Ian F. Benzie, Sheena Wellington, Rod Paterson, Isla St. Clair, Heather Heywood, Adam McNaughton, Dick Gaughan, Archie Fisher, Brian McNeill, Iain Mackintosh, Alan Reid, Davy Steele — this might be a good short list (though no doubt I've left out somebody's favorite singer!). Some who continue their Scottish singing from their base overseas in the U.S. include Tony Cuffe, Ed Miller, and Jean Redpath.

One remarkable fact about these modern singers is that many of them spend most of their time singing. There is enough appreciation for traditional music that they can even make a bit of a living into the bargain. This is a long way from the time when traditional singers were farmers, traveling people, and shepherds.

And yet, judging from the likes of Jeannie Robertson, it doesn't take a singing career to make a great singer. It requires a good voice, plus the heart and the dedication that were part and parcel of the thriving culture of Aberdeenshire.

30 ~ *Burns Complete*
winter 2003-04

If only he could join us for his 244th birthday this January, Robert Burns would flush with pleasure to know that every one of his songs can now be enjoyed by anyone with a CD player.

The *Complete Songs of Robert Burns*, from Linn Records, was completed this past year with the release of the last three volumes of the 12-volume series. Vol. 11 being a double CD, there are thirteen CDs in all, containing every song currently known to have been written by Burns – a total of 365. One for each day of the year — surely a Scot can invent a CD-playing calendar to play us our daily Burns song!

This monumental tribute to Scotland's national poet is also an homage to the extraordinarily vibrant community of traditional Scottish musicians. Over 100 of Scotland's finest performers participated in recording the series, including more than 40 singers and over 60 instrumentalists.

Despite this large number of artists, the quality of the performances is uniformly excellent. I attribute this partly to the professionalism of the musicians; partly to the musical and organizational ability of the producer and arranger, Dr. Fred Freeman; and partly to the inspiring lyrics of Robert Burns and the beautiful melodies he selected.

Burns composed his songs by first choosing (or being inspired by) a traditional melody, then having it firmly in mind when writing the words. This is why his songs flow, the syllables matching the music, and the music adding expression to the words. Of course, this was no free ride: Burns regarded his poems as the fruit of "labor, attention, and pains."

When sung by such fine artists as perform on these recordings, the songs flow effortlessly and with great spirit. This too results from "labor, attention, and pains," for the melodies selected by Burns span a broad range of emotion, from slow air to fast fiddle reel, and many are difficult to sing because of speed or a wide vocal range — up to two-and-a-half octaves in some cases.

The musical arrangements by Dr. Freeman are uncluttered and complementary to each song. Traditional instruments are used to accompany but never overshadow the songs. Often a guitar backs the singer, fingerpicked or rhythmically strummed; sometimes we hear fiddle and hand drum (bodhran). Here and there, we are treated to smallpipes, whistle, harp, cello, harpsichord, or even organ-like chording on accordion. Several songs are unaccompanied.

Dr. Freeman's intent was to allow each CD to stand alone, like an extended concert, with varied tempos and texture. In this he succeeds. There is a good balance of drama, tension, serenity, joy, humor, and spunk in the music, just as in the lyrics.

A multi-instrumentalist in his own right, Freeman is a piper, a pianist, and an Honorary Fellow of the Department of English Literature at the University of Edinburgh. Other recent projects of his include a CD tribute to Hamish Henderson, and several albums exploring music of the Borders.

The *Complete Songs of Robert Burns* was launched to celebrate the 1996 bicentennial of the death of Robert Burns. The first album was built around the singing of the late Tony Cuffe, because Dr. Freeman felt that Cuffe's clear enunciation and informal directness of expression represented the style of singing Burns preferred. Above all, Burns wanted his words understood and his feelings conveyed. Tony sings the opening and closing songs of the album, and four others as well. The other singers on that first album are all of the finest caliber: Rod Paterson of Ceolbeg, Billy Ross of Ossian, Christine Kydd of Chantan, Ian F. Benzie of Old Blind Dogs, Alan Reid of Battlefield Band, and Janet Russell.

Dr. Freeman brought on board many of Scotland's best singers and instrumentalists. For each song, he selected a singer that he thought would suit it best. In a few cases, he went through as many as six singers before finding the right singer for a particular song. Often, the singers were unfamiliar with their assigned songs, but learned them convincingly.

They then had to record in only one or two takes, in order to preserve the freshness of the performances.

The more famous Burns songs, such as "Auld Lang Syne", "A Man's A Man for A' That", "Comin' Thro' the Rye", and "Ye Banks and Braes" are sprinkled throughout the series, but there was apparently no master plan to spread out the "good stuff" among the various CDs. In fact, Dr. Freeman points out that there is "no rubbish," as he puts it, in Burns's work. All the songs are good, and many of the unknown songs are even better than the famous ones. Listeners may seek out the celebrated songs, but the not-so-well-known songs will never disappoint.

The songs with explicit lyrics are contained on one of the two CDs in Volume 11. Some are love songs with frank language; others are spunky or humorous exposés. Although there is a parental guidance label on this album, I'm not sure people need fret too much about the kids: the music is good, the singing spirited, the language is Scots, and the poet writes with plenty of indirect images and metaphors.

Volume 12 is a little different from the others in that the first half of the album contains a "cantata" with spoken words. Burns's "Love and Liberty: A Cantata" alternates brief poetic narration with songs, telling a story about a gathering of unsavory characters, revealing their humanity and distilling a few moral lessons for us all. Appropriately enough for this last album in the series, some of the songs are allusions or parodies of other Burns songs.

All lyrics are printed in the CD booklets. Ironically, my only frustration with the series is that the lyrics are the only information given about each song, other than a listing of performers. Despite the risk of too bulky a booklet, it would have been nice if the liner notes told us a little about each song; certainly most of the songs have tales to tell. For instance, we could learn about the melodies Burns selected, which were all tunes or older songs in their own right before he used them.

Some Burns songs are commonly sung to melodies Burns did not select, but this series remains true to the original tunes. Two examples are "Auld Lang Syne" and "My Love is a Red Red Rose." Once you hear the original melody, you will gain an appreciation for Burns's impeccable musical taste.

Burns made clear which melodies to use for most of his songs, but in a few cases, Dr. Freeman had to research Burns's letters for suggestions on which tunes to use. For the handful of songs without any indication of melodies, Freeman selected appropriate Scottish tunes, often ones used by Burns for other songs.

The significance of this project for Scottish culture cannot be overstated. About 60% of the works of Robert Burns were songs, and for the first time, we can now listen to Burns's works in roughly the way that he conceived of them. In addition, through the efforts of over 100 of Scotland's best contemporary musicians, we get a taste of the heart and soul of today's Scottish music.

Infused with modern freshness and spirit, yet true to the original works, the *Complete Songs of Robert Burns* recordings would surely thrill the author, if only he could make it to the birthday party. Come to think of it, what better way for him to join us than in a spirited performance of his works?

31 ~ Jean Redpath
summer 2005

The year 1937 saw two most notable comings and goings in Scotland: the death of James M. Barrie, author of *Peter Pan*, and the birth of singer Jean Redpath.

Always a singer from the heart, Jean Redpath has introduced to millions of radio listeners and concertgoers the beauty, drama, and wit of Scottish song. Some 30 of her CDs are currently available, spanning four decades dedicated to nearly constant touring. Throughout the recordings, her voice is consistently expressive: smooth, articulate, and pulsing with emotion. In person, she still speaks with the youthful and chipper voice heard in performances across the length and breadth of America and Scotland, and beyond.

One of Redpath's major projects has been to spread an appreciation for the songs of Robert Burns. It's almost been a mission of hers to present her audiences with a sense of the depth and variety of Scottish song, and move people beyond the few songs and stories that often stereotype Scottish culture.

In the 1980s, Jean worked with film and stage composer Serge Hovey on what was intended to be a complete recording of all 323 of Burns' songs. Unfortunately, Hovey died in 1989, having arranged 87 Burns songs (now on four CDs), taking care to match the songs to their original tunes. His arrangements place Jean's pure voice into a rhythmic texture, using piano, guitar, and orchestral instruments. Hovey's musical moods have an entertaining quality, almost like the soundtrack to a movie, as they vary between playful and brooding, complex and spare.

Jean also recorded 85 Burns songs with a very different sound, featuring only her clear voice with guitar. These are available on three

CDs on her own label, and recall the lovely atmosphere of her live shows. Robert Burns championed the use of the Scots language, and following his lead, Jean Redpath presents many of Burns' songs and other songs in broad Scots when in performance. For American audiences, she communicates through the beautiful melodies, along with a bit of cajoling and explanation about lyrics and story lines.

Of course, this is not without its difficulties and charms. After singing the Burns song, "Woo'd and Married and A'," one listener couldn't quite understand the song title, as was made clear when he asked Redpath about that interesting song he thought was called "Would America Know." Or after singing a song about the young man who "dried her cheeks and kissed her syne" ("syne" meaning "then" as in Auld Lang Syne), someone asked her exactly what it was that the young man had kissed.

Until college, Jean's experience with singing was pretty much limited to the songs her mother sang to help get the dishes or the laundry done, including parodies of Salvation Army songs, bits of classic ballads, and what Jean jokingly calls "Victorian hideobilia."

But at the University of Edinburgh, she heard a talk by the passionate Scottish folklorist and singer, Hamish Henderson. He had recently discovered the great Jeannie Robertson, and played tapes of her singing. Hearing one of her mother's songs sung to a different tune, Redpath excitedly sang to Hamish her mother's melody. Said he, drily, "That's an interesting variant." It was a rather deflating introduction to folklore academia. Nevertheless, Jean was inspired by Hamish Henderson and the School of Scottish Studies, and her singing was heavily influenced by Jeannie Robertson. Echoes of Robertson's commanding voice can be heard in some of the songs Redpath recorded early on.

One of the strongest influences on Jean's singing, though, came from Jeannie Robertson's daughter, Lizzie Higgins. Lizzie's singing moved Jean away from the impersonal voice of Jeannie Robertson to the more intimate side. "If I expected to reach emotions in other people," Jean realized, "then it was perfectly okay for them to reach emotions in me." Instead of focusing her performances on producing a perfect voice, she allowed herself to be affected by the story. It is this intimacy and emotion that makes Jean Redpath's singing timeless and compelling.

Amidst the sometimes dark emotions of Scottish song, Jean leavens the pathos with entertaining tales about Scots such as the minister who was vexed by a congregant who would come to church every Sunday morning after spending the previous night womanizing and drinking. "Iain, how do you reconcile the two?" asked the minister. Said Iain, "I've never tried."

Although she enjoys singing a wide variety of songs, the bulk of Redpath's repertoire is Scottish. Her style is very Scottish as well. Her voice holds onto syllables, and then gives a pulse with the consonants, in a way that reminds me of the ornamentation of a fiddler or a piper playing a march or a strathspey. In the fast songs, she sings with the lift and clarity of a good dance musician playing a reel or jig.

Jean Redpath's sound is so beautifully crafted that one might think she is a trained singer, but she appears to have developed her voice to suit herself. Often she carries off a song perfectly well with no accompaniment, or with simple fingerpicking on guitar. A lesser voice would wear thin without the benefit of an accompanist.

In 1961, when Jean first left Scotland to see America, singing folk songs for a living was not an option in Scotland. Just about the only folksingers getting by in Scotland were the MacEwan brothers. Groups such as The Corries and the McCalmans, and Celtic concert bands such as the Boys of the Lough and the Chieftains, were still several years away.

In Greenwich Village, New York, Jean found herself sharing spaces with then-unknowns such as Doc Watson, Mississippi John Hurt, Jack Elliott, Bob Dylan, Dave van Ronk, and the Greenbriar Boys. It was an exciting time. Perhaps the one thing she did not share with the folksingers of the time was her preference for a neat appearance. No grunge, no jeans, T-shirts, or unwashed hair for Jean. She has always felt that dressing for the stage honors her audience, her music, and herself.

Suddenly she got a rave review in the *New York Times* for one of her appearances, and the bookings became more serious. For about 30 years, Jean pretty much lived out of a suitcase, touring wherever she could perform. Despite the joys of the songs, the audiences, and the kind hosts who put her up at night, the traveling life was a "desperately lonely occupation." And yet, says Redpath, "Given a choice, I'd do the same thing again."

Finally, Jean "settled down" by purchasing homes in the U.S. and Scotland. She enjoys the warmth of winter in subtropical Florida, and the long daylight hours of the Scottish summer at home in Fife. Not that a house could tie her down. Commuting across the Atlantic continued, as did various shows elsewhere in the world. Only in the last few years has Jean taken more time off from touring, and discovered she enjoys it.

Redpath likes to encourage her audiences to sing; in fact, she likes to encourage anyone to sing. She taught in the 1970s at Wesleyan University and, for many summers, offered a singing course at the University of Stirling's "Heritage of Scotland" summer school. Her main advice to singers: Sing a lot, honor your own culture and language, and respect that of others.

Many students have asked her for a songbook, but selecting material for a worthy songbook has seemed a daunting task. Still, she is leaning toward producing a Jean Redpath songbook, if only to impart her own personal take on some of the songs in her repertoire. Of course, such a book would include an accompanying CD, to include a bit of the real thing.

Jean Redpath has been honored by many awards, including an MBE presented by the Queen in 1987. Her portrait was painted in 1998 and hangs in Scotland's National Portrait Gallery.

But clearly her greatest legacy will be her recordings, and the vast numbers of listeners whose ears she has helped open to the beauty and depth of Scottish song.

32 ~ *Eddi Reader*
fall 2004

One of Scotland's most evocative singers, Eddi Reader, has a richly colored voice which can begin a word in a breathy whisper and end it with full-bodied tone, or shift from a wail to a sigh at a moment's notice. In a concert I saw, she sang with eyes closed, fiery hair vibrant against a red dress, and hands fluttering like leaves, or dancing through the air, or circling like the hands of a rodeo rider preparing a lasso to rope us in.

And rope us in she does. Her voice is more compelling the more you listen to it. Reader is best known for her original and contemporary folk songs sung in pop style, including a number one hit on the British charts. But her current passion is Robert Burns. Bringing her powerful voice to bear on the songs of Burns sheds new light on Scotland's national poet and songwriter.

At first blush, *Eddi Reader Sings the Songs of Robert Burns* is a surprise because she takes some emotional liberties with songs that are so well known they have practically become institutions. But she brings to Burns a freshness entirely in keeping with his lyrics, drawing upon and enhancing the yearning, irony, humor and poignancy that fills his poetry.

Like Burns, Reader grew up poor and developed a deep need to communicate through song. The oldest of seven children, Reader recalls that singing was a key ingredient of any major family gathering, especially Hogmanay. Everyone would take their turn singing Elvis, the Beatles, Glaswegian music hall songs, songs from World War II, rude songs, songs of comfort, songs of tears. Sometimes there would be special themes, such as her aunt singing a song like "I Who have Nothing" pointedly at her husband, or her uncle singing "Too Many Chiefs and Not Enough

Indians" pointedly back at his wife. Oftentimes a song can say what conversation cannot.

Eddi knew she could change the atmosphere by opening her mouth and singing. And changing the atmosphere must have been a priceless talent in a family of nine living in a two-bedroom apartment in working class Glasgow.

Eventually the family moved to Irvine, a port town where Robert Burns lived and loved as a young man of 22. Eddi and her family were thrilled to leave the urban jungle and live near the sea. She soon found out that she could get in free at the Irvine Folk Club if she sang a song. She also quickly found out that Elvis didn't go down very well there. But the classic folk songs she learned at the club have stayed with her, as well as her enjoyment of sharing songs and tunes with like-minded musicians and singers.

Heading off to London and Glasgow while still a teen, Reader learned the art of busking. She could sing high, sing low, and loved the fact that she had a powerful voice. "I could sing at the bottom of the street and they could hear me two blocks away," she says. But once people gathered to listen, she would sing gently and passionately, and gather in her audience.

She caught the attention of Annie Lennox of the Eurythmics, who hired Eddi to sing harmony parts. At that point she entered the music industry, struggled at times with its impersonal demands, and backed by her band Fairground Attraction, she hit the pop charts. In recent years, she has produced a string of fine recordings and a sea of admiring fans moved by her voice.

Reader's favorite musical scene, however, is the small session, where a few good performers swap songs and tunes in a relaxed pub. This sense of musical community pervades her concerts and recordings.

Many of her songs have been written in collaboration with her friend and guitarist, Boo Hewardine, who will sometimes distill a first draft of a song based on communications between them. Their songs often explore restless longings, reflections and hopes, at odds with a desire for simplicity and peace — "where we're going, where we've been, when all that matters is in between" (from the song "Clear"). Reader's receptiveness to the people and world around her is present in her songs, as is, seemingly, a certain impatience that there is not enough peace, not enough love.

So she fell in love with a man, also from a poor family, who absorbed everything about the world around him and insisted there be more love and less duplicity — Robert Burns. Another Irvine lass loses her heart to the ploughman poet!

OK, maybe she is a couple of hundred years too late. Or perhaps one of them is a time traveler. As she was uncovering Burns songs for her repertoire, she noticed that the book kept falling open to a poem that began, "You're welcome, Willie Stewart." She found herself singing a melody for the words, but soon stopped herself. She didn't want to get hooked on the wrong tune. So she consulted the Burns recording by Jean Redpath, only to find that the correct melody was the same one she'd been singing! She swears she heard giggling from somewhere nearby — no doubt the spirit of Robert Burns, quite pleased with himself for monkeying with her mind.

As she recorded the CD, she liked to imagine Burns sitting in front of her, and sought to sense whether her rendition would please him. In the end, she felt he would have liked it, and I have to agree. She sings "Jamie Come Try Me" with whispering intimacy. "My Love is a Red Red Rose" is full of warmth and sincerity, "Willie Stewart" is effervescent and joyous, and "Charlie Is My Darling" is raucous and saucy. Reader's voice is compelling purely as a musical instrument. Add the words and the effect is magical.

Two thousand people experienced that magic in January 2003 at the Glasgow Royal Concert Hall during the Celtic Connections Festival. This was the premiere performance by Eddi Reader of the Burns repertoire later documented on CD, and featured Eddi's band, plus several top traditional musicians, and players of the Royal Scottish National Orchestra.

The vitality of the project owes much to the musical spirit of fiddler John McCusker and pals Phil Cunningham and Ian Carr, and to the sympathetic connections between Reader and her regular band members,

Boo Hewardine and Roy Dodds. The orchestral arrangements by conductor Kevin McCrae add energy to "Willie Stewart," set the tone for "John Anderson My Jo" and "My Love is a Red Red Rose," and clinch the beauty of "Auld Lang Syne."

For Reader, the passions and melodies of Robert Burns identify him as Scottish. She was happy to see, in the 1990s, a turnaround in Scottish pride and investment in Scottish culture. She now sees young people fired up and digging into their own traditions.

Central to those traditions is Robert Burns, who dared to be "brave with his intelligence," as Reader puts it. The immediacy of her singing helps reclaim the songs of Burns for the average Scot, and makes Burns come to life for any other listener as well.

Eddi Reader, at 42, is young and vibrant because she follows her passions, using her great gifts as a singer. "I'm a mother, so I have first loves and they're my children, but there's something really special about communicating by song."

33 ~ The Cast
winter 2009-10

It's anybody's guess whether Robert Burns, at the ripe age of 250, would enjoy the hit movie *Sex and the City*. But he certainly might enjoy his own song, "Auld Lang Syne." Sung by a Scottish duo called The Cast, the song lends emotional power to a crucial moment in the film.

The Cast is husband and wife team Dave Francis and Mairi Campbell. "We were touched to think that this old song, so firmly rooted in a Scottish tradition of folk music and folk poetry, could add a dimension to a movie with such a contemporary feel," says Dave, though he notes that the movie's themes, friendship and forgiveness, "are as old as the hills."

The Cast's recording of "Auld Lang Syne" was the first track on their first album, *The Winnowing*, released in 1995 by Culburnie Records. It came to the attention of film actress Sarah Jessica Parker about four years later, when the duo performed in Washington DC at the Kennedy Center's televised tribute to Scottish actor Sean Connery.

It is no surprise that their performance was memorable; Mairi's voice is warm and intimate, and Dave's fingerpicking accompaniment on guitar is thoughtful and uncluttered. The beautiful melody they use for "Auld Lang Syne" is the original one that Burns selected, which is different from the usual one we know, but is occasionally heard in renditions of the song by traditional singers such as Rod Paterson or Jean Redpath.

The Cast's first two albums came out in fairly quick succession in the mid-1990s. Both *The Winnowing* and *The Colour of Lichen* contain several Burns and other traditional Scottish songs, sung with enjoyable simplicity, relaxed timing, and interesting arrangements. Both Mairi and Dave sing, Mairi plays fiddle and viola, and Dave plays guitar. We hear "Ye Banks and Braes" in a fairly traditional performance, and "Green Grow the

Rashes" with a Latin feel. "Flowers of the Forest" and "Broom o' the Cowdenknowes" are among the traditional songs, while fiddle music from Scotland and Cape Breton, and several original songs, fill out the program.

The duo's first original song speaks of Mairi's wonder at observing all ages stepdance to Scottish music in Cape Breton, Nova Scotia. After discovering this strong Scottish-Cape Breton connection in the late 1980s, Mairi was among those who helped reintroduce stepdancing from Cape Breton back into Scotland, where it had originated.

These days, Mairi and Dave devote themselves quite seriously to songwriting. In January 2010, Mairi is releasing a new album of original songs written in collaboration with Dave, and performed by Mairi with a new band. Meanwhile, this husband and wife band continues its performing schedule as The Cast.

The Cast's most recent album, *Greengold*, contains an award-winning song. "Smile or Cry" rose above some 400 entries to join the ranks of the winners in the biannual Burnsong competition. Around the same time, Mairi was voted "Scots Singer of the Year" at the Scots Traditional Music Awards.

Beyond performing, both Mairi and Dave are very involved in community activities. Few musicians, especially traditional musicians, spend all their time performing. Playing trad music is not about having it as the "day job" (though they say you can end up with a million dollars by playing traditional music — if you start with two million!). In fact, Dave has a particular interest in researching the way traditional arts are intertwined with community. He points out that the modern traditional artist is not just about playing music but about being engaged in his or her culture, expanding cultural memory, strengthening the "fabric of community life" and helping give the community a voice.

Perhaps The Cast's most important community involvement is that they are raising two daughters. After their second album came out, Mairi and Dave took about ten years off from recording projects to focus on their family. Their *Greengold* album was released by Greentrax Recordings in 2007. A testament to their family efforts is that both their girls are passionate about traditional music, playing fiddle and harp.

Community work is a strong part of their lives. Dave served for three years as director of the Edinburgh Folk Festival (now no longer happening, though another venue for folk events, called Ceilidh Culture, has become successful as a springtime event in Edinburgh). He produced a report on traditional music in Scotland for the Scottish Arts Council, and has served as part-time music officer for the Edinburgh City Council.

He currently works as artistic director for Ceol Mor, a band project sponsored by the Aberdeen International Youth Festival, which brings together some 30 top young musicians from across Scotland, sometimes including a few players from Canada and the U.S. as well, to learn about selecting and arranging music, develop original pieces, and work with experienced composers and arrangers in the field.

Dave Francis is also codirector, with Simon Thoumire, of Distil, a project to help professional traditional musicians develop their creative skills both on their own and in collaboration with top musicians from other genres of music. Begun in Scotland in 2002, this project has since been extended into England and Wales.

Mairi's community work includes directing Sangstream, a community chorus of about 50 members, which is affiliated with Edinburgh's Scots Music Group (SMG). SMG is an adult learning project with some 500 participants exploring various aspects of traditional music, song and dance.

Mairi also teaches fiddle. She studied classical viola at Guildhall School of Music and Drama in London, but her visit to Cape Breton, Nova Scotia, and learning tunes from Dave Francis opened her eyes to the traditions of Scottish music. In a sense, she returned to the experiences of her childhood, when she summered on the island of Lismore. On this small western island near Oban and Mull, Mairi's family had a cottage, near where her great-great grandmother had a croft. She remembers going to the Lismore ceilidhs in a tiny hall packed with people, Gaelic songs, accordion music and ceilidh dancing.

Now, six weekends a year, Mairi Campbell returns to Lismore to take fiddle students on a retreat, where they can improve their playing while enjoying the beautiful surroundings.

Both Mairi and Dave play for ceilidh dancing as well, which is very popular throughout Scotland. They are part of a dance band called Bella McNab's, a fiddle-based band, with bass, piano, and Dave as guitarist and dance caller. What could be more about community than gathering people to celebrate a wedding or just to celebrate each other by getting up and dancing together in high spirits?

This blend of music and community spirit intrigues Dave in his research into the role of traditional arts in the community. It is also clearly lends warmth and emotional strength to The Cast's now famous performance of "Auld Lang Syne," experienced by millions of viewers of *Sex and the City* round the world.

34 ~ *Music Hall*
summer 2002

It's hard not to be swept away by the right combination of good music, high jinx and jokes. The old vaudeville artists were masters at it. Listen to a recording of Sir Harry Lauder and you can't miss the unwavering boldness, feel the twinkle of his eye, and sense the big crowd there to enjoy themselves.

Entertainment is the heart of show biz. I think of how I never got tired of playing fiddle every week for over two years at a restaurant/pub, mostly because of my crazy fellow musician, Jerry Bell, originally of Edinburgh, who could hold forth with preposterous jokes, high energy, contagious warmth and popular songs tossed in with good musical sets. He could even offend people with such high spirits that they could only laugh, and I won't try to justify his piping except to say it was brief, loud, unassuming and, like everything else, entertaining.

It's no wonder that ageless stars of show biz like Harry Lauder are still popular, especially for those who experienced them in performance. Lauder's creative energy is evident in the many hit songs he wrote, like "Roamin' in the Gloamin'", "Just a Wee Deoch an' Doris", and "I Love a Lassie."

He first recorded in 1904, and never stopped performing until his death in 1950. A CD is now out which makes available hit songs from his old 78 recordings. And the songs wouldn't be quite enough without hearing some of his banter with the audience. That's where you can feel the entertainer coming through and the audience smiling along.

But although the overall impression of an entertainer may be joy, warmth and fun, that feeling is not the result of unrelenting joy, warmth and fun in the actual performance. It's the masterful variety of moods that sets up the experience, and the best entertainers know they can reach the heights of hilarity only after wallowing in the depths of sentiment. Lauder's songs are not only entertaining but also full of passion and Scottish pride.

One contemporary of Lauder's was the actor and singer Will Fyffe, whose songs are like comic tales. He plied the circuit as a singer and comic, and ended up acting in a number of British films in the 1930s and 40s. Fyffe, like Lauder, wrote his own material.

His most famous song is "I Belong to Glasgow," which took shape one day when he encountered a drunk holding forth on the merits of drink and the rights of a working man to indulge after a hard week's work.

Fyffe asked the man, "Do you belong to Glasgow"? And the man lolled his head and drunkenly observed, "At the moment, Glasgow belongs to me." A hit song was born.

A CD of songs from Will Fyffe's old 78 recordings is available, remastered, like Lauder's, to clear up the sound quality. The album includes a comic sketch Fyffe performed for a group of shipyard workers during World War II, which brings to life the entertainer in action.

A couple of decades later, we find another great entertainer coming to the fore, full of humor, passion, patriotism, and a voice to beat the band. Andy Stewart became a household word in the 1960s, and like Lauder and Fyffe, his unflagging creative spirit contributed several hit songs to the Scottish repertoire.

His best known song is "A Scottish Soldier", which spent nine months on the British Top Twenty charts in 1961. A recent one-hour compilation CD, called *The Very Best of Andy Stewart*, is a perfect introduction to (or reminder of) his songs. And of course, the recording offers a bit of the banter as well. In "Donald Where's Yer Troosers" for example, he does a bold traditional rendition but also teases listeners about the popularity of rock and roll. He belts out a very convincing and funny rendition of the same song in the spirit of Elvis. But he ends with the Scottish version again, and makes quite clear, with good humor, his opinion that pandering to "international tastes" does nothing to improve the original.

The 1960s also saw the beginning of the Corries, a duo of folksingers whose blend of passion and humor made them among the most popular singers in Scotland. CD re-releases of the Corries original albums have just been completed this year, many of them single or double CDs that combine two old recordings into one new CD.

The Corries were Ronnie Browne and Roy Williamson, whose spirited voices and many instruments entertained audiences for 25 years, until Williamson died in 1990. Everyone knows at least one of their songs, "Flower of Scotland", which has become practically a national anthem for Scotland. It was written by Williamson and expresses an abiding dedication to those who have stood for Scotland in the past and will do so again.

Like the best entertainers, the Corries presented many moods, from sensitively rendered traditional ballads, Burns songs or originals about Scotland, to funny takeoffs on popular songs, always with a Scottish twist. And their live albums include some of their on-stage banter, sometimes with brief pauses and reactions that you know to be sight-gags. Yet even as you listen to the album, you can still picture what they're doing and join in the audience's enjoyment.

There are also countless imitators of great performers, but at best they can only offer a trip down memory lane. The original shows or recordings are where you can feel the real burst of energy, the embrace of the entertainer sweeping away his audience. You hear them singing their own songs with personal passion and pride, or teasing with an unstoppable twinkle in the eye.

Sir Harry Lauder, Will Fyffe, Andy Stewart, the Corries, these are just a few great Scottish entertainers, and they'll always be worth a listen, even as we look forward to new creative spirits with each generation. On with the show!

35 ~ Ewan MacColl
spring 2016

January 25 is well known as the birthday of Scotland's 18th century poet and songwriter, Robert Burns. Not so well known is that it is also the birthday of Britain's 20th century singer and songwriter, Ewan MacColl. Like Burns, MacColl was driven by passion and optimism. Both envisioned a future in which people could be respected for who they are, as most famously expressed in "A Man's A Man," the final song of MacColl's 1959 recording of the songs of Robert Burns.

In honor of MacColl's centennial, three of his children selected their favorite songs and invited great contemporary singers to arrange and sing them. Released as a double CD last fall, it was produced by Neill and Calum MacColl, and designed by Kitty MacColl. Their mother, American singer and multi-instrumentalist Peggy Seeger, was Ewan's third wife. For 30 years, she performed and recorded with him, and at age 80, is still going strong.

The new release, *Joy of Living,* features 21 songs, with a different singer on each track. Their unique voices and original arrangements create an enjoyable variety of styles, ranging from the bright and warm opener sung by Damien Dempsey, through the eerie "Cannily Cannily" by the Unthanks, to the theatrical, half-spoken version by Jarvis Cocker of "The Battle Is Done With." Norma Waterson sings of the callous treatment of gypsies, while Chaim Tannenbaum performs a gentle "My Old Man" about a father, presumably MacColl's, being left high and dry by the factory bosses.

Many of the songs celebrate workers: miners, truckers, fishermen, roadbuilders, and steelworkers. Others are about gypsies, probably inspired by Ewan and Peggy's adventures collecting songs from the traveling folk of Scotland and England in the 1960s and 70s.

Scottish singer Karine Polwart was one of the first artists approached by Neill and Calum MacColl for the project. She recorded "Terror Time," about living through winter as a gypsy. Her haunting rendition includes a pure and penetrating voice with drums and drones.

Dick Gaughan, who recorded an album of MacColl songs in 1978, here presents "Jamie Foyers," about fighting fascists in the Spanish Civil War. Christy Moore sings another song about armed struggle, "Companeros," honoring the Cuban revolution. These two songs are more overtly political and less personal than the others, but all are part of MacColl's dream that a system could be found to provide justice for working people.

MacColl's passion to improve living conditions of workers came from growing up in the heavily industrial town of Salford in northwestern England. His parents had moved there from Scotland to find work because his father, a third generation iron worker, had been blacklisted in Scotland due to his union activities.

MacColl recalled that each neighborhood in Salford could easily be identified by smell. When he was 15, an official inspection concluded that Salford contained the worst slums in the country, and yet the inspectors were "struck by the courage and perseverance with which the greater number of tenants kept their houses clean and respectable under the most adverse conditions."

"In spite of the bleakness of Salford itself," MacColl said, "there was a kind of life in us, that made us impervious to these things." This spirit infused MacColl's music and work. Several songs on the CD hearken back to his blighted home town, including the famous "Dirty Old Town," and "Alone," a meandering and pensive song from the point of view of a teenage Salford girl.

The situation in Salford was not new. Horrible working conditions, child labor, and squalor there had a major impact on the young German Friederich Engels, who worked in Salford in the 1840s at his father's mill. A few years later, he teamed up with Karl Marx to write *The Communist Manifesto*.

MacColl's father and his friends were working class intellectuals who debated about Engels, Darwin, Marx, Thomas Paine. Amid vast slums and the Great Depression, Ewan MacColl was inspired by his father's politics. He quit school upon turning 14, joined a Communist theater group, and never abandoned his optimistic struggle to expose and improve the lives of working people.

Ewan MacColl strongly identified with Scottish culture. Both parents spoke and sang in Scots, and his neighborhood was strongly Scottish. MacColl found that he could write poetry and prose much more easily in Scots than in English. In the 1930s, he was taken with the work of poet Hugh MacDiarmid and the Lallans Makars, who sought to make the Scots language the basis of a new literary genre. MacDiarmid had changed his name from Christopher Grieve to declare his dedication to Scottish culture. Ewan MacColl, whose original name was Jimmy Miller, did the same, choosing to take on the name of an 18th century Scottish songwriter.

In the 1950s, the American folksong collector Alan Lomax encouraged MacColl to help revive British folksong in the face of pervasive popular American music. Lomax also introduced him to Peggy Seeger. Over the coming decades, working with Seeger and others, MacColl performed, collected songs, wrote new ones, developed an innovative BBC radio program, started a folk club, and created a group to teach singers how to breathe life into folk music. His work had a huge impact on the British folk revival.

Through radio work, writing and teaching, MacColl honed sophisticated theories about authenticity in folk music, as the voice of the people. To some, his high standards seemed autocratic. Yet he provided wind for the sails of the folk scene, and showcased the earthiness, passion, and skillfully written lyrics of folk song, both traditional and modern.

MacColl may have been difficult to contend with intellectually, but his family found him emotionally warm. They loved his music. Peggy regularly worked with him, and sometimes the boys joined in. One song on the album is performed by his grandson Jamie, whose electro-indie band, Bombay Bicycle Club, has a huge following of its own. MacColl's most famous song, "The First Time Ever I Saw Your Face," was written for his wife Peggy, and is sung on the CD by Scottish singer Paul Buchanan. In 1973, it won a Grammy as Song of the Year, performed by Roberta Flack.

The MacColls often went hillwalking in Scotland and England, but at age 72, Ewan realized halfway up a mountain that he couldn't make it to the top. This led to the writing of the title song of the CD, *Joy of Living*, which bids farewell to those mountains, and passes along their pleasures to his children, that they should "never lose the thrill and the joy of living."

His children are already working on their next tribute to their father's work, a compilation of MacColl's own powerful singing. A boxed set of four CDs is planned for release by the end of the year on Topic Records, the same label that their father first recorded with in the 1950s. They selected 101 performances, half of them written by MacColl, the other half traditional. As they worked on the project, Neil and Calum discovered that Ewan MacColl sang more naturally in Scots than in English, so a majority of the traditional songs are in Scots. Robert Burns would no doubt have been well pleased.

Who can guess what kind of songs Burns might have written had he lived in the 20th century instead of in the shadow of the Jacobite uprisings and during the vibrant Scottish Enlightenment? We can sense that Ewan MacColl's songs draw upon an optimism born in the teeth of the Great Depression, in the wake of the Industrial Revolution.

The *Joy of Living* double CD is an enjoyable tour of his songwriting. The upcoming boxed set will take listeners to the source, with MacColl's own voice singing, as he once said, "an affirmation of life at its most poignant, its most beautiful, and its most rousing."

36 ~ *Dougie MacLean*
fall 2011

If you long to visit Scotland, or Caledonia, as the Romans called it, the words of this song may run through your mind:

> Let me tell you that I love you and I think about you all the time
> Caledonia, you're calling me, and now I'm going home.

For over 30 years, Dougie MacLean has been singing "Caledonia," his most famous song, to audiences in Scotland and throughout Europe, North America and Australia. Fans travel miles, even cross continents, to hear Dougie perform, whether with his backup band or solo, with just a guitar.

When not touring, MacLean lives in Perthshire, where he and his wife Jennifer have fostered Scottish traditional music by organizing Hogmanay parties, village hall ceilidhs, a summer day-long festival, an art and music gallery featuring his music and Jennifer's paintings, and for five years owned The Taybank, in Dunkeld, which in 2000 won the Music Pub of the Year award. Their son and daughter share in these enterprises, including the music, songwriting and studio work.

The latest home area project for the MacLeans is a ten-day multi-faceted event called the Perthshire Amber Festival. The 7th annual festival takes place this fall at some fifteen different venues within a 20-mile radius of Dunkeld. As hands-on host, Dougie MacLean will perform at some of the festival concerts, in addition to Phil Cunningham, Archie Fisher, Kris Drever, Jenna Reid, Breabach, and Buddy MacDonald. There are also workshops, open mikes, nature walks and other activities planned. Last year, some 6,000 people enjoyed the festival, hailing from about 20 countries.

Dougie's first instrument was the fiddle, which he learned from his father. In high school in Blairgowrie, he formed a band with Andy M Stewart and Martin Hadden, both of whom later joined Silly Wizard. In 1976, Dougie played fiddle and mandolin with the Tannahill Weavers, and toured Europe with them for some five years before moving on to develop his singing career.

Some two dozen solo albums by MacLean have been released on his own label, Dunkeld Records, featuring cover art by Jennifer. Only one, called *Fiddle,* particularly features his fiddling. His fiddle jig "The Gael" became popular from the theme music for the film *The Last of the Mohicans.*

Most of MacLean's recordings and career, however, are focused on his singing. His songs have a broad appeal, sustaining listeners who are hungry for warmth, poignancy, irony, and a bit of righteous indignation, but without finger-pointing, cynicism, or rage. They are spiritual without being religious. Many of the songs draw upon the Scottish experience, yet speak to audiences everywhere.

Some of the songs celebrate continuity: "On ancient wings we fly/Through aged rock we soar/It's in the beating of our hearts/And what has gone before." And: "But when everything has gone/The little ones must walk on."

Other songs reassure us about the future: "Our children growing graceful, strong/We feel it and we're certain that our way is clear." And respect for the wisdom of the past: "We trust to the smiles of the old and the wise/Uncovered in time to reflect in our eyes."

We hear humility towards nature: "You cannot own the Land. The Land owns you." And indignation about exploitation of the Highlands or of those who are less powerful: "You'll drink till our cup is empty." And: "They've cut down all the trees/No one can see what the old man sees."

Laments about modern life filter into MacLean's songs, asking "Where is the honest truth? Where is the open soul? Where is the simple smile?" Or: "There are things you don't know and without a little time they will never be revealed." Some songs mix despair with hope: "We are just passengers upon this godless, ghostly train... Oh, she helps me when I can't hold on."

Some of his songs speak about Scotland: "On Loch Etive they have worked with their Highland dreams/By Kilcrennan they have nourished in the mountain streams." Or: "Our answers they are somewhere in the Hebridean sky."

MacLean learned to sing several Gaelic songs phonetically, but never learned the language himself. In the song called "Stolen," he laments the widespread loss of Gaelic, which in his own family was last spoken and sung by his grandparents. As in many Highland families, the Gaelic has lost its cultural background, sounding as the song says, like "naked words without context" It continues with its sense of loss: "Rendered blind I cannot see/Back along the shining way we've come." He wrote music for these words that was very much inspired by Gaelic melody.

MacLean's modern heroes include songwriters Joni Mitchell and James Taylor, and he has a great appreciation for Robert Burns. MacLean feels that Burns's songs, "although written from a Scottish perspective, have universal human themes, and have touched people the world over. I like to think that in my wee way I do the same kind of thing."

Touring as a musician is a tough road to follow, but Dougie feels that the intense communication he shares with an audience is the "high end" of his art. "I'm very glad," he says, "that I did have the courage to develop this side of my music."

Dougie MacLean's success is apparent in his many recordings, tours, and popular events such as the Perthshire Amber Festival. Far along now in his career, but with many more years to come, he looks with pride upon some of his accomplishments, including the popularity of the song "Caledonia" and the tune "The Gael" but also the startup of his record label, touring the USA with Grammy-winner Kathy Mattea, and performing solo in Scotland for a sold-out show at the 2300-seat Glasgow Royal Concert Hall. In July 2011, he was awarded an OBE (Order of the British Empire) for services to music and to charity in Scotland.

With plenty of talent and energy to spare, and what he calls a "zennish" approach to developing business ideas as they become needed, Dougie MacLean and family are sure to come up with lots more musical activities and adventures.

In the meantime, if you have a yearning to go "home to Caledonia" in the fall, you might look into the Perthshire Amber Festival to experience not only Dougie MacLean's music but also a variety of fine Scottish musicians amid the autumn colors of central Scotland.

37 ~ *The Singing Kettle*
winter 2004-05

Has Artie's arm grown longer, or is it my imagination? Waving his arms like a conductor wearing huge white gloves, he's singing about leaving his luggage in the "*Left* Luggage" office and how that was the *right* thing to do, while his *left* and *right* arms seem to be — yes, definitely getting longer! And longer! Now they are so ridiculously long that you can't help laughing along with all the kids in the audience.

Full of pranks, good humor, ad-libbing, and above all, great singing, Scotland's Singing Kettle entertains families like no one else. The warm and boisterous voices of the husband and wife team, Cilla Fisher and Artie Trezise (rhymes with "size"), launch into every song with contagious energy, backed by upbeat music from Gary Coupland.

In Scotland, people know the Singing Kettle much the way Americans know Sesame Street or Disney. The group has performed for about 4 million children and adults since the 1980s, offering some 200 shows a year, mostly in Scotland, with annual tours throughout the UK and Ireland, and special events elsewhere in the world.

Their name comes from their hometown of Kingskettle in Fife (also referred to simply as Kettle), but it also ties in closely with the centerpiece of their shows: large teakettles with mysterious clues inside. In their stage shows, they discover or hunt for singing kettles, and when one is found, everyone exuberantly chants, "Spout, handle, lid of metal, what's inside the Singingggg... Kettle!" The kettle is opened and a clue is found, leading to the next song.

One year, the show was about pirates who had hidden the singing kettles on Devil's Island. Cilla and Artie had to find them before the pirates came back. Other years they found kettles deep in the jungle, or a medieval castle, or on a world tour. The 2004 show is a Deep Sea Adventure. Each March through October, the group tours a themed show of their own creation, and writes a Christmas show which they perform the last six weeks of the year. Their schedule may seem grueling, but their show sparkles, audiences are responsive, and everyone has a great time.

Most of their shows can be heard and seen via tapes, CDs, and videos, which, I must disclose, my own kids love without reservation. Perhaps most impressive is that as parents, we actually enjoy hearing the songs again and again.

What's their secret? "We're real people," says Cilla. When they started singing for children in schools and shows in the 1980s, most of what was available for children involved puppets. Singing Kettle filled a niche as an all-live, all-dancing, all-singing, real-people show.

But they're also "real people" in the sense that they convey a refreshing sincerity in performance. As a parent, I can think of children's performers who try so hard to be gentle that they practically lull you to sleep; other performers who patronize kids with simplistic talk; and still others whose attitudes or cynical side comments wink at the parents as if to say "we grownups know how to handle these wee ones." Singing Kettle is really a family show, treating kids simply as small people who enjoy laughing when you talk about monkeys or bananas or people's bottoms. Even grownups enjoy such silliness and good-hearted entertainment, especially when it is wrapped in quality singing.

Artie and Cilla were already successful folksingers when they began Singing Kettle in 1982. Their 1979 album, *Cilla and Artie*, was Folk LP of the Year. It was released on CD in 1998, launching the "Classics from Scotland" series on Greentrax Recordings.

Cilla comes from a famous Glaswegian folksinging family, including Archie Fisher and Ray Fisher, who were among the first professional folksingers in Scotland. Cilla recalls every kind of famous artist coming through their family home, from Pete Seeger to the Dubliners to Ravi Shankar.

Many of the songs Cilla learned as a child have found their way into the Singing Kettle repertoire. Sometimes Cilla takes simple nursery rhymes or street songs and writes additional words for them, turning them into full length songs.

Some songs Cilla and Artie have used or drawn upon can be heard in a new CD of classic field recordings by Alan Lomax, called *Singing in the Streets: Scottish Children's Songs*, on Rounder Records. These songs were recorded in various parts of Scotland in the 1950s, around the time that Cilla herself was first asked by BBC to record a street song. BBC had to set her up with an electrical cord to use as a makeshift jump rope so she could sing it right.

Artie was born and raised in Fife, where his Cornish father married a woman with the maiden name, ironically, of Fisher. He turned professional folksinger with Cilla in the mid-1970s. It was singing with and for their two children, Jane and James, that started them taking children's music seriously.

The third core member of the group is Gary Coupland, a virtuoso accordionist and multi-instrumentalist. He's worked with Cilla and Artie for over 20 years, and always provides varied and spirited accompaniment.

In the 1980s, Singing Kettle had a show for several years on BBC-TV, winning a BAFTA (the British equivalent of an Emmy) for Best Children's TV Program. In the 1990s they performed on ITV, British network television, and were seen by some 200,000 families each show.

Last year the group appeared at the Washington DC Folklife Festival, as Smithsonian Folkways released a Singing Kettle CD called *Singalong Songs from Scotland*. Most of the group's many recordings and videos are produced by their own family business, which employs some 12 to 20 people to put on their shows, run their popular store in Kingskettle, and maintain a website with information, games, and an online store.

The three original members of the group, Cilla, Artie and Gary, received the prestigious MBE (Member of the British Empire) medal from the Queen at Buckingham Palace in the Millenium New Year's Honours. Normally awarded to individuals, the Singing Kettle was the first to be honored as a group since the Beatles in 1965.

The original trio became a quartet in the 1990s. For six years, Cilla and Artie's daughter Jane performed with them, before moving into her own musical career with a techno punk band (characterized by Cilla as "exciting to listen to" and "not totally aggressive"). Now Kevin Macleod, formerly their stage manager, is the fourth member of the band, specializing in delightful characters such as Bonzo the Dog, who stands seven feet tall, with the 6'4" Mr. Macleod inside the costume.

Too often, producers of children's TV or other entertainment seem terrified of losing the attention of their audience. They make everything loud, flashy, and fast-paced, and in the end, it's all spectacle. Singing Kettle actually involves their audience, by being human, spirited, encouraging, silly, and very good at what they do.

When you watch Artie's arms get longer, or you see a sailor's pants fall down, or hear Cilla and Artie enjoying their own jokes with you, or listen to people who obviously love to sing, there's nothing left for you to do but relax and enjoy, and sing along yourself.

Hidden inside the Singing Kettle is one of the great treasures of Scotland.

38 ~ *Archie Fisher*
fall 2012

The resonant and gentle voice of Archie Fisher has a special place in my mind's ear. After 30 years, I can still remember his rendition of "The Flower of France and England" from an old cassette tape. His Scottish diction is crisp and easy to understand, his voice and guitar playing delivered with heart. Without fanfare or bravado, the steady ebb and flow of his voice on that song has remained with me all this time, much the way it has won the hearts of countless fans.

A professional singer for over 50 years, Fisher grew up singing with his family, whether at home or keeping time to the windshield wipers in their 1939 Ford Prefect. His father sang in the City of Glasgow Police Choir, and enjoyed a wide range of repertoire, from vaudeville to light opera to traditional folk. His mother sang in Gaelic just about any time she worked or walked from one place to another, though Archie never recalls her actually sitting down and singing a whole Gaelic song from start to finish.

Two of his six sisters also became professional singers. Ray Fisher honed in on learning ballads of the traveling folk such as Jeannie Robertson and Lizzie Higgins. Her first album was a duo with Archie, released in 1962 on Topic Records. In 1979, Cilla Fisher made an awarding-winning folksong album with her husband, Artie Trezise (now a CD in Greentrax's Scottish Tradition series). Cilla and Artie are best known in Scotland as "The Singing Kettle" for their popular Scottish children's music and touring show.

Archie Fisher continues to tour as a singer and songwriter throughout the UK, the US and Canada, with a spry stamina belying his 72 years.

Between 1968 and 2008, he recorded six solo albums, plus recordings with other musicians, such as Barbara Dickson and Garnet Rogers. He is currently at work on a new CD, to be released by Red House Records.

Windward Away, his 2008 CD, features 11 newly recorded tracks, plus 8 tracks from a 1988 recording that was never released because the master tape had been misplaced in the recording studio. Twenty years later, it resurfaced when the studio was moving to new premises. The old tape had to be specially heated to playable condition, after which it could only be played once before it fell apart. That one time was enough to make a digital transfer, allowing us, on *Windward Away,* to hear Archie's old songs alongside the new. In two decades, Fisher's voice really didn't change much; it remains rich and strong. One critic, tongue in cheek, remarked that there was "no improvement at all!"

The settings of the older recordings were different, however. Archie wrote string parts for some songs, and made use of flute, percussion and instruments, though the spotlight was still on his lilting voice and fingerpicking guitar.

A number of Archie's songs involve horses, a great passion of his. "Riding Through the Rainbow" on *Windward Away* is a tribute he wrote for his horse Sunny, who died at age 32. Archie rides Western style, and has competed in an event called barrel racing, which involves riding around three barrels and out a gate. In 1991 he won the Scottish championship with a time of 19 seconds. The following year, other riders despaired of beating him until they watched him ride to the first barrel, jump off, run around it himself, and jump back on. He was disqualified, but everyone had a good laugh, and he had left the championship open for someone new to win.

Although Archie needs no accompaniment other than his guitar, he has often worked with other musicians, including fiddler/mandolinist Allan Barty, the legendary Irish duo Tommy Makem and Liam Clancy, guitarist John Renbourn, and Tom Paxton. In 1988, he toured North America with the Canadian fiddler and singer Garnet Rogers, and last year they picked up right where they left off with another tour, and plans for more in the future. In conjunction with their 1988 tour, Garnet produced an album of Archie's, called *Sunsets I've Galloped Into*, featuring his original songs from 20 years of songwriting.

Fisher's songs have been performed by many artists, including Steeleye Span, Fairport Convention, and Stan Rogers. Recently, he was approached by musicians at a festival, who sang a song to him which he found very familiar. "It should," they told him. "You wrote it!"

Archie has considered putting together a book of his nearly 80 songs, but not as a typical songbook. He imagines it could be more like a novel, with songs telling part of the story. Inspired by the artistry of Liam Clancy, Archie likes to create a context for his songs during a show, and then let the songs speak for themselves. In songwriting clinics, he points out that he never once heard Liam Clancy say, "This song is about..." or "I wrote this song because..." The songs are part of the fabric of performance.

Although his mother spoke and sang Gaelic, Archie never learned the language. He has, however, recorded several Gaelic songs in translation, including the beautiful "Eternal Surge of the Sea" and "Joy of My Heart," both on *Windward Away*. His sister Cilla learned Gaelic in school and even competed in the Gaelic Mod, but Archie was not permitted to go to the same school she did. His father wanted him to be a lawyer, and sent him to a school where he could learn Latin, not Gaelic.

Needless to say, Archie Fisher did not become a lawyer. At 15, he left school and went to sea, where he learned a bit of guitar from a fellow crew member. One day, as his oil tanker unloaded in New Jersey, Archie heard some fantastic American music on a jukebox in town. Ironically, the performer turned out to be a Scottish musician, Lonnie Donegan, who hit the UK charts playing "skiffle" music. Skiffle was a hybrid of jazz, blues, and folk, and became all the rage in Britain in the 1950s. Even the Beatles played skiffle before developing their own songs. For Archie, skiffle opened his ears to American music, including singers such as Woody Guthrie and Pete Seeger.

Archie credits a Scottish schoolteacher, Norman Buchan, for impressing him with the value of his own culture. Over time, he also became friends with some of the great balladeers and tradition bearers of Scotland. In his turn, Archie has gone on to give Scots a greater appreciation of their own music, not only as a singer but also as a broadcaster. For 27 years, Archie hosted BBC Radio Scotland's folk program *Travelling Folk*, airing recordings and live interviews each week.

Fisher has contributed to Scotland's music in many ways, in addition to singing and broadcasting. He has worked as an instrument maker and repairer, ran a folk club, directed the Edinburgh Folk Festival for five years, and produced albums for bands such as Silly Wizard.

Archie Fisher was in the first group of six to be inducted into the Scottish Traditional Music Hall of Fame in 2005. Perhaps most outstanding of his honors was his 2007 receipt of an MBE awarded by the Queen for services to traditional music.

Without fanfare or bravado, Archie Fisher and his quiet, expressive voice have earned a place in the hearts of Scots and folk music listeners everywhere.

39 ~ Alan Reid
fall 2020 *(intended publication date)*

We twiddled with the Zoom settings, the voice/keyboard balance, the guitar connection, the internet cable. Though a veteran of over 50 years bringing Scottish traditional music to the world, Alan Reid had never done a concert like this before. He jokingly referred to it as a "reverse house concert" — performing at his own home for an internet audience.

As a founding member of the pivotal Scottish band, the Battlefield Band, Reid has played on five continents and recorded nearly 30 albums with the band. The band and its sound technicians were a good team. After 40 years with the band, Reid left in 2010 to tour with the band's sound man, Rob van Sante, a fine guitarist and singer in his own right. Online and in lockdown, though, performance as well as sound setup were pretty much a solo operation.

Recently, Reid has begun to play on his own anyway. Several solo tours and festival performances had been planned, but were cancelled due to the pandemic, so this online concert was a nice chance to perform, and for audiences to enjoy his unique voice.

In the online concert, Reid sang three songs. One was "The Road to Carradale," in which the songwriter feels increasingly sunny as he travels past Loch Lomond, the Rest and Be Thankful, Inverary, and arrives in Mull of Kintyre. The upbeat message is that although life can be a trial, you sometimes know just where you're going and how to get there.

Reid's voice is homey, friendly, and reassuring, his words always easy to understand. For Robert Burns's classic "My Love is like a Red, Red Rose" he used a beautiful melody that is not widely known but provides a refreshing and tender take on the song. This and his first song can be heard on *Rough Diamonds*, his fourth duo CD with Rob van Sante.

A third song in the online concert was an original that highlighted Reid's fascination with lesser known events and characters in Scottish history. "Baile an Or" describes the Scottish gold rush of 1869 in the far north of the Scottish mainland. He recorded this song with the Battlefield Band on their 2009 album, *Zama Zama: Try Your Luck.*

One of Reid's forays into the lesser known corners of Scottish history resulted in an original CD portraying the epic, triumphant and tragic life of John Paul Jones. Originally from the coast of Scotland south of Dumfries, Jones fought for America in its Revolutionary War, and became known as the father of the U.S. Navy. In *The Adventures of John Paul Jones,* Reid's entertaining and poignant songs and tunes are backed by Rob van Sante's guitar, along with top Scottish musicians on fiddle, cello, drums, flute, and accordion.

Reid considers himself a lucky man. At age 7, his grandmother gave his family a piano, and he was sent to learn from a nearby piano teacher who, though totally blind, could always tell whether he was using the correct fingerings! Years later, Alan taught himself to play guitar and immersed himself in the folk songs of the 1960s.

No doubt his greatest streak of luck took place at the University of Strathclyde, where he recalls meeting a loud, gregarious fellow named Brian McNeill. Together they started the Battlefield Band, naming it after the working-class neighborhood where Brian lived.

After graduation from university, the band continued playing music while taking teacher training courses and doing odd jobs. They were excited to travel from Glasgow all the way to the east coast (Edinburgh!) for one booking, followed by a tour of the Highlands with a comedian. The game changer came when Billy Ross, a founder of the band Ossian, convinced them to play at a music festival in Brittany, the Celtic part of France. This led to the Battlefield Band recording their first four albums over the next two years.

The band's fifth album, *Stand Easy,* was their first to include a piper and a female singer. This 1979 album really set the stage for decades of great albums from the band, some 35 in all. Their musical selection blended original songs and tunes with classic melodies and songs from

Scotland's rich heritage. Alan had begun to play electronic synthesizer (now simply called keyboards) for a better balance with the pipes, and Brian added his cittern (a cross between mandolin and lute). Together, they developed an innovative approach to vocal harmonies and musical arrangements, and managed it without percussion. Their sense of beat was made clear with bass notes from the synthesizer, plucked strings, and the strong pulse of the ensemble. *Stand Easy,* plus four tracks recorded the following year, was re-released as a CD by Temple Records in 1994.

Robin Morton of Temple Records was ultimately the driving force behind the Battlefield Band, as manager and producer of nearly all the band's recordings. The first time he met the band, he himself was, for a short time, a member of another very long-standing Celtic concert band, the Boys of the Lough. Those were the days when these bands and others, such as Tannahill Weavers and Ossian, were able to tour the world freely to enthusiastic audiences. In the last couple of decades, visa restrictions have made this increasingly difficult in the U.S., and with the implementation of Brexit, it's anybody's guess how well Scottish bands will get around in Europe.

While touring the world with the Battlefield Band, Reid enjoyed a surprising variety of cultures. At a Hong Kong shopping mall, the band's energetic music was met with total silence, and yet people hung over the railings to listen intently, and the crowd never dwindled. In India, the band was puzzled by applause that seemed to interrupt a slow air, until they learned that people liked to clap not just at the end of a number but any time they encountered a particularly beautiful moment of music. Meanwhile, back in the Scottish Highlands, the band was pleased if listeners loosened up enough to actually tap their toes during a sit-down concert!

One day in the early 1980s, Robin Morton informed Alan that a young woman who hosted an American radio show was coming to his home to interview him. When she showed up, Reid was pleasantly surprised to meet Fiona Ritchie, a down-to-earth Scottish woman whose parents lived only a few miles away. Their chat was Ritchie's first musical interview for her North Carolina radio show, which was to become NPR's longest-running program, *The Thistle & Shamrock*. Her inspiring program helped educate many Americans about Scottish music, and increased appreciation for bands like the Battlefield Band.

Over his long career, Alan Reid has seen many changes in Scottish music, including a growing number and quality of young musicians, who have responded to increased educational, performing opportunities, and a more confident culture. One noticeable change has been that many more women are playing now than when the Battlefield Band started out. The flip side of this vibrant music scene is that today's musicians often have many irons in the fire, with multiple bands and teaching gigs, and need to be more savvy about promoting their careers. This is not to say that supplementing music with a few extra gigs was new to Reid. One of his extra jobs involved spending two days as an extra on the set of "Outlander." This required that he shave off a 30-year-old beard so he could appear as a French merchant in a few seconds of the show. Recently, his voice played the lead in a podcast based on a series of graphic novels about the life and times of Scrooge McDuck!

In 2001, Alan published *Martyrs, Rogues, and Worthies,* a songbook of his own original lyrics and melodies. He has put together a second songbook and hopes to publish it as soon as the market permits. Those interested in his lyrics can find them readily available on his website.

Songs and tunes are custodians of culture and history. Alan Reid's long career and many recordings give us a window into Scottish history, whether through an original song about a little-known character or event, or a well-known song arranged to make it fresh again. Between his many CDs, potentially more "reverse house concerts" and the return of tours and festivals, we look forward to hearing more of this venerable Scottish musician.

SECTION FOUR
Instrumentalists

Iain MacFarlane and
Ingrid Henderson

Tony Cuffe

Aly Bain and Phil
Cunningham

Gordon Duncan

Photo: Nico Kaiser

Photo: Diane Neises

Pipe band

Sandy Brechin

ABOUT SECTION FOUR
Instrumentalists

Three instruments are often thought of as Scotland's national instruments: harp, fiddle, and bagpipes. As we take a look and listen to their music, we'll add a fourth contender, the accordion, and discuss them roughly in the order in which they appeared in Scottish culture. One more, the guitar, will fit into the section on harps.

We'll start with a look at Scottish harp music. The earliest depiction in the world of the triangular harp was in 8th century Pictish stone carvings in Scotland. The harp was central to music making for many centuries. It faded for a while, but has been revived and developed in exciting ways in recent decades. The guitar is included in the section about harps because this plucked string instrument is not very distant from the medieval lute that carried harp music and early Scottish tunes through the middle ages. One of the great musicians profiled, Tony Cuffe, built his own harp and transferred his skills on guitar to play harp as well.

The fiddle, a predecessor of the violin, was brought back to Scotland by Crusaders from the middle East, where bowed instruments appear to have been invented. Images of fiddlers date back to an image at Melrose Abbey from the 12th century. Once the modern violin was created in 16th century Italy, in an area closely linked with Scotland, the superior sound of the new instrument quickly took over from the older bowed instruments. We'll learn about some key fiddlers and makers.

Bagpipes have been promoted as a national instrument and symbol of Scotland. The sophistication and intricacy of the Scottish piping have come a long way since the instrument was first mentioned in Scotland in the early 16th century. In those early days, some Gaelic bards actually complained about the noise of the newcomer! Learn here about pipe bands and soloists, what they strive towards, and about the bellows-blown pipes as well.

The fourth candidate for consideration as a national instrument appeared much later, in the 19th century. The accordion is a veritable band in a box, and loud enough on its own to fill a dance hall. We'll take a look at how it came to take up residence in the Scottish scene.

SECTION 4a ~ HARP and GUITAR

40 ~ Heavenly Harps
spring 1999

The harp is the instrument of angels, or so we like to think. Satan marveled at this notion in his *Letters from the Earth* ("edited" by Mark Twain). How incredible, he wrote, that human beings could invent and desire a heaven full of things they don't even seem to like on earth — chastity, hymn singing without end, brotherly love, lack of intellectual challenge, and... everyone playing the harp all the time!

I don't suppose anyone would relish this portrayal of heaven, but then, it might be wise for us to hedge our bets and prepare for eternity by gaining an appreciation for the music of the harp. This way, we can hit the clouds running.

The world's oldest portrait of the familiar triangular harp can be found in Ross-shire, carved into stones by the Picts. The triangle has the strength to hold more strings than other forms of harp such as the lyre, and can withstand the pressure of strings under great tension. This allows for more volume and resonance, both in gut and metal wire strings. This is the Celtic harp.

A tune dedicated to those Pictish stones was written by Alison Kinnaird, a key figure in the modern revival of the Scottish harp. The tune, "Clarsach na Cloiche" (The Harp of the Stones), can be heard on her album *The Harper's Land*. Its first performance was at the 1991 Gaelic Mod during a visit by Prince Charles.

The Gaelic Mod, an annual series of competitions promoting many aspects of Scottish Gaelic culture, has helped foster the development of harpers who have, in turn, revitalized Scotland's ancient harp traditions.

Kinnaird is one such influential Mod winner. In the 1970s she pioneered an effort to reconstruct some of the lost oral tradition of the Scottish harp, finding old tunes and reforming playing techniques to suit them.

Kinnaird's first ear-opening album, *The Harp Key,* recorded in 1977, included two other harpers who have also made strong contributions to Scottish harping, Patsy Seddon and Wendy Stewart. Seddon, another Mod competition winner, has become well known as one half of the popular harp duo, Sileas, in which she plays the gut-strung harp. The other half of the duo is wire-string harper Mary MacMaster. The captivating sound of Sileas is available in three albums, as entertaining as they are informative, the most recent being *Play On Light.*

After her initial strong involvement in the harp scene, Wendy Stewart left the Edinburgh scene for some years, but on her return in 1990, she joined the folk band Ceolbeg, and soon made a beautiful solo album called *About Time.* Informed by tradition and a command of the instrument, this eclectic and enjoyable album includes such varied fare as a march/strathspey/reel set, a French bourée, a Danish harp song, a Gaelic lullaby and several original tunes. Wendy followed that with a new album of further musical explorations, entitled simply *About Time 2.*

Last summer, as organizer for the harp portion of the Edinburgh International Festival, Stewart helped in the production of a unique compilation CD called *Scottish Harps.* This fine sampling of the state of harp music in Scotland today is well worth a listen.

On *Scottish Harps,* you'll hear selections from a variety of harp CDs: Alison Kinnaird performing the bardic "Song to MacLeod of Dunvegan" with Gaelic singer Christine Primrose (from *The Quiet Tradition*); Wendy Stewart mixing traditional Scottish style with French and Spanish echoes (from *About Time 2*); Sileas combining bagpipe ornamentation and smooth harp technique, in an old lament praised by the duo's namesake, 18th century poet Sileas na Ceapaich (from *Play On Light*); and Savourna Stevenson offering eclectic virtuoso harp music on a track from her *Tusitala* album, a soundtrack commissioned for a BBC documentary about Robert Louis Stevenson.

Other tracks on *Scottish Harps* include harper/storytellers Fiona Davidson and Heather Yule, the classical harp and lute/guitar duo Rowallan Consort, and a nice if too brief harp accompaniment for bagpipes, by Ingrid Henderson.

This CD reveals some harpers exploring the ancient tunes and styles, while others seek to reenact a bit of the bardic tradition by including songs and stories with their performances. Still others, like Savourna Stevenson, are heard taking the harp in new directions by exploring its expressive potential.

Savourna Stevenson's virtuosity is astounding, and her compositions open new worlds of sound to the harp. Her album *Tweed Journey* traces the journey of the River Tweed by starting with solo harp and adding an instrument for each tributary. Another recording, *Cutting the Chord*, begins with eerie sounds suggestive of the wind-blown aeolian harp and includes jazzy rhythms of the African kora. A recent project of Stevenson's explores traditional musical forms of the Northeast, Highlands, and Borders for her Scottish Women's String Quartet, featuring violin, harp, viola and cello.

A new album, *Kiss the Wind*, by a student of Savourna's, Elise MacLellan, demonstrates the influence of Stevenson's teaching. Original tunes adorn this varied album, with instruments such as cello, bouzouki, gentle percussion, and even blues harmonica blending in with the harp.

My favorite recent release of straight traditional harp music is *The Ancient Music of Scotland* by the prolific harper and composer William Jackson. This CD presents an excellent selection of Scottish tunes, some well known as Gaelic songs, fiddle tunes, or lute pieces. Unlike most traditional harp recordings, this one has practically no liner notes, as if Jackson preferred to let the music speak for itself. Founder of the great folk band Ossian, and composer of a number of Celtic/classical suites, Jackson often features the harp on his recordings.

While a few harpers like Kinnaird keep close the traditional music, you will find that most harpers like to stray at least occasionally into contemporary or cross-cultural veins. Mary Ann Kennedy and Charlotte Petersen, for example, incorporate Gaelic song, Shetland tunes, Irish jigs, and even Pachelbel's Canon and the jazz standard "Take Five" on their album *Strings Attached*.

Hopefully, this is enough of a selection to make you feel heavenly, and we can pray it will whet your appetite for keeping up with today's flowering of Scottish harp music. I can't say that having an appreciation for harp music will necessarily help your chances with St. Peter at the holy gate, but you might ask him to wait while you fire up that one last compact disc. By then, you'll know just which one to choose.

41 ~ *Scottish Harpers*
fall 2013

Last December, harper Isobel Mieras quietly accepted the Hamish Henderson Services to Traditional Music Award, "mildly astonished but deeply honored" by this recognition of more than 40 years of performing, teaching and promoting the harp tradition in Scotland. It was the first time this award had gone to someone from the harp world.

The vitality of harp music in Scotland today is striking. There is a depth of technical skill, a variety of playing styles, and a large number of players, thanks in no small part to the work and encouragement of Isobel Mieras. Many harpers feel that Scotland has one of the most vibrant of harp communities. Its musicians seem particularly engaged in challenging listeners and players with the musical possibilities of the harp, as opposed to Ireland or the U.S., where there is often a greater focus on strictly competitive playing, or on gentler new-age Celtic sounds.

Scotland has long been fertile ground for the harp. The earliest known European lyre, dating to 2300 BC, was found on the Isle of Skye, and the earliest image of a triangular harp was carved in stone by 8th century Picts in the northern Highlands. But after Culloden in 1746, harps were practically forgotten until 1891. That's when the National Mod began its annual showcase of the Gaelic arts through competitions and concerts. At the end of the first Mod, Lord Archibald Campbell decided to make harps available for the accompaniment of Gaelic songs, by having copies made of several harps from the National Museum of Scotland.

Forty years later, the Caledonian Harp Society was formed, and then quickly renamed the Clarsach Society ("clarsach" being the Gaelic word for harp). Soon, however, harps became scarce, due to the disruptions of World War II. Isobel Mieras recalls that in the 1950s, her teacher, Jean

Campbell, "persuaded, coaxed and even bullied makers of other instruments to make small harps."

Today there are many makers and even innovators in harp design, which have contributed to the availability of instruments, and helped feed a growing community of harp players. School programs and the Clarsach Society help tremendously by lending or renting out instruments to students and Society members in need.

It is amazing what a range of musical sounds Scottish harpers draw from their strings with two agile and powerful hands – from ethereal to gutsy, from tinkly high strings to heart-stirring deep bass notes. Melody and accompaniment combine to give life to slow airs, fast fiddle tunes, proud pipe marches, and textural or jazzy effects.

Also quite amazing is the inspirational effect of players and teachers such as Isobel Mieras. All the harpers I've spoken with have sounded a bit like her: supportive of the art and of each other's efforts, and open to a broad range of playing styles and approaches. This is markedly different from some of the other arts in Scotland, Ireland and beyond, where competitive and territorial limitations often come to the fore.

For 30 years Mieras has worked for the Clarsach Society in Edinburgh and helped run the lively and influential Edinburgh International Harp Festival each April. Isobel's passion for fairness and inclusivity has pushed the festival to present a broad variety of soloists, ensembles, and workshops, making it one of the best of harp festivals. Judging by glowing comments from those who have worked or studied with her, her award for services to traditional music is well deserved.

Patsy Seddon speaks of Isobel's humor, enthusiasm, and kindness in nurturing people at their own level. Patsy performs in the legendary harp duo, Sileas, with harper and Gaelic singer Mary MacMaster. Together they combine the sounds of the gut-string and wire-strung harps, with vocals in Scots and Gaelic, and experimenting with electro-harps as well. Since the 1980s, Sileas has inspired listeners and fellow musicians with their heart-felt singing, unexpected harmonies, and throbbing rhythms on such CDs as *Play On Light* or *Beating Harps*. Sileas is slated to be inducted this coming December into the Scottish Traditional Music Hall of Fame. Both Patsy and Mary have recently joined Isobel Mieras as artistic planners for the Edinburgh International Harp Festival.

Catriona McKay, a former student of Isobel's, tells of her teacher's passion for bringing people together and working behind the scenes in homes and in the community. "I wouldn't be doing what I'm doing," said Catriona, "without her quiet support in my life." As a harper, Catriona plays with amazing technical and musical ability. She can be heard on recordings with the great Shetland band, Fiddlers' Bid, and with virtuoso fiddler Chris Stout. Her freedom of spirit encompasses jazzy grooves and jagged rhythms, but also traditional tunes and moving slow melodies such as her gorgeously meandering air, "The Swan." Catriona's solo album *Starfish* includes an exciting variety of solo and ensemble numbers, and also pays tribute to the innovative lightweight Starfish model harp that she uses.

Another former student, Maeve Gilchrist, describes Mieras as a very special teacher. "Embracing my excitement and enthusiasm for all kinds of music, Isobel would happily send me off to study with all different kinds of musicians, and when I came back, she would gently and skillfully reign me in, tightening up the loose ends of my playing while making sure the essence of the music shone through." Maeve has indeed strayed into various styles, including jazz, and currently teaches at Berklee School of Music in Boston. But the core of her music is Scottish. It shapes her playing and, as she puts it, makes her "a sucker for beautiful melodies." Maeve sings and has worked with various bands, but her latest album is pure solo harp: the *Ostinato Project,* an experiment in using two hands on the harp as separate voices. Snippets of old Scottish tunes mix into a stream of consciousness, exploring melody and rhythm, sometimes complex, sometimes simple and spare. In some ways, it reminds me of how Eric Satie's piano pieces played with the structure of melody a century ago, drawing the listener into the feeling of a personal musical diary.

Isobel Mieras herself ascribes some of her teaching qualities to the example of her mother, who was a well-known choral director in Edinburgh. "She had a great gift for taking keen but comparatively unskilled singers of all ages and turning them into good choirs. I hope I may have done the same with harp ensembles." Mieras has in fact taken groups of young and old harpers on tours around the world, and enjoys composing and arranging music for all levels of harp players, not only giving them a chance to play together but also featuring them as soloists. In 2006, she led an ensemble of 201 harps all playing together at the harp festival, a group so large that it made the *Guinness Book of World Records*!

Isobel's acceptance of her award last December was filmed in advance, because during the awards ceremony, she had to stay home and prepare a group of harpers for their annual "Harps of Gold" Christmas concert, in the Queen's Hall in Edinburgh. As Mary MacMaster said, "She's that kind of person. She wouldn't come here to accept an accolade when she can go and get those people playing."

Every musical tradition must be nurtured in order to grow. The harp scene is particularly healthy in Scotland today because of the dedication, energy, and inclusivity of people such as Isobel Mieras. Catriona McKay sums up the warmth Scottish harpers feel about their community when she says, "I feel very fortunate to be part of this tradition which has been carved and cared for since the first strum!" And we are very fortunate to be able to hear the results.

42 ~ *Scottish Guitar*
summer 2008

With a plink or a strum or a scream, the guitar has dominated much of popular and traditional music for several decades. In Scotland, guitarists have played folk melodies and accompanied songs for centuries.

The guitar has many sounds. It can sound like a harp or lute, can drive a song with rhythmic force, can deliver a melody, and in its electric version can create almost any kind of sustained sound (some might even say noise) at any volume.

In the hands of a Scottish fingerpicking master like Tony McManus or Tony Cuffe, a single guitar can provide the bass notes, the chords to accompany a melody, plus the melody itself in as complex and ornamented rendition as a fiddle — all at the same time.

Scottish singers such as Dick Gaughan or Bert Jansch back up their powerful voices with a range of guitar artistry, from simple and poignant accompaniment to intricate picking, between verses or in stand-alone selections.

A performing researcher such as Rob MacKillop can musically demonstrate the long history in Scotland of plucked stringed instruments, which stretches back throughout history. The first known triangular harps were represented in stone carvings in Ross-shire by the Picts in the eighth century. Scottish lute collections date back to medieval times, and the guitar can adapt to playing the old lute tunes beautifully. Some of those tunes may have been the sources for melodies such as "Highland Laddie" which are common to Scottish traditional music.

Early in the development of guitars, Scotland had them, as evidenced by carved images at Roslyn Castle from the 15th century, the use of Spanish guitars from the 16th century, and the pear-shaped English guitars in the 18th century, which resemble the citterns played in contemporary Scottish bands such as the Battlefield Band.

Yet the exact style of playing the guitar in Scotland has a murky history. It's not very clear how it was most commonly played or used. In 1783, Isaac Cooper advertised teaching a new method of fingering the guitar "never taught in this country before" which facilitated "the most intricate passages." It seems that guitarists have always had the freedom to reinvent the use of their instrument in Scottish music.

Tony McManus has been hailed by BBC Radio Scotland as "the finest guitarist Scotland has ever produced." He performs with a broad range of sounds and a mastery of the instrument, whether in straightforward accompaniments or complex solo pieces. McManus has released three solo CDs since his first, self-titled CD in 1995, and has made albums with artists such as Alasdair Fraser, or Alain Genty of Brittany. He is often called upon to represent Scotland at festivals featuring international guitar styles, and recently created an instructional DVD on the art of Celtic fingerstyle guitar.

One of McManus's key inspirations was Scottish guitarist and singer Tony Cuffe, who developed a distinctive and innovative sound of his own. Cuffe's long fingernails picked melodies which hint at the sound of the clarsach (wire-strung harp) while also playing a tapestry of colorful sounds blending bass notes and chord strums. As lead singer and guitarist of the great folk band Ossian during the 1980s, Cuffe also provided a driving accompaniment with quick rhythmic strumming and drone notes that sometimes meshed and sometimes clashed with the melodies, much the way bagpipe drones do. He even devised his own ways of tuning the guitar to accomplish this. Cuffe's guitar skills, as well as his compelling singing style, can be best appreciated in his two solo CDs, the 1988 *When First I Went to Caledonia*, and a posthumous album released in 2003, *Sae Will We Yet*.

Bert Jansch, originally of Edinburgh, has been one of the most influential of Scottish guitarists, especially alongside John Renbourn in the pivotal British folk rock band, Pentangle. This summer, from June 29 to July 14, Pentangle is coming together for a 40th anniversary tour of the

UK. Jansch's artistry on the guitar can be heard throughout a long career of solo recordings, from the 1960s through his 2006 release, *The Black Swan*. Most of his guitar playing supports his piercingly thoughtful singing, but some tracks spotlight his intricate guitar playing as well.

A number of guitarists can be sampled on a CD called *The Clear Stream* from Greentrax, a project spearheaded by musician Brian McNeill, who is also head of Scottish music at the Royal Scottish Academy of Music and Drama in Glasgow. This album presents tracks by Tony Cuffe, Tony McManus, Dick Gaughan, Rob MacKillop, Brian McNeill, and others.

Far from Glasgow lived one of Scotland's greatest guitarists. "Once every 300 or so years someone comes along with a talent like Willie's," said fiddler Aly Bain, speaking of guitarist "Peerie" Willie Johnson. Johnson lived most of his 87 years in the Shetland Islands, and following his death last year, a tribute CD was produced, simply called *Willie's World*, including 50 years of recordings dating back to the 1950s. We get to hear Willie playing a number of his favorite jazz standards, his jazzy style of accompanying traditional Scottish fiddling as performed by Willie Hunter, Aly Bain and Debbie Scott, and Willie's unique solo guitar arrangement of "Skye Boat Song."

Guitarists often cross genres in their careers, since the instrument is so popular in rock and pop music but can play almost any style. Chaz Stewart, originally from Stirling-shire, started off with rock and blues guitar, but got into Gaelic music when he became friends with Blair Douglas, the keyboardist with the Gaelic rock band Runrig. In recent years, Chaz has played guitar with Cliar, the traditional "Gaelic supergroup" featuring three traditional Gaelic singers with guitar, harp and fiddle. He also made an eclectic and mostly smooth listening album on the Gaelic label Macmeanmna in 2001. Currently, Chaz plays guitar with a band led by Donnie Munro, the former lead singer of Runrig.

One of today's finest guitarists playing traditional Scottish tunes is located over the water, in Nova Scotia, Canada. Dave MacIsaac's encyclopedic knowledge of Scottish and Scottish-based Cape Breton music is hinted at in his album *From the Archives*, where he brings to light some little-known tunes. His accompaniment is Mary Jessie MacDonald, the pianist who introduced the walking bass piano style into Cape Breton piano playing. MacIsaac plays both fiddle and guitar on the album. His earlier *Nimble Fingers* CD is a fascinating album on which he plays acoustic and electric guitar, fiddle, mandolin and dobro. It is amazing to hear Scottish tunes played sensitively on electric guitar or dobro.

The versatility and range of a guitar in the hands of this roster of brilliant players has not only preserved melodies of earlier centuries but also launched Scotland's guitar music into the 21st century. The instrument, whether as accompanist or soloist, allows for a freedom of exploration that holds great promise for any style of music.

43 ~ Tony Cuffe
spring 2002

We watched him sit quietly in his wheelchair last November, draped in a Scottish flag, smiling weakly, his pleased eyes taking in the unexpected outpouring of appreciation, a standing ovation. Guitar in hand, he was on stage for the last time. One of Scotland's greatest guitarists and singers, Tony Cuffe passed away a week before Christmas at the age of 47.

Tony's performances, most notably as lead singer and guitarist with Scotland's pivotal band Ossian in the 1980s, are as fresh today on CD as they were then. His solo album, *When First I Went to Caledonia*, easily bears repeated listening, and his fairly recent contributions of a number of songs to the first two volumes of Linn Records' *Complete Songs of Robert Burns* are captivating.

An inspired instrumentalist and a unique singer, Tony Cuffe's life and music were centered in the traditions of Scotland. Although he happily worked with colleagues and students playing Celtic music from Scotland, Ireland, Brittany and beyond, his own personal repertoire of songs and tunes was drawn from traditional Scottish sources. Many of the songs we hear in his recordings from the 1980s remained integral to his performances throughout his life.

Tony Cuffe was born and raised in Greenock, near Glasgow. His Irish surname comes from his father, who emigrated from Ireland at the age of 5. The oldest boy in the family, Tom, plays bagpipes, and made a strong impression on Tony's understanding of Scottish music. Tony taught himself whistle and guitar, and in the 1970s became known as one of Scotland's leading guitarists through his work in a succession of bands.

He founded the traditional band Alba, and soon after, joined Jock Tamson's Bairns.

"Jock Tamson" is the Scottish "John Doe," and "bairns" is Scots for "children," so the expression "we're a' Jock Tamson's Bairns" basically says that at the end of the day, we're all the same. The commitment of Scottish traditional musicians like Tony Cuffe has been to strengthen the common bonds of Scots by digging out gems from Scotland's traditional music and presenting them afresh to all who will listen.

In 1980, Cuffe joined Ossian, a well-respected band comprised at the time of talented multi-instrumentalists Billy Jackson, George Jackson, John Martin, and Billy Ross. Of their eight recordings, we'll take a closer look at two, *Seal Song* and *Borders*, to tell our story.

Ossian's third album, *Seal Song*, was the first to feature Tony Cuffe. It starts off with a pipe tune played on fiddle by John Martin. He is joined by Cuffe on guitar, with a fingerpicking rhythm that enlivens the entire medley. Tony picked the metal strings with long fingernails, much like the ancient players of the clarsach (metal-strung harp). His fingerpicking precision allowed for lively birls (quickly repeated notes, a common piping ornament), and his unusual tuning of the guitar permitted rich droning on open strings while he played a melody or chords on the higher strings.

The best way to appreciate Cuffe's mastery of the guitar is to listen to a solo guitar air such as "Coilsfield House" on *Seal Song*, or "Miss Wharton Duff" on his solo album. While playing the melody of the air, he also plucked chords, sometimes spreading out the chord notes to soften their impact, and sometimes plucking them all at once to give a precise beat. At the same time, he added drones or rhythmic arpeggios on the lower strings, often introducing unusual chords or bass lines that soothe or build tension and excitement. This may seem like a complicated description but that's because of how much Tony Cuffe actually accomplishes at one time with one instrument!

Cuffe's guitar work has had a great impact on other musicians. Many fine guitarists, such as Tony McManus, point to Cuffe as a major inspiration.

The songs on *Seal Song* are typical of Tony Cuffe's repertoire: two by Robert Burns (the lively "Corn Rigs," and the reflective "Aye Waukin-O"), one from a collection of Aberdeenshire bothy ballads, one a breathless Jacobite song telling of bold Highlandmen routing their enemy, and "The Road to Drumleman," for which Tony wrote the beautiful melody.

Tony's strong, resonant voice was unique, perhaps because it drew on his sensibilities as an instrumentalist. Like all good singers, he sang from the heart and could draw out plaintive notes, but he could also bring a sharp and rhythmic edge to his voice, with explosive syllables that perfectly suit the rhythm and power of many Scottish songs. Even the grace notes in his singing are more precise than most singers, and recall the rhythmic feel of pipes or fiddle. As a result, he was one of few singers who could easily sing for dancing. On many occasions, I heard him sing in performance with Laura Scott, a Highland dancer.

Ossian's *Borders* album was Tony's favorite. Although all the Ossian recordings are great listening, this one represents a kind of flowering for the band. By including piper Iain MacDonald, it brings together Scotland's three national instruments — pipes, fiddle, and harp — along with vocals, guitar, whistles and uilleann pipes.

Borders bristles with creative ideas. Cuffe composed a new melody for the traditional Scots words of the song "I Will Set My Ship In Order," and in "Bide Ye Yet," he added new verses in Scots, perfectly matching the sound and feel of the original lyrics. Iain MacDonald wrote a new part for the final pipe tune of the album, and the band beautifully arranged one of my favorite tracks, a medley of two Cape Breton reels, played slowly with rich instrumentation.

Tony's album, *When First I Went To Caledonia*, was truly a solo effort: he played all seven instruments on the recording! Other recordings that feature him, aside from Ossian's *Seal Song* and *Borders,* and the Linn Records Burns albums mentioned above, are Ossian's *Dove Across the Water, Light On a Distant Shore* (currently out of print), and *The Best of Ossian.* A number of other recordings include his guitar work accompanying other musicians, such as Billy Jackson and Jerry O'Sullivan.

In 1989, Tony Cuffe and his family moved to Boston, Massachusetts, where they lived for the rest of his life. Ironically, they were about to move back to Scotland last year when he learned he had cancer.

In the U.S., Tony proved to be a treasure, performing and teaching in the Boston area as well as elsewhere in the country. He was the only professional Scots singer for many miles around, and was often called upon to sing, play solo guitar, or to tour with the Windbags, Seamus Connolly, Bonnie Rideout, Laura Scott and myself, and others. His wry humor added to all occasions (e.g., "spam is the primary reason why Americans should never make fun of haggis!"). A dedicated family man with three children, he was always up for playing at ceilidhs and loved to pull out his wooden dancing man, Donald, for the children, or even in a concert.

It's no wonder that hundreds of people attended two concerts in Boston to benefit Tony Cuffe and his family. Musicians from far and wide came into town to perform. Unexpectedly, Tony himself was able to make it up on stage one last time to join in the final numbers. Like many hardworking musicians, Tony gave a great deal to students and listeners over the years without realizing how much it meant to everyone. Those last standing ovations managed to give a little back while he was still with us.

In a time when many musicians worry about impressing audiences with quick-paced variety, Tony Cuffe captured his listeners by tapping into the potential for freshness and vitality within traditional music. This is the legacy of Tony and his original circle of Scottish musicians, whose impact has broadened like ripples on a pool, helping revive Scottish pride and international appreciation for Scottish traditional music.

44 ~ *Tony McManus*
winter 2013-14

Big, quiet, thoughtful, expressive and musically powerful. These words describe both Tony McManus, the man, and the sound of his guitar. Whether finger-picking or flatpicking, Tony brings a musicality and virtuosity to Celtic music that is clear at first hearing. The great guitarist John Renbourn called him "the best Celtic guitarist in the world."

Born in Paisley, Scotland, Tony McManus fell in love with the guitar as a boy. He says he was nearly "struck dumb" by the experience of hearing the Bothy Band live in Glasgow when he was 10 years old. The power of the band's rhythm section, combined with the flair of fiddle, flute and pipes, left an indelible impression.

Totally self-taught, McManus drew inspiration from the melodic ideas of guitarist Arty McGlynn, the finger-picking and special guitar tunings of folksinger Dick Gaughan, and the deeply Scottish ornamentation and intricacy of singer and guitarist Tony Cuffe. He absorbed the originality and swing rhythms of The Easy Club band, and was also influenced by the crossover between Scottish traditional and classical chamber music in compositions by Billy Jackson of Ossian, such as "The Wellpark Suite."

With seven CDs of his own, there are plenty of opportunities to explore Tony's take on the music of Scotland, Ireland, and beyond. He also appears on well over 60 CDs by other artists, and has served as producer for albums by Gaelic singer Cathy-Ann MacPhee and pipers Gordon Duncan and Gary West, among others.

Tony's self-titled debut CD introduced his solo playing in 1995 on tunes such as the Scottish air "Hector the Hero," the beautiful Cape Breton strathspey "Sweetness of Mary," Irish jigs and reels, and Scottish pipe tunes. Several tunes from Brittany are included, and even a relaxed arrangement of a song made famous by Louis Armstrong, "What a Wonderful World." In the midst of simultaneous playing of bass strings, higher melody notes, and middle strings providing texture and rhythm, McManus manages to highlight exactly the notes he wants us to hear.

McManus is an instrumentalist, not a singer, but his music is very much melody-based, and he has often enjoyed working with melody players. "Every encounter with a different musician expands the horizon," he says.

In 1999, he toured and made a CD with Scottish fiddler Alasdair Fraser, called *Return to Kintail*. This thoroughly Scottish album focuses on fiddle music, though the guitar playing provides a thoughtful texture, much richer than mere backing chords. Fraser and McManus play off each other, trading melodies and counter-melodies. The guitar has solo moments, sometimes even backed up by the fiddle. The soulful playing of Alasdair Fraser meets its match in Tony's guitar renditions.

His 2002 album, *Ceol More*, spotlights solo guitar in remarkable arrangements of Scottish and Irish tunes. The playing is enjoyable and carefully considered, with obvious attention to detail, whether we hear an obscure traditional tune or the well known "Ye Banks and Braes." Sprinkled into the Celtic mix are a few Breton tunes and a swingy arrangement of Charles Mingus's "Goodbye Pork Pie Hat", plus a spare and beautiful performance of "Shalom Aleichem."

In 2005, Tony worked with Breton bassist Alain Genty, touring Scotland, France and Australia, and making a popular album called *Singing Sands*. His appreciation for the music and musicians of Brittany, the Celtic part of France, began in 1993 when he was completely taken by a performance of the band Gwerz, featuring bassist Alain Genty. Breton music often centers around seemingly simple melodies, with complicated and changeable rhythms. McManus was intrigued enough with this music that he ended up working with a number of Breton musicians. His first project was the intensely rewarding and memorable experience of learning a complex arrangement for a 12-piece Irish/Breton festival ensemble.

The *Singing Sands* CD mixes Scottish and Breton traditional tunes, with McManus playing melody and rhythm, and Genty adding a captivating sound with his 5-string fretless electric bass. The fifth string is lower than the normal lowest bass string, so low that it is almost felt more than heard.

Tony's lifelong love affair for guitars turned into a fascination with the instruments themselves. Guitar maker Paul Reed Smith even engineered a special McManus model of the PRS Private Stock acoustic guitars. It sold out, being a limited edition, but it is the model that Tony takes with him on tour.

McManus considers this the golden age of guitarmaking. One summer, he was teaching at the Swannanoa summer school in North Carolina when he noticed a student tuning up a different guitar each day. It was Paul Heumiller, owner of a nearby shop offering premium guitars by makers from around the world. Their relationship led to a recording called *The Maker's Mark,* on which Tony plays a different guitar on each track, and all of them on the last track! In many cases, the sound of each guitar suggested to McManus tunes appropriate to that guitar. The music kicks off with a pipe march and classic strathspey and reel, and moves on to a broad variety of traditional tunes, including the "Lea Rig," "Laird of Drumblair," and a haunting Irish air, "Sliabh Na MBan," plus others from elsewhere in Europe, and one from Africa.

Some of the guitars on the album are quite unusual, such as a miniature 12-string guitar, a low-sounding baritone guitar by a Scottish maker, and an amazing Canadian guitar with the sustained, buzzing sound of an Indian sitar. McManus likes to call it the "Dehlicaster." On the album, he used it to lend a bit of mystery to two Eastern European tunes, a Romanian-style doina (actually written by a Breton fiddler) and a Bulgarian tune.

McManus's 2013 release takes off in a whole new direction. It all began with hearing American mandolin virtuoso Mike Marshall play a beautiful rendition of a Bach violin piece. Marshall challenged Tony to learn the piece himself on the guitar. So he did. And he went on to learn more classical pieces, including spending 7 months to master Bach's

"Chaconne." The result was *Mysterious Boundaries,* an album of classical guitar music.

The title of this classical album came in part from a piece by Louis Couperin called "Les Barricades Mysterieuses," which McManus performs on the CD in two different ways. The title also suggests a question Tony says he has often wrestled with as a self-taught musician: Are the boundaries between genres real, or are they a result of our need to impose patterns and categories?

Perhaps it is thanks to his lack of formal musical training that musical categories do not define his playing. Tony McManus applies his heartfelt musicianship and discipline to all the music that moves him. As he explores this music, he gives us a chance to listen to a whole world of musical intricacy and powerful Celtic melody.

SECTION 4b ~ FIDDLE

45 ~ *The Fiddlers' House 1*
spring 1997

The night lights up when a good fiddler takes the stage. Fingers fly, the bow keeps time, and your feet just have to move. Along comes the slow air, and it chokes you up as if it were sung by a human voice. Such limitless expression drawn out of a carved wooden box by a horsehair bow.

The fiddle, along with the bagpipes and the harp, is one of Scotland's national musical treasures. Folk musicians in medieval and renaissance times played crude "fiddles", but the violin took over in Scotland almost as soon as it was perfected some 500 years ago in Italy. Since then, it has been a favorite instrument for listening and dancing wherever Scots may be found.

Nearly every culture has found a place in its heart for the violin. In contrast to the bagpipes, which are so strongly associated with Scotland, the fiddle can be heard in so many guises that it is easy for listeners to link it to classical music, Irish, Appalachian, or whatever fiddle music they have heard most.

The house of Scottish fiddling is just one door on a busy street. I invite you to do more than look in the window. By listening to the solo Scottish fiddling recordings available today, you can open the door and walk right into an astonishingly rich musical tradition.

Scots love drama, they love to dance, and when they dance, they like to get off the ground. Three required ingredients, then, for Scottish music are drama, drive, and lift. Listen for these when you hear a fine Scottish fiddler.

Two of modern Scotland's most brilliant fiddlers are Aly Bain and Alasdair Fraser. Both are solidly rooted in the Scottish tradition, and their recordings offer an excellent perspective into this music. The great concert violinist Yehudi Menuhin might as well have been describing these two players when he wrote, "the genuine Scottish fiddler has an infallible sense of rhythm, never plays out of tune and is master of his distinctive and inimitable style."

Be prepared for unbridled sentimentality in the slow airs and high drama in the marches and strathspeys, drawing you into a blast of unstoppable energy in the quick reels. In other words, get out your dancing shoes but keep your hankie handy!

Aly Bain is a member of the Celtic concert band, the Boys of the Lough, though in Scotland he is well known in his own right, and recently received an OBE from the Queen for his cultural achievements. He grew up in Shetland imbued with both Scottish and traditional Shetland fiddling. These styles remain at the heart of his playing, despite his love for many other kinds of music. His effortless virtuosity, and his ability to tuck expressive light and shade into every note, make his albums timeless and his playing tireless.

He is best heard on the solo albums, *First Album* and Lonely Bird, but he has also recorded extensively with the Boys of the Lough, with accordionist Phil Cunningham on *The Pearl*, with a classical chamber orchestra on *Follow the Moonstone*, and on many other recordings, including one from his BBC-TV series exploring the influence of Scottish fiddle music on the Canadian Maritimes, New England, Appalachia, and beyond.

Alasdair Fraser is a masterful performer with contagious energy, artistic creativity, and the persuasiveness and optimism of a good teacher. Each year he invigorates Scots at a summer fiddling school on Skye, and Americans at his fiddle camp in California.

Alasdair's solo recordings span a range of styles: his first, *Portrait of a Scottish Fiddler*, comes out of the classic accordion dance band tradition, with an aggressive and toe-tapping fiddle sound. In *Skyedance*, old Gaelic melodies are brought to life with traditional and improvisational fiddling, synthesizer and piano. *The Driven Bow* pares things down to fiddle and guitar, and particularly explores tunes that have found their way from Scotland to Cape Breton, Nova Scotia, where fiddlers cherish their direct link to the Scottish Highlands. His recent album, *Dawn Dance*, is subtitled "new music deeply rooted in the Scottish tradition." In 1997 it won an Indie award for Best Celtic Album of the year.

Once you are in the door, you will discover the house of Scottish fiddling to be a mansion, and the rooms we've looked into — Aly Bain's and Alasdair Fraser's — are two of the finest.

A look at the floor plan will help you plan your explorations: there's the J.S. Skinner drawing room, the Highland fiddle croft, the Shetlanders' lounge, the Cape Breton wing, the contemporary band pub, the country dance ballroom, and the American studio. A separate building is devoted to the hundreds of fiddlers who gather together into fiddle orchestras and rallies.

The window may seem small and frosted up from the warmth inside, the door a bit creaky because it's been around for a long time, but if you go inside, you'll find the house of Scottish fiddling abuzz with a powerful mix of great musicians, dancers, and friends. Hope to see you there!

46 ~ *The Fiddlers' House 2*
fall 2000

Before visiting the house of Scottish fiddling, it's good to realize how common the violin/fiddle is throughout the world, and how easy it can be for people to associate the fiddle or violin (yes, same instrument!) with whatever style of music they've heard most, whether it's Irish, Appalachian, classical or another style. Someone might hear a Scottish fiddler play a jig and think "Irish", or hear Shetlanders playing their traditional backbeat rhythm and think "Appalachia", or listen to a fiddler from the northeast of Scotland and think "classical", without realizing that these playing styles have been rooted for centuries in Scotland. The Scottish fiddler's house may seem like one among many, but if you stop in and listen, you will experience a rich brew of musical culture.

The two masters of Scottish fiddling that we visited in the earlier column, Aly Bain and Alasdair Fraser, are going strong, with impeccable virtuosity. Aly Bain has since put out another album with accordionist Phil Cunningham, called *The Ruby*, which gives a bit more of a chance to hear Aly's playing than the previous duo album *The Pearl*. Still, to appreciate his solo playing, I recommend his *First Album* or *Lonely Bird*, or perhaps the *Scottish Fiddle Rally Highlights* album, which has some unique tracks of Aly's traditional playing, in addition to performances of Alasdair Fraser and some top Cape Breton fiddlers as well.

Alasdair Fraser recently made a beautiful and straightforward recording with guitarist Tony McManus, called *Return to Kintail*, with a magical selection of traditional tunes. Alasdair has also explored new directions with his Skyedance band and its albums, *Way Out to Hope Street* and *Labyrinth*, blending his fiddle with pipes, flute, piano, bass and percussion, in a mix of rhythmic Scottish/new age/soft jazz sound.

With the flourishing of fiddlers in Scotland today, it is a good time to peer into some other rooms in the Scottish fiddling house. John McCusker is a key player, prominent in the Battlefield Band; their recent album, *Leaving Friday Harbour*, was named after one of John's tunes. John has a two solo recordings, his self-titled album, and a summer 2000 release called *Yella Hoose*, both well worth a listen.

One of the hottest fiddle bands today comes out of the Highlands — Blazin' Fiddles, with six great fiddlers, piano and guitar. Together, they fire up both the music and their audiences. Their first CD just came out this summer, called *Fire On!*

One of the Blazin' fiddlers, Catriona MacDonald, is from Shetland, and the remaining five are Highlanders: Duncan Chisholm, Aidan O'Rourke, Iain MacFarlane, Bruce MacGregor, and Alan Henderson. Blazin' Fiddles is making a splash with fresh energy, traditional Gaelic melodies and modern compositions. They play fiddle and pipe tunes in unison or with weaving harmonies, backed by Andy Thorburn's innovative piano style.

Each of the Blazin' Fiddlers can be heard on other albums. Catriona MacDonald's new album is *Bold*, with Shetland and contemporary tunes. Duncan Chisholm, formerly with the Celtic rock band Wolfstone, made a compelling solo album called *Redpoint* with Wolfstone guitarist Ivan Drever. Aidan O'Rourke and his compositions energize the group Tabache on their latest album, *Waves of Rush*. Bruce MacGregor plays several fine fiddle sets on the debut album of Cliar, an excellent Gaelic band led by singer Arthur Cormack. Iain MacFarlane has played on several albums, including CDs by box player Fergie MacDonald and Gaelic singer Anne Martin, but we can look forward to his solo album with piper Iain MacDonald in the coming year.

The sixth blazing fiddler, Alan Henderson, is featured on *Birlin' Fiddles*, a CD that brings together three contemporary Scottish fiddlers in the spirit of a spontaneous jam session. Alan hails from the western fishing village of Malaig, while Julia Legge, another member of this fiddle trio, comes from Montrose on the east coast. She is a member of the band Tannas. The third fiddler is Jennifer Wrigley, from up north in the Orkney islands. *Birlin' Fiddles* not only brings together a varied trio of players but also a broad variety of Scottish fiddle tunes.

Jennifer Wrigley and her twin sister Hazel, who plays guitar and piano, play in the band Seelyhoo, and also tour and record as the Wrigley Sisters. The Wrigley Sisters have two recent albums, *Huldreland* and *Mither o' the Sea*, both well played and creative, with moods ranging from fast and driving to dreamy.

Speaking of dreamy fiddling brings to mind a cut from west coast fiddler Eilidh Shaw's album, *Heepirumbo*, on which she plays a beautiful pipe march very dreamily, accompanied by spare jazz chords that quietly and pleasantly surprise the ears. She also includes quicker tunes on the album, of course, such as a long and wild ceilidh dance medley.

A number of today's Scottish fiddlers can be heard on *Heat the Hoose*, a live recording made at the Edinburgh Fiddle Festival. Included are Alasdair Fraser, Aidan O'Rourke, and Eilidh Shaw which have been mentioned above. Others on the album are the young Shetlander Chris Stout, northeast fiddler Paul Anderson, and Amy Geddes, who works with Julia Legge in the band Tannas — a fine cross-section of fiddling styles, presented with the obvious energy of live performance.

Chris Stout, like many Shetlanders (Aly Bain and the late Willie Hunter come to mind), has a solid violin technique put to the service of traditional Shetland and Scottish fiddling. He is a member of the 7-member Shetland band, Fiddlers' Bid, a quartet of fiddlers backed by harp/piano, guitar and bass. Their recent album, *Hamnataing*, is rooted in Shetland tunes, with a variety of moods but some especially memorable bursts of high spirits.

Paul Anderson is from Aberdeenshire, and offers what many listeners would regard as a more "classical" sound, though this violin technique is part and parcel of the fiddle style of the northeast of Scotland. Paul's album, *Journey Home,* is a virtuosic and enjoyable tour of some traditional favorites in the Scottish fiddle repertoire.

Another Aberdeenshire fiddler not usually thought of as a traditional player is Charlie McKerron, the fiddler with the Gaelic and world music band Capercaillie. Before joining that band, Charlie was a top competitive traditional fiddler, and a recording he made back in 1981 along with fiddler Keith Collins, has recently been released on a new "Music of the Fiddle" series from Aberdeen record label Ross Records. Charlie also has a new band project called Big Sky, far removed from the Aberdeenshire sound. He works with a singer, tape loops, guitar, and includes the two fiddlers of the band Deaf Shepherd, Marianne Campbell and Claire MacLachlan, mixing Celtic dance music with mainstream pop sounds. Big Sky's album is *The Source.*

Another recent recording bringing Scottish fiddlers together is *The Blue Lamp.* This one combines the considerable talents of Jonny Hardie of Old Blind Dogs, with Gavin Marwick of Iron Horse. These two fiddlers put to great use their skills at arranging enjoyable sets, using traditional fiddle tunes.

In this thick web of fiddling collaborations, you can sense how strongly the Scottish fiddlers today are weaving together a new tapestry of musical culture. In some ways it really seems like a big house, where fiddlers are venturing out of their regional rooms to jam together in the living room, bounce tunes off each other, and then go back to their rooms to explore new ideas with their own bands. If you haven't stopped into the Scottish fiddler's house lately, it's definitely time for a visit.

47 ~ Scottish Violin Makers
fall 2007

The violin was given to me by an old friend, who was told by a violin shop that it had been made by some 18th century German farmer on his time off in Aberdeen during the winter months. It had no strings or bridge, and lay under my piano for a couple of years before I had the opportunity to examine it, fix it up, and make some amazing discoveries.

The violin shop had made a lot of presumptions, not unlike many who encounter Scottish violins they know nothing about. Germany has for a long time been a prime violin-making area, so it was easy to suggest that the violin was German. Perhaps the shop even thought the maker's name, Joseph Ruddiman, sounded German.

In fact, Joseph Ruddiman was a prominent Scottish violin maker working in 18th century Aberdeen. In 1786, the famous fiddler and composer, Niel Gow, chose Ruddiman, some 70 miles away, to fix his expensive Italian violin, which had broken after a fall. My violin had been crafted by Ruddiman in 1774, the same year 15-year-old Robert Burns wrote his first song poem to a young lady he called "handsome Nell."

Last year, David Rattray, a Scotsman who works as Instrument Custodian for the Royal Academy of Music in London, published a new book called *Violin Making in Scotland, 1750-1950*. Measuring 10 x 13, with full-color photos and illustrations on nearly every page, the book lays out a history of Scottish violins, with detailed examples of work by about 50 key makers, and brief descriptions of nearly 400 makers, arranged by region. The book was launched in August 2006 at an exhibition showing many of the instruments, sponsored by the Edinburgh University

Collection of Historic Musical Instruments and the British Violin Making Association.

In his research for the book, Rattray discovered that per capita, Scotland has probably produced more violin makers than any other country. The violins were clearly popular in Scotland and beyond. Many of the owners and some of the makers emigrated, no doubt puzzling violin shops the world over about the origins of these instruments.

Although classical music has been important in Scotland's cities for centuries, it has generally taken a back seat to traditional music, so we can surmise that most Scottish violins were also used for fiddling.

Now comes the age-old question: what's the difference between a fiddle and a violin? The fiddle was one of the bowed instruments invented in and around Turkey, and brought to Europe by returning Crusaders about 1000 years ago. The instrument was popular enough in Scotland to be depicted in an image at Melrose Abbey circa 1140. King James IV employed fiddlers, as did James V, and Mary Queen of Scots, whose mother-in-law, Catherine de Medici, commissioned violins from the great Italian violin maker, Andrea Amati.

The age-old answer is, there is no difference today between a violin and a fiddle. Once the violin was invented and perfected by Amati, Stradivarius, and Guarneri, it quickly took over from the more primitive instrument known as the fiddle. For some 500 years, fiddle music (usually broadly defined as nonclassical music) has been played on the violin.

Still, some violinists call their instrument a fiddle, and vice versa. Charles Cramond, an early 19th century violin maker, was listed in the Aberdeen postal directory as a "fiddlemaker" by occupation. (He later emigrated to Nova Scotia, where there is to this day no shortage of fiddlers playing Scottish music.)

Edinburgh was an early center of violin making in Scotland by the 1750s, a time when the city was considered a European center of music. Matthew Hardie and his son Thomas were two of the most renowned of Edinburgh makers.

Aberdeen followed on the heels of Edinburgh and took over the spotlight as a musical center, beginning in the last half of the 1700s.

Glasgow became a prominent musical city in the mid-1800s. Violin makers flourished in each of these cities as the interest in music and the number of musicians grew, with Robert Duncan and Joseph Ruddiman establishing a northeast style in Aberdeen, and George Duncan, James Briggs, and Alexander Smillie among those who developed the craft in Glasgow.

Other parts of Scotland have fostered violin makers as well. Of the makers hailing from towns outside the major cities of Edinburgh, Glasgow and Aberdeen, some 13 makers are spotlighted in detail in Rattray's book, and nearly 200 are presented in brief. Rattray's book is full of photos of violins and parts of violins, showing the artistry and styles of different makers.

There is also some local history and many stories. We read of the dealings and disputes of Matthew Hardie, who spent his last days in debtors' prison, despite being considered the "Scottish Stradivari." One of the violins pictured was made by John Young of Aberdeen in 1844 and was owned by the late Scottish fiddler Johnny Cunningham. A photo of one of Young's "pochettes" demonstrates the small violins used by Scottish dancing masters to play fiddle as they taught their students. We read how Cramond's and Jamieson's instruments may look weatherbeaten because, as confirmed by the great fiddler and composer J.S. Skinner, musicians would often carry a fiddle (and drag a bass!) 8 or 10 miles in wet slush to play for a barn dance.

The maker of my regular violin (not the old Ruddiman) is listed in the book. Alexander Hume of Dumfries was an award-winning violin maker, but made some pretty poor life choices. He was hounded out of Dumfries due to scandals and lawsuits involving his children, including his son Jock, who was a violinist on the Titanic.

Today in Scotland, there is a burgeoning number of fine young musicians, especially fiddlers, so it is perhaps not surprising that there also appears to be a renaissance of violin making. One group, called "Violin Makers Scotland" consists of four makers and a bow maker from Edinburgh, Glasgow, and Shetland, who are making a go of the trade. The Shetland member of Violin Makers Scotland sold several of his instruments to members of Fiddlers' Bid, the virtuoso fiddle band from Shetland. Anniesland College in Glasgow offers a course in violin making attended by Scottish students, and there are several courses in England.

Meanwhile, my old Ruddiman violin from Aberdeen has undergone a renaissance of its own. Like many 18th century violins, a neck graft had been done in the 19th century to "modernize" the neck while retaining the artistry of the maker's carving on the scroll and keeping intact the pegbox, where the strings are tuned. Unfortunately, the neck graft burst apart recently, but the violin itself was unharmed. A master violin maker is carving a new neck and bridge, with advice from David Rattray, to return the old violin to its original condition.

In taking apart the old instrument for the repairs, we discovered that its 18th century Aberdeen violin maker was on top of his game in a number of ways. He was up to date on the newer trends in the art, tilting the neck back rather than keep it level as in baroque violins. He also used a screw instead of a nail to attach the neck to the violin body, in addition to the usual dovetailing and gluing. This detail is significant because screws did not appear in violins on the continent until after 1800, but in 1774, Ruddiman was already using them in Scotland, only four years after the first screw lathe was invented in northern England. Far from being an amateur German maker, he was a Scottish maker at the height of his art.

Soon, an old Scottish violin will be playing the tunes of its youth, with a sound to match.

48 ~ *Johnny Cunningham*
spring 2004

The youthful energy was barely containable, the two of them playing off each other with one topping the other – now accordion, now fiddle, now both – faster and faster until they joined note for note at lightning speed. Such was the amazing spectacle of the Cunningham brothers in the band Silly Wizard, with Phil on piano accordion, and the late Johnny Cunningham on fiddle.

And after that, singer Andy M. Stewart would deadpan, "That's nothing. When they play really fast, only dogs can hear them!"

Silly Wizard helped spur the revival of Celtic music in the 1970s and 1980s with a young approach to old traditions. Never pedantic, always full of heart, the band performed not only fast and exciting tunes but also rich ballads sung by Andy M. Stewart.

The electric connection between the Cunningham brothers extended also to their mercilessly uproarious jokes, stories, and retorts. They were really half music and half sit-down comedy.

Ten days before Christmas, a heart attack took Johnny Cunningham at the age of 46. While much can be lamented about this tragic and untimely loss, we can also celebrate the musical legacy Johnny left behind.

Some dozen albums feature Johnny's fiddling, including traditional and experimental Scottish and Irish music, new age, and rock. Unfortunately, some, dating as far back as the 1970s, are out of print, or seem perpetually out of stock, available only perhaps on used markets like Ebay.

Johnny was one of Scotland's most popular and influential fiddlers. He didn't exactly aim to be, but his virtuosity, spirit, and humor captivated everyone who enjoyed Celtic music. In fact, as a Scottish fiddler myself, I used to notice that just about the only Scottish tunes played at Irish sessions in America for many years seemed to be "Laird of Drumblair", "Angus Campbell" and a few others recorded by Johnny Cunningham – often played just the way he played them.

Four Silly Wizard albums spotlight Johnny's fiddling: their self-titled album, *Caledonia's Hardy Sons, So Many Partings*, and their last studio recording, *A Glint of Silver*. Tracks from these recordings can also be heard on the compilation *The Best of Silly Wizard*. All are built on traditional Scottish and Irish tunes and songs, or original compositions written in traditional style. The songs are stirring, the instrumentals well played and often high energy.

The Silly Wizard band developed in 1971 out of a group of musicians that lived on the edge. Johnny himself had left home at the age of 14 or 15 to make music his life, with the support of his parents.

Fortunately, the band took off. Johnny told *Dirty Linen* magazine, "We just wanted to make music that we were all happy with....We were always very honest in what we did, which is one of the reasons I think it worked."

And on and off stage, there were always the stories, keeping the light touch. Once after Johnny played the air "Cam Ye By Atholl," an audience member came backstage to ask the story behind "Come Eat My Apple." Without missing a beat at this complete mispronunciation, Johnny launched immediately into a tall tale about the significance of the apple to Scots, how they used to always offer fruit to their enemies in the midst of battle, until the English took advantage of this generosity at Culloden, which of course caused Scots to stop eating fruits and vegetables altogether!

In the 1980s, Cunningham moved to the U.S., and made a solo album called *Fair Warning*. Here we can easily hear the Scottish precision of his bowing, his ornamentation, his rhythm. There are airs, marches, strathspeys, reels, and jigs, all played with soul and spirit. Some have a simple arrangement with guitar, while others experiment with wild harmonies and drumming.

Silly Wizard faded in the late 1980s but by that time, Johnny was already playing in a new band called Relativity with his brother Phil and

Irish siblings Triona ni Dhomnhaill and Micheal O'Domhnaill, both formerly of the Bothy Band. Triona and Micheal are lovely singers as well as instrumentalists, so Relativity's two albums, *Relativity* and *Gathering Pace*, offer beautiful songs, and a mix of peaceful and driving medleys.

In the early 1990s, Johnny took a detour from traditional music to join the rock band, The Rain Dogs. Though highly appreciated, The Rain Dogs' two albums, *Lost Souls* and *Border Drive-In Theater*, never took off as some felt they deserved.

The roots of Johnny's playing were in Scottish fiddling, but he went where his muse took him. His violin was his home, and he never cared much for pretense. It would be difficult for anyone to put on airs in the presence of Johnny Cunningham, his lively and soulful music, his hilarious stories, and a drink or two, or three.

One of the best ways to hear Johnny's fiddling is on the three albums by the Celtic Fiddle Festival. This group was a trio that has toured over the past ten years, highlighting fiddling from Scotland (Johnny Cunningham), Ireland (Kevin Burke), and Brittany, the Celtic part of France (Christian LeMaitre). Each player performed solos as well as joining forces with the others, providing a fascinating glimpse into three very different styles of Celtic music.

Although he was often known for super-fast fiddling, Johnny was also appreciated for heartfelt slow airs, marches and strathspeys. He often accompanied singers as well, from the earliest days of Silly Wizard to the last days of his life on tour with Irish singer Susan McKeown.

In one of his last concerts with McKeown, last December, Johnny concluded with Auld Lang Syne, the great song by Robert Burns. He said he liked to sing it with his family at Hogmanay, even if over the phone from foreign lands. To him, the song was telling us that "the best thing we can do to help things along in the right way, is to be very kind to each other, take care of each other, the people round about us, whether we know them or not." This sentiment, he pointed out, is shared by Scots everywhere as they sing Auld Lang Syne at midnight on New Year's Eve, giving them a "great blast of optimism ... at least until about 12:15!"

McKeown worked with Cunningham not only on concert tours but also in the stage production, *Peter and Wendy*. Johnny wrote the music and lyrics for the show, inspired by the original book written by fellow Scot, J. M. Barrie. Barrie's *Peter and Wendy* was an adult story expanding on his popular children's play, *Peter Pan*. Cunningham's musical won two OBIE awards. A CD is available from Alula Records.

For Johnny, one of the saddest parts of the Peter Pan story is how the boys, after returning home, grow up and forget about Neverland — and even stop being able to tell stories about it. For a raconteur like Johnny Cunningham, forgetting how to tell stories would signal a dying spirit.

Ian Green of Greentrax Recordings mentioned aptly how Johnny "never lost that young boy sense of fun." His youthful spirit bubbled into his stories and his music. Or maybe it was the fiddle and the stories that kept him young. Either way, like Peter Pan, Johnny Cunningham will never grow old. And his youthful energy will stay with us in his recordings.

49 ~ *Alasdair Fraser*
winter 2012-13

Silhouetted against the glow of dawn, Scottish fiddler Alasdair Fraser lifts both arms in triumph, fiddle in one hand, bow in the other. This image on the cover of *Dawn Dance* proclaims the joy of Fraser's music, from the pulsing traditional Gaelic melodies to the smooth, powerful strathspeys. Even the stirring lamentations are filled with the joy of hearing rich tones from a well-played violin.

The *Dawn Dance* cover could also be the image of a victorious prize fighter – the champion of Scottish traditional music who has proved that this centuries-old music is very much alive. Or a champion of the arts who has delivered a blow to people's fear of doing what they love for a living.

Alasdair Fraser grew up in a musical family in Clackmannan in central Scotland. His brother plays and teaches fiddle, his father played pipes, and his grandfather helped found the nearby Stirling Strathspey and Reel Society in 1930. Alasdair has appeared in over 150 TV and radio programs worldwide, played on hit film soundtracks, and performed as a guest with top classical and folk groups. He currently tours the world with cellist Natalie Haas.

Seeing Alasdair Fraser in action today, as he plays fiddle with power and authority, flawless tone and control, and a deeply rooted Scottish style, you might not imagine him to have been a quiet child, who most enjoyed the predictable logic of science and math.

He earned a degree in physics (called "natural philosophy" at Glasgow University) and traveled to San Francisco to work for BP Alaska. Soon, his quest for Scottish music took him on a trip to Cape Breton, Nova

Scotia. He had heard that fiddling was thriving there, and he wanted to meet the great fiddlers in the band called "the Cape Breton Symphony."

The moment he arrived in Nova Scotia, wearing the kilt, running shoes, and holding a violin case, a man came up to him in the airport and asked what kind of music he played.

"Scottish," said Alasdair.

"So do I," said the man. He was Wilfred Gillies of the Cape Breton Symphony. Alasdair met the rest of the band, including Buddy MacMaster, Jerry Holland, and bandleader Bobby Brown, and that same night, shared the stage with them. It wasn't long before Bobby Brown produced Alasdair's first solo album, *Portrait of a Scottish Fiddler,* which presents Fraser in solid traditional form, backed by a lively dance band.

Moving to California, and marrying an American woman, settled Alasdair in America, but his roots were in the Scottish music. The trouble was, his roots also included what he called the "cultural cringe" of Scotland, a feeling that Scots were a little embarrassed in those days by their own culture. For example, Alasdair, twice winner of Scotland's National Mod Fiddle Championship, couldn't play Scottish music in some sessions in Scotland because people didn't know the tunes. He had a hard time finding old Scottish tune books. Other social constraints, such as the stifling of Gaelic and Scots, added to a feeling of being tongue-tied about his own culture.

It is perhaps this sense of injustice, seeing and experiencing the stifling of a people's pride about their culture, and the crippling fear people often have about expressing themselves, that has spurred Alasdair to become an inspiration, an enabler, a healer through music. Every performance, says Alasdair, is like a collaboration, not only with musicians on stage but also with the audience, "to see if we can get to a place that maybe we didn't think we'd get to that day." Over the years, Fraser has created and now directs four annual music camps. Each of them builds a community where people can learn the spirit of Scottish music, gain confidence with their instruments, and push traditional music forward. One camp is on the Isle of Skye, two are in California, and one is in Spain.

In California back in the 1980s, with the vibrancy of Cape Breton fresh in his memory, Alasdair Fraser set about teaching and playing Scottish music with the confidence and power that can be heard in all his recordings and performances. Soon, he began spending Wednesday nights with pianist Paul Machlis, playing pingpong and exploring how to play old Gaelic melodies with a modern sensibility. This led to a breakthrough album called *Skyedance.* Its powerful renditions of old tunes used piano, synthesizer, hand drums, and atmospheric fiddle harmonies. Paul and Alasdair continued to play for many years, pursuing new ways to work with traditional tunes in their album *The Road North* and with the Skyedance Band, which was named after their first recording together.

Fraser has always enjoyed collaborations. His third album, *The Driven Bow,* with American guitarist Jody Stecher, paid tribute to strong influences from Cape Breton style and tune selection. Ten years later, Alasdair made a beautiful CD called *Return to Kintail* with virtuoso Scottish guitarist Tony McManus, exploring Gaelic tunes, pipe tunes and Cape Breton tunes in a well-crafted performance. Fraser has joined with many other players as well, appearing as a guest on over 50 albums.

Dawn Dance was a departure from the duo format, focusing on original tunes and including piano, flute, Scottish and Irish pipes, and drums. This album won an Indie award for Celtic album of the year, and led to the formation of the Skyedance Band. Skyedance's three groundbreaking albums feature original compositions by band members and some improvisation within a traditional, mostly Scottish-based, context.

Alasdair Fraser experiments constantly but always comes back to his Scottish roots. With Paul Machlis on piano, he started a series of recordings of traditional fiddle tunes, called *Legacy of the Scottish Fiddle.* Volume 2 of this series focuses on the music of Burns, with legendary RSCDS pianist Muriel Johnstone and cellist Natalie Haas. Aged about 17 at the time, Natalie recalls entertaining Alasdair's two boys in one room while Alasdair and Muriel covered the next room with books, researching the music and times of Robert Burns for their recording.

Intellectual inquiry is a constant theme in Alasdair Fraser's artistry, and enriches his performances with stories and themes. For example, in his latest album, he traces the tune "Highlander's Farewell to Ireland" from its Scottish version to its settings in Ireland and America, using the talents of guest fiddlers Martin Hayes and Bruce Molsky.

That tune is the title track of *Highlander's Farewell,* the third album by Alasdair Fraser with Natalie Haas, his current musical companion. This duo not only seeks to return the cello to its former glory in Scottish music, but also to explore the possibilities of what they consider to be two fiddles – a wee one and a big one. Their sound ranges from gutsy rhythmic bowing, to soaring improvisation, to smooth, classical ensemble work.

Alasdair Fraser is always on a quest to unleash the wellspring of Scottish music, to renew and invigorate his music, and that of the musicians and students around him. In recent years, he has come to realize that he has succeeded in some of his goals. The era of reviving Scottish music may well be over. Young people today no longer need to be taught about how important it is to keep the music alive. They're doing it. In his ring, his camps and workshops, the prize fighter has won.

But after the fight, what then? Alasdair Fraser recalls a moment when he metaphorically gathered some of his well-worn exhortations about Scotland's cultural baggage, "tied it up with a big bow, and put it on a high shelf." Renewed, he felt ready to dive into the youthful musical scene of today. Several of his apprentices, such as Hanneke Cassel and Laura Risk, have launched their own fiddling careers. Cellist Natalie Haas is herself a product of Alasdair Fraser's music camps.

Together, Fraser and Haas are bubbling with new ideas, poised to bring joy to Scottish music in ways that we, and they, have yet to imagine.

50 ~ Twa Fiddles: Burns and Gow
winter 2019-20

If you walk through the old market cross of Dunkeld toward the Cathedral, you might notice a round, blue plaque on the last house on the right that reads: "The Old Rectory... Dunkeld's oldest surviving house. Fiddler Niel Gow and poet Robbie Burns entertained here 1787."

Last year, in January, some 232 years after Burns and Gow met in Dunkeld, their violins met and made music together, at the Gaiety Theatre in Ayr. Ayrshire fiddler Alistair McCulloch, dressed as Robert Burns, greeted Perthshire fiddler Pete Clark, who personified Niel Gow, in a concert called "The Twa Fiddles." They performed again in September at the Scottish Parliament building, sponsored by Deputy First Minister John Swinney, whose district includes the homes of Niel Gow and Pete Clark. The concert was attended by several members of Parliament and about 60 invited academics, musicians, members of the National Trust for Scotland, and friends.

The pairing of these historic violins was the brainchild of retired schoolteacher Paul Creighton of Ayr. "I knew Pete was one of the few fiddlers allowed to play Neil Gow's fiddle," said Paul, "and Alistair was one of the few to play Burns's fiddle. It occurred to me that we might have an opportunity to do something quite special." Bringing together the two historic violins is certainly something special, and Alistair, Pete, and Paul are hoping to raise funds to present more Twa Fiddles concerts, as well as produce a video and an educational package for schools, so that the unique connection of Niel Gow and Robert Burns can be more widely appreciated.

The original meeting between Burns and Gow took place in late summer, 1787. Perhaps Burns was seeking more melodies for his project, the *Scots Musical Museum*. The first volume of this six-volume series had just been published by James Johnson, and would ultimately total 600 traditional and contemporary Scottish songs, all collected by Robert Burns, many with lyrics written by Burns himself. To our knowledge, Burns did not write any of the melodies, but he had an impeccable ear and passion for preserving good melodies and lyrics representative of the Scottish tradition. Though known as a great poet, he was perhaps greatest as a songwriter. He wrote over 320 songs, nearly two-thirds of his artistic output.

Robert Burns was moved by Niel Gow's fiddling and his compositions, using several for songs such as "My Love's Like a Red, Red Rose" and "Braving Angry Winter's Storms." Gow was well known in his day for his powerful fiddling, and his son Nathaniel published an influential series of tune books that are central to the repertoire of Scottish musicians even today. The Duke of Atholl, who owned land from Blair Castle through Dunkeld and beyond, used to pay Niel Gow an annual retainer of £5 for his musical services – more than he paid his head gardener! At a time when classical composers like Mozart were patronized by aristocracy in mainland Europe, Gow and other Scottish fiddlers were patronized by Scottish aristocrats who cared deeply about their national music.

Burns's violin was not, strictly speaking, owned by Robert Burns but appears to have been handed down in his family, and might actually have been played by the poet himself. There is speculation that Burns learned a bit of fiddling, but no clear proof, though he did send a ballad under a fictitious name to a Mr Sharpe in around 1790, and wrote, "I am a fiddler and a poet." Burns was very musical, as is amply demonstrated by his ability to collect and preserve so many great melodies of Scotland. He could read and write music, and said himself that when he wrote a song, he first selected the melody and sang it to himself as he wrote the words. His songs are certainly a masterful blend of music and lyrics.

The violin associated with Burns was used by his dancing teacher, William Gregg. At age 17, Burns defied his father and went off to learn country dancing at the Bachelor's Club at Tarbolton Lodge, a small building that can still be seen not far from Ayr. He claimed he wanted to "give his manners a brush" despite (and probably in open rebellion against) his father's view that dancing was sinful. Like many dancing masters, William Gregg taught while playing the fiddle.

Made around 1750, the Gregg violin is beautifully and elaborately decorated on all sides. The violin fell into disrepair until 1995, when Wallace Galbraith, Alistair McCulloch's violin teacher and founder of the Ayrshire Fiddle Orchestra, learned that it was still in existence at a farm near Mauchline. The violin is now proudly on display in the Burns Birthplace Museum in Ayr. These days it is Alistair McCulloch who looks after the violin and keeps it in use several times a year, including Burns Night celebrations at the cottage where Burns was born.

Alistair learned classical violin formally, but his father played fiddle and pipes, and introduced him to the local strathspey and reel society. For many years, Alistair played with the Scottish Fiddle Orchestra, led the Ayrshire Fiddle Orchestra for nine years, and now teaches violin and Scottish fiddle both privately and as a faculty member of the Royal Conservatoire in Glasgow. His trio has toured and recorded, featuring whistle player Marc Duff, formerly of Capercaillie, and Aaron Jones of Old Blind Dogs on bouzouki, guitar and vocals. McCulloch's latest project is the annual "Land O' Burns Fiddle Weekend," which was launched this past fall. Four great Scottish fiddlers – Gordon Gunn, Kevin Henderson, Rua MacMillan and Alistair himself – provided instruction and performances.

The Burns Museum entrusts Alistair McCulloch with care of the Gregg violin and allows him to take it out of the museum for performances such as the Twa Fiddles concerts. In fact, in January 2020, McCulloch will be taking the violin over to the U.S. for a Robert Burns tour sponsored by the National Trust for Scotland in Boston, Washington DC, Chicago and Los Angeles.

Blair Castle displays Niel Gow's violin in the ballroom. Glued inside is a slip of paper inscribed "Niel Gow, 1787." Curiously, that is not only the year that Burns and Gow met, but also the year Henry Raeburn painted the famous portrait of Gow now hanging above the violin's display case. The only problem for the Twa Fiddles project is that Blair Castle will not permit the Gow violin to leave the premises.

Fortunately, Pete Clark found a way around this problem – by finding another violin belonging to Gow! One day, after discussing Niel Gow enthusiastically on television, Clark received a call from a retired clergyman in the Borders who asked Pete to come see an interesting violin. Accompanying the instrument was handwritten paperwork tracing it to a Peter Murray of Perthshire, who is known to have received directly from Niel Gow two violins and a cello. The label inside the violin is marked "Caspar de Salo" and links this violin with stories that Niel Gow played a violin made by the eminent 16th century Italian violin maker, Gasparo da Salo. The misspelling of the name inside the violin, however, has led experts to believe it was probably a German copy of a da Salo violin. And being a violin owned by Niel Gow, it allows Alistair McCulloch and Pete Clark to continue bringing together the music and the fiddles of Burns and Gow.

Since 2004, Pete Clark has organized an annual Niel Gow Festival in Dunkeld, offering concerts, workshops, and sessions on the weekend closest to Gow's birthday, March 22. Over the years, two of Clark's solo albums have featured Niel Gow violins. The first one made use of the violin at Blair Castle and is now out of print, while the more recent one uses a newly found Gow violin, with Muriel Johnstone on piano.

One of Clark's major projects has been to honor Niel Gow with a statue in Dunkeld. After years of fundraising, it appears that the dream may come true at the Niel Gow Festival. Scottish sculptor David Annand has made the clay sculpture, which is due to be poured in bronze by March.

Soon, before you pass through the Dunkeld market* and take note of the Old Rectory where Robert Burns and Niel Gow met in 1787, you might notice someone watching you – the new life-size statue of Niel Gow standing by the road, holding his fiddle and wondering which tune you'd like him to play.

Gow's statue, unveiled in late 2020 in Birnam, is located just across the River Tay from Dunkeld, not far from the cemetery where Gow lies buried.

51 ~ *Shetland Fiddle Frenzy*
winter 2017-18

As we boarded the Northlink ferry, it was fun to see the gigantic Viking painted on the side of the boat, pointing the way to the Shetland Islands. For six centuries, until 1472, Shetland belonged to the Vikings, and for the past six centuries has been a part of Scotland. Not surprisingly, its music, dialect, and traditions reflect a mix of local, Scottish, and Scandinavian influences.

On the ferry, an old Shetland tune, "Da Ferry Reel," came to mind. The "da" ("the") is just one of many unique Shetland words and pronunciations that are vestiges of Norn, a Germanic language related to Norse and Danish, which was gradually replaced by Scots, and died out (some Shetlanders say it was banned) in the 19th century.

"Da Ferry Reel" may refer to a ferryboat, but it is also said to honor the "fairy," one of the "little people" who made up or inspired the melody. Known in Shetland as trows or trowies, these fairies figure prominently in Shetland folklore. A word of warning to fiddlers: Beware of trowies who invite you into their knoll for a party. Legend has it that after playing music all night, you may discover in the morning that you've been away from home, not for a night, but for a century!

When we arrived in Lerwick, the capital of Shetland, we found our B&B located nearly opposite the park where a replica Viking longship is burned during the winter "Up Helly Aa" festival. This is but one of a number of local annual festivals, including the fall Shetland Wool Week, the spring Shetland Folk Festival, and the early August event we were looking forward to, Shetland Fiddle Frenzy.

Now heading into its 15th year, Fiddle Frenzy is an aptly named, week-long immersion in Shetland fiddle tradition, with daily classes for fiddlers and guitarists, and related events such as a tour of places linked to particular tunes, and workshops in silversmithing, drawing, and painting. Nightly concerts feature top bands and artists with Shetland connections, as well as showcases of local musicians, including excellent kids groups.

The headquarters for Fiddle Frenzy is the Mareel arts center on the Lerwick waterfront. Opened in 2012, the center hosts a multipurpose auditorium, two movie theaters, rehearsal rooms, a recording studio, broadcast facilities and a cafe bar. Its name comes from a special Shetland word for the phosphorescence of ocean waves on dark autumn nights.

Much of Shetland culture is centered around the sea and fishing. Next door to Mareel is the Shetland Museum and Archives, with a fantastic exhibition about Shetland history and culture. Some of the Fiddle Frenzy classes are held in the Museum's auditorium or in the boat hall, whose ceiling, several stories high, allows for historic boats to be hung on display from above.

One of the boats on display was a 19th century sixareen, so named because it was made for six oarsmen. A broad black boat with a single mast, it reminded me of a jaunty fiddle tune named "Da Sixareen." At the museum, I learned how Shetland fishermen had used sixareens in the 18th and 19th centuries to make a living beyond the control of the local lairds, rowing some 40 miles out to sea, against the wind, so they could fill their boats with fish and sail home.

The tune "Da Sixereen" was written by Tom Anderson, who was a driving force in the preservation of Shetland fiddle music. A fiddler and insurance salesman, Anderson used his business travels throughout Shetland to coax anyone who played fiddle into recording their tunes for him, and thus managed to preserve many traditional tunes while they were still within living memory.

The archives at the museum have a computer with digitized copies of all of Anderson's recordings. I listened to one recording of a fiddle lesson Anderson gave in the 1970s, in which he talked about how he came to compose one of his most famous tunes, the beautiful slow air "Da Slockit Light." Just after his wife died in 1969, Tom was up at night walking the grassy fields of Eshaness, his home town, in northwest Shetland. There is hardly a more dramatic coastline to be found in Scotland than at Eshaness, with its 200-foot cliffs by the sea, and geos cut into the land like inlets of a giant jigsaw puzzle piece. When the melody came to him, Anderson cut open a cigarette, unrolled the paper, and wrote the tune down. "Da Slockit Light" means "the light that went out" and although I've heard this referred to the darkened homes of Shetlanders off to work in the North Sea oil rigs, after listening to that tape I wondered if the light that went out had been his wife.

Tunes throughout Scotland have been named for places, battles, and people of note, but in Shetland, most of the tunes refer to the sea or everyday events. Often, the melody paints a picture of the story behind the tune. "Aandowin at da Bow," a tune about fishermen using oars to keep their boat steady in the currents, has a syncopated section that imitates the rhythm of the oars. "Doon Da Rooth," a jig in 21/8 time, perfectly mirrors the uneven rhythm of a foot on the treadle of a spinning wheel. In "Jack Broke Da Prison Door," a crashing high note highlights the moment Jack broke down the heavy wooden door. "Aald Swaara," named for the black waterproof sweater worn by fishermen, was played to honor those lost at sea. "Spootiskerry," originally called "Spoot o' Skerry," refers to the spoot, or razor clams, harvested on the skerries, small uninhabited islands off the Shetland coast.

"Willafjord" is one of the most popular of Shetland tunes, but until recently, nobody knew what its title meant. After a lot of sleuthing, fiddler Maurice Henderson found out. He's a member of a great band called Haltadans, which we heard at a Fiddle Frenzy evening concert, but for many years has played with one of Scotland's best bands, Fiddlers' Bid. Their four energetic CDs are well worth a listen, with lots of exciting arrangements of traditional Shetland tunes as well as originals by band members. Several fiddlers from Fiddlers' Bid are well known in the Scottish music scene today, including Kevin Henderson (no relation) who also plays with Session A9, and the innovative fiddle/harp duo of Chris Stout and Catriona McKay.

Maurice's book, *In Search of Willafjord*, documents his discovery, using the logs of whaling ships, that Willafjord was once the name of a settlement, now called Sisiumiut, on the west coast of Greenland. Many Shetlanders worked as whalers, "now beyond living memory, but remembered in the tunes," as Maurice says. The lavishly illustrated book shows amazing scenery including dramatic icebergs, native Greenland fiddlers, and describes local dance steps very similar to those of Shetland.

Shetland is so proud of its vibrant fiddle tradition that every schoolchild is provided with a fiddle and instruction. Some great Scottish fiddlers have hailed from Shetland, including Aly Bain, best known for years as the fiddler with the Boys of the Lough, and more recently in his duo with accordionist Phil Cunningham, or as host of the television series *Transatlantic Sessions*. Other great Shetland fiddlers, in addition to Fiddlers' Bid, include Jenna Reid of Blazin' Fiddles and Rant, and Catriona MacDonald, formerly also of Blazin' Fiddles.

It was exhilarating to hear so many great concerts, learn Shetland tunes from great fiddlers, and view breathtaking sights. But as I made my way to my little bedroom on the overnight ferry to Aberdeen, for some reason the Shetland tune that came to mind was "Sleep Soond Ida Moarnin" (Sleep Soundly in the Morning).

52 ~ *Bruce MacGregor*
spring 2011

Getting bayoneted on the field of Culloden is not the usual way to land a job with BBC Radio Scotland. But it seemed to work for Bruce MacGregor. Trained early on as a Highland fiddler in Inverness, MacGregor had never planned to make music his career, nor did he suspect he'd become a mover and shaker for Scotland's music, as a performer, organizer and radio personality.

At university, he pursued a major in Byzantine and Medieval Italian history, and attempted to follow up with a grad program in business. Unfortunately, he discovered a distaste for sitting in front of a computer doing accounting, and dropped the program.

Nevertheless, MacGregor's interest in business has ultimately led him to successfully found and direct a band, a music camp, a festival, and to convert his parents' farm near Inverness into a farm adventure resort called Bogbain. Offering a variety of fun activities for kids, Bogbain is also a small B&B, an excellent restaurant, and hosts musical events as well.

MacGregor's degree in Byzantine History could be said to figure into this tale, but only in the sense that "byzantine" usually means "convoluted." This best describes MacGregor's route to a productive career in radio. It all began when his rugby team was asked to appear in a film about the Battle of Culloden. During one scene, Bruce suddenly found himself underneath a rearing horse. Being a good rugby player and in a panic, he charged wildly down the field of Culloden until a searing pain in his leg alerted him to the fact that he had run into someone's bayonet. Another Highlander laid low at Culloden.

Crutches forced a reprieve from the film and his job, and led MacGregor to busk with his fiddle on the streets of Inverness. There he was informed by a passerby of a research job available at BBC Radio Scotland. Curiously, at the job interview, they only asked him questions about sports. It turned out the researcher's job had been filled, but they decided to use MacGregor for a sports program. Thus began his work in radio.

Over the years, BBC Scotland has given MacGregor the opportunity to create a number of radio documentaries, two of which won awards at the Celtic TV and Film Festival. These two were radio adaptations of fascinating theater productions written by actor Hamish MacDonald, delving into the lives of two giants of Scottish fiddling, Captain Simon Fraser (1773-1852) and James Scott Skinner (1843-1927).

MacGregor has produced nonmusical programs as well, but his main focus has been musical. One of his radio features celebrated the Battlefield Band's 30th year; another examined the pioneering traditional band Silly Wizard. A series of documentaries about young successful Scottish musicians traced performers such as piper Dougie Pincock, singer and harper Corrina Hewat, and fiddler Allan Henderson as they revisited the instructors of their youth to discuss tradition, music and teaching.

Last fall, Bruce MacGregor became the new presenter of BBC Radio Scotland's long-running traditional music program, *Travelling Folk*, which airs 32 weeks a year. He also contributes his crisp, articulate voice to *The Music Cafe*, where he interviews and samples the music of three guests each week. These programs can be heard in Scotland mid-week, and at any time online.

One of Bruce's more fateful programming decisions came about in the late 1990s when he attended Scottish fiddler Alasdair Fraser's fiddle camp in California. BBC let him bring equipment to record a radio program, and indeed the campers' enthusiasm for Scottish fiddling and colorful personalities made for great radio. But MacGregor noticed a curious phenomenon: almost none of the campers were aware of the current lively music scene in Scotland. One older fellow even said he thought fiddling was dying out in Scotland and being kept alive in America. This jarring opinion stuck in MacGregor's mind.

He realized that Scotland was doing a bad job of selling its own culture, even to itself. Scottish radio at the time seemed to be filled with Irish and Cape Breton music, rather than Scottish.

MacGregor returned home and made a bold proposal to the new Highland Festival: he would organize a showcase of some of the best fiddlers in the Highlands, and a Shetland fiddler, to demonstrate that their music was alive and well.

Joining Bruce in that 1998 showcase were fiddlers Duncan Chisholm, Iain MacFarlane, Aidan O'Rourke, Allan Henderson, and Catriona MacDonald. They became Blazin' Fiddles, one of Scotland's most exciting traditional bands. Still going strong, the band has played Albert Hall, Buckingham Palace, Royal Glasgow Concert Hall and countless village halls. In 2000, Bruce and his wife started "Blazin' in Beauly," a music camp taught by Blazin' Fiddles, with guest performers and teachers from Scotland and abroad. The camp was named "Music Event of the Year" at the 2005 Scots Trad Music Awards, the same year a Blazin' Fiddles CD won Best Album of the Year. The camp continues to enliven the small town of Beauly, near Inverness, every October.

Blazin' Fiddles has a number of recordings well worth a listen. Their virtuosity and irrepressible energy blend fast-paced arrangements with heartfelt slow airs, within varied traditions, from Gaelic to Scots, from centuries-old tunes to newly composed ones.

Bruce's own recordings include one of my favorites, *101 Reasons To Do Nothing* (a curious title and a long story involving his father's lawyer, some tractors, and cows). The clarity, energy, and resonant tone of MacGregor's fiddling are captivating. The album concludes with a mournful and unusual tune by his teacher, Donald Riddell, which he wrote to lament the death of King George V after playing pipes at the king's funeral in 1936.

MacGregor has recorded several other CDs, among them a book and CD spotlighting his teacher's compositions. For this project, he collaborated with other members of the Blazin' Fiddles band, most of whom had also studied with Donald Riddell.

His contributions to Scottish music seem to keep multiplying. In addition to working in radio, managing the Bogbain resort and events there such as the Northern Roots Festival, organizing the fiddle camp, and playing with the Blazin' Fiddles band, Bruce MacGregor has also worked with other groups, notably the big band The Unusual Suspects, and Cliar, which features three of Scotland's best Gaelic singers.

It would be tempting to say this was all thanks to taking a bayonet wound at Culloden, but Bruce MacGregor also has the talent of a well-trained and experienced fiddler, and the unstoppable energy and persistence of a rugby player. His knowledge of music from Scotland and beyond are complimented by the bright, concise voice of a good storyteller, making his radio interviews and musical commentaries nearly as much a listening pleasure as his fiddling. Building on the energy and talents of young players and organizers like MacGregor, Scottish music is entering exciting times.

SECTION 4c ~ BAGPIPES

53 ~ *Intro to Pipe Bands*
winter 1996-97

You've edged past the crowd, with the drone of warpipes buzzing louder in your ears until you come face to face with... a whole field of fierce Highland bagpipers marching straight at you. Okay, you're dipping into a bit of Highland Games fantasy. Who can blame you? If you have stood at the end of a field when the massed bands turn in your direction, you know what I mean.

A pipe band is a stirring sight, but the massed bands are awe-inspiring. Once you are safe at home, you can put on a pipe band album, close your eyes, and picture it again. The massed band albums, such as the Tattoos, or the recording of last year's giant Fields of Hope event, present the familiar tunes you've heard at Highland Games. Since massed bands include many pipers at varying levels, only the most popular tunes are selected so that everyone can play them together.

As you start to listen to pipe band recordings, you will discover the delights of great tunes, jazzy drumming, and sometimes a smattering of guitars, accordions, Caribbean drums, or even a symphony orchestra — but more on that later.

Traditional piping is a complex art. Pipers work very hard to attain a precision of timing and technique that is beyond the hearing of most listeners. It is very nearly a spiritual pursuit. In bands, this shows up in timing, clarity, and musicality. The best pipe bands contain great individual pipers who are able to learn interesting and difficult tunes, and play them well together.

Although there are excellent pipe bands whose names have not figured in recent world competitions, you can be most assured of listening to a fine album if you listen to championship bands. Some of the top names include Simon Fraser University, Shotts & Dykehead Caledonia, Field Marshall Montgomery, Strathclyde Police, 78th Fraser Highlanders, Scottish Power, Polkemmet Grorud, Vale of Atholl, Victoria Police, and Dysart & Dundonald. There are more, of course, but you can't go far wrong with these. All have released their own recordings, and there are compilation and competition albums can give you a taste of many bands at one shot.

There are also the regimental bands, including the Black Watch, the Scots Guards, and the Royal Scots Dragoon Guards. While both civilian and regimental bands perform in parades and concerts, the regimental bands actually use their music every day for military rituals and ceremonies. An album such as the Black Watch's *Proud Heritage* will lay out for you many of their traditional pipe tunes and their daily or monthly uses.

The heart of most pipe band recordings are the competition sets, which include the march/strathspey/reel medley and what's called the "selection," a free-form demonstration of versatility. The selection contains a creative mix of airs, marches, strathspeys, reels, jigs, and hornpipes — the "light music," as opposed to the "big music", which is the contemplative piobaireachd, or pibroch, the classical music of the Highland bagpipes.

The current World Champion band, Simon Fraser University, has made several albums. Their recent *Alive in America* spotlights solo pipers, drummers and small pipes in addition to the whole band. The best-selling pipe band album of all time appears to be *Live in Ireland* by the 78th Fraser Highlanders. Ironically, both of these bands are Canadian, and as of this writing are the only non-British bands ever to have won the World Championships.

Pipe bands are directed by their pipe major, who has an enormous influence on the band's sound. The pipe major seeks out interesting traditional tunes, creates harmonies, finds or writes new compositions, and sometimes arranges tunes originally written for other instruments.

Pipe Major Robert Mathieson, for example, writes many of the tunes played by his current band, Shotts & Dykehead. Under his direction in the 1980s, the Polkemmet Grorud was one of the first bands to record tunes using a new note in the bagpipe scale, the C natural. This year, Simon Fraser University chose to end its winning set with a fiddle tune, the "Cape Breton Visit to Shetland", which was successfully revised from its original 16-note range to fit the bagpipe's nine-note scale.

Pipe bands have ventured into many types of musical settings. The ScotRail Vale of Atholl Pipe Band collaborated with folk band Eclipse First in their *Names and Places* album. The Pipes and Drums of British Caledonian Airways recorded *Alba* with the BBC Symphony Orchestra. Shotts & Dykehead's *Another Quiet Sunday* includes the Battlefield Band. And MacUmba created a sensation with its *Don't Hold Your Breath*, featuring a Caribbean rhythm section.

Speaking of rhythm, look no farther than the pipe band to bring you the best. A famous jazz drummer, when asked by Johnny Carson to name the greatest drummer in the world, named Alex Duthart — the Scot who helped develop modern Scottish pipe band drumming.

Pipe band drummers energize every tune with bold, rhythmic ideas. Drum majors write arrangements for most tunes, playing the rolling or snapping snares off the booming bass drum. In slow airs, they gather and fade drum rolls to dramatize the mood.

Everyone has a different list of favorite pipe band albums, and even fine pipers I've spoken with are unaware of at least some of the many recordings now available. The world of pipe bands is as awe-inspiring as a massed band, and as complex as the bands and pipers within it. It's a world waiting for you to explore.

54 ~ *Listening to Pipe Bands*
winter 2001-02

The circle of pipers stands ready, the pipes silent, bags blown full. A sputtering salute from snare drums fills the air. The rich hum of drones kicks in. The pipers puff into their bags, again and again. Now the bright, biting song of the chanter lets loose with a swaying melody, drums ticking sharply in counter rhythms. We see the pipers' faces intense with concentration from playing, cheeks contorted from blowing air, arms letting air into the bags even as they force air out the drones and chanters, and on those simple round holes in the black wooden chanter, fingers snap at lightning speed in complicated patterns.

The sheer physical effort and volume of sound, the striving for the unison and perfect timing that breathes life into the music: in the presence of a good pipe band, this is an awesome experience.

You can hear pipe bands these days not only at competitions and parades, but in great concert halls, and even at home or in your car — on CD, of course. Many pipe band CDs are recorded live, no doubt in large part because it is not easy to fit 15 pipers and 8 drummers into a small recording studio and live to tell about it!

One of the most exciting live recordings of pipe bands is the annual World Pipe Band Championships album. In recent years, a second volume of this annual CD has been offered, in order to present not only the top half dozen pipe bands but also the remaining six or seven finalists. Unless you are very knowledgeable about pipe band music, you will hear little difference among all these great bands.

However, if you listen closely, you may notice that the best bands have a clear and strong unison sound, with no fuzziness on any notes, and their drum corps plays so well together that the drums come across sharp and clear, with exciting rhythms to offset the melodies. Above all, the band's musicality and spirit shine through, thanks to the leadership of the pipe major and the quality of the individual players.

The 2001 World Champion is the Simon Fraser University Pipe Band (SFU), of Vancouver, Canada. This is the band's fourth championship. SFU's latest CD is *Down Under*, recorded live in Australia in April at the Sydney Opera House. It's an excellent listening album, with not only traditional medleys but also jazzy selections, and a slow piobaireachd both played and sung (Canntaireachd) by the band to great effect. Fiddle, guitar and other instruments add nice texture.

Other recent albums by SFU include *Live in Carnegie Hall* and *At the Worlds*, a compilation of the band's performances at the Worlds during the 1990s. The band's video, *Legacy*, takes us behind the scenes as they prepare for competition and the Carnegie Hall concert.

Second in the Worlds this year was three-time world champion Shotts & Dykehead Caledonia. The pipe major of this band, Robert Mathieson, has made a splash with some of his solo work as well as innovative arrangements for band. Shotts & Dykehead's CD, *Another Quiet Sunday*, involves the popular Battlefield band, and *By the Water's Edge* offers a dramatic suite of programmatic arrangements. A third album, *Pipe Major's Choice*, presents fine historic Shotts performances otherwise unavailable on CD.

The Northern Irish band, Field Marshall Montgomery, took third this year. World champions in 1992 and 1993, this band has made two respected CDs, *Debut* (including a tune in 14/8 time!) and *Live*, which was recorded in concert at the Motherwell Civic Center in 1996.

Boghall & Bathgate Caledonia placed fourth overall, but its drum corps won the world drumming championships. The drum corps is featured in a drum fanfare on the band's 2001 CD, *InSpired in Belfast*, along with the full band, and some Irish fiddle and flute.

Fifth was the Scottish Power Pipe Band. Although this band's name may seem proud and patriotic, it actually refers to the band's sponsor, the Scottish Power utility company. They can also be heard on their 1995 CD, *Tartan Weave*.

The 78th Fraser Highlanders, from Toronto, Canada, placed sixth this year. This band made piping history in 1987 when it became the first non-Scottish pipe band to win the World Pipe Band Championships. Three days before that competition, the band was recorded in concert in Ireland. That CD, *Live in Ireland*, has proved to be the best-selling pipe band album of all time, and with good reason. Other fine albums include *Live in Scotland, Megantic Outlaw* and the recent *Flame of Wrath*. This last was a stage show recorded live as a CD and a video, featuring Scottish Highland and Irish step dancers.

Another Canadian band, Alberta Caledonia, took seventh, and fills out Volume 1 of this year's World Pipe Band Championships recording. Alberta Caledonia released *They Took Their Leave*, their 2001 CD, offering traditional piping, shuttle pipes, a drum fanfare, and Canntaireachd.

Three of these great pipe bands — Shotts & Dykehead, Field Marshall Montgomery, and 78th Fraser Highlanders — plus this year's tenth place band, Macnaughton's Vale of Atholl, can be heard on a unique album recorded at a millennium concert in the Glasgow Royal Concert Hall. Taking advantage of the gathering of pipe bands for the World Championships, this was the first concert to bring together four great pipe bands. The resulting two-volume recording, *A Pipe Band Spectacular*, showcases the bands both individually and together. Unlike typical massed bands, this one involves a rare gathering of great pipers who are capable of playing exciting and difficult tunes together, with infectious spirit.

An interesting introduction to the World Championships is a recent double CD called *A Decade of Champions*, which presents the winning performance of each world champion throughout the 1990s.

But missing in action here are the regimental pipe bands. Since they are on active military duty, they cannot take the time to travel and take part in pipe band competitions. Interestingly, the Victoria Police from Australia, the 1998 World Champions, has disbanded, apparently due to the conflict between the competition circuit and police duties. The band's last album, *Masterblasters*, is quite popular, and includes some rock arrangements as well as excellent traditional playing.

Some of the most famous pipe bands are military: the Black Watch, the Royal Scots Dragoon Guards, and the Scots Guards, for example. Some can be heard and seen in the annual Edinburgh Military Tattoo CD and video, and many have their own fine musical recordings. A few of these albums, such as *Proud Heritage* by the Black Watch, highlight the tunes played for reveille, working day calls, retreat marches, lights out, and other routine military duties. A sampling of regimental bands can be heard on *The Fighting Scot*, a new CD honoring these bands at a time when the British military has had to combine or disband some historic regiments.

New directions in pipe band music can be heard in recordings such as the millennium concert mentioned above, or in exciting albums like *Dedication*, by the St. Thomas Episcopal Pipe Band, Juvenile World Champions from Texas. A pipe band like MacUmba, which has replaced the traditional drum corps with Latin American percussion, is another story entirely!

If you have never seen a pipe band in person, go and experience one, especially a really good band. Then, when you sit back and listen to a pipe band CD, you can picture the intense teamwork striving for a single voice that is distilled in these stirring recordings.

55 ~ *Solo Pipers*
summer 1998

The telephone caller asked me four survey questions, as promised, but it was the fifth that had me stumped. "What is that music you're listening to?" she said. "I love that relaxing sound." Relaxing? A solo bagpipe album was on the CD player, and the tune that was playing was hardly a lullaby, or even a slow air.

Perhaps in this frenetic day and age, the unhurried, rock-solid timing of good bagpipe playing can come across as relaxing, as it pulses with rhythm for marching or dancing. It's one of the mysteries of the bagpipes that is well worth exploring, as you get to know the broad variety of solo bagpipe recordings available today.

The place to start is with relatively recent CDs, since many improvements have taken place both in bagpipe technique and in recording technology. And although a live piper is more exciting to watch and hear, there are benefits to CDs: you can invite the world's best pipers to your home, and you can set the volume!

Learn about the styles, moods, even the intent, of various pipers, to find what intrigues you. Some pipers are recorded to preserve their virtuoso technique and musical selections. Others offer musical ideas or technical innovations. Still others are oriented towards entertainment.

Thirteen award-winning pipers have been documented in Lismor's series, "The World's Greatest Pipers." If that seems overwhelming, there's one CD by the same title which samples eleven players. KRL's eleven-volume "Pipers of Distinction" series is similar. Five players can be found on both series, including such virtuosos as Alasdair Gillies and Gordon Walker. A new series of four albums from Temple Records features performances by eight legendary pipers during the past two years at Glasgow's new Piping Centre.

While many traditional piping albums are strictly solo, some add accompaniment for variety. For example, sprinkled in tastefully among the solo selections on Angus MacColl's *The Clan MacColl* are several tracks with electric keyboards, bouzouki, and congas.

Working with even more accompaniment, Pipe Major Robert Mathieson, of the current world champion pipe band Shotts & Dykehead, has charged up the piping world with *The Big Birl*. Traditional-style tunes (mostly written by Mathieson) are dressed in many colors, including a string quartet, calypso steel drums, piano blues, and electric rock guitar. His "Bells of Dunblane" is rendered gently, in an easy-listening mode. This is an enjoyable and musical tour de force.

While solo pipers try new ideas for accompaniment, concert bands such as the Tannahill Weavers and Wolfstone come from the other direction by highlighting their pipers in the context of a band sound. Having played with both these bands and a traditional pipe band, Gordon Duncan emerges as a lively presence in contemporary piping. His latest album, *The Circular Breath*, draws on his folk band experience, but also pays tribute to bagpipe tradition by including a pibroch. Similarly, piper Dougie Pincock, formerly of the Battlefield Band, offers innovative music on his *Something Blew*, and like Duncan, also includes a pibroch, this time with the unique touch of cello and harp.

Pibroch (the easy spelling for the Gaelic word "piobaireachd") is the classical contemplative solo music of the Scottish bagpipes. It can be an acquired taste, though some people are immediately drawn to its meditative quality. These slow and extended tunes carefully explore musical variations on a theme, the solid timing of held notes versus the pulse of explosive grace notes, and the continual shifts between the harmonizing and clashing of drone and melody notes. In a sense, they offer an opportunity in slow motion to appreciate the essence of solo piping.

Greentrax has just released a CD of historic pibroch recordings, including instruction, by Pipe Majors Brown and Nicol, the last of a line of instructors extending back to the 18th century MacCrimmons. Few recordings are devoted exclusively to this type of music, notably KRL's *Glendfiddich Piobaireachd Championship* and Lismor's *Piobaireachd.*

Bucking tradition, piper Hamish Moore has sought idiosyncratic styles in much the same fashion as do fiddlers and harpers. Moore struck a rich vein in Cape Breton, Nova Scotia, where some of the old Scottish piping traditions link up with social and step dancing. On his *Stepping on the Bridge,* Moore is accompanied by Cape Breton piano and guitar backup. He has also gone nontraditional in another direction by mixing bagpipes and jazz saxophone on the humorously but appropriately titled *Farewell to Decorum.*

Some of what Moore found in Nova Scotia can be heard on *Open the Door (Fosgail an Dorus),* by Cape Breton pipers Jamie MacInnis and Paul MacNeil. As you listen to this album, picture the piper sitting down, and stomping his feet like a fiddler to the powerful dance beat of his music.

The small pipes add another sound to the mix. Not to be confused with the Irish uilleann pipes, the Scottish small pipes are similar to the Highland pipes though much quieter, often using bellows instead of a mouthpiece to blow up the bag. Robert Wallace of the Whistlebinkies devoted his recent album *Breakout* entirely to the small pipes. Anna Mhoireach (Anna Murray) alternates between small pipes and Gaelic singing on her albums *Into Indigo* and *Out of the Blue,* supported by an enjoyable backup band throughout.

Listen for the players that can bring out the drive, the bounce, the sweetness or sadness of the music. The best pipers use a polished sense of timing and the pulse of grace notes (remember, changing the volume is not an option on pipes!) to bring out their musical ideas, whether playing solo or accompanied.

As you get to know solo bagpipe music, you will discover a rich variety, and perhaps even that relaxing quality that seemed to transcend the phone lines to my caller the other day. But don't expect it to put the baby to sleep.

56 ~ *The Three MacDonalds*
winter 2008-09

In the center of the west coast of Scotland lies the quiet fishing and crofting village of Glenuig, where Ronnie the Whaler used to live. His three sons, pipers all, have had an impact on Scottish music that no one could have foreseen growing up in a tiny village without electricity or even a road.

Ronald MacDonald was indeed a whaler before joining the Scots Guards in World War II, and his sons are still locally called the whaler boys, though they are now well into their 50s. Family and friends included pipers, box players, fiddlers, and Gaelic singers. A frequent visitor to the home was Ronald's cousin, piper Alexander (Sandy) MacDonald, as well as Sandy's son P/M Angus MacDonald, former pipe major of the Scots Guards.

The three brothers, Dr. Angus MacDonald, Allan MacDonald, and Iain MacDonald, have all brought heartfelt musicianship and strong Gaelic sensibilities to the piping world and to broader audiences. Dr. Angus mixes strong connections to Cape Breton with traditional award-winning piping; Allan's research, performance and teaching of the pibroch has infused the piping world with new ideas about an old form of music; and Iain's touring with great bands such as Ossian and the Battlefield Band has broadcast good piping throughout the folk music world.

Today, Angus, a medical doctor in Skye, is still a fine piper known for musicality, tone, and his long-time interest in mixing pipes with other instruments. He has won many top solo piping medals, including gold medals at Oban and Inverness, and the Silver Chanter.

In 1981, Angus started a movement that has had a profound effect on Scottish music. He and Father Colin MacInnes organized, on the isle of Barra, the first Fèis (pronounced "faysh"), an educational festival to revive traditional music on the island and inspire local youth. The idea grew into a movement: there are now about 40 Fèisean each year throughout Scotland, involving some 4,000 participants and 200 instructors. Many of today's top traditional musicians got their start or have learned some of their skills through these popular programs.

For a decade, Angus was a doctor in Cape Breton, Nova Scotia, and enjoyed the Scottish music scene there. This will be reflected in his new CD, which, in addition to solo piping, will include Cape Breton musicians and other guests such as Scottish fiddler Alasdair Fraser. Angus can also be heard on his classic CD, *A' Sireadh Spors* (Looking for Fun), and on a CD recorded at a Piping Centre recital in Glasgow. This was one of a series of recitals of top pipers celebrating the opening of the Piping Centre in 1996. Volume 3 of that first series of CDs features solo playing by Dr. Angus MacDonald and Willie Morrison.

Two years later, the Piping Centre recitals featured Angus's younger brother Allan (the CD is Series 3, 1998, vol 2). Allan is currently an instructor at the Piping Centre, where he delivers lectures and private lessons in piping to students from the Royal Scottish Academy of Music and Dance.

Allan has excelled in traditional piping; both he and Angus played with the British Caledonian Airways pipe band for some years, and as a solo piper, Allan won a gold medal and two clasps at Inverness. But his academic research took him in a new direction. He discovered connections between piping and Gaelic culture that led him to call into question the competitive style of piping, particularly in the pibroch.

Pibroch, the "big music" of Scotland, used to be a vital part of Gaelic culture until Culloden in 1746, but now is almost exclusively heard at competitions. A fairly common lament about competitions in the arts, whether in piping or other discipline, is that due to the requirements of judging, they sometimes foster winners who are missing something. They may be technically brilliant and yet passionless.

Sensing there was something missing in pibroch playing, Allan MacDonald did extensive academic research to place pibroch into its cultural context. He was able to demonstrate a close connection between pibroch and Gaelic song. As a result, he feels there should be more rhythmic and interpretive freedom in the pibroch, mirroring the way Gaelic is spoken and sung. Taking his musical cues from Gaelic song and language, Allan plays pibroch differently than those who place more value on written music and verbal descriptions.

Barnaby Brown, a piper who is also schooled in early classical music, writes that Allan's "refreshing, soulful interpretations have won the hearts of a much larger circle and helped to stimulate fresh thinking."

This comment was written in the introduction to Allan's 2007 CD, *Dastirum*, containing eleven pibrochs and some 70 pages of detailed notes. "Dastirum" is the first Gaelic word in a pibroch title which translates as "I Am Proud to Play a Pipe."

Other recordings of Allan's include two CDs, *Fhuair Mi Pog* and *Colla Mo Run* with Gaelic singer Margaret Stewart of Lewis and guest instrumentalists. These CDs are enjoyable musically, whether or not the listener is familiar with Gaelic or piping. Some of the tracks experiment with Allan's historical ideas. For example, one Gaelic song, about a Mackintosh chief fatally thrown off his horse on the day of his wedding, makes use of the melody of an old pibroch called "Mackintosh's Lament," giving the pibroch a special emotional context.

Other projects of Allan's include his tunebook, *The Moidart Collection*, with some 100 tunes and a CD recording of all the tunes for learning. He's hoping to bring out a new tunebook around Christmastime. Allan has also worked on a number of television projects, such as the recent six-part series called "Highland Sessions" linking the music of the Scottish Highlands and Ireland.

For some of these projects, Allan, like many musicians in Scotland, has called upon the expert services of his younger brother Iain.

Iain MacDonald never went for the competitive piping, and yet he had excellent training, starting like all the brothers with P/M John MacKenzie at school, plus lessons from cousin Sandy MacDonald, Roderick MacDonald of South Uist, and Duncan Johnstone.

Iain's work has mostly been in the context of Celtic touring bands and theater, playing pipes as well as flute and whistle. With several others, he co-founded the first Gaelic Repertory Theatre Company, based in Harris, and following that, joined the great Scottish folk band Ossian, with which he toured for nine years. Later he played with Wolfstone, and toured for six years with the Battlefield Band.

He has also worked in film and television, has produced many recordings for fellow traditional musicians, and has done quite a bit of teaching as well, currently at Lews Castle College in Benbecula. For many years, Iain has served as the Artistic Director for Ceòlas, a summer Gaelic music school on the isle of South Uist. Ceòlas runs for a week in early July, offering classes in fiddle, song, dance, pipes (including Allan MacDonald as a tutor), and Gaelic language.

Iain made a CD called *First Harvest* in 2002 with Iain MacFarlane, a fine Highland fiddler from Glenfinnan, and a member of the Blazin' Fiddles band. The Scotsman newspaper considered it the "best traditional album of Scottish Music to emerge in a decade from two of the foremost instrumentalists in the country."

Sadly, Iain was diagnosed a few years ago with MS. Mostly he's continued as busy as ever, although earlier in 2008, Iain had to take a few months off to regain his strength.

There are rumblings about a recording of all three MacDonald brothers, if only they could be pulled into one place! On occasion they've been known to play together, such as at the 2001 Celtic Colours Festival in Cape Breton or this past fall at the Blas Festival, a week-long festival held in various venues throughout the Highlands in early September.

The MacDonalds' home town of Glenuig built a new hall in 1995 to offer more space for events than the old village hall (which was once the elementary school attended by the MacDonald brothers). In spite of the small but slightly growing population (it helped that electricity arrived in 1983!), the Glenuig Hall has kept up an admirable schedule of musical and other events benefiting its whole neighborhood in Moidart. Perhaps some day it will welcome home the now famous piping MacDonald brothers for a little recorded concert.

57 ~ *Gordon Duncan and Ross Ainslie*
fall 2016

As I watched piper Ross Ainslie flawlessly playing a wild, syncopated tune based on the AC/DC rock song, "Thunderstruck," I reflected that this was a pretty nice tribute to his mentor, the late Gordon Duncan. For a CD released in 2003, Duncan had arranged the same song for bagpipes and recorded it as his title track.

Until Ainslie met the legendary piper and composer Gordon Duncan, he had been a reluctant student of the bagpipes. There were not many pipers in his home area near Perth; he was the only piper in his school. His good friend, Ali Hutton, was likewise the only piper in his school. Both boys joined the juvenile level of the Vale of Atholl pipe band in Pitlochry, a half hour north, in order to participate in the band's excellent feeder system, which accommodated nearly a hundred players, from teenage beginners to Grade 1 pipers.

Gordon Duncan's older brother Ian was the Pipe Major of the Vale of Atholl band from 1974 to 2000, moving it in only seven years from Grade 4 to Grade 1, and eventually into World Championship competitions. Ian directed the band, but relied upon Gordon's musical genius to craft the band's famously adventurous repertoire. At the time Ross Ainslie joined the juvenile level band, it was led by Gordon Duncan, whose quiet and intense musicianship fostered respect and commitment from the young players, to the point of winning the juvenile world championships.

Duncan used to take Ross aside at each band rehearsal for a half hour of instruction to bring him up to speed. Often Ross would spend time at Gordon's house, where he was exposed to all sorts of music – Scottish, Irish, rock, blues and more. Gordon's musical mind was always switched on. As they listened to music, Gordon would challenge the boys to imagine how they might play along if they were a banjo player or a fiddler. He encouraged them to learn guitar, whistle, or cittern, and showed them that music was about more than being in a pipe band. Sometimes he would get them to play along with rock bands like AC/DC and struggle to make the notes work, even if they were playing an instrument tuned to the wrong key.

Ross Ainslie was inspired by Gordon Duncan's leadership and musicianship to pursue music in all his spare time. His favorite album was Gordon's 1994 CD, *Just for Seamus.* For his part, Gordon Duncan not only played traditional pipe band music but also toured with some of Scotland's top folk bands, including Capercaillie, Wolfstone, and Ceolbeg.

One day, complaining that he was 17 and jobless, Ross found himself hustled by Gordon Duncan into a taxi to Dunkeld, where they played pipes in the Taybank bar until the owner, singer Dougie MacLean, walked in. MacLean ended up hiring Ainslie to tend bar, work in the kitchen, and play sessions. For two years he practically lived at MacLean's house, and landed some gigs with him as well.

In 2002, at age 19, Ainslie was a finalist in the BBC Scotland Young Traditional Musician of the Year award, the first of his many high-profile award nominations. Singer Emily Smith won that year and invited Ross to join her band. He soon acquired a taste for touring the world.

The following year, Ainslie began a long-lasting duo with uillean piper Jarlath Henderson, who had moved from Ireland to Scotland to attend medical school. They eventually recorded two albums, *Partners in Crime* (2008) and *Air-Fix* (2013), and were nominated Best Duo in the 2014 BBC Radio 2 Folk Awards. Their upbeat tunes are very melodic and mostly traditional-sounding, effortlessly mixing in eclectic flavors as well. Border and uilleann pipes, whistles, fiddle and voice are backed tastefully by guitar, piano, bass, and percussion.

Ainslie's big break came in 2005 when he was asked to join Salsa Celtica. This band mixes Cuban salsa music, jazz and traditional folk, and was so popular at the time that it provided him with full-time work.

2005 was also a tough year for Ainslie, as it was then that Gordon Duncan, struggling with alcoholism, took his own life. The sudden, inexplicable loss of this brilliant player and tunesmith came as a shock to the Scottish piping and traditional music communities. Gordy Jr, Duncan's son, gave his father's chanter and some of his whistles to Ross Ainslie, who ended up placing them with other memorabilia into a display case on his living room wall. Though the chanter might be usable again some day, the whistles were beyond repair. It didn't help that one of them had doubled as Gordon's fireplace poker!

Ainslie's first solo album, released in 2013, is called *Wide Open*. He was joined by his old piping buddy, Ali Hutton, on guitar, with other backing instruments. Although it is imbued with fascinating rhythms and drive, the tunes are, above all, melodic explorations. The album was nominated for Best Album of the Year in the Scots Trad Music Awards, and was among the top ten in the Sunday Herald's list of the best Scottish albums of 2013.

His second solo album derived from a New Voices commission by Celtic Connections, and was influenced by his decision a few years ago to stop drinking. Alarmed by a sense of dependence on alcohol, Ross quit over the course of a year, and found himself with more time on his hands and a need to face his new self squarely. To do this, he used music. "Music's a kind of thing that saves you in a way," Ainslie said, "Especially writing, and that's my favorite thing with music – writing, working on music on my own." He pulled together a group of eight great musicians to work with him in performance and later on a live recording. The CD, *Remembering*, was released in 2015, and unlike his other albums, features primarily songs. An instrumentalist and non-singer himself, Ainslie writes flowing and compelling melodies for his thoughtful lyrics, and frames them with exciting, precise instrumental backup. Perhaps the best description of the album comes from fiddler Laura Wilkie, who speaks of it glowingly as "honest music."

One of Scotland's busiest musicians, Ross Ainslie has many irons in the fire, including annual performances with Dougie MacLean at the annual fall Perthshire Amber festival, a new recording with his old friend Ali Hutton, and cross-cultural explorations with his international quartet, India Alba.

Much of his time, however, is devoted to Treacherous Orchestra, the epic eleven-piece band of which he was a founding member. This band grew out of the camaraderie of Glasgow's traditional music sessions during the early 2000s. After one of their lively late-night festival club performances, Celtic Connections Festival director Donald Shaw invited them to be an official part of the next festival. Their January 2009 Celtic Connections show sold out, and Treacherous Orchestra was born.

A high-energy crowd pleaser, Treacherous Orchestra comprises two pipers (Ross Ainslie and Ali Hutton), accordion, fiddle, flute, two guitars, banjo, drums, bass, and bodhran. Their first album, *Origins* (2012) and their 2015 release, *Grind,* present moments of solo piano, flute or fiddle, broad textural grooves, and climactic, full-band wildness. Their musicianship is impeccable, modern, and yet schooled by Scottish tradition.

Gordon Duncan built a bridge between high quality traditional and modern Scottish music. Ross Ainslie crossed that bridge, and has moved on to inspire growing numbers of young musicians and audiences. To them, he is a leader by example.

"I'm definitely not a leader," Ainslie says. "I'll make things happen but I'm not a leader. I just get stuff together." Then he confesses, "I'm probably a quiet leader." While honoring the quality and discipline of traditional piping, he follows the lead of his mentor Gordon Duncan, and helps keep Scottish music vibrant with new ideas, excellent musicianship, and a sense of community.

58 ~ *Hamish Moore*
summer 2012

The power and drama of the great Highland bagpipes will always make it an iconic symbol of Scotland. But for much of the 20th century, it stood pretty much alone. The harp had virtually disappeared, fiddle styles were limited, Gaelic song marginalized, and a previously popular type of bagpipes, the bellows pipes, seemed to have gone into hiding.

Certainly, the major wars of the last century caused social and economic dislocations, and the media helped solidify certain stereotypes. But the media also helped diversify Scottish culture by quickly spreading new research. In the 1970s and 80s, a generation of impassioned Scots uncovered and revived many musical traditions of Scotland, including the harp, fiddle, Gaelic music, and the bellows-blown bagpipes.

If you're not familiar with bellows pipes, their primary characteristic is the pumping of air into the bag using a set of bellows under the elbow, as opposed to blowing the air in by mouth. Their sound is far quieter than the Highland pipes, and more compatible with playing indoors for dancers, singers, or with other instruments.

The year 1981 was pivotal for the revival of the bellows pipes in Scotland. It was then that pipers Mike Rowan, Hugh Cheap and Gordon Mooney first met to form what later became The Lowland & Border Pipers Society, to explore and promote the traditions of the bellows pipes. The Society's primary interest is in music of the borders, but the fact that there is a Gaelic word for the bellows pipes indicates that these pipes were also played in the Highlands.

That same year, a veterinarian and Highland piper named Hamish Moore returned to Kingussie from a journey to Ireland, wondering why Scotland, the home of the bagpipes, did not appreciate the bellows-blown pipes as extensively as the Irish valued their uilleann (pronounced ILL-an) pipes. Hamish's next-door neighbor, John MacRae, quietly answered this question by pulling out from under his bed some 19th century Scottish smallpipes and Lowland pipes.

Hamish had MacRae's old pipes restored by Northumbrian pipemaker Colin Ross. Northumbrian pipes are bellows-blown and are an important part of the musical traditions of northern England. But they, like the Irish pipes, are quite different from Scottish pipes. Northumbrian and Irish pipes can stop their sound by closing all the finger holes, but Scottish pipes have an open end, so their sound is continuous.

At around the same time, in America in the early 1980s, I had the good fortune of having a band that included Scottish smallpiper Jamie MacDonald Reid. His Highland smallpipes used the same fingering as Highland pipes, and therefore could play the same tunes. Being quieter and tuned in concert pitch, they were easy to incorporate into a band with fiddle, harp and Gaelic song.

Jamie's pipes were a family heirloom he had restored in 1965. Rural traditions of smallpipers and Lowland pipers never died out, though they generally kept to their own communities. The traditions were surviving, but marginalized by Scottish society as a whole. It took someone with drive and imagination to bring bellows pipes back into Scottish culture in a way that has allowed them to grow and develop as a vibrant tradition once more.

Hamish Moore was so smitten by the bellows pipes that he left his trade as a veterinarian in the mid-1980s and leaped headlong into the world of the bagpipes as a performer, organizer, and maker. In 1985, he recorded *Cauld Wind Pipes,* an album whose title refers to the cold air of the bellows. It presented the mellow sound of the Scottish smallpipes and Lowland pipes, along with clarsach (traditional wire-strung harp), guitar and fiddle.

Unfortunately, this debut album and his next, *Open-Ended,* are out of print. One early bellows pipes album that is still available is *O'er the Border,* recorded in 1989 by Gordon Mooney on Scottish smallpipes, Borders pipes, and Northumbrian pipes.

Hamish's father, a wood-turner by trade, tried his hand at making pipes, and showed Hamish how as well. In 1986, the firm of David and Hamish Moore began making Scottish smallpipes available once more in Scotland. Eleven years later, the firm added a third generation when Hamish's son Fin, a fine piper in his own right, came on as an apprentice. The company is now run by Fin, with seven workers, and over a thousand sets of pipes have been completed.

Part of the appeal of the smallpipes for Hamish Moore was their freedom of musical expression, as compared with the highly prescribed technique developed in the regimental pipe bands and competitions. James MacGillivray, a Canadian Highland piper whose solo CD is Volume 10 of Lismor's *World's Greatest Pipers* series, said of Hamish's instruments, "I own three sets of his pipes and they are superb.... One of the aspects I enjoy about playing smallpipes is getting to use whatever gracing I want!"

Moore's interest in expanding musical expression on the pipes was stoked by hearing Buddy MacMaster, the great fiddler from Cape Breton, Nova Scotia. His interpretation of Scottish music, particularly strathspeys, made Hamish wonder whether this was a window on how the bagpipes might have played those tunes before modern piping techniques were developed. The ideas he developed working with Cape Breton musicians and dancers led to his 1994 recording, *Stepping on the Bridge.* In this album, Hamish played Highland pipes, Scottish smallpipes, and Border pipes, backed by a unique gathering of Cape Breton and Scottish musicians. The album's tune selection includes many fiddle tunes, some of which were old pipe tunes which have come to be played primarily on the fiddle. Now they could be reclaimed by the pipes.

In the mean time, Hamish Moore also experimented with presenting the bagpipes as an instrument in its own right by working with soprano saxophonist Dick Lee. Their CDs, *Farewell to Decorum* and *The Bees' Knees,* offer an intriguing blend of two reed instruments interwining their sounds on traditional and modern tunes.

While many recordings now include Scottish smallpipes, one album showcases a variety of pipes made by Hamish and Fin Moore. Just before the 2003 Glenfiddich Piping Championships, Hamish pulled together a concert of 12 pipers playing music on a variety of bagpipes made by his own firm. The concert was recorded and released as *The Piper and the Maker*.

The Moores' most recent involvement in a recording project was *Seudan*, a bold musical presentation released in 2011 using a matched set of four Highland pipes. These instruments were made by the Moores based on exact measurements of the 1785 Black Set of Kintail from the Inverness Museum. After fitting their modern copies with reeds, the Moores found that the bagpipes played in concert pitch (A440), as opposed to most Highland pipes today, which play higher than concert pitch by a half-step or more, for the sake of producing a brighter sound in competitions. The *Seudan* album has a rich sound quality, the four Highland pipers playing with a Cape Breton-style immediacy. Allan MacDonald adds smallpipes and sings pibroch, Mac Morin plays Cape Breton piano and provides the sound of stepdancing, and others add guitar, percussion and Gaelic song.

Since Hamish Moore began making smallpipes, other makers have helped make these instruments even more available, and bellows pipes have become common among young Scottish musicians and bands today.

The revival of this type of pipes is perhaps best summed up by Gary West, an accomplished piper on Highland and smallpipes, who can be heard on *The Piper and the Maker* CD. Of Hamish Moore, Gary notes, "He has done so much to bring the bellows tradition back into the mainstream of Scottish folk music once again since it disappeared in the 19th century, and it's now back where it belongs."

59 ~ *World Pipe Band Championships*
winter 2005-06

Bagpipe music is stirring. It can evoke nostalgia or can provide fodder for logical analysis. It can stir up pride, romance, awe, determination, or even despair (as in "why don't they go outside?").

True, some people have had unpleasant experiences with bagpipers, such as the well-meaning fellow in our downtown district, who happily dresses in mismatched tartans on Tartan Day and plays a semblance of pipe music to afflict passersby. Still, he is appreciated, if only for sentimental reasons.

If you want to be stirred musically, however, treat yourself to performances by the world's top pipe bands. A good place to start is a CD of the World Pipe Band Championships, recorded live each August. Every pipe band that makes it to the Worlds is made up of excellent individual pipers, a musically energetic pipe major, and a top-notch drum corps. They play with clarity, precision, expressive timing, supported by exciting and atmospheric moods set up by the drummers. And because the pipers in these bands are so good, they play more interesting and challenging tunes than the average pipe band can handle.

Volume 1 of the World Pipe Band Championships CD contains the winning performances of the six best bands. From there, you can explore some of the concert and studio recordings of these bands, or solo albums by their pipe majors, key soloists, or small groups. Volume 2 presents the next seven bands, and a third CD even gives afficionados a chance to hear all the qualifying heat performances.

The bands on these CDs are competing at the height of the Grade 1 level. Lots of lesser bands are well worth hearing and supporting, but if you listen to the best Grade 1 pipe bands, you can better appreciate what the others are seeking to do.

There are well over 400 pipe bands worldwide in Grades 1 to 4 (and many others which are ungraded). Of these, fewer than 30 are currently in Grade 1 — ten in Scotland, six in Canada, five in Australia, three each in the U.S. and New Zealand, and one each from Belfast and Dublin. These numbers change from time to time, as bands can be upgraded or downgraded, but what does not change is that the winners of the World Pipe Band Championships are the crème de la crème.

Only six different bands have won the World Championships in the past 20 years, and five of them are still top contenders. The one past winner that didn't place this year is no longer in existence: the Australian band, Victoria Police, was disbanded partly because the police force couldn't afford the personnel required to maintain a world-class pipe band. The CD they made at the time, *Masterblasters,* remains an enjoyable and accessible album.

Not all great pipe bands compete. Fine regimental bands as the Scots Guards, Black Watch, and Royal Scots Dragoon Guards, are generally kept out of competition by military obligations. All three of these regiments, for example, have recently served in Iraq.

The winner of the 2005 World Pipe Band Championships was The House of Edgar Shotts & Dykehead Caledonia Pipe Band. Traditionally known as Shotts & Dykehead, the band's name was adjusted a few years ago to acknowledge its sponsor, a producer of tartans and Highland gear.

Imagine putting a great pipe band together and keeping it running. It's no mean feat to find and inspire top-quality pipers to put in the time required for serious practice and travel. Some pipers travel over 100 miles just to get to band practice. Nor is it easy to arrange and pay for uniforms, logistics, and a performance schedule that keeps the band in shape. This is why many top bands have corporate sponsorship.

Shotts & Dykehead, based in a coal mining area between Glasgow and Edinburgh, has won the Worlds fifteen times since the Royal Scottish Pipe Band Association began the World Championships in 1947. The band's latest CD, called *The Legendary House of Edgar Shotts & Dykehead,* is a historic tour of Shotts performances since the 1950s, which was a decade of innovation by the band. It was then that Shotts drum major Alex Duthart developed the virtuosic snare drumming that is the hallmark of today's pipe bands. The band's current pipe major, Robert Mathieson, is innovative in his own right. His solo album, *The Big Birl,* for example, features bagpipes played in settings ranging from rock to classical.

Field Marshall Montgomery Pipe Band, of Belfast, came in second in the Worlds this year, losing by only one point. Founded in 1945 and named after the British World War II hero, the band has won the Worlds four times, including last year. Its most recent CD is *Unplugged,* recorded live in the Glasgow Royal Concert Hall just before winning the Worlds in 2002.

These two top finishers can be heard together in a concert setting on a 2-part CD called *A Pipe Band Spectacular,* along with two other bands, the 78th Fraser Highlanders and the Vale of Atholl band (then called MacNaughton's Vale of Atholl, and now known as Robert Wiseman Dairies Vale of Atholl). While the Worlds CD has the edge of competitive excitement, concert settings allow bands more freedom to be creative and entertaining.

Third place this year was won by Simon Fraser University Pipe Band, of Vancouver, Canada. This band has won the Championships four times, and often performs in concert, with an entertaining repertoire. The newest SFU recording, the 2005 CD *On Home Ground,* provides a fine sampling of this versatile and energetic pipe band. SFU's pipe sergeant, Jack Lee, is an award-winning soloist who can be heard on many CDs such as Volume 15 of Lismor's *World's Greatest Pipers* series.

Fourth place went to the venerable Strathclyde Police Pipe Band, of Glasgow, which won the Worlds every year from 1981 to 1991, except for 1987. In 1986, after six straight wins, Strathclyde Police put out a traditional recording called *Six in a Row,* and in 1991 an album called *The Strathclyde Police Pipers* offered a nice spotlight on small piping ensembles, such as quartets, from this band.

The fifth place finisher for 2005 is the only one that has not yet won first place in the Worlds. The St. Laurence O'Toole Pipe Band hails from

Dublin, where it was formed in 1910 with the famous playwright Sean O'Casey as its first secretary. Since 1991, the band has won many major prizes, and has introduced a lot of traditional Irish tunes into standard piping repertoire. The band's newest CD, released in October 2005, is called *Live from the Glasgow Royal Concert Hall*, and offers both traditional piping and a fun mix of singing, congas, guitars, and flute.

The sixth and final band presented in Volume 1 of the World Pipe Band Championships is the exciting Canadian band, the 78th Fraser Highlanders, which wowed the piping world in 1978 by being the first non-Scottish band to win the Worlds. The band's *Live in Concert in Ireland* CD from that year is still a classic album, and one of the best-selling pipe albums ever. Since then, the band has made a number of CDs that make for great listening, such as *Flame of Wrath*, which also came out in video. The band's pipe major, Bill Livingstone, while continuing as pipe major, is now retiring from solo piping competition as the most successful piper in North America, and the only pipe major of a World Champion pipe band to have won the solo piping clasp at Inverness. He is featured on Volume 9 of Lismor's *World's Greatest Pipers* series, and recently released four CDs called *A Piobaireachd Diary*.

Keeping an eye on the World Pipe Band Championships will tune you into some of the world's greatest pipe music, whether you listen to the competitive performances, concert recordings, or CDs by individual members of the bands. You'll be sure to find bagpipe music there that will stir you with wonder at what this ancient instrument can do.

SECTION 4d ~ ACCORDION

60 ~ *Accordion: the 4ᵗʰ National Instrument?*
summer 2014

There's an elephant in the room when we speak of Scotland's national instruments. The usual suspects are the harp, fiddle, and bagpipes. But there's a newcomer lurking, well, just about everywhere: the accordion.

Accordions are enjoyed throughout Scotland and beyond, at dances, festivals, sessions, on radio, and at monthly meetings of more than 70 Accordion and Fiddle Clubs throughout the country. The instrument has had a colorful history during its relatively short life, and seems due for a vibrant future, if listening to today's fine players is any indication.

Perhaps in time, the accordion will be considered the fourth national instrument of Scotland. The first known appearance in Scotland of each of the first three national instruments took place roughly 350 years apart: the harp in 8th century Pictish carvings, the fiddle in an image from 1140, and the bagpipes mentioned in writing in 1509. Some 330 years later, the accordion arrived, first patented in 1829 and imported into Scotland about ten years later.

One possible reason the accordion has not been accorded the same honors as the other three is that there has never been a native accordion-making industry in Scotland. Another reason might be that it simply hasn't had time to develop the proud historical tradition the others had, whether with clan chieftains, aristocracy, or in battle.

An early form of the accordion was the melodeon, with one or two rows of buttons for melody playing. Limited to a few musical keys, the melodeon was relatively inexpensive, and considered suitable to both men and women because of its modest size and playing position.

A CD called *Melodeon Greats* allows us to hear some of the top Scottish players between 1909 and 1920. Two notable inclusions on the CD are tracks by Willie Hannah, whose playing inspired that of a younger melodeon player, Jimmy Shand, later to become the great dance band accordionist; and several tracks by Peter Leatham, whose daughter Chrissie was pivotal in the development of the accordion in Scotland.

Chrissie Leatham was a small and lively woman whose father didn't realize she always stood by the door during band rehearsals and absorbed all the tunes and techniques. When she left home at 15 for a job, she picked up the accordion and piano and soon began to perform at silent movie theaters, and toured with a band. In 1932 she began a 50-year teaching career in Edinburgh, inspiring accordion greats such as Jim Johnstone in the 1940s, Phil Cunningham in the 1960s, and Sandy Brechin in the 1970s. Two tracks of Chrissie Leatham playing Scottish accordion can now be heard online at raretunes.org. Her playing is full of the lightness of touch and the musical lift characteristic of great Scottish dance music. Leatham's son, Owen Murray, became a professional classical accordionist and the first professor of accordion in the UK. Since 1986 he has taught at the London Academy of Music.

In the 1920s, melodeons faded out in favor of newly designed accordions with large bellows and many more notes, some with buttons for keys, and some with piano keyboards. Sir Jimmy Shand eventually helped design his own four-octave accordion, with special engineering for more consistent tone, and 117 bass buttons for playing the bass notes and chords along with the melody.

The 1920s was also when Scottish country dancing was developed and standardized. It is perhaps no surprise that accordions have dominated country dance bands, usually featuring a lead accordion plus a second one for rhythm and chords. Laid on top of this sound is often a fiddle, not always easy to hear, but present for the flow of the music, and underneath, a bass, piano and drums. This is the kind of sound you'll hear when listening to bands led by Jimmy Shand, Jim Johnstone, Bobby MacLeod, and other great Scottish country dance musicians. The clear punch of the accordion and articulate, tidy ensemble playing can be heard throughout this exuberant music. It's a staple on Robbie Shepherd's weekly BBC Radio Scotland program, *Take the Floor*.

Ceilidh dancing, less formal and a bit wilder than the country dancing, attracts a different and often younger crowd. Its musicians can be found crossing over between dance and folk music. The "Ceilidh King," West Highland accordionist Fergie MacDonald, switched over from Scottish country dance music to ceilidh dance music in 1965 and has promoted and played it tirelessly. Freeland Barbour, an original member of the great folk band Silly Wizard, moved into ceilidh dance music in the 1970s. His piano accordion sound is flowing and clean, blending the country dance sound with his own original ideas for tunes and arrangements. His 25-year old ceilidh band The Occasionals is still going strong, and Barbour just completed a solo 6-CD set of *Music for Old Time Dancing*.

Barbour's 1976 replacement in the Silly Wizard band was Phil Cunningham, now one of the great movers and shakers in Scotland's traditional music. His clear, bright sound on the accordion, and effortless flying fingers, lend themselves equally to heights of joy and to mournful and contemplative slow airs, including many tunes of his own composition. One of the most popular settings for listening to Cunningham's accordion is in his duo with fiddler Aly Bain. Their congenial and entertaining duo albums, *The Ruby*, *The Pearl*, and *Another Gem*, remain highlights among their many recording and touring projects.

Phil Cunningham has been an inspiration for many younger players, such as Sandy Brechin. Brechin was determined to be a crazy and happening guy, and not a tartan-trouser type, although now that he's reached middle age, he finds himself occasionally doing just that! Playing mostly traditional tunes, Brechin incorporates contemporary sounds in his arrangements. He has played with some exciting contemporary folk bands such as Seelyhoo and Burach, and has a great sense of humor, as can be seen in his album title, *The Accidental Death of an Accordionist*, or his ceilidh band, The Sensational Jimi Shandrix Experience. His solo albums include *Out of His Box* and *Out of His Tree*, both picturing himself as a crazed accordionist on the cover. The craziness is reflected in the high energy, but the tunes are well played, with strong, rhythmic accompaniment.

Brechin tours and teaches accordion and sees a growing number of young people taking to the instrument. What does he look for in a student or performer? Excellent control of the bellows; creative use of the left hand on the buttonboard, where choices are made about bass notes and chords; the ability to support the melody with anything "from basic vamping to complex rhythms, plus syncopation, unison and harmony." Good players are also able to make good use of the couplers, or registers, which act like the stops on an organ to select different sets of reeds for different moods and voices.

Accordions are not always played with subtlety in mind. And yet, the instrument has that capacity. Listen to the west Highland accordionist Iain McLachlan playing his famous waltz, "The Dark Island" (Springthyme Records 1979) and you'll hear an emotional breathiness that mimics the breath of a singer baring his soul with each note.

Today's Scottish accordionists make clear that the instrument has a bright future. Box Club is a band formed in 2008 to feature four young accordionists, bass and drums, and provides a good starting point for tracking some of the up-and-coming players. Look for Mairearad Green (often touring with Anna Massey), John Somerville (with the Treacherous Orchestra), Gary Innes (with Runrig and others, when not playing shinty), and Angus Lyon (6-time British accordion champion and pianist with Blazin' Fiddles).

With its growing vibrancy and popularity, its versatility of sound and effect in melody and accompaniment, the accordion seems on track to one day finding its place as one of Scotland's national instruments. And considering the speed of modern life, it might not take a few centuries, as with the harp, fiddle and pipes!

61 ~ Devilish Accordions
spring 2001

The accordion reigned supreme in Scottish dance music during the 20th century. Its popularity made the squeezebox not only broadly celebrated but also frequently maligned — mostly in the form of bad jokes. In writing about harps, I described the heavenly harp, preparing faithful readers for the music of the next life, but now the time has come to go the other route, as we recall the instructive two-part cartoon by Gary Larson: Panel 1 caption — "Welcome to heaven, here's your harp!" Panel 2 caption — "Welcome to hell, here's your accordion!"

Through versatility and sheer volume, the accordion made it possible for a single musician to play for a dance where a whole band might otherwise have been needed. When it was introduced in the 19th century, it must have been quite a novelty to have a portable instrument that could play both melody and accompaniment at the same time, with its bellows capable of a breathy variety of expression. Older breeds include the smaller melodeons and concertinas, but now we most often see and hear the larger accordions with a piano-style keyboard for melody making, or various types of button-keyed accordions.

Although there are some fine listening albums by Scottish accordionists, most recorded accordion music has been made for dancing, either the high energy of ceilidh dancing, or the more formal Scottish country dancing.

Just before last Christmas, the most famous of Scotland's accordionists passed away. Sir Jimmy Shand was born into a poor coal miner's family in 1908 and went on to become a household name through numerous radio broadcasts. He topped the popular charts with his "Bluebell Polka" (for which he earned £12!), and once drew a crowd of 20,000 in Aberdeen, causing several young ladies to swoon with hysteria (a full decade before the Beatles). A year before his death, Jimmy Shand was knighted.

Shand's sound is sunny, bright, and clear, his bold rhythms irrepressible, and above all, very danceable. In fact, in the playing of a strong dance musician like Jimmy Shand, danceability often takes priority over melody. All the music, including sustained notes in slow waltzes, is strongly pulsed in order to bring out a dance beat that even a rhythmically challenged dancer would have a hard time ignoring.

Still, the music has plenty of heart, and can hardly help put a bounce in your step. And Shand's love of the music shines through it all. This was clear even when he retired and decided to sell his accordion. Canadian pipe major and dance band accordionist Reay MacKay managed to buy the accordion, but first had to pass an audition! Shand would only sell his instrument to someone who could do it justice.

One excellent CD of Jimmy Shand is *The Golden Years* (Moidart Music), with over 75 minutes of music from Shand's most productive decade, 1955-1965, beginning with his famous "Bluebell Polka." Another fine album is *The Legendary Jimmy Shand MBE* (REL Records), which offers an hour of great medleys drawn from various recordings. There is also a video available, featuring Jimmy and his son with the band, called *Dancing with the Shands*. This video was made in 1990, long after Shand had retired, and it nearly met a tragic fate. At first, Shand was left unpaid, the video company went out of business, and the tape was lost. Fortunately, it was tracked down and released in 1994, and proceeded to surprise everyone by reaching the top 10 of the pop video charts.

Because of the nature of the instrument, nearly all accordionists have done their share of dance gigs, and some specialize only in dance music. Jim Johnstone figures high on the list; his *Tribute* album (Temple Records) spotlights music of Jimmy Shand. John Ellis, Bill Black, Ian Holmes, Freeland Barbour of the Occasionals, Michael Philip and many more are worth a listen.

In the west of Scotland, there are some players with notable energy and expression, primarily for ceilidh dance music. Fergie MacDonald of Moidart offers great tunes and unpretentious high spirits. His *21st Album*

(Greentrax Recordings) features his accordion playing clearly, but also a host of Highland musicians from the Moidart area. Fergie stopped playing for some 10 years but was lured back to music by the accordionist Phil Cunningham. If you've ever seen a live show by Phil Cunningham and Aly Bain, you've heard plenty of hilarious stories about Fergie MacDonald.

On *Kings of the Button-Keyed Box* (Lismor Records), Fergie is joined by accordionist Iain McLachlan of Benbecula, composer of the famous and beautiful tune "The Dark Island." The two accordionists trade tracks and play a few duets, and McLachlan adds some Gaelic music and pipe tunes to the repertoire. For more of a home-style sound from the Western Isles, try Iain McLachlan's *An Island Heritage* (Springthyme Records), which, though well recorded, has some of the roughness of a field recording. Amid the Gaelic and pipe music played on accordion, fiddle, melodeon, and goose (bagpipe chanter without drones), you will hear one of the most moving accordion airs — McLachlan playing his Dark Island as an air, then as a waltz, then back to air. You can hear the effort and feeling as each note is squeezed out, yet the tune flows quietly and without a hint of hurry.

Phil Cunningham is one of the best-known Scottish accordionists, having toured widely with the Silly Wizard band, where he engaged in dazzling musical (and verbal) duels with his fiddling brother, Johnny. Phil's music includes many original tunes as well as a strong base of Scottish traditional tunes, ranging from broad sentimental airs to sizzling hot reels. He is probably the fastest accordionist in the west, when he wants to be.

Apart from the Silly Wizard recordings, Phil has two solo albums, *Airs & Graces* and *Palomino Waltz* (Green Linnet), and in recent years, has teamed up with the great fiddler Aly Bain for tours and recordings. On tour, Phil sometimes soups up his accordion with computer MIDI connections that allow him to sound like many instruments, becoming quite a one-man band. This is what accordions must have seemed like when they first appeared on the scene in the 19th century, but now they really can play just about any sound, at least in the hands of a virtuoso like Cunningham. Aly Bain and Phil Cunningham can be heard together on three recordings: *The Pearl, The Ruby,* and the brand new *Another Gem.*

Another player breaking stereotypes for the accordion is Sandy Brechin. Brechin has played with the popular contemporary bands Seelyhoo and Burach, and ought to win a prize for the title of his other band, The Sensational Jimi Shandrix Experience. His solo albums are *Out of His Box* and *Out of His Tree* (Greentrax), which, as the titles suggest, offer music on the wilder side. The tunes are traditional or original tunes in a fairly traditional vein, but with innovative and striking harmonies and syncopations. Speed is not his game; Brechin's albums captivate with interesting and tight arrangements of intriguing melodies.

Finally, mention should be made of a related instrument, the concertina. Scotland boasts a terrific concertina player who is very active in the music scene: Simon Thoumire. In the 19th century, the concertina came into its own and spawned a number of virtuoso players, but around 1910, the accordion superseded the concertina as the squeezebox of choice, and not too many musicians specialize any more in the concertina.

Simon Thoumire works both in the traditional side of the music and in the experimental modern side. He established a record label, Tartan Tapes, to offer budget-priced albums such as *Trip to Scotland* and *Scottish Love Songs,* featuring contemporary players, because he feels strongly that great traditional Scottish music is too often underrated. On some of these albums, he goes by the tongue-in-cheek name of Hamish MacGregor and the Blue Bonnets. But he is such a virtuoso on the concertina that he easily embraces a mix of traditional, jazz, and what I want to call urban-frenetic experimental music. Some of his album titles tell the tale: *March Strathspey and Surreal* (Green Linnet), or *Fast and Furious: Traditional Music for a Modern Generation* (Foot-Stompin' Records).

Accordion music has a habit of livening up anybody's day and making you want to dance, and yet, it can also be moving and plaintive. There's really nothing very devilish about it, despite the message of the cartoon I mentioned at the beginning. That was just a joke, and you should be glad it was the only one. I had to leave my other accordion jokes out of the column, because not only would it have been a tight squeeze, it could have risked a lawsuit. And a lawsuit, like an accordion, makes everyone happiest when the case is closed.

SECTION FIVE
Regional Music

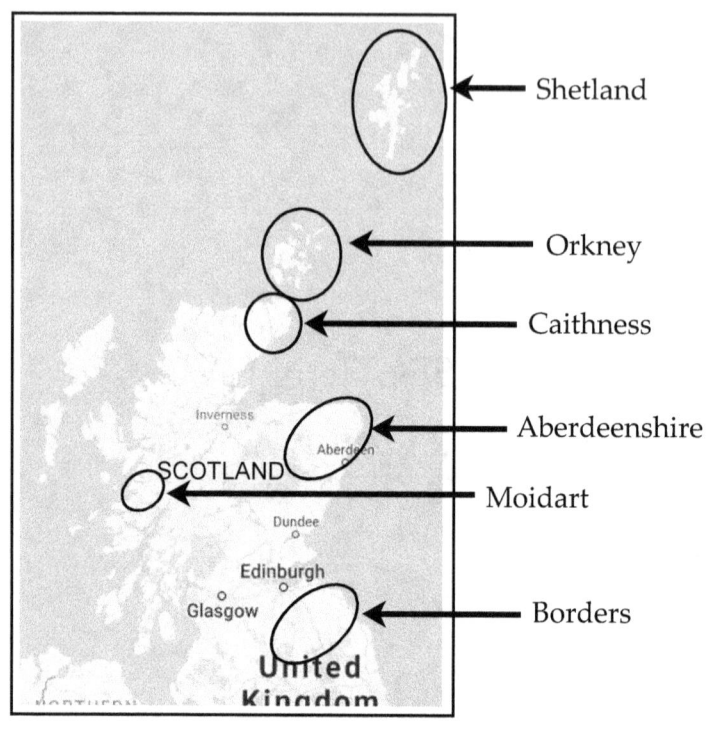

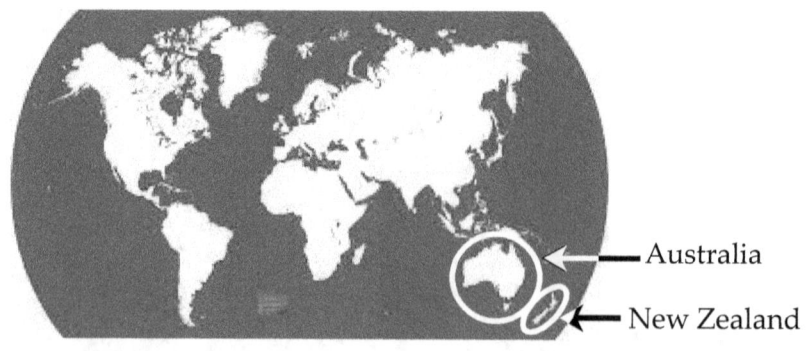

ABOUT SECTION FIVE
Regional Music

Here we'll examine geographical differences in the music, starting in Scotland with regional musical accents from the somewhat insular western Highlands, and the remote northernmost points of the mainland in Caithness. We'll voyage to the northern islands of Orkney and Shetland, and return to the mainland to explore the riches of Aberdeenshire in the northeast.

Aberdeenshire has been protective of its culture, but the opposite is the case with the Borders, where maintaining an indigenous culture has seemed nearly impossible, with all the constant exchanges of territory between Scotland and England throughout the centuries. And yet there are local traits of even that region, an area where some historically kept a law unto themselves.

Then we'll travel farther afield with the emigrants who populated North America, infusing their music into the lifeblood of American folk music and preserving Highland music and dance in Canada. We'll finish with a trip to the other side of the world, Australia and New Zealand, where Scottish descendants continue to keep their heritage alive and well.

62 ~ *Moidart*
summer 2015

My perch atop the Glenfinnan Monument was surrounded by scenery, history, and music. In one direction I could see the soaring Glenfinnan Viaduct, with its 21 arches, and in the other direction, the waters of Loch Shiel cutting through wooded mountainsides. History stood right next to me in the shape of a giant statue of a kilted Highlander. He is often mistakenly presumed to be Bonnie Prince Charlie, for here is where Charlie landed, raised his standard, and gathered the clans to begin the uprising of 1745.

Music was happening less than 500 yards away, but I couldn't actually hear it. The musicians were playing inside of a long temporary tent set up on the broad lawn of the Glenfinnan House Hotel for a BBC Alba television special featuring the Glenfinnan Ceilidh Band. No doubt they were playing Highland waltzes, schottisches, two-steps, barn dances, jigs, and reels, on fiddle, accordion, piano, and banjo, as can be heard on their 2010 CD, *Glenfinnan Gathering*.

One member of the band is fiddler Iain MacFarlane, who actually grew up in the Glenfinnan House Hotel. His family purchased the house in the 1970s and fixed it up into both home and hotel. The house dates to 1752, just six years after its original owner, Alexander MacDonald of Glenaladale, was wounded at Culloden.

MacFarlane plays pipes, like many Highland musicians, but his main instrument is the fiddle. He learned to play from his father Charlie, and from the great Inverness-shire fiddler and piper, Donald Riddell. Iain was a founding member of the Blazin' Fiddles band, which has toured internationally, giving the world a chance to hear that Highland fiddling is very much alive and well. His wife, Ingrid Henderson, not only plays piano with the Glenfinnan Ceilidh Band, but is also one of Scotland's best traditional harp players. Her 2005 CD, *The Little Beauty*, highlights her virtuosic and lilting harp playing, as well as her accompaniment skills. In addition to their many other musical projects, Iain and Ingrid created Old Laundry Productions, converting the former laundry building of Glenfinnan House Hotel into a state-of-the-art recording studio.

A fine sampling of west Highland music can be heard on MacFarlane's 2003 CD, *First Harvest*, with another Iain, Iain MacDonald, on pipes and flute. At the time, it was called by the *Scotsman* newspaper the "best traditional album of Scottish music to emerge in a decade from two of the foremost instrumentalists in the country."

Iain MacDonald is one of three famous piping brothers who have had a major impact on Scottish music. They grew up in the Gaelic-speaking village of Glenuig, which is located on the coast about 20 miles from Glenfinnan. He played for many years with the folk bands Ossian, Wolfstone, and Battlefield Band, and is currently director of Ceòlas, a summer school in South Uist which gives students a chance to explore connections between the pipes, fiddle, song, and dance. In 2013, Iain was inducted into the Scottish Traditional Music Hall of Fame for his contributions to the music. His older brother, Dr Angus MacDonald, is a gold medalist piper who organized the first Fèis in Barra in 1981. The Fèisean (FAY-shen) have grown over the years into a huge educational movement with over 40 annual events teaching music and Gaelic arts. The third brother is Allan MacDonald, also an award-winning piper, who teaches at the Piping Centre in Glasgow. He is particularly interested in the intersection of piping, Gaelic song, and the music of pre-Clearance times when, as he says, "the fiddle and its counterpart of step-dancing were part of a dynamic matrix of song, instrumental music and social behaviour/ritual." In 1990 and 2011, he published *Music of Moidart*, two books of original and traditional bagpipe tunes.

The MacDonalds' village of Glenuig had no access road until 1968. Their district, Moidart, is the center of an area traditionally called the "Rough Bounds," because of its remote and wild location. The Rough

Bounds extends along the west coast from just north of Mallaig, south through Moidart, to the Sound of Mull.

Moidart itself stretches roughly from Glenuig to Glenfinnan, southwest along Loch Shiel to Acharacle, and out to the sea. The area's history is very much present, whether in names such as Acharacle, recalling the defeat of the Viking Torquil by Somerled in 1120, or in ancient tales of the 8th century Queen of Moidart, whose army of female warriors cleared nearby islands from intruding missionaries. More recent events include Bonnie Prince Charlie, who is celebrated each August 19 at the Glenfinnan monument, where he raised the standard in 1745. Part of the celebration is an annual Highland Games, which always concludes with a dance at the hotel. The history of the Highland Clearances of 1780-1850 weighs heavily on Moidart, since a large percentage of the area's population emigrated, many of them to Cape Breton, Nova Scotia.

The relative remoteness of the west Highlands has helped keep many traditions intact, and may also have kept outsiders from knowing very much about those traditions. For example, Highland fiddling has continued, without fanfare, despite a presumption by some that it died out in Scotland and survives only in Cape Breton. Similarly, it appears that Scottish stepdancing, a strong part of Cape Breton culture, generally died out in Scotland as a result of the Clearances, continuing possibly as late as World War I. But according to Allan MacDonald, Farquhar MacRae, a great box player and leader of the Roshven Ceilidh Band, used to call up stepdancers to show their steps at afternoon teas in Moidart as late as the 1970s.

The music of the west Highlands is rooted in Gaelic traditions of song, piping, fiddling and dancing. Tunes are traditionally played with a light, rhythmic style suitable for dancing, and in addition to the Scots Gaelic repertoire, there is also an Irish influence, in part because for many years, the only radio reception available was Radio Athlone from Ireland. Few songs are known to have originated in Moidart, but one of the most famous was written by Father Ranald Rankin for the children of Moidart before he and his parishioners emigrated to Australia in 1855. Translated from the Gaelic as "Christ Child's Lullaby," its haunting melody can still be heard at midnight masses in the Hebrides, online, and on several recordings, most notably as sung by Irish singer Christy Moore on the Boys of the Lough album, *Midwinter Night's Dream.*

All these Gaelic, Cape Breton and Irish influences can be heard in the music of the Moidart-based band, Daimh (pronounced "dive", the Gaelic word for kinship). The band's first album, *Moidart to Mabou,* calls to mind the Moidart/Cape Breton connection, as well as the fact that the band's piper, Angus Mackenzie, is a Gaelic speaker from Cape Breton. The band's fiddler, Gabe McVarish, grew up in California, but has moved back to the area; his ancestors were originally from the village of Morar, just north of Moidart, before leaving for Canada, and then moving to the U.S. Ironically, after coming to the Highlands to study with fiddler Angus Grant, Gabe ended up living in the same village his family had emigrated from. Other band members include local guitarist Ross Martin, and musicians from Loch Lomond and Glenelg. The band's full and energetic sound can be heard on four albums, and at festivals and venues all across Scotland.

Today's visitors to Moidart and Morar can enjoy Thursday night traditional music sessions at the Glenfinnan House Hotel, where there might even be a song, story, recitation or someone dancing on a table. Sunday afternoon sessions in Lochailort are not far away, along with sessions in Arisaig and Mallaig. Several festivals make themselves felt in addition to the Glenfinnan Highland Games in August, such as the Blas Festival in September, and Mallaig's Fèis na Mara in October. There are some pub sessions around, but historically, the music making in this area took place in halls and homes. In the old days, pubs that hosted music were considered morally suspect!

As you marvel at the beauty of Loch Shiel, or climb to the top of the Glenfinnan Monument, or listen for the chugging of the Hogwarts Express across the Glenfinnan Viaduct, be sure to keep your ears open for some of the exuberant traditional music of the west Highlands taking place all around you.

63 ~ Caithness
spring 2017

If you drive seventy miles north from Inverness, you come to the border of Caithness, the northernmost corner of mainland Scotland. Within another hour you can cover the whole of Caithness, including the capital city of Wick on the east coast, and Thurso and John o'Groat's on the north coast. Historically a tough place to make a living, Caithness is nevertheless a source of much joyous and sweet music. Often it seems that people in the toughest places create the happiest music.

Think of the hardship of living in Badbae in the old days, when during rough weather, children and animals were tethered so as not to be blown off 200-foot cliffs into the sea. Or imagine working as a herring girl in Whaligoe, packing your creel with fish from the boats, carrying it on your back up 330 steps cut into the cliffs, and walking eight miles to the market in Wick. In the 19th century, Wick's harbor was packed with over a thousand fishing boats on a bay that Robert Louis Stevenson called the "baldest of God's bays." He wrote of watching the Wick fishing fleet put out to sea "silently against a rising moon," strangely and beautifully turning the horizon into a forest of sails.

And yet the rugged, treeless beauty of the Grey Coast has produced some wonderful music. (Perhaps not coincidentally, it has also provided fine whisky as well! Wick's Old Pulteney distillery was awarded World Whisky of the Year in 2011.)

Those who view Scotland as centered in Glasgow and Edinburgh might think Caithness to be far from the mainstream, but in the days of the Vikings, when long-distance travel was by sea, Orkney was a central hub, and Caithness, only twelve miles away, was within easy reach. By the time the Norse arrived in Caithness in the ninth century, the Picts of the kingdom of Cait had been living there for eight centuries. The Norse called the area the headland ("ness") of the Caits, or Caithness. But even the Caits were newcomers in an area where burial cairns of past inhabitants date to 5,000 years ago.

Many place names and family names in Caithness come from the Norse, including the popular name Gunn. Neil Gunn, who grew up in Caithness, was one of Scotland's most influential 20th century novelists. In 1937, Gunn sailed the west coast of Scotland and wrote about it in his book *Off in a Boat*. In 2014, multi-instrumentalist Mike Vass (another Scottish-Norse name, in this instance from Nairn) recreated Gunn's voyage by sea and in music, composing a suite of music which fuses acoustic folk with atmospheric and evocative riffs on keyboard, oboe, fiddle, guitar and other instruments. Called *In the Wake of Neil Gunn*, the project was performed at the Celtic Connections Festival, on tour, and on CD.

Also in 1937, Neil Gunn published *Highland River*, a novel about the effect of World War I on Caithness. A project by Wick fiddler and composer Gordon Gunn (a distant relation of the author), and playwright and poet George Gunn (no relation), will tie into celebrations of the novel's 80th anniversary this year, featuring original songs, storytelling, a performance and a film centered around the beautiful strath of Dunbeath.

An earlier collaboration by Gordon and George Gunn produced *The Musical Map of Caithness*, a CD which alternates colorful narrations with original tunes and songs. The music, played on fiddle, keyboard, drums, and whistle, is sweet, driving, and rhythmic. In addition to being an interesting introduction to Caithness, the recording has proved popular in the primary schools, where children enjoy learning songs about home.

Gordon Gunn is one of Scotland's finest fiddlers, and though based in Wick, he travels the breadth of Scotland to play and teach. He is a member of the great fiddle band, Session A9, and regularly teaches at the Plockton High School's Centre of Excellence in Traditional Music, a 3-1/2 hour drive from home. He occasionally ventures beyond Scotland, this spring heading to New Zealand, and in August to Boston. In addition to gigs and teaching, Gunn also composes music for television, promotional videos, and radio plays.

Gunn's *Shoreside* CD is a dazzling performance of traditional Scottish fiddling, with ideas from jazz and bluegrass sprinkled in. You can't help smiling as you listen to him play from the heart. His latest CD, *Wick to Wickham*, spotlights strong and playful fiddling backed by two of Scotland's top accompanists, pianist Brian McAlpine and guitarist Marc Clement.

A huge inspiration for Gordon and other kids growing up in Caithness was fiddler Addie Harper, leader of the Wick Scottish Dance Band. This band was one of the top touring dance bands in Scotland in the 1950s, 60s and 70s. They appeared frequently on BBC Radio Scotland and made records for the EMI label. In addition to fiddle, Addie also played banjo and added the soulful sound of a Hawaiian guitar, which he would lay in his lap and strum with his left hand while stopping the notes by sliding a whisky glass along the fretboard.

Addie recorded dozens of albums and composed more than 70 boisterous and danceable tunes. Published in three tune books, his tunes explore playful or thoughtful ideas, many with a west coast feel. Some are quite well known, such as "Barrowburn Reel," "John Keith Laing," and the pipe march "Pipe Major Jim Christie of Wick."

Addie's childhood fiddle teacher, Margaret Henderson of Wick, taught several generations of Caithness musicians, including Addie Jr and Gordon Gunn. She also taught piano to Addie's future wife, Isobel. Though focused on classical technique, Margaret made an exception for Isobel after catching her with a Jimmy Shand tune book in her bag! She agreed to let her study both Scottish and classical music.

Addie Harper was active in monthly meetings of the Wick Accordion and Fiddle Club, which, along with the Thurso Accordion and Fiddle Club, still provides players of all ages a chance to learn and play traditional music. He and Isobel also worked with the Wick Fiddlers, a performing group of about eight teenagers, and the Young Traditionals, a group of about five.

Isobel started playing piano with Addie's dance band in 1962. Addie passed away in 2002, but Isobel still plays and teaches keyboard and piano accordion. In January, she and Addie Jr were featured guests at the Skye Accordion and Fiddle Club. Addie Jr meanwhile has made a living as a fiddler and accordionist, often playing with west coast accordionist Fergie MacDonald or with his own band, Addie and Friends. He also teaches at Caithness schools and in Skye.

A number of other excellent musicians have come from Caithness, such as pianist James Ross who joined the faculty of the Royal Conservatoire in Glasgow, and Jim Sutherland, who got involved in traditional music as a teenager well aware of Addie Harper and his Scottish dance music. Sutherland has gone on to a stellar career firmly rooted in Scottish music but embracing other folk traditions and styles as well. His True North Orchestra blends prominent members of Scottish symphonies, jazz orchestras, and folk musicians playing bagpipes, concertina and clarsach, to create an orchestra that reflects a more Scottish sound. Jim has written music for more than 70 TV and film productions, including two songs for the Disney movie *Brave*. He also directs and writes for La Banda Europa, which includes 35 virtuoso musicians representing various European folk traditions.

Caithness may be tucked away in a northern corner of Scotland, and the Grey Coast may not be the easiest place to live, but Caithnessians have certainly contributed their fair share of spirited music throughout Scotland and beyond.

64 ~ *Orkney*
fall 2008

The Orkney islands in the north of Scotland may be windswept and treeless, but they are also friendly and full of music. Hundreds of musicians of all ages gather weekly in the largest city, Kirkwall, to learn and play traditional tunes. These islands, home to about 20,000 people, host music festivals in April (jazz), May (folk), June (classical) and September (blues).

Back in the early 1980s, BBC radio decided to open a local station in Orkney but were at a loss when they sought to play local music. Usually we take for granted that if people are playing music, we can hear it on the radio, but first, the music has to be recorded. In those days, there was no recording studio in Orkney.

Last year marked the 25th anniversary of Attic Records, Orkney's record label and recording studio. Its owner, Owen Tierney, a musician himself, owes the quality of his recordings to the generous advice of an expert who understood what goes into making a good recording studio. This expert happened to be visiting Tierney's sister shortly after she landed a job with the BBC Orkney radio station.

With excellent advice in hand, Tierney built a recording studio in his attic with acoustics that rivalled the best in Scotland. He then proceeded to record local artists.

A 25th anniversary compilation from Attic Records, called *Gems from the Attic*, highlights some of Orkney's artistry, including the Wrigley Sisters, Ivan Drever, Douglas Montgomery, the Kirkwall City Pipe Band, and Angus Findlater.

Jennifer and Hazel Wrigley are among the most famous ambassadors of music from Orkney, having toured the world as a duo, and also performed with the contemporary Scottish band, Seelyhoo. Jennifer plays fiddle, and Hazel guitar and piano. Their interconnected sound shows great musicianship, and being twins, that extra bit of playful sibling connection.

One of their recordings, *Skyran*, spotlights Orkney music and local folklore about Pictish runes and tales of the little people, the trowies. Another CD, *Orkney After Sunset*, in collaboration with storyteller David Campbell, includes traditional tunes mixed with mythical stories. Earlier Wrigley albums such *Huldreland* and *Mither o' the Sea* feature traditional Scottish playing with innovative jazzy rhythms. With their Edinburgh band Seelyhoo, they worked with Gaelic singer Fiona MacKenzie and the whimsical accordionist Sandy Brechin, as well as drums and bass. One of Seelyhoo's two CDs, *Leetera*, is still available on the Greentrax label.

After years of touring, the Wrigleys have settled back in Orkney and set up The Reel, a shop, pub/cafe, and music studio where Jennifer and Hazel teach and help keep the traditional music alive with lessons and music sessions.

The gentle, compelling voice of singer and guitarist Ivan Drever took off from Orkney into the successes of the Celtic rock band Wolfstone. He often tours with one of Scotland's finest fiddlers, Duncan Chisholm of the Wolfstone band and formerly a member of Blazin' Fiddles. The best of Drever's earlier songs from his Orkney years were compiled on two CDs available from Attic Records.

Ivan's son Kris Drever grew up on Orkney but came into his own in the Scottish music scene with the bands Fine Friday, and currently Lau. Kris has a strong singing voice, presents thoughtful and moving songs, and in Lau, works with top fiddler Aidan O'Rourke of Blazin' Fiddles, and accordionist Martin Green in a dynamic and energetic trio. In 2008, they won the BBC radio folk awards for Best Group.

About the same time that the radio station and Tierney's Attic Records were organized, the Orkney Folk Festival began bringing top folk acts in from all over the UK and beyond. A few years later, in 1985, a 16-year-old fiddler from Shetland named Debbie Scott took the Orkneys by storm at that festival, and turned young people on to the excitement of traditional music. She was accompanied by master guitarist Willie Johnson and a jazz bass player. While in town, the trio popped over to Tierney's studio and recorded a popular album on Attic Records, called *Selkie's Song*. After taking time off to raise two daughters, Scott ultimately released a second album (self-titled) on Veesik, a Shetland label.

Helped along by the popularity of young Debbie Scott, and players and teachers such as Jennifer Wrigley, increasing numbers of young Orcadians have taken to the fiddle. It's cool now for kids to play traditional music! The Orkney Strathspey and Reel Society coaches young players for an hour before its regular musical meeting and session on Thursdays in Kirkwall. The Traditional Music Project brings together up to a hundred young players every Saturday at music sessions led by a retired music teacher. The Accordion and Fiddle Club also meets weekly on Wednesdays, though not with all the same people, since it's made up of nearly all accordions (it's hard for a fiddler to get a note in edgewise among a bunch of accordionists!).

Some 75 recordings have been put out by Attic Records on Orkney. According to Tierney, many have been well supported by local residents. Interest by tourists used to be strong but has probably been dampened in recent years by internet habits. Attic hasn't made its own website yet but some of its offerings can be found online, where I found a number of items such as Wrigley Sisters CDs, the *Gems from the Attic* compilation, a recording from the Orkney Folk Festival, heartfelt songs by the late singer Angus Findlater, several dance band albums, the Ivan Drever compilations, a tour de force by fiddler Douglas Montgomery and multi-instrumentalist Stewart Shearer, Tierney's band Hullion, and a recording of an excellent group of young Orkney fiddlers called Shoramere.

The leader of Shoramere is a Shetland fiddler, Jenny Keldie, who took the group back to Shetland to perform there, and surprised the Shetlanders with the musical quality of the young Orcadians. Shetlanders are known for their fiddling, and have a long tradition of preserving their own music thanks to the collection of recordings and teaching by the late Tom Anderson.

Orkney has had no similar traditional bearer for its native music. Like Shetland, it was Norse until 1472, but because Orkney is only ten miles from the Scottish mainland, its music has been dominated by Scottish music for as long as people can recall.

One CD tries to simulate older Orkney sounds, though not specific native melodies. It's called *Out of the Stones*, by Bob Pegg and Bill Taylor of Ross-shire, who recorded musical sounds that might have been heard throughout 5000 years of Orkney history, using shells, whistles, drums, Pictish and Viking tunes, and a variety of harps, pipes, and songs. (A charred hazelnut shell from a human fire, found last year, appears to push Orkney's earliest settled history back to 8500 years ago.)

For many generations, Orcadians have been entertaining themselves with music for listening and dancing. Fiddler Tommy Mainland is in his 70s and playing strong, often visiting the Orkney Strathspey and Reel Society meetings. He likes the three-tune sets they often play and is happy to see slow airs coming back into fashion. He likes to point out that the airs are not as easy to play as the quick reels — you have to have the feeling for it.

Tommy appreciates the Wrigleys, fiddler Douglas Montgomery and other recorded Orkney artists, but adds that there are lots of great musicians in the area, few of whom are even semi-professionals, and most have no recordings out at all.

It seems the best way to really hear the music of Orkney is to brave the winds and a two-hour ferry ride, and experience the warmth of the people and their music first-hand.

65 ~ *Shetland*
spring 2003

Some of the most upbeat and easy-going tunes in Scotland come from a patch of islands halfway to Norway — the Shetland Islands. You might have heard about Shetland ponies or sweaters, or read about their offshore oil rigs, but if you haven't caught an earful of Shetland music, you are in for a treat.

Nearly every traditional Shetland tune seems to paint a picture: one describes a fisherman keeping his boat steady with the oars ("Aandowin' At Da Bow"), another portrays the way you might limp along a sandy beach that tilts down to the sea ("Shingly Beach"), and yet another tune cycles through notes that can speed up and slow down like a mill grinding grain ("Da Mill").

Shetland is a land of fiddlers. In the old days, they played reels for dancing, or hymn-like slow tunes for listening. With the wind howling off the sea and treeless fields, there could be no better way to warm up a winter's night than to fit three couples and a fiddler into a kitchen for a dance. For weddings, there was always a fiddler leading the procession, eventually playing the newlyweds right into their bedroom.

In the dialect, place names, and some of the music, the Norse influence is clear. One of the most popular Shetland fiddle tunes, for example, is called "Willafjord". The Norse took over from the Picts and Celts over a thousand years ago and ruled the islands for 500 years. Then, in 1469, Scotland's King James III married the daughter of the King of Denmark, and Shetland was given to Scotland as a dowry. Such was the power of kings.

The two World Wars were disruptive to Shetland. Especially after the second World War, people sought out new ways and ideas, and musical tastes were broadened by visitors, radio, and records. Aberdeen being the nearest Scottish city, it's not surprising that Aberdeenshire fiddling had a strong influence on Shetland fiddlers. Some left their native music behind and took to the novelty of the Scottish airs, marches, strathspeys and reels, and the romantic northeast Scottish style of playing them.

Perhaps the best recorded examples of this are two albums by the late Willie Hunter Jr: *Leaving Lerwick Harbour* and *The Willie Hunter Sessions*. Willie's traditional fiddling spirit (his father was a fine old-style fiddler) drew upon his classically trained, impeccable technique to grab listeners with powerful playing.

Aly Bain, Shetland's (and arguably Scotland's) most famous fiddler, is a master of the northeast Scottish style of fiddling. But he also knows the traditional Shetland tunes well, because he was taught both styles by his mentor, Tom Anderson.

In the 1950s, Tom Anderson worked as an insurance salesman throughout the islands, which gave him a chance to haul his clunky reel-to-reel tape recorder with him and record every traditional fiddler he could find. In 1959, he founded the Shetland Fiddlers Society, setting the stage for the resurgence of Shetland traditional fiddling. Aly Bain was the youngest founding member of the group, at age 13.

A fine fiddler himself, Anderson taught many students, and composed beautiful slow airs and jaunty reels. He and Aly Bain can be heard together on the classic album *Da Silver Bow*, playing traditional Shetland tunes.

Aly Bain has many recordings to his credit, a number of them with the great Celtic concert band, Boys of the Lough. Although he is a master of Shetland and Scottish fiddling, he also has eclectic musical interests which he explored as host of multiple BBC TV programs. French Canadian, Cajun, and Texas swing tunes amiably join the Scottish and Shetland music on Aly's solo albums, *First Album* and *Lonely Bird*. In recent years, Aly recorded four duo albums, three with accordionist Phil Cunningham (*The Pearl, The Ruby,* and *Another Gem*) and one with Swedish musician Ale Moller, called *Fully Rigged*. On the *Scottish Fiddle Rally Highlights* CD (disclaimer: I produced this album), Aly plays several tracks of straightforward, traditional Shetland as well as Scottish fiddling.

Follow the Moonstone spotlights Aly Bain as a solo fiddler with a chamber orchestra, the BT Scottish Ensemble, performing three works by a Finnish composer. One of the works is built on traditional Shetland tunes, one is based on Scottish fiddle tunes, and one uses Scandinavian themes.

My current favorite band from Shetland is Fiddlers' Bid. This group of three fiddlers, backed by guitar, harp, piano and bass, is incurably lively much of the time, though they do like to wallow in a few lush waltzes and slow airs from time to time. Their recent albums, *Hamnataing* and *Da Farder Ben Da Welcomer*, are both great listening.

Catriona MacDonald, who was one of Tom Anderson's many students, keeps up her Shetland repertoire whether touring with the Highland band, Blazin' Fiddles, or as a soloist. Her album *Bold* includes traditional Shetland tunes as well as a nice variety of other tunes. One track begins with an old recording of a Shetland fiddler and blends right into Catriona's own rendition of the same tune.

Of course, there is more to Shetland's music than the fiddle. During the last century, the piano and guitar became popular for accompaniment. The accordion arrived to substitute for, or supplement, the fiddles, providing the needed volume for larger dances. And in such a musical culture, music filtering in from elsewhere perked up local ears with a penchant for Scottish and Irish tunes, country, bluegrass, and rock.

One of Scotland's most popular bands is the Shetland group Rock Salt & Nails, which is a rock band of sorts, with lively songs, and as might be expected for Shetland, some fine traditional fiddling thrown into the mix. Their most recent CD, *Boxed*, offers good songwriting and instrumentals; their other albums, *Waves,* and *More & More* are equally good, with a diverse selection of music that they like to call "Shetland sheboogie."

Other Shetland bands to look for include the versatile Drop the Box, and the bluegrassy Hom Bru. A ceilidh band called Da Fustra has several lively dance albums, as does the Cullivoe Ceilidh Band, which featured the late fiddler, Willie Hunter Jr.

Shetland's rugged hills and coastlines are home to only 23,000 inhabitants, who nevertheless manage to host two major music festivals each year. The Shetland Folk Festival has presented island artists and major performers from around the world every April since 1981, and the Shetland Accordion and Fiddle Festival offers concerts, dances, workshops and music sessions every October, including the "Grand Dance" with about a dozen bands playing nonstop music for some 1500 dancers and music lovers.

Despite its 100 islands, most of Shetland is connected enough to be accessible by car, with a few larger islands only a short ferry ride away from what they call the "mainland." Of course, mainland Shetland itself is an overnight ferry ride, or a 90-minute plane trip, north of mainland Scotland.

The small population of these northern islands has made a happy musical imprint well beyond their shores. Many wonderful Shetland tunes are now common repertoire throughout the Celtic music scene. But beneath the surface of those tunes lie the spirit of the old dance tunes and airs that will always tell the tale of fishermen and crofters from Shetland.

66 ~ *Aberdeenshire*
summer 2017

The 25th anniversary CD of the band Old Blind Dogs, just released this spring, is a celebration of the energy and pathos of traditional Scottish music. It also evokes both the richness and mystery of the music of Aberdeenshire, which has been something of a closely held secret.

Old Blind Dogs began in the early 1990s as a ceilidh dance band rooted in Aberdeenshire. The only founding member still with the band today, fiddler and guitarist Jonny Hardie, lives in a house built in 1604 that belonged to his mother's family.

Fraser Fifield, who joined the band in 1997 at the ripe age of 20, recalls dancing to Old Blind Dogs when he was a teenager; he and his friends were even bussed to the events from school. Ceilidh dancing was becoming very popular, and everyone liked this local band that could play traditional music with a groove.

One point of pride was the Aberdeenshire songs at the core of the band's repertoire. Singer Ian F. Benzie performed and toured with Old Blind Dogs until 1999, bringing to it a clear, passionate and yet calming voice, with a pronounced Scots accent.

It is estimated that nearly half the residents of Aberdeenshire can speak Doric, the northeast dialect of Scots, and there are efforts to bring the language into acceptance at businesses and schools in the area. Robbie Shepherd, the long-time host of a dance music program for BBC Radio Scotland, also wrote a regular column in Doric for the Aberdeen newspaper. He saw language as integral to the culture, saying, "Our dance, our song, our poetry, our music and our landscape – it needs the language too."

The treasury of songs and tunes of Aberdeenshire has not always been widely known or understood. This could be ascribed to a somewhat insular culture, with strong dialect and a largely rural population. Between 1902 and 1914, Gavin Greig and James Duncan set out to collect the songs of the area, and were shocked to come up with no fewer than 3,000 songs, including about one-third of the ballads catalogued by Francis Child from the whole of Britain. Many songs had been carried on by tradition bearers such as Jeannie Robertson, Lizzie Higgins (whose daughter played violin with Old Blind Dogs for a time), Jock Duncan and others.

In the 1970s, a trio called the Gaugers showcased some of these songs and inspired many local singers and listeners with their repertoire. And yet their pride of place, to the point of insularity, was expressed by one member of the trio when he said, perhaps only half-jokingly, that "anything from south of Stonehaven would be considered 'World Music'. Broad-mindedness has always been our enemy."

In this context, the Old Blind Dogs were a unique ambassador from Aberdeenshire, touring Scotland, Europe, the USA, and beyond. Their sound has included hand percussion, fiddle, vocals, guitar, whistles, bass, bouzouki, and when they added Fifield as their fifth member in 1997, bagpipes. One distinctive feature of the band's sound is that it has never used a drum set. Davy Cattenach, the percussionist on the band's first few albums, used hand drums and particularly liked a relaxed reggae rhythm. This has created a non-rock sound palette that is very complimentary to traditional Scottish music. Texture, melody, countermelody, and a careful selection of tunes and songs provide plenty of drama.

Over the years, the band explored many great Aberdeenshire ballads. Jonny Hardie likes to joke that the band includes songs from elsewhere because it has used up all the Aberdeenshire songs. Building around their song repertoire, the band has blended local and national music with hypnotic tunes from Brittany, where they toured early in their career, plus an occasional old-timey tune from America, all supported by the boom and slap of the African djembe drum. It's a mix that works effortlessly and yet remains, at heart, Scottish traditional music.

The name of the band came from an Appalachian tune called "Old Blind Dog," which happens to sound a lot like the Aberdeenshire song "Back of Bennachie". This may be no coincidence, as many Appalachian songs and tunes were carried overseas by Scottish immigrants, even after some of them spent a generation or two in northern Ireland.

The band's first album helped launch a sublabel of KRL Records called Lochshore, which was formed specifically to feature the popular folk band phenomenon in Scotland in the early 1990s. Old Blind Dogs' first few album titles humorously referenced dogs, as in *New Tricks*, *Close to the Bone*, and *Tall Tails*. Their fifth album was simply called *Five*, because it was both their fifth album and honored the addition of their fifth band member.

Through the 1990s and 2000s, Scotland developed an astonishing coterie of brilliant young musicians, and Old Blind Dogs has taken advantage of it, bringing on board some top players. As time went on, fewer of the band members were actually from Aberdeenshire, and the band took on a broader Scottish sound. Many of the current and former musicians have been integral to the Scottish music scene, composing music or playing with bands such as Capercaillie, Deaf Shepherd, Shooglenifty and Treacherous Orchestra. Old Blind Dogs was twice named Folk Band of the Year at the Scots Traditional Music Awards.

Aberdeenshire has historically been a powerhouse of traditional solo fiddling in what's called the "northeast" style, with players and composers such as J.S. Skinner, William Marshall, Peter Milne, and Hector MacAndrew, but this style is not particularly featured in the Old Blind Dogs. Instead, though instruments are often featured during arrangements, you can hear above all the chemistry of the band and how well they like to work together rather than as soloists.

All Old Blind Dogs recordings are great listening, with a mix of high energy and quiet quality. One of my favorite CDs of theirs is called *Fit?* which in Doric means "What?" Made in 2001, it has some fine instrumental playing and great songs including Burns's "A Man's A Man for a' that", "Awa' Whigs Awa", and "Tatties and Herrin". As usual, hand drums, bass, and guitar lay the foundation for vocals, pipes, fiddle and whistles. Dramatic moments in songs are marked by furious but quiet countermelodies on whistle, or sudden a cappella voices in rich harmony.

The new 25th anniversary CD, the band's first in six years, is called *Room With a View*. Its humorous cover shows an easy chair looking out at an Aberdeenshire hillside from the ruins of a stone house, with only the fireplace and chimney still standing. The music is polished and varied, including exciting tunes on pipes as well as quieter tunes with harmonies on whistles and fiddle, performed by some of Scotland's best musicians — Jonny Hardie, Ali Hutton, Aaron Jones, and Donald Hay. Songs include a grizzly old ballad, a newly composed ballad in traditional style, and an old song that taunted Napoleon for his defeat at the hands of the Russians. A dance tune from Brittany figures in the mix, along with a number of well-blended arrangements of Scottish traditional tunes.

Founder Jonny Hardie finds that the band's sound on its new album harkens back to the sound of its second album, *Close to the Bone*, released in 1993. There is certainly an admirable continuity in the sound and energy of Old Blind Dogs throughout its quarter century. Its energetic style of presenting music and songs of Aberdeenshire, and spotlighting great Scottish talent, has earned it a well-loved niche in the development of Scottish traditional music.

67 ~ Borders
spring 2015

The music of the Scottish Borders is not easily defined, but shared repertoire and stylistic preferences are certainly present, and there is a strong orientation toward community involvement. We can see this clearly in the music used for the Common Ridings. At the heart of these summer events is a special selection of traditional songs and tunes connecting each town to its history.

The annual Ridings date back to times of lawlessness, from the late 1300s to the early 1600s, when King James VI gained control of the area. To protect their common grazing grounds, riders toured the boundaries to make sure they remained intact. Once quite a serious undertaking, they are now symbolic and ceremonial. For locals, these events are a highlight of the year, with ritual ceremonies, brass bands, flute bands (fife and drums), and songs. Throughout the year, many residents learn Riding songs at school or at home, with lyrics linked to the Borders, including "The Souters of Selkirk," "Ettrick Banks," "Braw, Braw Lads," and "Blue Bonnets O'er the Border."

In Selkirk, the musical routine of the Riding has been recorded by the Selkirk Silver Band on its CD, *The Souters – A Common Riding Celebration*. The music matches the celebratory activities, starting with "Auld Lang Syne" and later proceeding to Burns's "Of A' the Airts the Wind Can Blaw" as everyone marches to the River Ettrick. The mood changes when the procession approaches the old town with "Flowers of the Forest," recalling Selkirk's role in the horrendous Battle of Flodden in 1513, where Scotland's king and 10,000 Scots were lost. Of all the Selkirk men who left for battle, just one returned — a weary young horseman carrying with him a captured English banner. This sad melody is followed by few more upbeat tunes, and the day concludes with "Home Sweet Home" and "Auld Selkirk Toon."

The Hawick Riding features its own special march, a song called "Teribus." The lyrics recall the Battle of Flodden while touting the virtues of Border bowmen and an independent Hawick. Interestingly, the song calls upon the Norse gods Tyr and Odin (to which we owe the words "Tuesday" and "Wednesday"), possibly harkening back to the 11th century, when Vikings occupied the area.

The Ridings illustrate a strong sense of community despite a turbulent history of lawlessness and war. Local allegiances have been defined more by work and social groups than by the political border, with many residents having lived on both sides of the border. Some towns, such as Berwick, have switched between England and Scotland multiple times throughout history.

This tension between fluidity and sense of place is present in the music of the area. Border fiddle tunes and songs are drawn from all over Scotland and northern England in addition to locally written works. Many Northumbrian pipe tunes have found their way into the Scottish repertoire and vice versa.

In 1995, Border piper Matt Seattle published a very old collection of pipe tunes from Northumberland, in northern England, which turned out to be mostly music for the Scottish Border pipes. Dating to the 1730s, the Dixon Collection is the oldest known manuscript of bagpipe music. Many of the tunes are rants, 4/4 hornpipes, and triple-time hornpipes, which are not common outside of the Borders, and Seattle discovered that more than half the tunes have too many notes for the Northumbrian pipes. The title of his book, *The Master Piper: Nine Notes that Shook the World,* refers to the fact that 18th century Northumbrian pipes only played 8 notes, while the Scottish pipes could play 9, allowing for a distinctively Scottish way of changing keys within a tune. Tunes written for 9 notes were intended for the Scottish pipes.

Being bellows-blown, the Border pipes are quieter than the mouth-blown Highland pipes, but otherwise they sound quite similar, and play the same notes. The Scottish smallpipes, also bellows-blown, are smaller and play an octave lower, but they look much like the Border pipes, with the drone pipes resting across the chest of the player.

The popularity of this form of bagpipes seems to have collapsed around 1800, around the time when Borders towns ended the custom of having an official town piper play in the streets each morning and sound the curfew at night. In the past 30 years, this instrument has seen a lively revival in manufacturing, performing, and research. A number of key players stepped in enthusiastically, such as Matt Seattle, Hamish Moore, and Gordon Mooney. Mooney helped found the Lowland & Border Pipers Society. His album *O'er the Border* is a classic sampling of Border tunes on pipes.

The uncle of Sir Walter Scott was a fine Border piper. We don't know whether he passed his piping skills along, but we do know that Sir Walter himself was instrumental in preserving another part of Border culture. In 1802, he published *Minstrelsy of the Scottish Borders*, a collection of Border ballads and newly composed songs in the ballad style, some by Scott himself.

These songs have recently been performed in a fun way by Border fiddler and singer Lori Watson, in collaboration with folklorist, singer, and storyteller Margaret Bennett. Known as the Fireside Music Company, they present songs, tunes, and stories by and about Sir Walter Scott, quite informally, as if sitting in a living room. An upcoming version of their performance will include stories and songs of the Border poet James Hogg as well.

Lori Watson has become an expert in Border music, after growing up in various parts of the Borders, learning to play the music and then studying it as a graduate student. She is currently a lecturer in Scottish music at the Royal Conservatoire in Glasgow.

In 1998, Watson was one of five Border fiddlers pulled together for a fiddle festival in Edinburgh, including piper Gordon Mooney's daughter Shona, who has made her own career in Border fiddling. They formed a band called Borders Young Fiddlers. In Watson's view, the band became a sort of training ground to explore musical traditions and repertoire of the Borders. By the time of their 2004 self-titled CD, a congenial and enjoyable album, the band had apparently grown old enough to drop "Young" from their title, and become known simply as Border Fiddles.

Watson describes their music as cooperative and homey, or as she puts it, "nonflamboyant." In defining the Border qualities of the band's music, she notes their preference for moderate tempos, a broad sound, and weighted rhythms, not to mention a fair share of raucous moments.

This might serve as a somewhat vague description of the Border style, and perhaps that is as it should be. Watson observed that when asked, many people at the band's performances could not say exactly what a Border sound was, but felt that Border Fiddles had found it. In a nonacademic way, the musicians had brought their local music to life in a social setting, and developed a living sense of it.

While some in the Borders have clear notions of what they want from their music, as in the Common Riding bands, others explore the legacy of those who have gone before, such as Sir Walter Scott and his ballads, or the late fiddler Tom Hughes, who along with his father and grandfather were all dance band fiddlers.

Whether hearing or participating in the music of the Ridings, or at events such as the Innerleithen Music Festival, there is plenty of Border music around. But there are also people delving into Border culture, researching and playing the Border pipes, and participating in the concerts, workshops, ceilidhs, panel discussions and youth competitions of the annual Border Gaitherin festival in Coldstream. All are keeping Border music alive and creatively healthy.

68 ~ Off to America: Wayfaring Strangers
fall 2014

The power and richness of a river flowing through the woods or past a city sometimes makes us wonder where all that water came from, and where it might be going. So it is with the currents of culture: the music, song, dance, and stories that enrich the daily lives of those who share in it.

The river of American folk music comes from many tributaries, but one of its key sources is Scotland. A new book by Fiona Ritchie and Douglas Orr offers a readable and epic tale tracing the flow of Scottish music, much of it via northern Ireland, to the hills and hollows of the American Appalachians, and from there into the mainstream of American culture.

Wayfaring Strangers: The Musical Voyage from Scotland and Ulster to Appalachia is almost encyclopedic as it sifts through the flowing river of Scots-Irish-Appalachian culture and shares stories about its course and some of its key tradition bearers. It is a tale gently, even lovingly told, despite the trials and tribulations of the wayfarers we read about. Hardly a page goes by without a beautiful photo of a place or a face, or a painting or drawing. Numerous boxed sidebars allow casual readers to dip into brief articles about a key person or issue, or to read an informal, personal perspective taken from an interview with a musician or researcher. A decade in the making, the book is available this fall.

Fortuitously, the book comes with a CD, which is perhaps not surprising, since the book is co-authored by Fiona Ritchie, host of NPR's long-running Celtic program, *The Thistle & Shamrock*. The CD gives us a first-hand listen to the connections and differences between American music and its primarily Scottish ancestors. Selections include the ubiquitous ballad "Barbara Allen" sung by both Dolly Parton and northern Irish singer Mairead Ni Mhaonaigh of Altan; a Scots Gaelic song of the type that can be heard in the melodies of American folksongs; an Appalachian song that speaks of Glasgow despite Scotland being beyond the memory of the Appalachian singers; as well as some instrumental playing from both sides of the "pond."

Divided into three broad sections, the book first lays out for us the background of balladry and instrumental music in the old country, takes us along on perilous, desperate, yet hopeful journeys across the waters, and finally gives us a good look at how the old music has been both preserved and transformed in America.

We learn of the origin of the ballad in medieval times and its travels into Scotland, the development of Scottish fiddle and bagpipes, and tales of Niel Gow and Robert Burns. Meanwhile, the authors shed light on related topics, including a look at who the Celts were, their connections to Picts and Vikings, and the Gaelic language.

The 16th and 17th century brought King James's "plantings" of Scots in Ulster, across the narrow waters between Scotland and northern Ireland, where many Scots settled but never quite felt comfortable. Their rents were often hiked unreasonably, and the Anglican church was imposed upon them, despite the fact that they were Scots Presbyterians. This did not bode well for a peaceful and productive life.

Large numbers of these unhappy Scots became "wayfaring strangers," never at home with their surroundings. Yet they were always at home with their traditional songs, tunes, and dances. Along the way, they composed new songs to express their experiences, and it is often through the lyrics of these songs that the book tells its story.

Taking a one-way ticket across the rolling waves required these travelers to be packed into American ships, many of which sought human cargo for their return voyage, after having unloaded American flax for the Irish linen industry. A key member of the ship's crew was the fiddler, who provided exercise for the cramped travelers by playing for dancing. Music, dance, and shared songs kept travelers entertained and hopeful during an endless and sometimes terrifying voyage.

Who were these travelers? Sometimes they weren't sure themselves. They came over from Ireland, but many of their songs reveal a homesickness for Scotland, or an adaptation of old Scottish ballads to new circumstances in America. Arriving mostly in Philadelphia, some tried to fit in, but many moved on, often following the Great Philadelphia Wagon Road south into the Appalachians of Virginia and the Carolinas. They took on many names, sometimes referring to themselves simply as "frontier inhabitants," but eventually came to be known as "Scotch-Irish" and later on, "Scots-Irish."

One Scots-Irish frontiersman by the name of Daniel Boone blazed a new trail from the Philadelphia wagon road west into Kentucky. There we come across a new kind of folk instrument played on the lap, with strings for melody and drone strings reminiscent of the bagpipe. We know it as the mountain dulcimer. The book traces the dulcimer's journey from the original, boxy "sheitholt" of the Pennsylvania Germans, to the rounded Scots-Irish version found along the wagon trail in Virginia, and finally to its hourglass shape found yet further down the road, in Kentucky.

As we follow the broad "carrying stream" of music from Scotland to Appalachia, many tributaries came together to enrich the scenery. *Wayfaring Strangers* does not shy away from examining any and all of it. There are few places where the book mentions an instrument, aspect of tradition, or personality, without taking some time to tell us more.

In this way, we learn of some of the African and Native American influences upon the Scots-Irish music and dance in America. African-American musical traditions are best known for blues and jazz, but also contributed to traditional old-time music through widespread appreciation for the black dance bands with their own caller, fiddler and banjo player. In Appalachia, the driving beat of Scottish fiddle music was tempered by the syncopations of the African-American style of playing. This style also introduced the bluesy flattened third we hear in old-timey music, and its descendant, bluegrass. The rhythmic stepdancing that later emigrated from Scotland to Cape Breton, Nova Scotia, can also be seen in Appalachian clogging, with the addition of African shuffle steps and Native American stomps.

Native Americans influenced the Scots-Irish in other ways as well. While there were certainly confrontations between frontiersmen and

Native Americans, there were also commonalities. Apart from shared cultural ideas between clan and tribe, a deeper story is told by the surnames found among the Creek and Cherokees (including some of their chiefs): MacGillivray, McPherson, Mackintosh, and Ross. Some Scots-Irish referred to the Native Americans as Coilltich, Gaelic for "forest folk."

The book traces the pathways of older music leading to the folk and popular music we hear today. The current technology of each era always found a way to spread local songs and tunes, whether through broadsheets during colonial times, vinyl records and radio in the 20th century, or the internet of today. We read about songcatchers and tune collectors, about connections between Robert Burns and Woody Guthrie, and how country and bluegrass developed from old-timey music. We glimpse personal tales, such as the story of the gig Jean Redpath shared with Bob Dylan in Greenwich Village in the 1960s. During her set, she found herself singing an old Scottish version of a song Dylan had incorporated into a song of his own earlier in the show.

We learn of the influential and hugely popular Carter family of the 1930s, and how Pete, Peggy and Mike Seeger brought traditional songs and tunes to the American mainstream. We read about singer and song collector Jean Ritchie; a poor, blind Appalachian guitarist named Doc Watson; Presbyterian hymns and shape-note singing; and of the Scottish heritage of Elvis Presley and Johnny Cash.

Fiona Ritchie was captivated by these Scottish-Appalachian connections as a Scottish student abroad in North Carolina back in the 1980s, where she launched the radio career that led to her NPR program, *The Thistle & Shamrock*. Doug Orr, formerly president of Warren Wilson College near Asheville, North Carolina, founded the highly successful Swannanoa Gathering, where musicians of all ages work each summer with top instructors from the Celtic and American traditions.

Together they tell a story remarkable for its breadth and depth, conveying the drama of Scottish emigration via Ulster to Appalachia, by a people who clung to the music and song they held dear, and bequeathed it to America. It is for us to keep our eyes and ears open to see how this musical river carries on.

69 ~ *Cape Breton Island, Canada*
fall 1998

One day last winter, I witnessed Cape Breton fiddle music become a contender in mainstream American culture. I was at the health spa, wishing I had remembered to bring my tape machine to drown out the obligatory pump-you-up disco music, when my beleaguered ears perked up to hear strains of the old Scottish reel, "Sleepy Maggie," as played by Cape Breton fiddler Ashley MacIsaac on his popular album called *Hi How Are You Today?* Cape Breton fiddling had arrived!

To be sure, this recording has a modern edge, symbolized by Ashley's performance outfit: a kilt with combat boots. But there is some traditional fiddling included, and now that Americans have been exposed to Ashley MacIsaac's name, his two traditional CDs have also been picked up by a major label.

Interestingly, many people assume that traditional albums are the earlier ones, that players start traditional and go commercial. In fact, Ashley's latest album, *Fine Thank You Very Much*, is an answer to *Hi How Are You Today?*, paying homage to the traditional fiddlers who inspired Ashley to play the music he loves.

Another young Cape Breton fiddle star, Natalie MacMaster, has come out with a new all-traditional album, called *My Roots Are Showing*. Her previous release, the brilliant *No Boundaries*, included some eclectic tracks, suggesting that she was moving in new directions. But her latest album, and her hugely successful road shows, demonstrate that Natalie's playing is deeply and comfortably rooted in tradition. Her concerts spotlight her unparalleled zest for traditional tunes, and her Cape Breton step dancing, danced while playing, brings down the house.

This love of traditional music can be felt everywhere on Cape Breton Island (eastern Nova Scotia, Canada), the home of thousands of Scottish families escaping the Highland Clearances of 1780-1850. Bringing with them their music, Gaelic songs, and step dancing, these emigrants preserved some of Scottish Highland culture that was later diffused in Scotland. The Highlanders who remained in Scotland suffered serious suppression of their culture because of politics and religion, while the Cape Bretoners were free to protect and develop their Scottish heritage. Lately, some of the Cape Bretoners have been traveling back to Scotland to teach their style of fiddling and stepdancing to interested Scots. (To give them their due, the humble Highlanders are not prone to publicizing themselves, so there is usually more to their story than we are led to believe. For instance, contrary to popular belief, there is a small but ongoing tradition of fiddling in the Highlands that is not far off from the Cape Breton sound. Some tunes, such as "West Mabou Reel," widely thought of as Cape Breton tunes, are still played in the Scottish Highlands under their old Gaelic names.)

Cape Breton today is a treasure trove of musical events, dances, and summer festivals, plus the new Celtic Colours International Festival held in mid-October. These events draw not only many visitors but also native Cape Bretoners of all ages. Even teens hang out at the traditional dance halls, and up on stage you might as easily see a 14-year-old fiddler as a 75-year-old.

Cape Breton's vital musical culture is reflected in a growing output of recordings, a rich repository of primarily Scottish music played on the fiddle. To sample this upbeat music, listen to an album such as *The Bridges of Cape Breton County*, featuring fifteen traditional and old-style Cape Breton fiddlers, or *The Cape Breton Connection*, which presents ten fiddlers with a traditional but more modern sound, including traditional tunes performed on electric guitar, piano, bagpipes, and by the Barra MacNeils and Slainte Mhath. The *Atlantic Decade*, just out this summer, includes Ashley MacIsaac, Natalie MacMaster and PEI fiddler Richard Wood plus singers and bands such as the Rankin Family, Great Big Sea, Rawlins Cross, Barra MacNeils and Rita MacNeil. *Traditional Music of Cape Breton* on Nimbus Records features thirteen of Cape Breton's finest, and the *Scottish Fiddle Rally Concert Highlights* album mixes Jerry Holland, Natalie and her uncle Buddy MacMaster with top Scottish fiddlers Alasdair Fraser and Aly Bain, plus some fine group playing.

Once you decide to delve into the recordings of individual players, you will be rewarded with some irresistibly lively music. The music of the best older-generation fiddlers includes the strong sound and uplifting beat of Buddy MacMaster (try *Judique on the Floor*), the twinkle of joy in the playing of Joe Cormier (his recent *Informal Sessions* is excellent), the great selections of tune medleys by Carl MacKenzie (*Highland Fiddle and Dance* is his latest), and the down-home fiddling of old-style players Alex Francis MacKay and Joe MacLean (each has a new album).

One of the best known of Cape Breton fiddlers is Jerry Holland. Originally from the Boston area, his mastery of this music is such that many of his own tunes are now standard repertoire, and his sweet, expressive and highly danceable playing style has influenced many younger players. His newest album is *Fiddler's Choice*, which is highly unusual in that it features solo fiddle and no accompaniment. Jerry is one of those fiddlers who can capture your ear with a pure fiddle sound.

Another expressive, strong player is Howie MacDonald, whose name as a soloist is not well enough known outside of Cape Breton because he is part of the Rankin Family band. His recent album *The Dance Last Night* places music in the humorous story, like a radio play, of two fellows going to a Cape Breton dance, combining great music with hilarious comedy (all instruments, voices and sound effects by Howie!).

Cape Breton is rightly proud of its strong native culture of music and dance, where younger players are always growing into the scene. As their compatriots tour the world, there is also increasing international interest in their music. So keep your ears open, whether in your health spa (perhaps) or on your radio (more likely), for a hint of old Scottish music as transmitted by a new generation in Cape Breton. Better yet, pick up a few albums or go to see these fine players in concert or at a dance in Cape Breton, and experience this bit of Scottish heritage for yourself.

70 ~ Glengarry County, Canada
spring 2007

Like a scene from *Brigadoon*, the pipers and drummers came out of the mist onto the field, except, unlike *Bridagoon*, there were nearly a thousand of them. A field full of dancers performed a choreography of Highland and Cape Breton stepdance, and some 75 fiddlers of all ages took the stage to play Scottish fiddle.

Within a 20-mile radius of where we were, in Canada, there are towns named Dunvegan, Dalkeith, Dalhousie, Glengarry, and Glen Robertson. In one area you could find about a mile of mailboxes with MacLeod names, followed by an array of MacDonalds, and a clan of MacGillivrays.

This pocket of Scots can be found in Glengarry county, Ontario, just west of Montreal. It is home to about 25,000 residents, including well-known performers of Scottish music such as the Brigadoons, Hadrian's Wall, Glengarry Bhoys, and four pipe bands. It has hosted the North American Pipe Band Championships for over 50 years.

The Glengarry Highland Games celebrates its 60th anniversary this August in Maxville, Ontario. Maxville may not seem like a Scottish name, but in fact it derives from the town's former name, Macksville, which in turn came from Mac's Corners, known for being the place where everybody's name started with "Mac"!

The county's surprisingly strong Scottish culture has been passed on continuously since the late 1700s and early 1800s, when several waves of Highland immigrants swept the area. The strength of the local Scottish culture is all the more remarkable for not being isolated from other cultures. The first Scots in Glengarry were actually placed there by government officials who wanted a buffer zone between the French Catholics of Quebec and the English Protestants of Ontario. They chose

Scottish, English-speaking Catholics, and succeeded in establishing a peaceful community.

Since Glengarry in Scotland was home to clan MacDonnell, it's no surprise that the Scots who named Glengarry, Ontario were MacDonnells. They were primarily loyalists fleeing upstate New York following the American Revolution in 1786. Soon, other Scots followed directly from Scotland, such as MacLeods from Glen Elg in 1794, MacGillivrays from Lochiel, Campbells and MacNabs from Breadalbane, and others.

Glengarry County has lots of pipers. The Glengarry Pipe Band musters both a Grade 2 band and a Grade 4 band, both of which have placed well in recent years in their respective grades in the World Pipe Band Championships in Scotland. Two other pipe bands, the South Glengarry Pipes and Drums, and the Quigley Highlanders, are also active in the county.

One of the giants of the piping world, John T. MacKenzie, former Pipe Major of the Scots Guards and personal piper to the Royal Household, became the first head instructor of the Glengarry School of Piping and Drumming after moving to Canada to be a pipe major with the Royal Canadian Air Force in the 1950s. The school later was headed by world-class piper Colin MacLellan, and currently by Colin Clancy, formerly of the world champion Simon Fraser University Pipe Band.

Scottish fiddlers can be found throughout the county. The director of Scottish fiddling at the Games, Donaldson MacLeod, has been a member of the Glengarry Strathspey and Reel Society for some 25 years. Dairy farmer Ian MacLeod, the fifth generation of Scots working the same farm, learned fiddling from local fiddler Malcolm Dewar, and after playing in several of the local fiddling groups, started teaching in 1993. The demand for learning Scottish fiddle has been such that Ian now teaches about 45 kids, with a little help from his older son to keep the farm going.

Ian says that when you hear a fiddler play well, "you can almost hear the people talking in Gaelic." Gaelic was commonly spoken in the area until about two generations ago, and there are still Gaelic classes and a Gaelic choir.

Ian's daughter Ashley MacLeod has become a hometown fiddling star. She has toured with the Brigadoons, Hadrian's Wall, and the Simon Fraser University Pipe Band. Ashley now has two solo CDs, in addition to having recorded with the SFU pipe band.

The Brigadoons are probably the best known export from Glengarry county. For the past 35 years, they have entertained at Highland Games and Scottish events around North America, performed ten years in a row at Disney World, and toured the world as musicians with the Rae MacCulloch Dancers, also of Glengarry. The Brigadoons offer popular Scottish songs and tunes, with accordion, guitar, bass, and often a fiddle. They have over 15 recordings plus a DVD with the MacCulloch Dancers.

For dance musicians, Rae MacCulloch, director of the MacCulloch Dancers, often makes use of the Brigadoons, and occasionally the Glengarry Pipe Band as well. In 2004, she celebrated the 50th anniversary of her dance school with an event so amazing that it made the Guinness Book of World Records. She invited all her dancers, past and present, to join in a massed dance, a choreography of Highland and step dance on the field at the Glengarry Games. Over 500 dancers participated.

This dance school grew out of and reinforced the area's love of Scottish culture. Aiming to teach the art of Scottish dance for its own sake rather than for competition, Rae MacCulloch has built a hugely popular school. The way she sees it, competition makes winners out of a few, while a good performance makes winners of everyone. In recent years, the group has toured to Scotland, France, Mexico, Bulgaria, and performed for the Queen.

The Glengarry Bhoys are a high-energy Celtic folk rock band with strong roots in the county. Featuring songs, guitars, pipes, and fiddle, they've made six CDs since 1999, and sold nearly 100,000 copies, touring widely in North America. In recent years, they even added a female fiddler/singer (a Glengarry ghirl?), and include some French Canadian songs in honor of the French heritage of Glengarry as well. The Bhoys' lead singer, Graham Wright, hails originally from Scotland.

Hadrian's Wall is another very popular Glengarry band, offering up Celtic rock for the past ten years, with strong vocals, guitar, drums, fiddle and bouzouki. The band has made three CDs, one of which is available, song by song, on iTunes.

Cape Breton musicians are well appreciated in Glengarry, and there have been exchanges of young fiddlers, as well as guest Cape Breton performers such as Natalie MacMaster, and workshop leaders. As in Cape Breton, Scottish events in Glengarry attract participants of all ages, from teens to grandparents. Yet Glengarry, only one-eighth the size of Cape Breton, has its own style, its own historical connections to Scotland, and a vital Scottish musical culture in its own right.

St. Andrew's is one of the most celebrated holidays in the county each year. Among other events, there is a major concert at the high school, with amazing young talent on pipes, fiddle, English and Gaelic song, Highland dance, and Cape Breton (Scottish) stepdance. Some of that talent is likely to provide tomorrow's performers and teachers in the Scottish arts.

Apart from listening to CDs or concerts by touring musicians, probably the best way to experience the culture handed down through six generations of Scottish settlers in Glengarry, Ontario, is to visit the Highland Games in Maxville in early August. Local performers — pipers, fiddlers, dancers, Celtic rockers and the popular Brigadoons — along with some 70 competing pipe bands, will show you the way to your own bit of Brigadoon.

71 ~ Down Under
summer 2006

Wherever the Scots have lived, you'll find Scottish music. Even at the opposite side of the earth from Scotland — Australia and New Zealand, where many Scots since the early 1800s sailed in search of jobs and a better life.

About 10% of Australians today are of Scottish heritage. New Zealand's percentage is higher, probably even higher than Canada's 14%. By comparison, only about 4% of Americans claim Scottish ancestors, though in actual numbers, this translates into more than twice as many people as there are Scots in Scotland!

It is not too surprising, then, that there is a great deal of interest in Scottish culture in the Down Under. There are actually more grade 1 pipe bands in Australia and New Zealand than in the US and Canada. One of them, the Victoria Police Pipe Band, won the World Pipe Band Championships in Scotland in 1998. Their creative CD from that year, *Masterblasters*, presents excellent traditional pipe music alongside original compositions and toe-tapping arrangements.

Highland Games in Australia take place from spring to fall (September through May), and in New Zealand from November through February. There are a number of festivals as well, such as the Port Fairy Folk Festival in March, and in June the National Celtic Festival and the Kilmore Celtic Festival not far from Melbourne in the south. The Australia Day Celtic Festival takes place in late January in Sydney, and the Australian Celtic Festival is in April at Glen Innes.

These Highland Games feature fine native pipers and pipe bands such as the Dalewool Auckland & District Pipe Band, which won nine New

Zealand piping championships. This band's CD, *Southern Gael,* is varied, with full band, mini-band, and solo numbers.

Solo piper Mark Saul, formerly with world champion Victoria Police Pipe Band, is a fine composer as well as piper. His album *Mixolydian,* on Greentrax, offers precise and thrilling piping harmonies in a rich atmospheric setting.

A relatively new resident in OZ, as the natives like to call Australia, is piper Roddy MacDonald, originally of Inverness, who has composed tunes played by many top pipe bands and folk bands, including the 78th Frasers, Royal Scots Dragoons, Simon Fraser, Tannahill Weavers, and Slainte Mhath. His solo album is *The Drying,* available from Greentrax Recordings.

Popular acts at the Celtic Festivals include Australian Celtic bands such as Dalriada, a bagpipe-based rock band, and Claymore, a Celtic folk rock band with a Scottish lead singer. The folk band Colcannon is also well-known as a band with a slightly Celtic flavor, with Scottish guitarist and songwriter John Munro.

Celtic music mixed with jazz is offered up by smallpiper Jimmy Young and guitarist James Wilkinson of New Zealand. Young is Scottish but lived in New Zealand for some time and recorded with his band "Rua" there; on his return to Scotland, he made a beautiful album called *Pipeworks* in collaboration with several top Scottish musicians.

Some of the festivals feature The Melbourne Scottish Fiddlers. This ten-year-old group has made two lively CDs, *Red Hot Scots* and *Reel Cool.* Similar, smaller groups are based in Adelaide, Canberra and Sydney; and Scottish fiddling is taught at summer camps in Australia, Tasmania and New Zealand by Cathy Fraser, Chris Duncan and others. It's great to discover how busy the Melbourne Fiddlers have been; I'm pleased to disclose that the group was launched after its director, Judy Turner, enjoyed two years with the Boston Scottish Fiddle Club under my direction in the U.S.

One of Australia's superstar performers is the folksinger Eric Bogle, who left his native Scotland back in 1969 at the age of 25, and after an attempt to become a respectable accountant, threw caution to the wind and developed his talents as a songwriter and performer. He has become famous the world over for his witty, incisive, and effusive songs. His most famous song is probably "And the Band Played Waltzing Matilda," a devastating antiwar song inspired by Anzac Day, in remembrance of the bloody battle of Gallipoli.

Eric Bogle tours regularly in Australia and beyond, accompanied by fellow Scot John Munro. Every other year, including this August, Bogle performs in Scotland, where eight of his recordings are available on the Greentrax label, plus a new 5-CD boxed set called *Singing the Spirit Home*, which offers Bogle's most popular songs from the past 30 years.

Many musicians from Scotland make the long trip to tour the friendly lands of Australia and New Zealand, including guitarist Tony McManus, singer Dick Gaughan, fiddler Alasdair Fraser, the Wrigley Sisters, the band Fine Friday, and Shooglenifty, one of whose members hails from Tasmania, the large island south of Australia.

Of course, today's 24-hour plane ride from Scotland is nothing compared to the 4-8 months of sailing required by the ships of the 18th century settlers. By the time Harry Lauder visited Australia in 1914, the boat ride was only 19 days from San Francisco. Lauder was greeted by thousands of Scots as he steamed into Sydney to begin a successful tour of Australia and New Zealand, traveling with his wife and son. Unfortunately, World War I began during his trip, and his son was called up for service, never to return.

For those of us living in Europe or North America, it is difficult to grasp the geography of Australia's latitudes and size. If we could transplant Australia to a spot exactly opposite its position on the globe, it would practically fill up the North Atlantic Ocean, with its southwest corner in Venezuela and northwest corner near New Jersey, while its eastern border would reach the Cape Verde Islands off Africa. New Zealand would superimpose itself on Spain and western France.

Scots had a strong hand in the development of Australia, even in naming the continent after the Latin word for "southern" (renaming it, really, because the Dutch had reached it in the 17th century and called it New Holland). After the American Revolution, the British could no longer send prisoners to the American colonies, so they started prison colonies in Australia. But probably less than 5% of those prisoners were Scottish.

Among the prisoners were the "Scottish Martyrs" of 1792, who had been inspired by the French Revolution to seek parliamentary reforms in the U.K. It was the unjust treatment of these political prisoners that inspired Robert Burns to write the song "Scots Wha Hae."

The drama of Scottish history did not fade with settlers in such faraway places. If anything, the long distance made the heart grow fonder. Scottish societies there have long supported Gaelic song, piping, and Highland dancing. Even though most of the settlers were from the Lowlands of Scotland, they took upon themselves the mantle of the romantic Highland saga.

Nothing could portray that drama better than music. One of the most popular singers from New Zealand is Steve McDonald. His blockbuster album *Sons of Somerled* touched hundreds of thousands of listeners worldwide with over an hour of musical theater portraying the 12th century Scottish hero Somerled, who defeated the Vikings and became King of the Isles. His grandson Donald became the father of the first MacDonalds.

McDonald followed up his first CD with two award-winning albums, *Highland Farewell* and *Stone of Destiny*, continuing his passionate portrayal of Highland history.

If you have the chance, fly Down Under and visit the festivals and Games, and attend Celtic summer schools and music clubs. Or by the magic of CDs, listen to great music from the faraway land they like to call OZ, a land enchanted by musical wizards from Scotland.

SECTION SIX
Festivals and Events

Hebridean Celtic Festival, Lewis

Puppet "Storm"
in Glasgow

Transatlantic Sessions in
recording session

ABOUT SECTION SIX
Festivals and Events

Immersing yourself in a festival is a joyful inhalation of culture. You experience top performers at their best as they bring their favorite music to the stage. We'll begin and end this section with a visit to the great Celtic Connections Festival, which warms up Glasgow in the dead of winter. First, we'll time-travel back to the 2001 event, and end up in 2020 to enjoy the festival before the pandemic forced it to go virtual.

In between, we'll see the Celtic Colours Festival in Cape Breton, Nova Scotia, patterned after Glasgow's festival, with a spotlight on the beauty of Cape Breton island and its culture. Held in October during peak fall colors, this event features the vibrant local music scene while also importing top players from abroad.

The Hebridean Celtic Festival in the western Isle of Lewis is notable for its close-knit community support, its environmentally friendly innovations, the beauty of its surroundings, and a fantastic blend of top musicians from near and far.

We'll also take a look at the most local of "festivals" – the music sessions that are held weekly in Scotland, and in at least one pub daily. Here's where you can enjoy a classic pub scene while you experience the quality and informality of musicians having a great time sharing tunes.

A new festival that's grown very popular in Glasgow is Piping Live!, which grew out of the annual influx of pipers and enthusiasts attending the nearby World Pipe Band Championships. We'll learn how this event, sponsored by the National Piping Centre, has grown into a well-rounded presentation of piping styles from around the world, including related musical performances, talks, tours and whisky tastings.

A different sort of event, made for television but also presented live and in recordings, is the Transatlantic Sessions. This popular concert and TV series brings together musicians from Scotland and America in a unique and high-quality showcase.

As we tour through these events, you might start making plans for your own adventure to experience them first-hand. Prepare to enjoy a variety and quality of live music available in no other way.

72 ~ *Celtic Connections Festival 2000*
winter 2000-01

Glasgow in January? If you love Scottish music, that's the place to be. The Celtic Connections Festival is an astonishing brew of the world's best Celtic music, and in particular, a perfect showcase for Scotland's finest musicians.

People didn't think it would work, of course. Until the 1994 debut of the Festival, many doubted that people would care to visit Glasgow in the dead of winter, especially just after the big Hogmanay parties for New Year's were over and done. Well, they were wrong!

Glasgow is now looking forward to its 8th annual Celtic Connections Festival this winter, and the growth of the festival is amazing. Last year, the festival offered 250 events at a dozen venues over the course of 3 weeks, mostly concerts, but also workshops, lectures and debates. Over 65,000 people attended.

Yes, you might find yourself in a gray, misty, and chilly Glasgow, but the spirit of the continual flow of musical celebrations more than makes up for any winter bleakness. And it's a wonderful reason to take advantage of low winter airfares.

The Quality Hotel on Gordon Street next to Central Station is the place to stay if you really want your fill of music. That's because as a guest there, you can get into all the nightly performances at the "Festival Club" in the hotel's Kintyre Suite. Every night, after the Festival's scheduled concerts are over, great performers play 40-minute sets between 11pm and 3am, including many that have played at larger venues during the Festival. In order to take in the Festival Club as well as evening concerts, I ended up living a bonafide musician's schedule: waking close to noon and staying up till 4am. One unexpected fringe benefit for me of keeping that schedule was that when I returned to the U.S., I had zero jet lag! But of course, there are so many wonderful events over the course of this three-week festival that you can pick and choose your favorite events to suit your own schedule.

One day, I almost got up early to catch an 11:00 am "Community Program" at the Glasgow Royal Concert Hall. Although not specified in the Festival's 100-page program book, this concert was to feature top artists, including fiddler Aly Bain, singer Rod Paterson, guitarist Tony McManus, and others. It was an example of how the Festival can pull together some of the country's best artists for a free community presentation, since all these performers are already present for their own concerts.

The availability of these great performers has proved to be one of the unexpected benefits of holding the Celtic Connections Festival in January. Who else would book them at that time of year? As a result, Celtic Connections offers an unbelievable lineup of the world's finest Celtic and related artists, and it is not surprising to note that many Celtic event organizers from Europe and North America attend this Festival to decide who to hire for their own events.

The Glasgow Royal Concert Hall, at the end of Sauchiehall Street, is the hub of the festival, with major evening events held in the Main Auditorium, and other concerts upstairs in the Strathclyde Suite. On the first floor is an Exhibition Hall which hosts a daily Open Stage for up-and-coming musicians, and participatory events such as ceilidh dances.

The Concert Hall also has a cafe, a booth selling CDs by festival performers, and the box office where you can purchase tickets to any event. Other venues include the Piping Centre, the Old Fruitmarket, the Tron Theatre, Waterstone's Bookshop, the Barrowlands, and several churches. Most venues are within walking distance of the Concert Hall, or a short taxi ride away. Ticket prices this year ranged from £3.50 to £12, though some programs are free, and a few high-profile concerts charged more for better seats.

There are five or six programs each evening, most of them featuring two performing groups. You will want to select one, or possibly two, and then go for a drink at the Festival Club to hear lots more!

Here are two of my Festival days:

Tuesday, January 25. With my press pass, I was able to sample more concerts in more locations than was reasonable, but who's counting? I went first to the big Runrig concert in the Main Auditorium. This Gaelic rock band had the audience on its feet several times, and their show was professional and exciting, as you would expect from a 27-year-old band that put Gaelic music on the British pop charts. It was nice to hear a strong performance from their new lead singer, Bruce Guthro of Cape Breton, Nova Scotia.

Another concert began a half hour later upstairs in the Strathclyde Suite — a reprise of the classic "Wellpark Suite" by William Jackson, featuring many of the artists who originally performed the work 15 years ago. It was an exciting performance that stirred the memories of many who recall this work as one of the first to present traditional Scottish music in the almost classical setting of a composed suite.

William Jackson and his friends from the band Ossian performed again that night at the Festival Club, joined by Gaelic singer Mairi MacInnes, and Mae McKenna, whose rich singing hushed the crowd. Other performers at the Club included singer Buddy MacDonald from Cape Breton, Eric Rigler's "Bad Haggis," and a new, young, energetic band called "Daimh" (pronounced "dive," Gaelic for "kin"), with band members from Scotland, Ireland, U.S. and beyond.

Wednesday, January 26. I couldn't quite get up in time for the 11:00 am free program with Aly Bain, Rod Paterson, and Tony McManus. After a bit of visiting and sightseeing, my first real event of the day was to have an early dinner with some friends at the Piper's Tryst, a very nice small restaurant next door to Glasgow's Piping Centre. We were planning to see the fiddler Duncan Chisholm and singer/guitarist Ivan Drever at the Piping Centre, but I decided to first catch part of the "Celtic Notes" performance down the street, featuring writer William McIllvaney and fiddler Aly Bain.

"Celtic Notes" is a literary series within the Celtic Connections Festival, offering about a dozen programs spotlighting Celtic writers and poets, sometimes joined by a musician. In the one I saw, McIllvaney and Bain talked, read poems, and played tunes relating to different stages of their own lives.

I had to slip out of the presentation to make it to the Duncan Chisholm/Ivan Drever concert at the Piping Centre. An intimate hall at the Centre allowed for a warm and friendly concert of fantastic Highland fiddling, warmly sung ballads, and hilariously silly stories.

Becoming an inveterate concert-hopper, I took a short taxi ride to hear the band Big Sky at the Old Fruitmarket. This old market in a formerly open courtyard has been enclosed and outfitted with a stage, lots of tables, a bar, and probably holds up to 800 people. Big Sky was performing with a big sound, about seven band members dancing as they played fiddle or guitar, with colorful lighting, a show that was worthy of the setting. The band is a Celtic/pop group led by Capercaillie's fiddler, Charlie McKerron, and for this show, he included the two dynamic fiddlers from the band Deaf Shepherd, a cross-fertilization of musicians and bands typical of the Celtic Connections Festival.

I had missed the earlier act at the Old Fruitmarket, a flute and whistle-based band called Flook. But they played again later at the Festival Club, and I was glad to catch their ingenious and versatile performance. At this festival, and especially at the Club, you go to see one group you know, and end up mesmerized by others you never heard of before. This is the hope of the organizers, as they not only feature the best Scottish performers, but many top Irish musicians, and interesting performers from Galicia (Celtic Spain), Brittany (Celtic France), Scandinavia, Cape Breton, and the U.S.

In the next few days, I managed to see the Highland fiddle band Blazin' Fiddles, which filled the Old Fruitmarket with a blast of irresistible energy from their six fiddles; piper Fred Morrison's band Ceolas with its fresh take on piping and Gaelic song; virtuoso harper Savourna Stevenson and Friends, featuring a number of her fellow musicians from other groups at the Festival; and a gala celebration of Phil Cunningham's fortieth birthday. This included a stream of great musicians, finishing with a performance of Cunningham's Highlands and Islands Suite — a grandiose and beautiful composition performed by some 150 musicians: the Scottish Opera Orchestra, the Glasgow Phoenix Choir, Aly Bain, Sileas, Iain and Allan MacDonald, Manus Lunny, the Inverness Fiddlers, Blazin' Fiddles, Charlie McKerron, and many more.

There were, needless to say, many other incredible programs: a folksinger's dream concert with Eric Bogle, Archie Fisher, Dick Gaughan, Brian McNeill and Tom Paxton; the Gaelic Women concert, presenting the best female Gaelic singers; the String Sisters concert, with fiddlers Catriona MacDonald, Natalie MacMaster, Liz Carroll, Mairead Ni Mhaonaigh and more; Alasdair Fraser; Boys of the Lough; Shooglenifty; Arlo Guthrie; Carlos Nuñez; La Bottine Souriante; Sharon Shannon; Davy Spillane; Altan; Anam; Whistlebinkies; Wolfstone; Old Blind Dogs; Iron Horse, and lots more.

In addition to concerts by well-known musicians, and the literary "Celtic Notes" series, there were two other kinds of events. The "New Voices" series included commissions by Celtic Connections of new works by traditional musicians. This has resulted in five exciting compositions over the past few years, drawing on traditional music and infusing it with new ideas. For example, Andy Thorburn's "Tuath Gu Deas" for 12 unaccompanied voices singing in Gaelic, Scots, English and Welsh, was described in *The Scotsman* as "the distillation of 2000 years of Scottish history into a polyphonic choreography of sound and words."

The other remarkable series of events were the debates and master classes, more than two dozen of them over the course of the Festival. Master classes included a day of discussing and teaching pipes, accordion, and fiddle by top players. The debates covered topics such as Scottish Identity, Interpretations of Robert Burns, Land Reform, Who Owns Scotland, the Scots Kitchen, Scottish Filmmaking, and Gaelic Politics.

In short, Celtic Connections offers something for everyone, and nearly all the offerings are top drawer. Whether you try to catch everything you can, or select a few key events, it is a most rewarding time to visit Glasgow. By the way, don't try to get a press pass and see too many concerts; you'll need a vacation when you get home!

73 ~ *Celtic Colours International Festival*
summer 2002

The highway from my inn gave way to a quiet, hilly road through occasional farms and the candy colored trees of fall. I was headed over the mountain to a concert in Mabou, on the west coast of Cape Breton Island. Out of five concerts offered throughout the island that night, I selected "Gaelic Roots" at Mabou's new Strathspey Place Auditorium. Great music, spectacular scenery, and tough choices welcomed me to the nine-day Celtic Colours International Festival.

"Celtic Colours" refers both to the beautiful October foliage and to the many shades of music offered by Celtic masters from Cape Breton, Scotland, Ireland, Wales, Brittany, Spain and beyond, about 200 performers in all.

Located on the east coast of Canada in Nova Scotia, Cape Breton is home to a strong musical culture that traces its roots directly to the Highlands and Islands of Scotland. Over 25,000 Scots immigrated to Cape Breton during the Highland Clearances of 1780-1850, and their Gaelic language, music and dance have shaped the culture of the island.

"Celtic Colours was designed to celebrate a living Celtic culture that exists in Cape Breton," explained Festival producer Max MacDonald, "and to increase tourism – to bring people here to experience something that is real."

As I spoke with last year's festival artists, it became clear that, especially for musicians from Scotland, Celtic Colours is not just another gig. One of Scotland's best known musicians, brilliant accordionist and composer Phil Cunningham, noted his astonishment on arriving in Cape Breton. "People look the same, everything's laid out the same. You're driving past little townships and you see stuff that just looks like the Isle of Skye or outside of Inverness. It's more than I could ever have hoped for."

And the experience works both ways. "Whenever I'm in Scotland," said MacDonald, "I see my cousins, I see my neighbors, I see the shopkeeper from down the street. I get a sore neck the whole time I'm there. We're still wearing their genes."

Highlander Ingrid Henderson, pianist and clarsach (harp) player with the Gaelic band Cliar, spoke of the similarities still present in the music. "So many tunes they're playing over here, we know from old fiddlers where we live back home. We have old standards at home, and they're the standards here as well, and actually in the strathspeys and reels, they're not that dissimilar, the way they're played."

Scots from outside the Highlands have less of a direct connection to Cape Breton and its music. The progressive concertina player Simon Thoumire of Edinburgh felt that "the music here is very different from what we play in Scotland today. Cape Breton music is very dance rooted, very rhythmic. I think music in Scotland is far more performance-related."

The Festival encourages listeners to appreciate a broad variety of styles, often in the same concert. Thoumire performed with jazz and folk pianist David Milligan at an intimate concert in North River, and the appreciative audience loved their playful virtuosity built around traditional Scottish tunes. They were joined for an evening of contrasts by members of the Gaelic band Cliar and Welsh triple-harper Robin Huw Bowen.

Festival concerts are programmed around themes of music, culture and community. Last year's events included a piping concert; a tribute to Cape Breton fiddler Winston Scotty Fitzgerald; a dinner reading from a novel about emigration from Scotland, with Gaelic song and fiddle; a huge array of musicians playing for the "world's largest square dance"; a blast of fiddling from women of Cape Breton, Scotland, and Ireland; a candlelit dinner concert at the Louisburg Fortress; a songwriter's circle with top folksingers; the world premiere of a work performed by bagpipes, fiddle, and Symphony Nova Scotia; and many more concerts, not to mention the numerous workshops as well.

In Mabou, the "Gaelic Roots" concert highlighted connections rather than contrasts. Strathspey Place was built to showcase and promote Cape Breton's Scottish cultural heritage at a time when its Gaelic roots have been seriously threatened by assimilation. I settled into my seat in the new auditorium and listened to the MC welcome us in both Gaelic and English. We were about to hear piper Allan MacDonald of Glenuig, the Cape Breton band Beolach, and the band Cliar from Skye.

Allan MacDonald is a fine piper who has researched the strong relationship between Gaelic song and pipe music. He and his well-known piping brothers Iain and Dr. Angus were all featured at the Festival last year.

Beolach is an exciting band comprised of six young veterans of the bustling Cape Breton music scene, with two fiddles, guitar, pipes, piano and drums. The band's Gaelic name aptly means "lively youth."

Like most Celtic Colours events, Cape Breton artists were presented in this concert, partly to showcase the world-class talent of the island, and partly to serve as hosts. "When we invite performers to Cape Breton," Max MacDonald told me, "we think of inviting them to our house." In Cape Breton, the local yokels include such stars as Natalie MacMaster, Buddy MacMaster, the Barra MacNeils, Ashley MacIsaac and Mary Jane Lamond.

One of the two fiddlers in Beolach is Mairi Rankin, who is among Cape Breton's best young players. Mairi is half Scottish; her mother is from North Uist and her father one of the many Rankins of the Mabou area. The most famous of these is the Rankin Family, a band that toured internationally for ten years. The Strathspey Place stage is dedicated to one of their key members, the late John Morris Rankin.

"We brought the Rankin Family over," said Phil Cunningham, speaking about his BBC program, which introduced the music of Cape Breton to many Scots. "We burst into tears when they sang 'Ho Ro Mo Nighean Donn Bhoidheach' because it's normally a fast tune and they sang it slow to us."

Cunningham's radio show aired in the late 1980s and early 1990s. Since then, Cape Breton musicians have stirred a lot of interest in Scotland.

Here were representatives of a living Gaelic culture playing Scottish tunes, and stepdancing in a style that died out in Scotland as late as World War I.

Many young Scots were inspired by Cape Breton's fresh take on old Scottish tunes. A few, however, felt resentful that these foreigners seemed to be telling them how to play their own music. "But it has changed," observed Scottish guitarist Tony McManus. "And I guess the main thing that really got over that hurdle are the friendships that have been cemented between the musicians of Scotland and the musicians of Cape Breton."

The Celtic Colours Festival has been clearly part of that glue. "I see a lot of exchanges going on," said artistic director Joella Foulds. "What continues to amaze me is the energy that can be created by music and what a positive influence it is on people's lives."

The cultural exchanges have affected Cape Breton as well. "There was a time when in order to protect our own culture, Cape Bretoners were saying — this is the right way to do something and this is not," commented Foulds. "I see that changing. I see people opening up and being thrilled that — oh, that is a tune we know, but it's played differently and that's okay!"

One of the most important exchanges at the Festival has involved the Gaelic singers. The number of Gaelic speakers in Scotland has statistically declined to around 50,000, but there is a revival of Gaelic education and culture, and the new parliament gives some hope that this indigenous language may be protected and nurtured.

"There's no doubt over the last 20 years that there are many more young Gaelic speakers now," said Gaelic singer Arthur Cormack, "and that's because of Gaelic regional education. You can hear Gaelic on the streets of Portree, which you never ever heard when I was a kid." Cormack has been very involved in efforts to carve out a vital niche for Gaelic in Scotland.

By contrast, Cape Breton's Gaelic speaking population has declined by possibly 90% in the past decade alone, to as few as 500 speakers. Clearly, the impact is on more than the language itself. Allan MacDonald has shown how integral the Gaelic language is to piping, and many have said the same about the fiddling. As Hector MacNeill of the Gaelic College points out, "We can call it Celtic and put all kinds of larger names on it, but it's Gaelic culture we're talking about."

No doubt the sense of a dwindling Gaelic culture in Cape Breton made Cliar's appearance at the "Gaelic Roots" concert that much more thrilling. Arthur Cormack's smooth, mesmerizing voice joined with two other Gaelic singers and top Highland musicians on harp, fiddle, piano and guitar.

Near the front of the audience was an enthusiastic group of Gaelic speaking teenagers on holiday from the Highlands. Said Cormack, "They're staying with families. That's a deliberate attempt to show that Gaelic is still spoken amongst young people at home."

One of the hopes of the Celtic Colours organization, according to Joella Foulds, is "to help, if possible, to prevent the loss of the Gaelic language. We think that one way we can do that is by bringing over people from Scotland who still do have the songs, and do have the language and speak it, and this hopefully will inspire people of this generation to keep it alive."

Gaelic singer Mary Jane Lamond is known for her progressive interpretations of traditional songs. Because of her deep appreciation for the tradition, she has dedicated herself to helping preserve Gaelic in Cape Breton. As a Festival artist-in-residence, Lamond helped coordinate the Gaelic programs last year, one of which was a fascinating, informal exchange of songs and stories between Gaelic singers from Scotland and Cape Breton.

After the performance, the singers continued at the "tune shack," a nearby building where musicians often gathered to play tunes until dawn.

"We went over there and sang for two hours," said Lamond. "People from thousands of miles away and people from here, who never met each other and who completely understand each other, sang together for two hours!"

Arthur Cormack also enjoyed that song swap and marveled at the similarities. "There's one difference in the Gaelic where we use a thick L sound and they actually place a W sound. Other than that, it's just like speaking to somebody back home. It's incredible." The Cape Bretoners he was singing with traced their family back to the Isle of Barra in 1802. "That's 200 years ago. It's just amazing to me that they still have such pure Gaelic. Most of the old songs that we sing, they know a version."

Like most Highlanders, Cormack has always wanted to visit Cape Breton, but he never had a chance to go until he was brought over for the Festival. Now he plans to come again and bring his Gaelic-speaking family. Both he and Lamond mentioned the hope of collecting and preserving some of the thousands of songs in the memories of Cape Breton singers now in their late 80s. There is also the great hope of inspiring young people to incorporate more Gaelic into their lives.

My inn was located in Baddeck, near the beautiful Bras d'Or (pronounced bra-DORE) lakes. After some evening concerts, I bypassed my beckoning bed and headed towards the Gaelic College in St. Ann's for the late night Festival Club, with food, drink and lots more music into the wee hours. The idea is to "bring everyone together in an informal setting," said MacDonald, "and that's when magic happens." Many of the performers who played at the events I couldn't get to would be there, sometimes joining forces with others making surprise appearances. And sometimes listeners would jump up for a bit of step or ceilidh dancing.

While the chilly nights of October required a warm jacket, the mild days could be bright and sunny, perfect for seeing the sights before the evening events. Some concerts required a drive of as much as two hours, but this was not a burden in a place voted "most scenic island in the world" in a poll of Condé Nast readers. There were also many daytime workshops open to the public, taught mostly by festival artists, in dancing, Gaelic language, song, culture, and a variety of musical instruments.

What makes Celtic Colours unique for both audiences and artists is that it is "not a site-based festival where you create a place and bring in the performers and an audience," as MacDonald put it. "This festival takes place in a community where the culture is very vibrant."

The vibrancy of the culture clearly gave Scottish musicians something valuable to take home. "I've been seeing how happy people are with their own thing here," said Phil Cunningham. "It's amazing to watch. They love their own musicians, they support their own musicians, they have a network set up to support Cape Breton music."

Ingrid Henderson agreed about the "fantastic support for their own artists here. The home crowd were just so proud of Natalie MacMaster, they were just so behind her, it's amazing."

But there's more to the vitality of the Cape Breton music than supportiveness. "It seems to me the music is more valued here," said Tony McManus. "It's more woven into the fabric of everyday life here than it is in Scotland. There seems to be a deep understanding of the music in the general population here. You mention a tune, and they nod their approval." And, he added, "This is the only place in the world where you can get tapes of fiddle music at gas stations!"

Still, McManus pointed out that the "music scene in Scotland is far more healthy than it has been in years," and Henderson echoed that sentiment. "A whole lot more people are playing and we're having a whole lot more fun with it," she said.

Phil Cunningham painted a happier picture now compared with when he was growing up. "I do a lot of work with children and adults who are just learning to play, and the current climate in Scotland is just great. I'm not worried about being an old person any more, because I know there's going to be music for me to listen to."

"Cape Breton and Scotland have remade a very strong bond," observed Brian McNeill, a folksinger and songwriter, perhaps best known as the fiddler for the Battlefield Band for many years.

"Although it seems like two sides of one very old culture, really this revival we're talking about is a young thing," said MacNeill, now serving as head of Scottish music for the Royal Academy of Music and Drama. "These festivals, Celtic Connections and Celtic Colours, they are its first real flowering. You don't know which way the branches are going to grow, and that's very healthy."

We may not know which way the branches will grow, but the Celtic Colours Festival is certainly helping to water the roots.

74 ~ *Hebridean Celtic Festival*
winter 2015-16

A long time ago on an island far, far away, a new Celtic music festival was born. It was 1996 on the Isle of Lewis, and this past July, the Hebridean Celtic Festival celebrated its 20th year.

Festival director Caroline McLennan recalls chatting with workmate Fiona Morrison back in the spring of 1995 about the new Celtic Connections Festival in Glasgow. Could such an event could happen in the Outer Hebrides? It did not take long for them to find six or seven others who shared their vision and made a plan to try it out. They had hoped to use a site near the spectacular ancient standing stones at Callanish, but ended up situating the event in Stornoway, on the Castle Green in front of Lews Castle.

The first Hebridean Celtic Festival took place in the summer of 1996, featuring great performers such as Davy Spillane, Dougie MacLean, Wolfstone, Natalie MacMaster, Iron Horse, and Shooglenifty. Fiddler Jennifer Wrigley, piper Rory Campbell, and Gaelic singer Christine Primrose, among others, were recruited to tour the local schools as an educational part of the festivities.

In recent years, HebCelt, as the festival is fondly called, has been named one of the UK's top summer festivals (it's the only Scottish one on some lists). Around 14,000 people are estimated to have attended last year, half from the Outer Hebrides, 30% from the rest of Scotland, 10% from elsewhere in the UK, and another 10% from around the world. In many cases, people born in Lewis use the festival as an opportunity to come back for a visit, and sometimes, people meet there, fall in love, and stay on.

HebCelt always brings in a critical mass of great Celtic musicians, a guarantee that it's worth the trip. It also features many musicians with a connection to the isle of Lewis, some of them top names in their own right, while others are local artists, part of the community which supports the event.

On opening day you can feel the excitement in downtown Stornoway. Musicians are playing outside; people are dancing a Strip The Willow in the middle of the street. The Lews Pipe Band plays a set of tunes in a circle, and marches down the street, leading an ever-growing crowd across a footbridge and up to Castle Green for the start of the evening's concerts.

As you follow the pipe band to the festival, you'll see two gigantic circus tents looming ahead, with broad stripes on taut roofs sloping up to high poles in the center. Inside each is a large stage, fully equipped for the bands, with sound systems, smoke and light shows, TV monitors, and standing room for huge crowds, plus a curtained platform to the side for those who need seating. When the music starts, and the tent fills with listeners and dancers, you will find yourself in another world, with joyous fellow travelers alongside.

Some of the artists heard this past summer included the wild drum/bodhran exchanges and hybrid music of Afro-Celt Sound System, the mellow Gaelic singing of Karen Matheson with Donald Shaw of Capercaillie, cross-cultural music by the Scottish band Salsa Celtica, a blend of electronic grooves and traditional instruments by the band Shooglenifty, and high-energy tunes from Treacherous Orchestra.

Among the Festival musicians with a Lewis connection was one of the fastest rising stars of the Scottish music scene, the band Mànran, whose lead singer came from Lewis. This band hit it big in its first year, back in 2010-11, and has continued to be hugely popular in Scotland and beyond. Sweet Gaelic songs, lively mouth music, and songs in English are backed by fiddle, accordion, flute, uillean and Highland bagpipes, and drums, blending traditional music with funk, jazz, and rock.

For its 20th festival, HebCelt commissioned a work by Lewis native Alasdair White, the fiddler with the Battlefield Band. White grew up inspired by HebCelt every summer, and remembers especially the time fiddler Alasdair Fraser called him up to play a tune for the huge audience when he was only 13. Jovial and mustachioed, White opened the festival this year by introducing his commissioned work, entitled "An Iuchar (The Key)." This suite of some 30 melodies traded off between danceable and contemplative moments, with Alasdair himself on fiddle, joined by colleagues on Highland pipes, bouzouki, accordion, drums, uilleann pipes, and guitar/banjo. Hopefully White will find funding to record his one-hour composition.

Another Lewis native, singer Alyth McCormack, invited White to join her and a few other musicians in a performance celebrating her new CD, *Danns an Rathaid (The Road Dance)*. Her rich voice, singing both Gaelic and English, was also featured as part of her trio, Shine, with singers and harpers Corrina Hewat and Mary MacMaster.

One band with an unusual Lewis connection was Raghu Dixit from India. Their presence underlined longstanding ties between Lewis and India, dating to the 18th century, when Col. Colin Mackenzie of Stornoway became the first man to map all of India, as Surveyor General.

The musical acts at HebCelt alternate starting times between the two primary tents, so people can catch some of everything if they wish. There is also a smaller tent with an Acoustic Stage for instrumental duos, singer/songwriters, and other smaller-scale acts, while listeners try out the wide selection of Scottish whiskies and gins at the bar opposite the music. Another tent provides cover in case of rain for those wishing to grab a bite and a beer from the food vendors, or to sit on hay bales in the summer breeze.

New this year was a smaller tent for circus acts, magicians, and mask making. Given that some 20% of the audience is under 16, it is no surprise that this kid-friendly entertainment was well received.

HebCelt offers some of its activities offsite, including late night performances by many of the top bands of the day, in two different Stornoway locations. Everything is walking distance in town, but there are also a few offerings in other parts of Lewis and Harris during the four-day festival.

Community support for the festival is strong, as evidenced by the 140 volunteers putting in some 3700 hours to help, local businesses providing in-kind support, and community groups such as Highland dancers, the pipe band and others adding activities of their own. Gaelic is an important part of the event, not only in the musical acts but also in language classes. A group of students from a local school circulated in the crowds and taught simple Gaelic phrases to visitors. In return, the festival creates a huge sense of pride and excitement in the community, while injecting a much-needed £1.5 million into the local economy each year.

By December, HebCelt's website begins listing some of the major artists confirmed for next year's event, and continues adding names as more are confirmed. While the 20th festival honored a number of the artists who have appeared in its first two decades, the upcoming HebCelt plans to focus on becoming 21 years old: a coming of age. What that means in terms of music is something we'll have to wait and see. If past is prologue, it's sure to be a great experience for all ages.

75 ~ *Pub Sessions*
spring 2012

All across Scotland, you might step into a pub for dinner or to have a pint with a friend, and be greeted by the pulse of live music. Often the music is played by a booked band, but if you're lucky, you'll happen upon a traditional music session.

Fiddlers, guitarists, a pennywhistle player, and a singer or two may be sitting round a table, enjoying the tunes they know together and eyeing each other for cues as to what's coming next. The music ebbs and flows but rarely pauses for long before it's off and running again. You can't help but appreciate the good spirits and camaraderie, and the slice of Scottish culture that you've happened upon.

One of the most famous traditional session haunts is Sandy Bell's pub in Edinburgh. Here sessions have taken place every night since 1982. Sandy Bell's was the hub of the Scottish folk revival, with the first gatherings held in association with the University of Edinburgh Folk Society in 1942. The pub is relatively small, so on any given night there might be only 3 or 4 players, but there can be up to a dozen or more.

Sandy Bell's and the Captain's Bar are two Edinburgh sessions held nightly, but there are a number of other pubs which host sessions on certain days of the week. For example, if it's Tuesday, the "craic" is at the Reverie. Here, there can be more than a dozen players around a long table, with the lead musician at one end. Some pubs will hire a lead musician to make sure there's a critical mass of musicians and quality music for the pub's patrons to enjoy. The leader will encourage fellow musicians to show up, and keeps the music going through the evening. Often the lead musician is well known locally or nationally. At the Reverie, for example, the leader is usually Angus R. Grant or Luke Plumb, members of the band

Shooglenifty. Since Angus's father is a famous west Highland fiddler, he often plays classic Scottish fiddle repertoire or pipe tunes, in addition to contemporary favorites.

Many sessions happen without a lead musician. People show up just because they like to be there with friends, have a pint (sometimes given free to musicians), and share favorite tunes, or challenge themselves by learning new tunes on the fly. Most groups welcome newcomers and various levels of players, though some favor the regulars, and are particularly conscious of presenting good quality music to the listeners. At Hootananny, a popular pub in Inverness, the sessions are not open, but the booked traditional bands on Mondays, Tuesdays and Wednesdays often invite players to come up and sit in with them.

Glasgow's session scene is thriving, with many pubs hosting informal traditional gatherings. Some of the Glasgow musicians are students in the traditional program at the Royal Conservatoire of Scotland (formerly the Royal Scottish Academy of Music and Drama) and always on the lookout for chances to play music.

One Glasgow pub, the Ben Nevis, has regular music sessions Wednesdays, Thursdays, and Sundays starting around 9:30pm. This little pub is so popular and welcoming for musicians that it was named Venue of the Year at the Scottish Trad Music Awards last December. Most of the music is instrumental, with sometimes 8 or 9 fiddlers showing up, but on occasion several Gaelic singers will pop in for a song.

Not all the sessions happen at night. For example, Glasgow's Babbity Bowster has a session every Wednesday afternoon, as well as on Saturday nights.

If you're up in Aberdeen, you might stop in at The Blue Lamp, frequented by Jonny Hardie, leader of the popular traditional band, Old Blind Dogs. Jonny even named an album of his after the place, and a number of musicians have named tunes after the owner of the pub, Sandy Brown. Every Monday a session starts there around 9pm with whoever shows up, mostly fiddles and guitars. On Wednesdays you'll hear more music, mostly singing, sponsored by the Aberdeen Folk Club.

Every session has its own etiquette, though you may not always notice it as a listener. At some sessions the lead musician will start most of the tunes, but there's always a chance for others to kick off a favorite of theirs, with the expectation that others will join in. Regulars get to know the local repertoire and choose tunes that are popular with the group. It is through regular playing at such sessions that many musicians build a repertoire of thousands of tunes. Once in a while, a musician will play a tune nobody knows, and everyone will listen, while perhaps the guitarists provide backup.

Part of the magic as an observer is to see how connected the musicians are to each other. How do they know when to move on to a new tune, or stop at the same time? In some ways they have a sixth sense about these things. Often there are visual signals, or someone will give a little shout to indicate a change of tune.

It is possible to spend time in Scotland without happening upon a session. You might just hit the wrong pubs, or the right pubs at the wrong time. One way to keep track of where to go is to consult the annual Event Calendar published by the Traditional Music and Song Association of Scotland (TMSA) each January. It is available in print form to members, or can be consulted online as well. Many sessions, as well as festivals and other cultural events in Scotland, are listed there.

During the Homecoming Year in 2009, TMSA organized a special program to create over 300 sessions throughout Scotland, counseling and cajoling pub owners to host a regular session, and helping line up musicians to lead them and attract players. Many of these sessions were successful enough to keep going after the experiment was over.

Taigh na Teud, a publisher of Scottish music books, maintains a website with information including guides to sessions and festivals. The owners, Alasdair and Christine Martin of Skye, update their session listing each spring, as seasonal changes can affect the accuracy of the listing. Or new sessions can be added. One new host this year, for example, is the Edinbane Inn on Skye, which welcomes musicians on Tuesday nights and Sunday afternoons.

The presence of a music festival will spur offshoot sessions at local pubs as well, so you might check out a good festival and ask around for where the sessions are happening. Throughout the year, hardly a week goes by without a festival being offered somewhere in Scotland, from Ayrshire to Shetland, from Edinburgh to Skye or Lewis. The huge Celtic Connections Festival spawns many a January session in Glasgow, but a guide such as the TMSA's calendar can lead you to many events at other times and places, with lively sessions nearby.

If you're headed into a pub intent on having a focused conversation, you might prefer a place with recorded music, which is often so carefully crafted that it's easy to take for granted as a backdrop. But if you'd like some high spirits and a connection to Scotland's culture, I'd recommend a pub with a session. There, the music, the musicians, and the listeners are all live and engaged, and anything can happen.

76 ~ *Piping Live!*
summer 2018

Every August, Glasgow is abuzz with bagpipes. This is partly due, of course, to the annual World Pipe Band Championships. But it's also due to the week-long "Piping Live!" festival that leads into the Worlds, and is sponsored by The National Piping Centre.

Last year, the Piping Centre estimates that over 40,000 spectators enjoyed the festival. There were more than 150 offerings at ten venues throughout Glasgow, ranging from major concerts to informal participatory events held outdoors in Georges Square or under large tents. There were academic talks, tours of the Piping Centre's museum, a pub quiz, competitions, a trade show for reedmakers and pipemakers, and a city tour tracing the history of the local scene for piping, folk and roots music. Every night at 10pm, the Piping Centre hosted a Festival Club, with short performances by many of the day's top musicians. There were even whisky and gin tastings, and a chance for people to try their hand at playing the bagpipes.

Now entering its fifteenth year, "Piping Live!" is the popular name for what is officially the Glasgow International Piping Festival. When it began, in 2003, the festival was called "Piping Hot," a catchy pun that unfortunately was already in use by someone else, as it turned out, so the following year the moniker was switched to "Piping Live!" and it's been known by that name ever since.

The director of the festival, Roddy MacLeod, MBE, has been principal of The National Piping Centre since helping create it, essentially from scratch, in the spring of 1996. The Centre has had a major impact on the teaching and presentation of bagpipe music in Scotland, offering a degree in piping since 2000, in collaboration with the Royal Conservatoire (formerly the Royal Scottish Academy of Music and Dance). The Centre's faculty are all top pipers who are active in performing and research. Roddy MacLeod himself has won all the major solo competitions in Scotland, many of them multiple times. Lismor Records devoted Volume 6 of its *World's Greatest Pipers* series to MacLeod's solo playing.

In addition to Piping Live! and its degree program, The National Piping Centre sponsors the National Youth Pipe Band, offers outreach workshops round the country, presents programs in schools throughout Glasgow, gives free piping instruction in low-income areas, and publishes tutoring books and a magazine. The Centre's instructors travel to the U.S., Germany, and Italy to teach pipes at seasonal schools. And closer to home, the excellence of the Centre even extends to its own restaurant, the Piper's Tryst, where I enjoyed a particularly delicious haggis dinner!

Being an international piping festival, one of the unique features of Piping Live! is the presentation of various types of bagpipe music from around the world. Last year, there were concerts spotlighting the gaita, which is a type of bagpipes from Asturia, in the Celtic part of northwest Spain. There were Breton pipes from Brittany, the Celtic region of northwestern France, and many other types of bagpipes in addition to the Highland pipes. These included the Scottish lowland and Border pipes, the Northumbrian pipes from northern England, the zampogna pipes of Italy, the Sardinian launeddas, Nordic drone music from Sweden, Bohemian pipes from the Czech Republic, and Estonian bagpipes.

Although some of the festival's events spotlight a variety of instruments and musical styles, many of the events are focused purely on presenting Scottish piping at its best. These concerts and competitions are very popular, and well worth attending. Even those who are not great fans of the pipe music should give at least one of these concerts a try. Everybody has heard mediocre piping played casually in parades or other events, but few have had a chance to listen to an excellent player. Of the thousands of pipe bands in the world and the more than 300,000 individual pipers, there are only about 40 Grade 1 (top quality) pipe bands, and it is only in these relatively few bands, as well as in solo competitions or special performances, that people actually hear the best pipers. The top players have superior timing, tone, and musical expression, and because of this, they are capable of playing the most exciting and beautiful tunes.

Piping Live! features some of the piping world's best players in lunchtime solo recitals, as well as the Pipe Major Alasdair Gillies Memorial Recital Challenge, the Masters Solo Piping Championships, the Gordon Duncan Memorial competition, an International Pipe Quartet competition, and the Pipe Idol competition for players under 21 years old.

Not all the concerts focus on the bagpipes, although nearly all include pipers. Many pipers are multi-instrumentalists, and when they perform with a band, they may switch to pennywhistle, low whistle, bellows pipes, or guitar. Research by piper and former Piping Centre faculty member Allan MacDonald uncovered the strong connection between bagpipe music and Gaelic song. As a result, Gaelic song is an important part of Piping Live! and there is even a daily Gaelic language class offered during the festival.

One Piping Live! concert presented last year paid tribute to piper, whistle player and composer Fraser Shaw, who had been very active in the Glasgow music scene, playing in sessions and with various bands. Because he passed away from a rare disease in 2015, many of his former bandmates joined together to perform a spirited and varied concert launching a CD of music written by Shaw. Excellent musicians on a variety of instruments participated, including Eilidh Shaw, Ross Martin, Innes Watson, Adam Sutherland, and piper Ross Ainslie. A portion of the concert was offered again later at the Piping Centre's late-night Festival Club, along with performances by other bands.

Other concerts that were not purely piping events last year included a musical play paying tribute to musicians of World War I during its centennial; showings of archival films of artists among the piping, folk, and traditional arts; a concert by the Peatbog Faeries, and another by the Battlefield Band.

Georges Square in the center of Glasgow has been traditionally used by the festival for some of its outdoors events, but this summer those activities, including public performances by pipe bands from around the world, will be moved to a new tent alongside the Piping Centre. In fact, the whole festival, usually held the second week of August, will take place a little later than usual, on 13-19 August. This displacement is due to the fact that Glasgow will be hosting the 2018 European Sports Championships, 2-12 August, featuring triathlon, golf, rowing, gymnastics, biking, and aquatic events.

Visitors to Glasgow during the Piping Live! festival this August will be hard pressed not to run into a great piper or pipe band performing or practicing in the open air. But that's just a teaser, compared to attending some of the festival's concerts. It is not often that you find yourself in the middle of such a concentration of the world's finest piping talent, so if you are in Glasgow in August, give yourself the treat of attending a concert or five!

77 ~ *Transatlantic Sessions*
summer 2013

Listeners love it, but so do the performers. Transatlantic Sessions is a dream concert series that regularly brings together about 25 of the best folk musicians from Scotland, Ireland and America in television programs, recordings, and live concerts.

"Where you have great musicians all gathered together into one room and making music, a sum bigger than the parts happens. You get magic in the room," said the sound engineer for the project, Iain Hutchison. "It all comes together and you're sitting there with goosebumps."

Scottish fiddler Aly Bain has been co-hosting the series since 1995. That year, Aly's musical codirector was American fiddler Jay Ungar, who played with the house band and contributed musical selections such as two of his most famous compositions, "Ashokan Farewell" and "Lovers' Waltz." Totaling more than three hours of music, the programs included amazing pairings of performers from both sides of the Atlantic, such as Dougie MacLean and Kathy Mattea, or Dick Gaughan and Emmylou Harris. To mention just a few of the other musicians, the Scots that year included Rod Paterson, Karen Matheson, and Simon Thoumire; Americans included Mark O'Connor, Iris DeMent, and Rufus Wainwright; and from Ireland came Cathal McConnell, Manus Lunny, and Davy Spillane.

One of the Americans performing in the first series was Nashville dobro player Jerry Douglas, who went on to become Aly's musical codirector on all the subsequent shows, starting with the second TV series in 1998. Douglas Eadie, producer of the series, especially appreciated Jerry Douglas's experience not only as a top Nashville musician, winner of 11 Grammies, but also as a working producer. For Eadie, the two lead musicians complement each other: "Aly has a deep sense of what tunes are; he's more instinctive, and Jerry's more disciplined."

Six half-hour TV episodes are recorded for each series and aired weekly on BBC, usually from late September to early November. Following these broadcasts, DVDs and CDs are made available. Since 2009, many of the Transatlantic Sessions performers have come together to perform live at Glasgow's Celtic Connections Festival in the dead of winter, as part of a sold-out tour around Scotland.

After the second series in 1998, it took a while for BBC and RTE, the Irish broadcaster, to take up the project again. The third Transatlantic Sessions was finally produced in 2007, and since then the programs have come out every other year, in 2009, 2011, and 2013. This year's series was recorded in March at a lodge on the (bonnie, bonnie) banks of Loch Lomond, and is expected to be aired in the fall, with DVDs available for Christmas, and CDs to come out on Aly Bain's Whirlie Records label.

Many great musicians have taken part in the Transatlantic Sessions over the years. To give a sense of the show, it may help to list this year's performers for those who are familiar with these top players. The all-star "house band," which backs up the guest soloists, includes fiddler Aly Bain MBE; dobro player Jerry Douglas; venerable Scottish fiddler John McCusker; young Scottish multi-instrumentalist Matheu Watson; American guitarist Russ Barenberg; virtuoso Irish flutist Michael McGoldrick; Capercaillie pianist and artistic director of the Celtic Connections Festival, Donald Shaw; English bassist Danny Thompson, a founding member of Pentangle; and Scottish percussionist James MacIntosh.

The guest artists this year include Scottish soloists Julie Fowlis, Karen Matheson, Phil Cunningham, Ewan McLennan, and Allan MacDonald. The American guests are Mary Chapin Carpenter, Aoife O'Donovan, Tim O'Brien, Teddy Thompson, and John Doyle. Irish musicians include Maura O'Connell, Cara Dillon, Andy Irvine, and Donal Lunny.

A few of the special guests that have been featured in the past are James Taylor, Eddi Reader, Sharon Shannon, Alison Krauss, Bela Fleck, Bruce Molsky, and Mary Black.

One of my favorite sets was performed in the second series, in 1998. Scots and Gaelic singer Karen Matheson gave a heartfelt rendition of Burns's song "Ae Fond Kiss" sweetened by the fiddling of Aly Bain, and rounded out by an emotional duet by Matheson and Irish singer Paul Brady.

Part of the reason that viewers and audiences love the Transatlantic Sessions performances is the obvious joy the musicians take in playing with each other. James Taylor said of the musicians and crew, "This group of people that surrounds you, their talent is only matched by their warmth and their welcome." American singer Joan Osborne said it usually takes "months of playing together to be able to get that kind of group mind cohesion. And these guys are right there after just three or four times of running it."

"If we had done this in America, it wouldn't have the same feeling to me," said Jerry Douglas. "We're taking all this technology into places that were built in the 1500s, 1600s." The recordings were all done in beautiful and historic surroundings, including hotels in Ayrshire, Aberdeenshire, and a hunting lodge in Perthshire.

TV director Mike Alexander and producer Douglas Eadie first tapped into the transatlantic traditions with Aly Bain in 1985 and 1986, when they filmed a series of programs called "Down Home." These shows explored the roots and regional styles of fiddling in North America. Aly and the film crew visited prominent traditional musicians in Nova Scotia, French Canada, the Appalachians, Nashville, and Texas. Said Aly, "We were asking about their music and playing with them, finding where the roots of it came from, and of course a lot of it came from over here."

For the Transatlantic Sessions programs, Aly said the idea was to "bring these Americans we'd met, many of them, over here so we could introduce them to Celtic players in Scotland and Ireland. It's grown into something else now, much bigger than we thought it would be."

Audiences enjoy the performances for their high quality musicianship, and the musicians enjoy, as Jerry Douglas says, the chance to "make the music we want to make, not the music we have to make."

But Aly Bain also views the program as a historic effort to make connections, "not only to promote folk music but to bring young Scottish artists into the company of Alison Krauss and Mary Chapin Carpenter and James Taylor and let them learn from these great artists. And that's to my mind what the Transatlantic Sessions are about."

Originally an exploration of the roots and connections between Scotland and Ireland and North America, Transatlantic Sessions has developed into a mix of accomplished musicians, young and old, that is creating new cultural connections in its own right on both sides of the Atlantic.

78 ~ *Celtic Connections 2020*
summer 2020

The January sun rose midmorning in Glasgow. Surface ice on the walkway along the River Clyde began to thaw and allow a firmer grip for the small crowd waiting and watching intently. Several cameramen stood ready to record the big moment. "Storm," a gigantic sea goddess puppet designed to call attention to climate change, was about to wake up and begin her long stroll through city streets to the Glasgow Royal Concert Hall, the hub of Celtic Connections Festival 2020.

Workers in sky-blue raincoats kept watchers at a safe distance while a team in yellow raincoats marked STORM untied veils and took hold of ropes. Ominous whooshing and popping sounds emanated from a sound truck. Music by Mairi Campbell and Dave Gray sketched mysterious sounds, bits of melody and the chant, "Pure sound. It's a mantra." As if speaking for Storm, a voice intoned, "I come from the sea. My memory is long, and my children are strong..."

Slowly, Storm rose from kneeling to her full height of 30 feet. Her huge blue eyes opened and looked about, knees lifted, and she took her first steps, arms swinging much more naturally than might be expected for a puppet three stories tall. Police escorted her as she walked between tall buildings, pushed by a vehicle, her movements controlled by ten puppeteers pulling coordinated ropes.

After heading into the city from the river, I was about to walk the last block of Buchanan Street to the Glasgow Royal Concert Hall when I spotted the distant figure of Storm towering over the cars and crowds, slowly making her way toward me. It could have made a good horror movie except that Storm had such big friendly blue eyes.

I stepped into the concert hall building to check out an experimental new festival within the Festival, open from noon to 6pm, called "Coastal Connections." In celebration of Scotland's Year of Coasts and Waters, five venues within the Glasgow Royal Concert Hall simultaneously presented music of the west coast, Easter Ross, the Hebrides, Orkney, Ireland, and Cape Breton, Nova Scotia. In the main auditorium, I saw performances by Capercaillie, Fara, Daimh, Skerryvore, and a show by young musicians from the Outer Hebrides who wrote and performed music that represented a different aspect of each island's culture. Audience members in one of the smaller halls sat on the floor or stood by the wall as I did, to enjoy harper Ingrid Henderson's collage of original tunes, songs, and historic photos from west coast life by the sea. Singer Josie Duncan sang in Gaelic and English about ferries and fairies, and in another hall, Anna Massie and Mairearad Green played accordion, fiddle, guitar and song. There was lots more, and nobody could see all of it, but there was something for everyone, much like the Festival itself.

It had been 20 years since I'd last attended the annual Celtic Connections in Glasgow. Back then, at the seventh annual festival, people still recalled the skepticism that greeted the first proposals for having such an event. Some doubted whether musicians or audiences would want to come to Glasgow in the dead of winter to hear music. As it turned out, all the best musicians were available at that time, and listeners have flocked to the event from all over Scotland and the world. A nonstop party three weeks long, the Festival offers six times as many events now as it did 20 years ago. Over 300 events at 29 different venues now attract nearly 150,000 people to experience performances by about 2,000 international artists.

"We've tried to focus on creating relationships with international artists," says the Festival's creative producer, Donald Shaw. "We think about traditional music, and Gaelic music, as forms of world music. Engaging with other indigenous cultures, and other folk styles, helps us appreciate our own music."

While the Festival always includes some of the world's best Celtic, and particularly Scottish, artists, there were this year many samplings of non-Celtic cultures represented in the concerts, sometimes in fascinating combinations. The lush voice and physically powerful performance by Portuguese fado singer Anna Moura was paired with the Scottish band Moishe's Bagels playing klezmer, Celtic, Latin and classical music. The octet Kokoroko mixed West African music with players from the London jazz scene. Mali singer Fatoumata Diawara shared a show with a Nordic duo. Concerts were presented by the West African female supergroup Les Amazones d'Afrique, banjo superstar Bela Fleck and friends, the Seamus Eagan Project, and a star-studded tribute to Bruce Springsteen. Shetland fiddler Kevin Henderson and American pianist Neil Pearlman played a double bill with Alistair Anderson's Northumbrian band.

Cross-cultural sharing has also been the basis of Transatlantic Sessions, the Scottish-American television and recording series, which appropriately enough presented its 17th annual live concert at Celtic Connections. American, Australian, Irish and Scottish performers were backed by all-stars Aly Bain, Jerry Douglas, John Doyle, Donald Shaw, Michael McGoldrick, John McCusker and others.

To do justice to the sheer quantity of events and artists at the Festival would require a very long list. To give a sense of the quality of the events, however, I'll take you with me to a few selected concerts, focusing especially on a few of the many brilliant Scottish traditional musicians.

As the audience for the opening night concert filled the 2500-seat main auditorium, the stage was filled by the Grit Orchestra. Conducted by violinist Greg Lawson, the orchestra blends the talents of about 80 folk, jazz and classical musicians. It was launched at the 2015 Celtic Connections Festival and named after the last studio album by the innovative piper, fiddler, and composer Martyn Bennett. Before his untimely death at age 33, Bennett had produced an influential and irreverent fusion of musical styles built upon a deep knowledge of Scottish tradition.

The first half of the opening concert premiered "The Declaration," a six-movement work in honor of the 700th anniversary this April of the Declaration of Arbroath. Each of the movements was composed by Scottish folk, classical or jazz musicians, including Donald Shaw with Karen Matheson, Catriona McKay and Chris Stout, Patsy Reid, Fraser

Fifield, and Rudi de Groot, some of whom also performed. Epic walls of sound from the huge orchestra were interspersed with quiet solos, and all was enhanced by dynamic lighting, including a dozen illuminated pillars placed throughout the stage.

The second half of the show featured the Grit Orchestra's arrangements of Martyn Bennett's acclaimed and quirky music. Beautiful sounds blended with ear-provoking juxtapositions and social commentary. Fiona Hunter sang "Blackbird" in the style of traveler Sheila Stewart, curiously interwoven with a hymn sung by a choir. "Nae Regrets" involved audience participation, and the piece called "Aye" was built around guitarist Innes Watson having an imaginary cellphone conversation in which he periodically spoke into a phone to someone, saying nothing but "Aye" throughout the music, until he punctuated the end of the music by finally saying "Nah!"

On January 25, Robert Burns's birthday, an all-star roster of singers paid tribute to Burns, backed by the BBC Scottish Symphony Orchestra and a band of top traditional musicians. The show was broadcast by BBC, with a BBC presenter introducing the acts, chatting with performers, and telling kitschy jokes. Karen Matheson and Eddi Reader moved the audience with a duo rendition of "Ae Fond Kiss," Shona Davidson intoned Burns's "A Slave's Lament," and Jarlath Henderson sang "Green Grow the Rashes." At the end of the night, we were treated to a stirring sight and experience when 2500 audience member took hands with their neighbors and swayed to the singing of "Auld Lang Syne."

One venue I frequented was the recital room at the City Halls, where up to 100 listeners could listen to musicians in an informal and personal setting. Here I saw fiddler Bruce MacGregor, founder of Blazin' Fiddles, launch a new book of his original tunes and stories. Accompanied by a few friends, Bruce played tunes with colorful backstories, such as "101 Reasons to Do Nothing," about his father's encounter with a lawyer, and "The Cambridge Caravan Catastrophe" about an afterparty so boisterous that it collapsed the trailer where it was held.

Innovative fiddler Adam Sutherland, a member of Session A9, Peatbog Faeries, and Treacherous Orchestra, made his recital personal, charting his own musical progress from childhood (he fell in love with fiddling because he liked his first teacher's cat!) and how he has challenged himself in creating tunes, such as one tune where he blended the ominous mood of an air by J.S. Skinner with musical ideas from a horror film soundtrack.

Crazy sounds and popular melodies fused in the brilliant recital by concertina and piano duo, Simon Thoumire and David Milligan. Their humorous, virtuosic, and entertaining music made it clear that these musicians are so capable that they can experiment successfully with just about any musical idea that comes to mind. David also did a solo concert on a different day, bringing together Scottish tradition with his jazz training. Sometimes he dipped phrases of Scottish melody into a texture of jazz to create improvisatory musicscapes.

Behind the City Halls, where the recital series was held, is the Old Fruitmarket. A vast dance hall, this was just the right place for listeners to rock out to the energy of a 15-piece band led by the legendary whistle and flute player Michael McGoldrick. His all-male ensemble was offset by a reunion performance by Dochas, an all-female band (plus a male bodhran player) featuring Gaelic singer Julie Fowlis and fiddler Jenna Reid. Ten years earlier, the two bands had played together on a tour of double bills, so the whole show was a reunion of top musicians, many of whom have since gone their own ways as soloists or members of other bands.

Other trips down memory lane included Phil Cunningham and friends celebrating his 60th birthday in concert (20 years ago, I saw his 40th birthday concert at this festival!) and venerable folksinger Archie Fisher performing for his 80th. Breabach, one of my favorite Scottish bands, celebrated their 15th year by bringing on several past members to join them, and announcing the launch by Glenturret of a new whisky, which, like the band, was 15 years in the making and named "Breabach."

I saw many concerts, but nobody could get to them all. There was a tribute to women pipers, a guitar summit, great bands performing in venues large and small, ceilidh dances, a series of dementia-friendly concerts, and a stage for up-and-coming musicians. Students of the Royal

Conservatoire performed a range of traditional and original music, and a heartwarming tribute to the late improvisatory trombonist and well-loved teacher Rick Taylor brought together 25 great musicians, with evocative slides, stories, tunes and songs. Gaelic singer Flora MacNeill presented a heartfelt concert, and the unique Irish singer Dabhagh (Davy) Stuart sang captivating songs in Irish, English and Scots Gaelic.

During the day, concerts took place in many venues, but there were also educational opportunities, such as the "Come and Try" workshops offering everything from whistle, fiddle, or djembe for beginners to jazz, blues, and Gaelic song classes. Fiddler Alasdair Fraser and cellist Natalie Haas taught a two-day traditional strings master class.

And late at night on weekends, two venues presented short sets by five or six bands drawn from Festival artists, from 11pm to 3am. The longest running late night venue is the Festival Club, located this year at a dance club near the Concert Hall. It has standing room for up to 600, plus a few seats round the edges. The other late venue, which began about ten years ago, is simply called "Late Night Sessions." The Drygate Brewery played host, offering some 20 tables, about 50 additional seats, and plenty of standing room in a relaxed setting.

Back in 2007, Donald Shaw came on as artistic director of Celtic Connections Festival. Shaw was already at that time a well-known keyboard player, composer and arranger. He had founded the band Capercaillie in 1984 with his wife, Gaelic singer Karen Matheson, and explored the musical connections between the rhythmic and melodic heart of Gaelic music and complementary traditions in world music. Capercaillie has toured the world and sold over a million albums.

Shaw works on the event year round with Festival manager Jade Hewat and associate producer Lesley Shaw. As the event draws closer, many others come on to manage the logistics of travel, venues, accommodations, equipment, publicity and more. Shaw's title is now Creative Producer, which perhaps reflects the kind of vision he brings to Festival leadership.

"This country's an incredible place musically," says Shaw, "where musicians are coming out of music courses and they're familiar with traditional music, but they're also familiar with orchestral music, or jazz, or electronica, and that's something we've really embraced.... We try to be a vehicle for artists' aspirations. So although folk music is absolutely at the heart of the Festival, we're like the branches stretching out from a very old and large tree, trying to find what the new directions are."

His team crossed their fingers as they prepared for this upcoming 28th annual Celtic Connections Festival, at first hoping it could come off as usual, but the pandemic forced them to create an entirely virtual festival for 2021. Donald Shaw remarked that "one of the hardest consequences of the Covid virus for musicians this year has been the loss of live audiences in venues, so like many festivals we have had to look to an alternative way of presenting the Celtic Connections experience." Observing the plight of the professional musicians we all depend upon to provide quality entertainment, David McDonald, chair of Glasgow Life, commented that "now more than ever it's important we do what we can to support live performers and artists who have lost their income entirely because of the Covid-19 pandemic."

For its virtual version, Celtic Connections planned online events every night from 15 January to 2 February at reasonable prices. An early bird ticket cost only £30 for all 19 nights, and the video of each concert was scheduled to be available for one week following the show, to accommodate global viewers in all time zones.

No doubt everyone will be grateful when Celtic Connections once again offers an amazing in-person festival in 2022, but this year's digital experience will be shared by viewers around the world, and may well lead to selected future events to be enjoyed online from afar. Time will tell.

SECTION SEVEN
Making the Music Happen

Ian Green

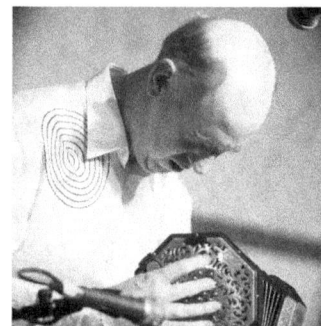

Simon Thoumire

Fiona Ritchie

ABOUT SECTION SEVEN
Making the Music Happen

One sentence in the article about Ian Green, the founder of Greentrax Recordings, says it all about this section of our journey through Scottish music: "Talent and tradition mean little in themselves, unless the talent is developed and the tradition explored."

However great the performers, they need a chance to play, and however wonderful the tradition, it needs to be brought into the open in order to be appreciated.

In this section, we take a look at some of the people who have helped make the music happen. Agents, producers, record labels, radio presenters, developers of programs to train and spotlight musicians, and publishers of traditional music, are all integral to the effort to bring Scottish music to our ears and our dancing feet, and to allow us to appreciate its vibrancy and depth.

We'll start with the story of one of Edinburgh's top traditional music agents, whose commitment to the music extended to creating a popular newsletter, a major folk festival, and helping hundreds of musicians perform throughout Scotland, despite having a day job teaching high school physics.

We'll take a look at the life of a policeman who built a premier Scottish record label, recording and promoting great musicians and documenting traditions of the past. Several other important record labels have filled out the market with excellent traditional music, and we'll be following their stories as well.

Radio announcers have kept the music alive and educated huge audiences both in Scotland on BBC Scotland and in America on NPR. They also have fascinating back stories. One important radio program not given special attention in this section is "Travelling Folk" on BBC Scotland – for more on this show, see Chapters 38 and 52.

Being a successful musician involves many skills in addition to being able to play music well, but one virtuosic Scottish musician continued his performing career while also developing a host of organizations to support traditional music, helping musicians, audiences, and the industry that presents the music in live concerts and recordings. He also explores ways to make the best of use of the internet for the sake of music. We'll learn about Simon Thoumire in two chapters of this section

The internet has also been a tremendous resource for locating original editions of old Scottish music books that long ago fell out of print. We'll discover some of these options, and will meet an elderly couple who dug out copies of old Scottish music and reprinted it in handsome new editions, making the richness of Scotland's three centuries of published music more easily available to today's performers.

These are just some of the key individuals who have been helping make Scottish music happen so we can all appreciate it, enjoy it, and carry it forward.

79 ~ *John Barrow*
winter 2018-19

Much has happened in the world of Scottish music during the past 45 years, and Dr John Barrow has been in the middle of it. Based in Edinburgh since the 1960s, Dr Barrow has worked as an agent for well over 400 traditional musicians, helping arrange concerts, tours, visas, and producing events.

It all began in 1964, when Barrow moved from his home town, about 50 miles south of the Scottish border, to attend Edinburgh University. At home, his father was a choral singer and loved classical music, his mother taught folk dancing in the schools, and John secretly sang folk and rock music, playing a guitar stashed under his bed. At university, John decided to volunteer for charity, and was fortuitously given the task of raising money by organizing concerts. In the process, he met many musicians, who in turn appreciated his talents for helping them out. Barrow's scope expanded as he gained experience and discovered that in order for some musicians to be able to travel to Edinburgh for a concert, he had to make it worth their while by arranging tours for them elsewhere in Scotland.

Around 1970, he discovered Sandy Bell's pub, which is still today a center for traditional music in Edinburgh, offering live sessions every night of the week. John frequented Sandy Bell's so much that he questions whether he would ever have graduated from university if he had learned of the pub while he was still in school!

Two of his best friends at Sandy Bell's were police sergeant Ian Green (later the founder of Greentrax Recordings) and journalist Ken Thompson. In 1973, the three decided to start a folk music newsletter. They were annoyed at the lack of attention given folk music in the regular media, and disturbed by the lack of communication about events, which sometimes resulted in double bookings. Their 6-10 page newsletter, the legendary *Sandy Bell's Broadsheet*, was launched in August 1973 and lasted ten years. They wrote articles, announcements and reviews, listed opportunities for musicians, printed letters and debates by readers, and included a diary of bookings. Every other week, Kenny would hop off the train from Glasgow after a day writing for the Scottish *Daily Record*, and the three of them would man typewriters until the wee hours of the morning, crash on the sofa, and take their work to the printer. About 800 copies would be distributed to folk clubs, postal subscribers, and sold for the grand price of 4p, mostly at Sandy Bell's. A full collection of the *Sandy Bell's Broadsheet* is kept in the National Library of Scotland; some issues can be viewed on the website of Barrow's agency, Stoneyport Associates.

In October 1973, this trio came to the rescue of the Edinburgh folk scene after one of the three folk clubs in town was forced to close. In response, Barrow, Green, and Thompson founded the Edinburgh Folk Club, which is now in its fourth decade of presenting regular performances of traditional music.

In 1979, John was invited by the Scottish Tourist Board to direct the first Edinburgh International Folk Festival. The Tourist Board had money and personnel to help, but knew nothing about folk music. John took on the full-time job of running the event, brought in his friend Ian Green as chief steward, and together they pulled together a dedicated army of volunteers. It didn't hurt that John and Ian had often dreamed of such a festival and had even charted out some of the bookings they'd like to make. The ten-day festival was a great success, being the biggest of its kind in Europe at the time. Its high profile spurred many in the public and the media to take traditional music seriously. Barrow ran the festival for about six years, and it flourished into the 1990s, though financial woes made the 1999 festival the last.

During his time with the Edinburgh Folk Festival, many things happened both for Dr Barrow and for Scottish music. In 1982, he took a full-time position as a high school physics teacher at the prestigious Edinburgh private school, George Watsons College, a job he kept until retirement in 2010. In his "spare time," on weekends and after 3:30 on weekdays, and when not grading schoolwork or preparing for class, Barrow continued his work on behalf of traditional music.

John recalls discussions among folk festival organizers about where Scottish traditional music was headed and how they could help it along. He noticed that younger music teachers were starting to include traditional music in their playing and teaching. It seemed that Scots had taken note of the growing popularity of Irish music, and had begun embracing their own music in earnest.

A group of organizers from the folk festival took particular interest in a new development happening in the Outer Hebrides, so John and a friend went out to the Isle of Barra to investigate. The event was the first Scottish Fèis. Pronounced "faysh," this is an educational Gaelic culture and arts festival. A priest in Barra, along with piper Dr. Angus MacDonald and several parents concerned about the decline of local culture, had decided in 1981 to bring in folk musicians to the island to teach local music, singing, and Gaelic language and culture. The event was enormously successful and is still going in Barra every summer. The idea of a Fèis also spread to other parts of Scotland, particularly the Highlands and Islands. Today there are nearly 50 Fèisen working with thousands of young learners, and presenting their music to tens of thousands more.

Barrow observed that Arts Councils were taking notice, and over the years, traditional music began to take off in the schools, eventually supported by a degree program at the university level in the Royal Conservatoire. "A whole raft of interlocking things built a big change in the music and a big change in attitude toward it," says Barrow.

During his time at the Edinburgh Folk Festival, Dr Barrow also teamed up with Ian Green and John Allen to start a venue for traditional music during the Edinburgh Fringe. Called the Acoustic Music Centre, this venue is still directed by Barrow and his team, and offers about 50 performances during the Fringe. Although the Fringe is not primarily devoted to folk music as the folk festival was, it does offer hundreds of traditional music concerts, which is a significant offering, though only a small percentage of the 52,000 shows the Fringe presents each summer!

Many of the musicians he's worked with over the years have been pivotal to the Scottish music scene, including singers Archie Fisher, Davy Steele, Karine Polwart, Eric Bogle, Dick Gaughan, Emily Smith, Andy M Stewart, and Michael Marra; bands such as the Easy Club, Battlefield Band, the Poozies, Tannahill Weavers, and Ceolbeg. He has arranged gigs for pipers and pipe bands, worked with guitarists Bert Jansch, Tony Cuffe, and Lulo Reinhardt (grandnephew of Django), and helped Scottish fiddler Alasdair Fraser, English concertina wizard Alistair Anderson, and Irish artists such as Altan, Frankie Gavin, Gerry O'Connor, and De Danaan. Fine musicians rooted in the traditions of Brittany, Italy, Hungary, the Andes, Australia and klezmer have also benefitted from John Barrow and his agency, Stoneyport Associates.

Stoneyport Associates is not only a way for Dr Barrow to help touring musicians but also a way for him to mentor and share his knowledge with others. Some of his associates are well-known musicians who help out while learning much in the process.

In 2009 John Barrow was inducted into the Scottish Traditional Music Hall of Fame, and now, at 73, he continues his work with musicians, still a part of the vibrant Scottish traditional music scene he helped to build.

80 ~ Ian Green
summer 2003

Back in the 1940s in Forres, a town between Inverness and Aberdeen, a boy named Ian Green used to watch his dad and his uncle march up and down in front of the house, playing the pipes together for hours. Musicians would drop in at the house to play fiddle, spoons, and other musical implements, and ceilidhs in the village hall would provide yet more music.

Though he never really took to an instrument himself, Ian developed a passion for traditional music that "has changed the face of Scottish music, permanently and hugely for the better," according to Brian McNeill, Head of Scottish Music at the Royal Scottish Academy of Music and Drama in Glasgow.

Brian was speaking of Greentrax Recordings. The brainchild of Ian Green, this record label now offers well over 200 recordings that spotlight the vitality of Scotland's music and many of her finest musicians.

Green did not set out to start a record label. After serving in the army in Korea, he joined the Edinburgh Police, where he remained on the job for a full 30 years. But during that time, he became hooked by Scottish music, first by seeing the Corries and other folk artists on TV, and then by frequenting the thriving folk clubs of Edinburgh. In the 1960s, he founded the Edinburgh Police Folk Club, which became one of the best folk clubs in Scotland, and ten years later co-founded the Edinburgh Folk Club, still recognized as among the best.

There were times during the 1960s and 70s when "folkies" and policemen didn't always see eye to eye, but sharing music at the Edinburgh Police Folk Club (fondly known as "Fuzzfolk") certainly promoted a greater understanding. Ian learned years later that some senior officers actually eyed this "folkie" policeman as a possible "left-wing threat" and even held up his promotion for a while. He retired in 1985 as a Police Inspector (equivalent in the U.S. to a lieutenant).

One year after retirement, he launched Greentrax Recordings. By the mid-1980s, the Scottish folk clubs had spawned many excellent traditional singers and instrumentalists, yet recordings were maddeningly sparse, outside of a few small labels with local or in-house musicians. Green felt that the British music industry was largely neglecting the traditional music of Scotland in favor of stereotypical pipers, and singers spun off from the music hall era of Harry Lauder. This was about to change dramatically.

Ian Green sank his police pension into recording the contemporary musical talent of Scotland, and to the surprise of many, his record company filled a need and took off. The initial impetus was a new book of tunes by fiddler Ian Hardie, which Green thought would make a fine recording. Then the great folk duo, the McCalmans, offered to record an album, the first of ten they made for Greentrax.

An exciting panorama of music followed. A quick tour of the catalog might begin with beautiful Gaelic songs from Cathy-Ann MacPhee, Billy Ross, Mairi MacInnes (including an album of Gaelic children's songs), and waulking songs from the women's group, Bannal. A sampling of some of Scotland's best Gaelic singers can be heard on *Gaelic Women,* a recording that capped three years of work, and was followed up by a unique and moving concert at the Celic Connections Festival.

Pipe bands on the Greentrax label range from the Black Watch regimental band to MacUmba, which blends traditional pipe band music with Latin percussion. Top solo pipers can be heard on the *World Masters of Piping* album, and a set of four CDs preserves historic oral instruction in classical bagpipe piobaireachd. Contemporary piping albums include high quality, accessible CDs from, among others, Iain MacInnes, Hamish Moore, Dougie Pincock, and Gordon Duncan, who debuted on Greentrax and just put out his third album, *Thunderstruck,* in April.

The broad range of Scottish folk singers on Greentrax includes two of the most influential, Dick Gaughan and Eric Bogle. Both have new CDs on the label. Gaughan's *Prentice Piece* is a double CD representing three decades of this hard-hitting songwriter's best work, and Bogle's *Colour of Dreams* contains poignant songs typical of this well-known Scottish emigre to Australia, including a song about 9/11.

The historic posthumous CD by singer and guitarist Tony Cuffe, *Sae Will We Yet,* came out in March, offering some of Tony's favorite Scottish and Irish love songs, plus other previously unreleased material.

Scots Women, a double CD with glorious multi-voice and solo singing, is a Scots complement to the *Gaelic Women* album. Last fall, Jacobite songs were highlighted in a CD called *The King Has Landed,* featuring a broad cross-section of singers from Ewan MacColl and the Corries to Rod Paterson and Jim Malcolm.

Sheena Wellington, whose bold Scots voice enriched the opening of the Scottish Parliament, released her latest work, *Hamely Fare,* this spring. Her singing of Burns's "A Man's A Man For A' That" at the Parliament provided one measure of the growing appreciation for Scottish traditional music. A few decades ago, prevailing tastes might have selected a classically trained tenor.

The broad selection of Scottish music on Greentrax Recordings extends also to ceilidh bands, guitarists such as Tony McManus, harpers such as Wendy Stewart (whose new album, *Standing Wave,* was issued in April), and fiddlers such as the powerful Willie Hunter, the snazzy Gordon Gunn, or the playful virtuosity of Jennifer Wrigley. Greentrax has also brought out recordings of Cape Breton artists, including fiddler Natalie MacMaster and the band Slainte Mhath.

Some of the most exciting and popular albums on the label come from Celtic touring bands, including the venerable Whistlebinkies, Jock Tamson's Bairns and Ossian, as well as debuts by Deaf Shepherd, Malinky, Burach, and the cutting edge Shooglenifty.

Many Greentrax releases have been debut albums, because of Ian Green's commitment to supporting young Scottish talent, even if some of their titles barely break even. Guitarist Tony McManus underlines that Greentrax "has provided me and many other musicians with a platform to develop our talents." An upcoming debut project features an award-winning quartet of teenage sisters.

Ian Green's broad musical tastes allow Greentrax to stray from traditionally based music, though for his label, "it all has to have some Scottish connection." A new sublabel called G2 was set up especially for these experimental forays, which include the hot Latin sound of Salsa Celtica, and the dance beat of Keltik Elektrik.

Not all Greentrax albums are contemporary. Ian Green said he practically fell off his chair with pride when Edinburgh University's School of Scottish Studies asked him to make available their Scottish Tradition series. These historic albums draw on some 8000 hours of field recordings to document many aspects of Scottish culture. About 20 CDs and accompanying booklets are now available, exploring Gaelic songs, traditional fiddling styles, pibroch, bothy ballads, storytelling, Gaelic psalms and other topics.

The universal respect musicians have for Ian Green and his record label is remarkable. Singer Ed Miller expresses the views of many when he touts Greentrax's "taste, honesty, decency and great selection of Scottish music." Even Green himself remarks, "I have always been dead straight with people, and in business, especially, this can be seen sometimes as unusual and refreshing."

Talent and tradition mean little in themselves, unless the talent is developed and the tradition explored. Ian Green's passion for Scotland's rich musical heritage has helped make Scottish talent and tradition shine by providing practical support and exposure. Radio stations, musicians and listeners around the world are now able to appreciate the vitality of Scottish music in a way never before possible.

Who could know that a young boy surrounded by dedicated musicians, who didn't even play an instrument or work in a related field, would end up, in his second career, opening so many doors for the flowering of Scotland's music?

81 ~ *Robbie Shepherd*
winter 2010-11

Take the floor. It's what dancers do when the music starts up. It's also the name of a radio program that has brought the bounce and good cheer of Scottish dance music into Scottish homes every weekend for 30 years. *Take the Floor* and the energetic voice of its presenter, Robbie Shepherd, is a mainstay of Scottish culture.

Shepherd's enthusiasm for the dance music is contagious, and many Scots have been introduced to the genre through his program. Jimmy Shand, Ian Powrie, and Jim Johnstone are some of the icons of Scottish dance music from the 1950s and 1960s that can still be heard on the show. Their danceable accordion music, with its strong swing, is the core of the program, but a variety of singers and contemporary musicians are also heard and interviewed during the programs. Shepherd considers himself an enthusiast of fiddle music as well, and has served as the emcee for performances of the Scottish Fiddle Orchestra throughout the U.K.

The original version of the radio program was simply called *Scottish Dance Music*. Begun in 1936, it was BBC Scotland's first entertainment program. Some four decades later, it was renamed *Take the Floor* by a new presenter, David Finlay, who was a pianist with the Olympians dance band. In 1981, after Finlay's tragic death in a car accident on the way home from the radio show, BBC turned to the talents of Robbie Shepherd, who was known for hosting an Aberdeen-based radio program called *Shepherd's Tartan*.

Take the Floor airs on Saturday evenings and repeats on Sunday afternoons in Scotland, but each show can be heard at any time online until the next week's show comes on. On occasion, Robbie enjoys taking the show on the road, which has proven very popular. One time, *Take the*

Floor attracted 1600 people to a midsummer show featuring the Iain MacPhail band at the Princes Street Ross Memorial Bandstand in Edinburgh.

Shepherd often brings on musicians to talk about and play recordings of their work. During the summer, he enjoys meeting up with musicians at their homes, and visiting their favorite places to have an on-air chat. This is a great way to learn more about the musicians than they might discuss in a studio setting. For example, last summer, Shepherd traveled to Oban and Loch Etive to chat with Donald Shaw and Karen Matheson of the band Capercaillie. As they walked along the beach, they came across the very spot where a cover photo for an early album had been taken, and as a result, carried on a spirited conversation about their early musical work.

Summer interviews on location used to be a regular feature that Shepherd included in another weekly radio program of his, *The Reel Blend*. For a long time, *Take the Floor* focused mostly on traditional dance music, while *The Reel Blend* included a variety of music and culture. Shepherd once said, "*The Reel Blend* is all about tradition, all about the different aspects which includes the dialect, includes the genuine tongue." The two programs were folded together into *Take the Floor* in the fall of 2009.

When Shepherd first was proposed as the presenter for *Take the Floor*, some at BBC wondered whether Robbie's strong Aberdeenshire accent might be an impediment to the show. He was born in Dunecht, about 12 miles west of Aberdeen. His language is Doric. Some consider it the Aberdeenshire version of Scots but Robbie calls it Doric for a simple reason: that's what his father and grandfather called it.

An advocate for the language, Robbie writes "The Doric Column" regularly for the *Aberdeen Press & Journal*. Here's a wee sample: "I jist hid tae see it for masel fin pickin up last Setterday's paper tae read that the Broch wis in the tap three seaside toons on the crest o a wave for gettin the best oot o life." For more, take a look at his book compilation, *The Doric Columns*, or one of Shepherd's collections of stories in Doric, featuring the wit and wisdom of Scotland's Northeast.

Connecting his passions for language and music is essential, Shepherd says. "It's interwoven with our culture. Take our dance, our song, our poetry, our music and our landscape – it needs the language too." Needless to say, 30 years on, worries about his accent proved groundless. Shepherd's warmth and enthusiasm, and the music itself, made *Take the Floor* a long-lasting success.

Outside of the music and the language, Robbie is well known for another pursuit: for over 40 years he has served as a commentator at Highland Games, including more than 30 years at the famous Braemar Gathering, which is attended by the Royal Family.

Over the years, Robbie has seen Scottish music grow and change, and his program has reflected that to some extent, but still the thread is the same. He dismisses talk of a musical divide between east and west in Scotland. He cites the prevalence of festivals, traditional music schools, the Accordion and Fiddle Clubs, and similar venues where tunes and styles are swapped back and forth with mutual appreciation.

If there's any divide in the dance music, he says, it's between the style and attitude of village hall (ceilidh) dancing versus that of the Royal Scottish Country Dance Society (RSCDS). Shepherd grew up with the village hall dances, high energy community events with a grand march, Gay Gordons, Strip the Willow, Eightsome Reel, and other popular dances, along with old-time round-the-room dances such as slow foxtrots. The RSCDS dances are more formally structured, and standardized so as to be available round the world. Top RSCDS dance bands travel abroad, though at home some also play for ceilidh dances.

Shepherd was honored in 1998 with an award from the RSCDS for his loyal support of their dance music. He often plays RSCDS dance music on his program, though he doesn't partake in that style of dancing himself, preferring the greater freedoms of the village hall dances he attended as a youngster.

About once a month, his father used to bring home records of some of the great dance bands. By the time Robbie became part of the music scene himself as a radio presenter, he was in awe of the great musicians. He tells of his first meeting with the famous Sir Jimmy Shand. Before the radio show, he explained that he would announce the tune and then Jimmy would play. Jimmy replied that unfortunately this would not work, as the name of his first tune was far too long! But Robbie practiced, announced it, and to this day has never forgotten "Dr. Ross's 50th Welcome to the Argyleshire Gathering."

Subsequently, he and his wife became good friends with the Shands. In fact, Shepherd says he has seldom met any musician he has disliked. "Scottish music is a great leveler," he says, "as is golf."

For his services to Scottish dance music and culture, Shepherd has received many awards, including an MBE from the Queen, and induction into the Traditional Music Awards Hall of Fame. Other recognition has come from the National Association of Accordion and Fiddle Clubs, the RSCDS, and Aberdeen University, which gave him a Masters for his work with Doric and culture of the Northeast.

While working tirelessly to promote an appreciation for Scottish music and culture, Shepherd has himself become an integral part of it. When there's no dance hall nearby for you to take the floor, you can always *Take the Floor* with Robbie Shepherd.

82 ~ KRL Records 30th
winter 2007-08

Nearly 40 years ago at a record shop in Glasgow, a young woman's life was about to change, with reverberations that still affect Scotland's singers, pipers, and bands. It happened the day Gus MacDonald, a sales manager with CBS Records, took young Isobel Waugh aside and said, "You're the only one who works hard in this shop — do you not fancy opening your own record shop some day?" And he made her an offer: if she could save up a certain amount of money, he'd match it.

Three years later, they did it. Just as cassettes were coming on the market in 1972, they opened a shop, and soon expanded to open two more, plus a wholesale music company.

In 1977, they started their own record label, Klub Records, which in 1978 became Klub Records Limited, or KRL. Their first album was a single by comedian Andy Cameron called *Ally's Tartan Army*, celebrating Scotland's 1978 World Cup football/soccer team. It sold 360,000 copies and rose to #6 in the British charts.

Now celebrating its 30th anniversary, KRL is best known for two major sublabels: Monarch Records, which is exclusively devoted to recordings by pipers and pipe bands; and Lochshore, which covers a broad range of Scottish traditional, pop, folk and world music.

KRL's most significant project is its release, every September since 1990, of the World Pipe Band Championships. Now produced on three CDs and a DVD, one CD contains the winning performances by the world's top seven pipe bands, with the second CD presenting the other seven finalists in the competition. The third CD allows us to hear and judge for ourselves the march/strathspey/reel medleys performed in the qualifying heat.

This year's winner of the Worlds was Field Marshall Montgomery, followed by Simon Fraser University, Shotts & Dykehead, 78th Fraser Highlanders, and Strathclyde Police. Of the fourteen finalists this year, eight of them have recorded CDs of their own on Monarch Records.

The Monarch sublabel of KRL began in the late 1980s as a project of Gus MacDonald, to take his mind off the loss of his 3-year-old granddaughter to leukemia. Its first release featured one of Scotland's top solo pipers, William McCallum, the start of a series called the "Pipers of Distinction." Monarch then brought out a recording of the Dysart & Dundonald pipe band, followed by many other well-known bands such as Vale of Atholl, Boghall & Bathgate, Scottish Power, and the Black Watch. A fascinating selection of great pipe bands from overseas is available on Monarch as well, including world champions Simon Fraser University (Canada) and Victoria Police (Australia), and the up-and-coming Los Angeles Scots.

Monarch's catalog includes some 75 piping albums, a tremendous resource for pipers and other knowledgeable listeners. However, it doesn't take a connoisseur to be stirred by the virtuosity, musicality and expressive drumming rhythms of the world's top pipe bands and solo pipers. We may be used to hearing the pipes at various events and festivals, but rarely do we have a chance to hear pipers and bands at the top level of Grade 1, as is offered in these recordings.

Some of KRL's piping albums are found on its other major sublabel, Lochshore. This is because, unlike Monarch, which is reserved for traditional piping, Lochshore presents pipers such as Chris Armstrong, Rory Campbell, Fred Morrison, and Anna Murray, who experiment with new ideas in piping technique, or mix them with other instruments in creative musical arrangements.

The Lochshore sublabel began with the idea of tapping into the enthusiasm for contemporary Scottish bands that make use of traditional music in new ways. The first band on the label was Old Blind Dogs, which continues to be a strong and exciting presence in the Scottish music scene, though no longer recording for Lochshore. Their first six albums on Lochshore, however, continue to be great listening.

Other contemporary artists picked up by Lochshore included Iron Horse, led by singer and piper Annie Grace; Tannas, an exciting Gaelic band; and Craobh Rua (pronounced kreeve ROO-ah), from Belfast, a fine folk band with humorous CD titles such as *If Ida Been Here, Ida Been There*.

Compilations are often a good means of sampling a record label. KRL's double-CD, *New Celtic Dimensions*, includes Old Blind Dogs, Iron Horse, Craobh Rua, the Whistlebinkies, Cape Breton fiddling and more. Several compilation albums are event-related, such as *Scottish Parliament*, celebrating the opening of the parliament with contemporary bands, ceilidh bands, bagpipes and folksingers. A CD commemorating the 550th anniversary of the University of Glasgow came out in 2001, featuring pipers, singers, and harpers, mostly focusing on original compositions. There's also a series with more generic album titles such as *Celtic Airs*, *Celtic Soul*, and *Celtic Spirit*, which pull together a selection of contemporary and traditional music drawn from Lochshore titles.

Hundreds of recordings were made by KRL in the early years and went out of print, featuring singers in the tartan-and-heather tradition of entertainment. These are being released periodically on CD each year on ELM, KRL's budget label, which now has over 150 titles, including singers such as Calum Kennedy, Valerie Dunbar, and Peter Mallan. Some of these fine singers are mixed into the Lochshore label as well, such as Anne Lorne Gillies and her romantic album *The Hills of Lorne*.

The label has also ventured into producing some videos, in addition to DVDs of the World Pipe Band Championships. Some videos were done in conjunction with Grampian TV, such as *Music of the Fiddle*. A stirring set of three videos called *The Blood Is Strong* uses a soundtrack by Capercaillie and tells the story of the Gaelic-speaking Highland Scots, their dispersion throughout the world, and efforts to maintain and revive the Gaelic culture.

As befits a record label begun by two people from the retail music business, KRL has been drawn to record artists that they hope will sell well. Their roster of musicians covers a full gamut of Scottish music, plus a few experiments in pop music, world and roots music, and even a couple of jazz titles. It can be a tough business. Artists sometimes are not pleased by the rough-and-tumble of the economics, while labels sometimes support a band by recording them, only to see the group split up and let the band name sink into oblivion along with its album.

A special trouble today for a traditional label such as KRL is the prevalence of digital copying. Some titles are purchased by one person in a group and copied instead of being purchased for others. CD sales are down significantly, and record shops in Scotland are closing in favor of supermarkets, which carry only top selling titles.

But the internet seems to be picking up the slack to some extent, and KRL, like most other labels, is moving into offering downloads of its music catalog.

Isobel Waugh is thinking of making a celebratory CD for KRL's 30th anniversary. My guess is that it will be dedicated to Gus MacDonald, the former record sales manager who cajoled her into going into business, and helped create and guide KRL with her for three decades. Gus passed away last December 23, after a long illness, one day after his last day of work at KRL.

But Waugh is carrying on with a small staff, putting out the annual World Pipe Band Championships recordings, and a selection of other CDs for KRL, including some of the irreplaceable older masters that have long gone out of print. The Monarch and Lochshore catalogs are a growing treasury of music by Scottish artists, and well worth exploring.

83 ~ *Robin Morton's Temple Records*
summer 2010

In 2008, thirty years after founding Temple Records, Robin Morton was inducted into the Scottish Traditional Music Hall of Fame. He was cited as a pioneer and visionary in his services to traditional music. As I spoke with him this spring, he was hunkering down for a predicted 50cm of snow in his village of Temple, just south of Edinburgh. The last time this had happened, he was told, was some 35 years ago. I calculated that Morton probably doesn't remember that blizzard because he wasn't home. During the 1970s, he was on tour all the time, as both player and manager with the Boys of the Lough.

Robin Morton's pioneering spirit has often been on display. In Northern Ireland in the 1960s, he had formed the Ulster Folk Music Society, researched and written two books on Irish songs, worked in radio, and in 1967, started the group that became Boys of the Lough. Since 1969, he's lived in Scotland, and has become, especially through Temple Records, an especially strong promoter of Scottish musical traditions.

Morton became manager of the Boys because it didn't seem to him anyone else was suited to the job. He filled that role, and after a hectic decade managing and establishing touring networks for the band, he was ready to move on and step into the fray on a new front.

The new front turned out to be Temple Records. Having produced many recordings for Topic Records, he struck out on his own after Topic turned down what Morton felt would be a very promising project. The harper Alison Kinnaird, who happened to be Morton's wife, had done significant research to revive the lost art of Scottish traditional harp, and had developed a versatility in harp performance to match her research. Topic didn't think it would sell, but Robin Morton proved them wrong.

He did the same with his next few releases, including two albums of Gaelic singers, Flora MacNeill and Christine Primrose. At the time, people didn't understand why someone would release such music on recording, but its beauty and expression rose above all objections. Primrose has remained with Temple for other releases, and won "Gaelic Singer of the Year" at the Scots Traditional Music Awards last November.

Soon after starting his label, Morton struck a deal to record and manage the Battlefield Band. He had first met them while he was performing with Boys of the Lough. As Morton recalls it, the Battlefield Band was raring to blow the Boys off the stage with their fresh and energetic playing. He says they couldn't outplay the Boys, who had their own high energy, world-class talent, and tight arrangements, but he admired their attitude. He has since recorded some 25 of their albums and has kept them touring the world despite a gradual shifting of band personnel.

Some 20 different musicians have been members of the Battlefield Band at various times, with four typically performing together at any given time. Only one, keyboardist and singer Alan Reid, stuck with the band the entire time, but there are others who provided continuity by staying with the band for long periods of time. Some stayed for over ten years, including founding member Brian McNeill, who is a singer and fiddler, or singer and guitarist Alistair Russell, fiddler John McCusker, and current band piper Mike Katz. Named after a suburb of Glasgow which was home to the band's founders, Battlefield Band has served as a platform for many other musicians as well, among them pipers Duncan MacGillivray, Dougie Pincock and Iain MacDonald; and singers Davy Steele and Karine Polwart. Its current fiddler, Alasdair White, won two independent music awards in 2008.

Although the group's sound has adjusted to the tastes of its members, it has always featured vocal harmonies, pipes, fiddle, flutes, and plucked instruments. The lack of a drummer has kept them away from ever having a rock sound, though their arrangements can be adventurous. Their mission has been to interpret traditional tunes and songs in a contemporary way, and yet stay true to the feel of the tradition. Hence the band's motto: "Forward with Scotland's Past."

One of Robin Morton's fonder memories as a producer is selling out Usher Hall for a gala show of Scottish traditional music in the early 1980s, including the Battlefield Band, Cilla Fisher, forty Shetland fiddlers, Christine Primrose, and dancers, with introductions by actress Gerda Stevenson. Some of the audience told Morton they never knew before that Scotland had music like that. A simulation of the concert was produced in the studio on Temple's *A Celebration of Scottish Music*.

Gaelic singers on Temple include the sweet voice of Arthur Cormack and the clear, innocent sound of Eilidh MacKenzie. Morton combined these two singers with Christine Primrose to form a trio called Mac-Talla. Their beautiful and uplifting triple harmonies came naturally, Morton recalls, and were a pleasure to work with.

Temple's offerings of bagpipe music encompass top traditional players and bands as well as good players outside the spotlight of the piping world. World Champion bands such as Shotts & Dykehead and Dysart & Dundonald, and solo pipers such as Iain MacFadyen, Dr. Angus MacDonald, and William McCallum are available, plus recordings of other top pipers in recitals at the Piping Centre in Glasgow. One album gives us a window on world-class Scottish drumming from the masters championship competition, "accompanied" by bagpipes. An early Temple release called *A Controversy of Pipers* deliberately promoted the playing of good pipers who were involved in the folk band world rather than the pipe band world, and another CD features smallpipes played by Gordon Mooney.

Robin Morton's career as a producer makes him the hidden glue behind the recordings. The producer is the one who patiently listens, records, urges, prods, and pulls together the artist's best work. He cited his early training as a social worker as one of his credentials for being a good producer. Rather than shy away from tension in the recording studio, he feels he was able to work with it and shape it into good musical results.

In one early recording, Morton brought five good fiddlers together and recorded them in a session setting. They were skeptical at first, but it didn't take long for them to appreciate what came out of it, an album called *Fiddlers Five*.

A broad range of music is covered in Temple's catalog. One historically significant release is a remastering of the legendary fiddler James Scott Skinner's early 20th century recordings. Other albums reach out to present Irish flute and uilleann pipes, Scottish Renaissance music, singer/songwriters, blues, and fine Cajun music by a Scottish band. Morton has experimented with enhanced CDs, which in addition to music, also include special photos and videos when inserted into a computer. He has compiled recordings into boxed sets and published music books related to the recordings. Today, he is struggling with the internet behemoth, and experimenting with offering single tracks online, with CD compilations of those tracks to follow at a later time.

After a lifetime of intense work with top musicians, Morton has little patience for those who stereotype traditional music. A great musician may play an old tune, but by putting his own expression into it, or arranging an interpretation of it with a band, the tune is made fresh and contemporary. And don't get him started about the deadening effects of calling all Scottish and Irish music "Celtic." While "Celtic music" as a genre might be a convenient marketing tool, it is particularly maddening to Robin Morton, who feels that this overused term blandly lumps many strong and diverse traditions into one generic label.

When Morton was inducted into the Scottish Traditional Music Hall of Fame, what probably pleased him most was that the award he received was named after one of his heroes, Hamish Henderson. Henderson, one of the great movers and shakers for Scottish traditional music, received the honor posthumously in 2003, and the award has continued to carry his name since then. The Hall of Fame bio cites Morton's service in the recording industry and his three years as director of the Edinburgh Folk Festival.

Robin Morton's feisty imagination, professionalism and dedication to traditional music have enriched Scotland's heritage through the offerings of Temple Records, the touring of musicians such as the Battlefield Band, and all the influences this work has fostered among young musicians and those yet to come.

84 ~ *Greentrax 20th*
winter 2006-07

The year: 1985. Police Inspector Ian Green's last night on the job. The song cycling through his mind was a Scottish one. No piano bar jazz, no cigars, slick dames, or "Here's looking at you, kid." Just an Edinburgh police inspector putting on his coat one last time, after 30 years on the job, and sauntering out into what appeared to be the golden sunset of retirement...

Fast forward to 2006. Former police inspector Ian Green releases a triple CD commemorating the 20th anniversary of his Greentrax record label. In July, he was awarded an honorary doctorate by the Royal Scottish Academy of Music and Drama. Last year, he received the Hamish Henderson Services to Traditional Music Award.

There were hints, back in his police days, that this kind of thing might be in the offing. Green organized the Edinburgh Police Folk Club, fondly known as "Fuzzfolk," in the 1960s, and went on to co-found the Edinburgh Folk Club. Greentrax Recordings was a natural extension of his passionate pastime. But its success in fostering Scotland's music could not have been foretold.

Green has always been close to the Scottish music scene. When he spots a promising new formation of musicians, he'll approach them to offer encouragement and a chance to record. "We have had a commitment," he says, "to offer debut albums of new talent who deserve to be heard by a wider audience."

The result is astonishing: over 350 recordings representing the cream of Scottish traditional music. The new triple CD samples 59 Greentrax albums, with two discs representing a decade each of traditional music releases, and the third disc spotlighting the "cutting edge," innovative and experimental takes on Scottish music.

Every track is a quality performance, and very listenable. Such a broad range of performers could have been thrown together in an arbitrary smattering of disparate sounds, but these CDs flow well from track to track, without dwelling for long on any one style — a tribute to Ian Green and his knowledge of the music.

Green's view is that Greentrax has "tried to cover every aspect of Scottish traditional music and the contemporary approach to this music, and I think the result is a label which has greater breadth and depth than any other Scottish label."

For those familiar with Scottish music, the three CDs comprising the Greentrax 20th anniversary album will be a rewarding tour de force through the sounds and sentiments of Scotland's best musicians, including some artists you probably haven't heard before. Listeners not conversant with a broad range of Scottish traditional music can hardly help but feel energized by such a display of national talent.

Most of the two traditional CDs feature vocal selections, backed by excellent musicians. These include the clear Gaelic voices of Catherine-Anne MacPhee and Mairi MacInnes, ballad singer Heather Heywood, Isla St. Clair, Jean Redpath, and the rough-hewn Jeannie Robertson. We are stirred by the sonorous Rod Paterson singing Burns, the modern folk sound of the late Davy Steele, and the strong voices of Dick Gaughan, Jim Reid, Archie Fisher, Eric Bogle, and Ed Miller. For an antidote to the dour, there's the Glaswegian humor of Adam McNaughtan. Perhaps the most exciting song is the final track of the album, the live recording of Sheena Wellington singing Burns's "A Man's A Man" at the opening of the Scottish Parliament.

A track from the ever-popular folksingers, The McCalmans, was taken from their first Greentrax album, which gave the fledgling record label a boost in its first year of existence. The McCalmans have happily stayed on through the years, releasing their most recent album, *Scots Abroad*, on Greentrax in September 2006.

Piping selections offered on the anniversary CDs include performances by two accomplished musicians who tragically passed away last year, Gordon Duncan on Highland pipes, and multi-instrumentalist Martyn Bennett playing Scottish smallpipes. Australian Mark Saul, formerly with the world champion Victoria Police Pipe Band, plays a wild piping composition of his own. Two of Scotland's top Grade 1 pipe bands, Scottish Power and the Vale of Atholl, offer up fine piping with creative arrangements. One track on the cutting edge CD presents the unique pipe band MacUmba, with South American drums and rhythms backing up the Highland pipers.

Fiddle enthusiasts will enjoy listening to Aly Bain's duo with accordionist Phil Cunningham, Alasdair Fraser with cellist Natalie Haas, Shetlander Chris Stout, Orcadian Jennifer Wrigley, the high energy of the band Fiddlers' Bid, Gordon Gunn's eclectic virtuosity, and the beautiful tone and soulfulness of the late Willie Hunter. A track from the label's very first release features original fiddle tunes by Ian Hardie.

Varied hues of musical moods radiate from the many accomplished folk bands included on these CDs, such as Deaf Shepherd, Malinky, Easy Club, Ceolbeg, the venerable Whistlebinkies, the atmospheric Shooglenifty and Peatbog Faeries, the young band Slainte Mhath of Cape Breton, and the Australian-Scottish Colcannon. One of Scotland's most experienced folk bands, Jock Tamson's Bairns, and one of the youngest, GiveWay, can also be heard.

High energy ceilidh dance music is present and accounted for, led by accordionist Fergie MacDonald on one track, and Freeland Barbour of the Occasionals on another. The wild accordionist Sandy Brechin does his thing as well, mixing a dance beat with lively contemporary tunes.

Scottish Latin from Salsa Celtica, Scottish lute, Scottish and Breton guitar music from Tony McManus and Alain Genty, and party music from Keltik Elektrik add intriguing glimpses of the vital music scene in Scotland that is represented on the Greentrax anniversary celebration CDs.

So what's missing from this seemingly comprehensive roster of musicians? Ian Green admits he knows nothing of pop or rock music, and as a result does not record those genres. He also generally steers clear of straight classical and jazz, "although these influences have entered the Scottish traditional stream," he says, "and no bad thing, too!"

When Greentrax began, there was a feeling that much of Scotland's real traditional musicians were neglected by the British music industry, with a few exceptions such as Temple Records. Scotland's musical image was often limited to the "heather and haggis" music derived from the music hall scene, and from films such as *Brigadoon*. In Green's opinion, this stereotyping of Scottish music "caused untold damage to Scotland's real traditional music, which has taken years to recover."

After some 350 Greentrax albums, and vital developments in Scotland's educational and performing circuits, perhaps that recovery can be considered complete. Donnie Munro, former lead singer with the Gaelic superstar band, Runrig, recently signed on to Greentrax for an album released this past summer. "I am delighted to be signing to one of Scotland's finest record companies," said Munro, "and one which has played such a major role in developing and sustaining the industry here in Scotland."

Brian McNeill, singer, writer, fiddler, a founding member of Battlefield Band, and Head of Scottish Music at the Royal Scottish Academy of Music and Drama, put it simply: Greentrax "changed the face of Scottish music, permanently and hugely for the better."

85 ~ *Simon Thoumire's Footstompin' Records*
fall 2010

Scotland's concertina virtuoso, Simon Thoumire, is seen in a video sitting on his couch playing a tune by J.S. Skinner, with a snare drummer. They appear serious and focused and their music continues uninterrupted as the doorbell rings, the TV starts up, and Thoumire's 7-year-old son wanders in and out brandishing a light saber or dressed as an alien.

This is part of the UK's first recording released, not on CD, but on YouTube as a video playlist, under the title "Self Portrait 2009." It is perhaps emblematic of the way Scottish traditional music and culture persist amid the whitewater rapids of shifting demands from our internet-connected world. At a time when the music industry is confronting a flow of changing interests from music fans, Simon Thoumire and his Foot Stompin' Celtic Music business have been at the forefront of experimenting with new ways to promote Scottish music and culture through an array of online services.

At the same time, Thoumire has worked hard in the "real world" to help Scottish musicians develop their art, working with both young people and professional musicians through organizations such as Hands Up for Trad, and Distil.

Foot Stompin' was originally a record label, but a few years ago, after putting out about 40 titles focused mostly on new artists, the label stopped releasing new recordings and moved into promoting the full range of Scottish music and culture, exclusively online. As Thoumire points out, the internet environment was not exactly crying out, "Please make more records!"

The Foot Stompin' website now offers recordings by some 650 artists (each with a bio and audio samples) in all Scottish genres of music, plus

DVDs and hundreds of books, including not only music books but also books on Scottish history, culture, language and even comics and cookbooks. It's a family business run by Simon Thoumire along with his parents.

All of the content is Scottish. Thoumire says he has "really loved and believed in Scottish music." Although he has eclectic tastes in his own playing and listening, he feels Scotland needs and deserves the support. "There is lots of support for Irish music everywhere," says Thoumire, "but Scottish music itself is a massive genre, and to do it properly you have to concentrate on that."

The Foot Stompin' site builds community through free services. Its forum has many posts written each day and thousands of viewers, as people discuss Scottish music, gigs and festivals, plus occasional forays into urgent topics such as Scotland's performance in the World Cup. There are free guides to Scottish festivals, musicians, songs, sessions, pipe band championships, and history. Free podcasts present a half-hour of Scottish music every two weeks, DJ'd by Thoumire. More than 5,000 listeners download each podcast either from Foot Stompin' or from iTunes. A biweekly newsletter brings people up to date, and the site even offers ringtones with Scottish music. Foot Stompin' also maintains a Facebook page with well over 3,000 fans.

For aspiring musicians, there is an affiliated website, cleverly named Ayepod.net. Here, online video courses are available in Scots song, Scottish harp, five different styles of Scottish fiddle, concertina, and beginning whistle, taught by some of Scotland's best musicians.

All of this is, of course, demanding work for Thoumire to keep up with, as we can see in "Give Me Peace," another video in his "Self Portrait" playlist on YouTube. Here, he is besieged by endless requests for his time, and at one point his cartoon head spins round the screen, a feeling most of us can sympathize with at some time or other.

Simon Thoumire first learned music on recorder, and then took to the bagpipes, eventually winning piping awards, and performing at the Edinburgh Tattoo and in Usher Hall. But his music career took off after he learned the concertina. In 1989 he won the Young Tradition Award (now called the BBC Radio 2 Young Folk Award).

He has became a virtuoso, coaxing out of that little octagonal squeezebox the most astonishing array of traditional Scottish tunes. Yet he has the ability to move unexpectedly from a traditional tune into free improvisation, building melodic ideas or letting them peter out, or allowing his concertina to hiccup or bray like a mule. Then suddenly, after a foray into improvisation, the traditional tune will resume effortlessly. His playing is intense and expressive, and always articulate.

His eclectic musical interests trace in part to the musical tastes of his father, but Thoumire also credits the vitality of the Edinburgh music scene during the 1990s, where musicians of all genres often explored music together. That's how music came together such as, for example, Hamish Moore's blend of bagpipes and jazz saxophone on Moore's album *Farewell to Decorum*.

Thoumire has recorded many CDs of his own over the years, including two duo CDs with jazz/folk pianist David Milligan, and two with his band Keep It Up. He has also performed on many albums by others, such as John McCusker, Pipe Major Robert Mathieson, Alan Reid, and Thoumire's wife, fiddler Claire Mann. Several recordings feature his own compositions, such as his bagpipe concerto, or "Music for a New Scottish Parliament." And, of course, he can be heard on YouTube. When not wrapped up in Foot Stompin' and other projects, Thoumire is currently playing with the innovative English guitarist Ian Carr.

Thoumire's experience in winning the Young Tradition Award in 1989 led him to appreciate the importance of meeting other musicians and learning the craft of becoming a successful musician. Hands Up for Trad is an organization Thoumire created to allow for such opportunities. It hosts the annual BBC Radio Scotland Young Traditional Musician Awards, with a semifinalists concert in October, and the finalist awards concert at the end of January. However, the focus is not just on winning a contest but on educating young musicians through workshops and touring experience, giving them the tools to build a career in Scottish traditional music.

Hands Up for Trad also hosts the MG Alba Scots Trad Music Awards in early December, which celebrates Scottish traditional music in all its forms, including members of the traditional music industry. One portion of this ceremony weekend is the induction of notables into the Scottish Traditional Music Hall of Fame.

Another activity sponsored by Hands Up for Trad is the Tinto Summer School in Lanarkshire, a residential summer school with top Scottish musicians as teachers.

Although Thoumire cares deeply about helping young musicians succeed, he has also organized educational opportunities for professional musicians. Distil is the name of this project, co-directed with David Francis of the duo The Cast. This project began in 2002 and has grown to expand into England and Wales, as well as Scotland. Its premise is to spur the development of new ideas and skills by placing professional traditional musicians in workshops with leading musicians from other genres. For example, they may work with a classical composer, an accomplished improviser, and a traditional musician from another culture. The Distil showcase concert in October presents about ten new compositions each year.

Keeping track of Simon Thoumire's varied activities, whether online or in the real world, is a little like keeping up with all the apps on a smartphone. We can pick the ones that appeal to us, and be grateful that a tireless musician and supporter of other musicians continues to make it all happen.

Thoumire says he's always looking for new ideas, but is well aware that once a new activity gets started, it takes a lot of work to keep it going. While managing his own music and family, plus Foot Stompin' Celtic Music, Hands Up for Trad, and Distil, he likes to retreat to his favorite camping spot overlooking Loch Tummel in Pitlochry. You can view it in his video "And Relax," another part of his "Self Portrait" album on YouTube. But as always with Thoumire, expect surprises. That seemingly still photo of the beautiful loch is not really a still photo. Towards the end, as you listen to the slow air played on concertina and guitar, you'll see the distant silhouette of Simon Thoumire leaping for joy.

86 ~ *Compass Records*
spring 2008

When you think of Nashville, what kind of music comes to mind? Scottish, by any chance? Believe it or not, the home of the Grand Ole Opry is also home to one of the world's largest Celtic record labels, Compass Records.

The first releases on Compass in 1995 featured primarily American songwriters, but within a few years the label began including Celtic music. The owners of the company, Alison Brown and Garry West, are themselves musicians, and when they toured the UK and Ireland in the late 1990s, they discovered such fantastic Celtic musicians that they soon expanded musical friendships into business relationships back home.

Brown made her musical mark playing with Alison Krauss' band, Union Station, and now tours with her own band. She also happens to have a degree from Harvard and an MBA from UCLA, with a bit of investment banking experience to boot. Garry is experienced in record production, and together, they sought to create a company that was both business-savvy and musician-friendly.

A number of Scottish musicians have found in Compass a doorway to North America. Some had self-produced CDs at home and were pleased to have an American label. Others had earlier releases in the US on the major Celtic label, Green Linnet, but felt themselves to be on a sinking ship, and were just scrambling for the lifeboats when Compass steamed by and offered a ride.

In fact, Green Linnet was struggling, and after several deals fell through, it was Compass who came to the rescue a few years ago, and bought the label, around the time of Green Linnet's 30th anniversary.

With that purchase came the opportunity to revive and expand the recordings of a number of great Irish and Scottish musicians. Excellent older CDs are being reissued, some new ones are using the Green Linnet label, and several Green Linnet artists are releasing new albums on the Compass label.

The acquisition of Green Linnet enabled the venerable Scottish band, the Tannahill Weavers, to add a new CD last year on Compass, *Live and In Session*. This is no less than their twelfth release on the Green Linnet/Compass labels. This year the band celebrates its 40th anniversary of touring Scotland and the world. The Tannahill Weavers offer a classic fare of traditional Scottish music, with pipes, fiddle, whistle, and guitar, but with driving energy, strong vocal harmonies, and a generous dollop of comedic talent (this last is not available on their CDs, unfortunately!). In their US tour this summer, they'll be visiting the Midwest and New England, including dates in Hartford and the Maine Highland Games in mid-August, and the Celtic Classic Festival in Bethlehem, PA in September.

Another active and exciting Scottish band helped out by Compass Records is Old Blind Dogs, which this past year put out its tenth album, *Four on the Floor*. Originally based in Aberdeen, the band includes many tunes and songs from the rich traditions of Scotland's northeast, with creative arrangements and instrumentation.

One of my favorite Compass albums from the past couple of years is *Downriver* by Karen Matheson, the singer with the Gaelic band Capercaillie. Her rich, compelling voice and her selection of some of her own favorite English and Gaelic songs is both moving and entertaining.

Last year, Compass released *Black Water* by the versatile young singer and guitarist Kris Drever of Orkney. Drever's clear voice, intriguing lyrics and intricate guitar style are complemented by well-known Scottish musicians such as Phil Cunningham, Donald Shaw and John McCusker. Another Compass release features Drever as a member of Lau, a high-power trio formed in 2005, which was nominated in four categories for the 2008 BBC Folk Awards. Their album, *Lightweights & Gentlemen*, is well worth a listen for the intelligent songs and the professional polish, not only of Drever but also fiddler Aidan O'Rourke of Blazin' Fiddles and accordionist Martin Green.

Another recent CD on Compass is *Peacetime* by singer Eddi Reader. Her unusual and exciting rendition of Robert Burns songs came out on this label as well. Her new album includes new songs and traditional ones such as "Leezie Lindsay" and "Ye Banks and Braes," sung with Reader's unique, sensuous vocal style. Both this recording and Drever's *Black Water* were produced by Scottish fiddler John McCusker, whose musical arrangements in these CDs are personal favorites of Compass's owner, Alison Brown.

Bringing Scottish recorded music into the US is difficult to sell unless the artists can be heard live. For this reason, artists from overseas appreciate that Compass has made it a priority to support touring artists.

Owners Brown and West have an interesting take on how people relate to the label's Celtic music. They regard Celtic music as a "lifestyle" music, as opposed to what they call "fashion" music. Fashions are highly popular for a short time until people move on to other fashions, whereas "lifestyle" music is something people live with, even define themselves by. Brown suggests that people interested in "lifestyle" music like to own real CDs, see concerts, and know who plays what song and why. This may explain why Compass was interested in acquiring rights to Green Linnet's physical recordings, while another company bought the digital rights. Time will tell how this will play out, as the music industry adjusts to the changes wrought by the internet.

One thing the test of time tells us is that a good recording doesn't go bad. Considering the number of fine older Celtic recordings on the Green Linnet label, it is a relief to Celtic music fans that Green Linnet's recordings are now in good hands.

Scottish artists formerly on Green Linnet, and now available through Compass, include the Tannahill Weavers, Old Blind Dogs, Johnny and Phil Cunningham, Andy M. Stewart, Relativity, Silly Wizard, Capercaillie, Sileas, and Wolfstone. Many of the world's top Irish artists can also be found on this label.

Compass has also released recordings of Scottish musicians in its own right, including fiddlers Aly Bain, John McCusker and Catriona MacDonald, the edgy Gaelic singer Alyth McCormack, and guitarist Tony McManus, and as mentioned above, Kris Drever and Eddi Reader.

Brown and West didn't set out to make their company one of the world's largest record labels in Celtic music. They seem to have moved in that direction due to their relationships with top Celtic musicians. Last fall, in addition to picking up Green Linnet and honoring its commitments to Celtic artists, Compass took another step toward expanding its service to Celtic music, by acquiring Tayberry Music. This small company retails thousands of hard-to-find Celtic and folk recordings, focusing primarily on music played by Fiona Ritchie, the Scottish host of *The Thistle & Shamrock* radio program. Her National Public Radio program airs throughout the US. Alison Brown credits Fiona Ritchie with going a long way towards educating Americans about quality Celtic music.

Although it's a challenge to get the music of Scotland out to people in the US, Compass Records sees the potential. Garry West views the Scottish music scene as "incredibly vibrant, really creative," fostering a lot of the changes coming about in Celtic music today. "There's a fire and energy there among the newer Scottish artists that resonates, that really engages the audience."

These are encouraging words for Scotland's music, coming to us from one of the world's leading Celtic music labels, located just a five-minute drive from Nashville's Country Music Hall of Fame.

87 ~ *Preserving Printed Music*
fall 2015

Scottish music, like any living tradition, requires both an engaged community to support and develop it, and a knowledge of the past to nourish it. Listeners and dancers make use of the songs and tunes, while musicians learn from each other and bring fresh ideas to old music. And yet Scottish music is also a remarkably literate tradition, with great respect for what has gone before.

We often hear performers announce the names and even composers of the tunes they play. They certainly learn a great deal from other musicians, but they also like to consult books, both new and old, to learn more good tunes, or to gain a better appreciation of ones they already know.

Scottish music books date back to the 18th century, when traditional musicians and their publications were supported by aristocrats. At the same time that Mozart was hired by an Austrian prince to compose classical music, Niel Gow was employed by the Duke of Atholl to play and compose strathspeys and reels, and fiddler and composer William Marshall to do the same in the service of the Duke of Gordon.

Between 1780 and 1810, Niel and Nathaniel Gow published about 20 collections of traditional tunes, dedicated to no fewer than ten different aristocrats – dukes, duchesses, earls, marchionesses, countesses. One publication was simply dedicated to "the Nobility and Gentry of Scotland." Generously sprinkled with compositions by the Gows, the Gow Collection primarily features tunes composed by others, or traditional melodies commonly played in their time. The Gows even stated their intention to standardize the tunes by writing them down.

These books have not been easy to find. For many years, people had to buy photocopies at libraries or from enterprising publishers selling copies, but finally an edition of the Gow Collection was typeset and published. It contains hundreds of tunes selected by the editor, and alphabetized for ease of use. While this is helpful for finding tunes, the editing and reformatting leaves out commentary, bowing, ornamentation, and arrangements of tunes for dancing, as found in the original books.

Thanks to the internet, we are fortunate to be able to view the original Gow Collection, however. The International Music Score Library Project (IMSLP) allows us to see or download the publication in its entirety. There, we can find charming and informative commentary omitted from the modern book, such as an explanation about the book's "Medleys – a Strathspey and Reel following alternately in their respective Keys, as the frequent changing the Key more or less has been found to offend the Ear." We also learn which dance tunes the publishers felt were best played slowly when not danced.

Another important old Scottish music book available from the IMSLP website is the Fraser Collection of 1816, which preserves songs and tunes from the Jacobite uprisings, as well as some written by the editor, Captain Simon Fraser. The influential Skye Collection of 1887, with over 400 tunes drawn from a variety of sources then available, is now available online for free from Google Books.

Fiddler James Scott Skinner, the "strathspey king," published hundreds of his own tunes, along with traditional or contemporary compositions, in important books such as *The Scottish Violinist* of 1901, or the *Harp and Claymore* of 1904. These books are not difficult to find in their typeset and reprinted editions. However, the original manuscripts, with a great deal of background information, can also be found on a website from the University of Aberdeen.

Starting in the mid-18th century, many Scottish musicians managed to publish their own tunes. One of them was Angus Cumming, whose book of 60 tunes came out in 1780. He lived in Strathspey (strathspey is Gaelic for "valley of the river Spey") in the northeast of Scotland, and his family included players such as John Roy Cumming, who apparently was a highly regarded musician in the early 1700s. The Cummings may have been among the originators of the strathspey, which Angus Cumming described as "an old Highland reel." The strathspey is a type of tune unique to Scotland, with strong dotted rhythms and four beats per measure. It is essential to Scottish dance music, whether social or Highland dance, and seems to have a strong connection to the rhythms of Gaelic song and speech, which would have been the everyday language for the Cumming family.

This June, Angus Cumming's music was celebrated as part of the 250th anniversary festival of his home town, Grantown-on-Spey. Hamish Napier, a native of the town and an accomplished traditional musician, performed a concert of Cumming's tunes drawn from a book called *Highland Collections*. This reprint compiled, in one volume, seven 18th and 19th century books by fiddlers from the eastern Highlands, east of Inverness.

Highland Collections was published in 2005 by the Highland Music Trust. It is a hefty 8x12 publication on high-quality glossy paper, and is one of the Trust's best-selling books, probably because Scottish musicians were excited that they could find great old tunes that were nevertheless new to today's traditional music scene.

The Highland Music Trust has published four other classic music collections in high-quality editions. Their first was the *Athole Collection,* a compilation of nearly 900 tunes from 1884. The *Glen Collection,* from the 1890s, contains just under 300 tunes, plus composer biographies and source information. The *Mackintosh Collections* pulls together four books published in the late 18th century by "Red Rob" Mackintosh, the great fiddler and sophisticated composer to whom Niel Gow sent his son Nathaniel in order to study music. The *Marshall Collections* presents a readable reprint of the brilliant compositions by William Marshall (1748-1833), whom Robert Burns regarded as the finest composer of strathspeys of their time. Burns used some of Marshall's tunes for songs such as "Of A' the Airts the Wind Can Blaw", which Burns wrote for his wife on his honeymoon.

Eric and Helen Allan, who run the Highland Music Trust, have been members of the Inverness Fiddlers for some 30 years. They were inspired to start the publishing project in the 1990s after hearing fiddler Alasdair Fraser speak about how difficult it was to find old Scottish music books in Scotland. Eric, now 80, is a retired lawyer, but has always been a fiddler, and lately a publisher, on the side. Using funds earned from a client following the sale of a Highland estate, the Allans started the Trust to support Balnain House, a center in Inverness for traditional music lessons, concerts, exhibitions, and a cafe. After Balnain House closed its doors in 2003, Eric and Helen decided to continue publishing old collections, and added a few modern books as well, including a book of original tunes by Paul Anderson, one of the finest Northeast fiddlers, and several by Eric himself. They have also used funds to provide travel assistance to students headed to the Ceòlas summer school on Uist, and to help musicians such as Sarah-Jane Summers to make an instructional fiddle DVD, and fiddler Lauren MacColl to record music from *Highland Collections* on a CD called *Strewn With Ribbons*.

While the Highland Music Trust continues to sell its books, and has added a couple of trustees to ensure that it will continue, the Allans have stopped publishing printed books, and moved online for their new projects. To date, they have put 18 old Scottish music collections on their website for free download. One of these is the smallest of the books, and a rarity, in that it features compositions by a woman. It is comprised of 14 tunes by Magdelina Stirling (1766-1846). Notable in this tiny book is the powerful and growly tune "Perthshire Hunt," which has become a standard in Scottish and Irish sessions everywhere.

Thanks to the Trust and various internet projects, some of the most important of the classic Scottish music books are now available. The living culture of Scottish music is strong today, and nourished by the voices of the past.

88 ~ *Hands Up for Trad*
spring 2018

Like the Oscars or the Grammies, the annual "MG Alba Scots Trad Music Awards" represents something more powerful than the glitz and pageantry of live TV, something more meaningful than winning and losing. These ceremonies embrace and promote a community of artists and the whole culture of traditional music in Scotland.

Behind this awards ceremony is a small organization called Hands Up for Trad, led by its Creative Director, concertina player Simon Thoumire, who has tirelessly supported the music, musicians, and music industry of Scotland for the past 20 years. Hands Up for Trad manages more than 20 projects, with funding from Creative Scotland, a Scottish governmental organization promoting the arts. Captivated by tradition and tuned into technology, Thoumire seems to work nonstop managing projects and dreaming up new ones, and yet he still finds time twice a week to personally mentor musicians and help them solve problems in their careers or musical projects.

Thoumire recalls when he himself competed in a prominent competition for young musicians back in 1989. He arrived in London primed for an intense experience, only to be astonished at how friendly all the competitors were to each other. The same congenial atmosphere impressed him when he judged a similar competition 10 years later. It's a cooperative spirit that now pervades his events and builds community spirit.

The Scots Trad Music Awards ceremony first took place in 2003, and is held every year in early December in various locations throughout Scotland. Since 2008, it has been called the MG Alba Scots Trad Music

Awards in honor of its sponsor. MG Alba partners with BBC Scotland to broadcast BBC Alba, Scotland's Gaelic TV channel.

The ceremony airs live, with announcements in Gaelic and English, and sometimes in Scots as well, so that it is accessible to everyone. The glamorous evening includes performances by a variety of musicians, in addition to the much anticipated awards presentations. Last December, awards were given for Album of the Year (*All We Have Now* by the Elephant Sessions), Scottish Pipe Band of the Year (Inverary & District), top live act (Skippinish), Gaelic singer of the year (Robert Robertson), and Scottish Folk Band of the Year (Talisk). All nominees and winners were selected by the public in a process that tallied over 100,000 votes from around the world. As Thoumire points out, it's the public that goes to the gigs, buys the CDs, and generally supports the music, so the public should make the decisions. Only the Album of the Year category makes use of an expert panel to whittle the list of nominees from about 45 to 20 semifinalists, with the finalists and winner chosen by public vote.

To help people choose the Album of the Year, and also to promote some of Scotland's top bands, Thoumire released a free podcast on November 1, which is still available from Hands Up for Trad. Containing well over an hour of music, the podcast presents one full track from each of the 20 semifinalists for the prize, along with links to each band's website. This is one of over 160 free monthly podcasts, allowing online visitors from some 140 countries experience the best in Scottish music. In addition to these audio broadcasts, Thoumire has also published videos on the Hands Up for Trad YouTube channel, including interviews of musicians, collations of Scottish music videos (with whimsical introductions by Thoumire himself), and a very fun Trad Awards Quiz show pitting one band against another in a humorous game-show setting.

Hands Up for Trad runs two other major awards ceremonies. One is a dinner at which musicians and music industry professionals are inducted into the Scottish Traditional Music Hall of Fame to honor lifetime achievements. Awards are also presented for Services to Community, Services to Scots (support for the Scots language and culture), and Services to Collecting (of traditional music and songs).

The other awards ceremony is the BBC Radio Scotland Young Traditional Musician Awards, which began in 2000 and was so successful that it inspired the launch of the Trad Music Awards. The Young Traditional Musician Awards was started by Simon Thoumire along with Clare McLaughlin and the TMSA (Traditional Music and Song Association), in 2000.

This event, focused on honoring and encouraging younger musicians, begins each year with a series of performances. Twelve semifinalists emerge after the first round, at which point they are taken on a music retreat to meet, play music, and learn about marketing and other aspects of the music business. Another competitive performance follows, narrowing the competitive field to six finalists, who perform at the Celtic Connections Festival in late January to determine the winner. Though winning is the hope, there's a supportive atmosphere throughout the event. If you want to hear the future of Scottish traditional music, keep an ear out for the six annual finalists from these competitions. The 2018 winneres were bagpiper David Shedden, singer Amy Papiransky, singer Hannah Rarity, pianist Rory Matheson, guitarist Luc McNally, and whistle player/bagpiper Alexander Levack.

The educational side of the Young Traditional Musician Awards is only the tip of the iceberg for Hands Up for Trad. Three other major projects focus almost entirely on education. Distil is a unique project allowing professional Scottish traditional musicians to work with professionals from very different genres, such as jazz and classical music, to mutually broaden musical horizons. Tinto is the name of a series of residential summer music schools held in the countryside for high school kids. A weekend program is offered for adults, as well as some "taster" weekends of instruction and fun given free of charge to kids aged 8-14. A similar program, the Edinburgh Youth Gaitherin, gives urban kids a chance to study with professional traditional musicians.

Some of the other projects run by Hands Up for Trad are not primarily physical events. The Inspiration Award is presented to spotlight musicians who innovate with Scottish music. The Business Limelight Award recognizes one business each month that contributes to the arts and culture of Scotland. Landmark Awards recognize institutions who demonstrate longstanding support of live music; for example, the Irvine Folk Club was honored for 50 years of producing concerts. Another honor, called Scotland Live, rewards producers who establish new regular venues for live music by providing financial help and professional mentorship.

The list of supportive programs includes the Chorus Awards, which highlight musical offerings within local communities. Originally focused on community singing, this project has grown to recognize musical community work of various kinds. Recent Chorus Awards went to a fiddle instructor, a charity fundraiser, a youth brass band, a public ukelele and singing group, a singing group for people with respiratory ailments, and a Shetland effort to teach schoolchildren to sing in their local dialect. Another community-based project is Scotland Sings, which runs five workshops a year, with local workshop leaders teaching people to sing, join a choir, or even start a new one.

In addition to teaching, encouraging and recognizing achievements, Thoumire's organization also provides online services for musicians. Folkwaves makes available tracks by Scottish musicians to radio stations for airplay. The Music Hub gives composers of new tunes a chance to upload and share them with others – over 400 tunes have been shared publicly since 2015. The Tour Directory is a listing of venues and promoters for those planning tours in Scotland. Finally, there's TradLive, launched in September 2017, which Hands Up for Trad calls the world's first online trad music festival. Presented on YouTube, this event featured a full day of live Scottish musicians performing and talking about their music.

Hands Up for Trad is running so many programs to promote, educate, and boost traditional music in Scotland that Simon Thoumire and his Hans Up for Trad deserve an award for many years of tireless support of Scottish music – if there were only some other organization to present it!

Then again, perhaps the increasingly vibrant and tight-knit community of musicians, industry professionals, and listeners that keeps Scottish traditional music alive and growing is the best reward of all.

89 ~ *Fiona Ritchie*
summer 2009

In the early 1980s, Scottish radio host Fiona Ritchie attended her first Highland Games in America, and was at first baffled by the passion Americans showed towards her home country and its traditions. Then she caught sight of a poor Appalachian family, the children "sitting quite reverentially as their father recorded the sound of all these pipe bands on his little tape recorder." It was at that moment that she "realized that magical musical connections exist between my part of the world and many others."

Those magical connections between Scotland and the US have been strengthened all across America for millions who listen to Fiona Ritchie's National Public Radio program, *The Thistle & Shamrock*. For nearly 30 years of weekly radio shows, Ritchie has actively explored with her audiences the vibrant music of Scotland, Ireland and related traditions.

Ritchie pioneered for listeners a new and compelling way of listening to Scottish and Irish music. She molds her shows around themes of culture, traditions and artists. An early April show called "For Freedom Alone" was devoted to music related to the April Arbroath Declaration, in honor of Tartan Day. A March show was devoted to solid Irish music in celebration of St Patrick's Day. One program was entitled "Under the Stars," and explored music and songs inspired by ancient landscapes under the sun, moon, and stars. Program themes devoted to Celtic love, Robert Burns, Celtic rock, and Welsh music give a small window into the endless variety of Ritchie's method of tying together Celtic music in a fascinating collage of musical samples. She selects music based on quality and her own personal taste, which has been well honed by listening to the best music for decades. Even if the lyrics of a song are unintelligible to most listeners because it's sung in Gaelic, its beauty is still aired for all to enjoy.

The popularity of her radio show has both reflected and amplified a tremendous resurgence in the quantity and quality of Celtic music.

"I have seen such a change in the Scottish cultural climate since I first came to the US in 1980 and started my radio work," says Ritchie. "There is confidence here, a fluency in expression, and a real sense of cultural identity which is both contemporary and deeply rooted in our history and heritage."

When she was growing up in and near Greenock, west of Glasgow on the river Clyde, television programs used to display a "very prettified version of our heritage," says Ritchie. "Let's be honest — that was some programmer in London deciding how to represent Scottish culture."

The Thistle & Shamrock has helped move the media representation of Scottish and Irish music in a new direction. "It took a while," says Ritchie, "for people who appreciated the cultural importance of the music to actually get control of the ways of sharing it."

Her first radio program aired on WFAE in Charlotte, North Carolina, in March 1982, while she was in the US for graduate studies. Since then, *The Thistle & Shamrock* has grown to enchant the listeners of nearly 400 radio stations throughout the USA, plus Armed Forces radio and worldwide internet streaming.

Wisely brushing off initial skepticism from some that Americans might not take to her foreign accent on radio, Ritchie went on to host one of America's most popular and long-lived radio programs. She presents music she is passionate about, including both new releases and older titles in order to explore the context of songs, tunes, styles and artists. Her interviews of musicians offer in-depth portraits of those who dig out and interpret music from the Celtic traditions.

Her first radio interview was with Battlefield Band pianist and singer Alan Reid. Reid says the band quickly learned that many listeners in their audiences had been educated and intrigued by Ritchie's radio show. Paddy Moloney of the legendary Irish band, The Chieftains, said that "her show widened our audience tremendously." If a CD was played on *The Thistle & Shamrock*, most stores wanted to carry it. They knew their customers would come looking for it.

Outside the radio station, Fiona Ritchie has also been active. In 1989 and 1990, she organized a tour of Scottish musicians through the US, going beyond radio to bring live music to many audiences. She was a host at a tribute to Scottish music at the Smithsonian Folklife Festival in Washington DC and at the huge Fourth of July celebrations there as well.

After moving back to Scotland in the early 1990s, Ritchie presented music for many BBC Radio Scotland and BBC Radio 2 programs, as well as producing a number of live concerts, including one for Prince Charles at Holyrood Palace.

From her current home base in rural Perthshire, Fiona Ritchie now devotes most of her time to her long-time passion, *The Thistle & Shamrock*, with the help of her administrative colleague back in North Carolina, Margaret Kennedy. She also works on Thistleradio.com, which offers a broad spectrum of information, interviews, playlists, links to streaming stations, audio clips, and even podcasts with previews of new music before it's broadcasted on the show.

Ritchie's latest project, however, is a book. Entitled *Wayfaring Strangers*, the book will trace the musical migration from Scotland to Appalachia, including excerpts of conversations with musical icons such as Jean Ritchie, Doc Watson, Archie Fisher and Pete Seeger. (See Chapter 68.)

Fiona Ritchie hopes some day to go beyond the book and find a way to "breathe life into that historical connection between Scotland and Appalachia." When that happens, she'll complete a circle of sorts, better grasping that yearning for heritage that first struck her when she saw a poor Appalachian family recording pipe bands on a little tape recorder at her first Grandfather Mountain Highland Games.

SECTION EIGHT
Summing Up the Future

David Francis

Young Musicians

Nobody Wants Covid!

The World Is Listening

Independence Campaigners

ABOUT SECTION EIGHT
Summing Up the Future

The future of Scottish music will grow from knowledge of its past. The folk revival was exciting because musicians discovered the vitality of old tune books, dances, vocal and instrumental traditions that had been sequestered in local communities or swept under the rug by media portrayals of Scotland.

The rededication of the Scottish Parliament in 1999 was a symbol of the revitalization of Scottish culture, and the government has supported its own traditions and languages in ways that London never did. It is hard to know whether music has reflected or helped spur the growing confidence of Scots in their nation and its history. Time will tell whether the United Kingdom is able to hold together the four nations it has tried to keep under one aegis, but it is apparent that each nation's culture is its own, and the musical contributions of Scotland are more complex and vibrant than most have given it proper credit for.

In this section, we "sum up the future" by reviewing the past and inspecting signs of coming changes.

We'll begin with a government-sponsored institution intended to bring together and nurture the makers of Scottish traditional music. Then we'll glimpse the future by taking note of the young musicians, how they learn, what their aspirations seem to be, and where their careers are aiming.

In 2020, musicians everywhere were hit with a total loss of gigs and income due to the coronavirus pandemic. We'll take a look at its impact and how the musicians, listeners, and institutions adapted to the scourge.

Not to conclude on such a dour note, we will look at various signs of great hope. The internet has shaken up the music industry but also provided many opportunities for musicians and listeners alike.

Finally, we'll look back at many of the chapters in this book and review how far Scottish music has come in rising to the challenge of alerting a nation and the world to what it has to say to us all. Its richness of musical expression has, with the help of good gardeners, grown out of the fertile soil of the past and breathes fresh ideas in today's sun, wind, and sea.

One musician told me he believed that artists help create and shape change, and judging from the tremendous fear that dictators seem to have of powerful folksingers and popular musicians, perhaps this idea is right on target. Music can help us honor and understand our past and thereby shape the future.

At the beginning of this book, we discussed Handel's choice to honor his adopted nation, rather than the nation of his birth. Like Handel, we don't have to be born Scottish to enjoy and appreciate Scottish music, and to help it grow. But only Scots have the right to be proud of their music, and it is they who share the responsibility to see their players flourish.

Music is there to celebrate victory and to lift up the oppressed. It will always be with us, if we nurture the musicians.

90 ~ Trad Music Forum
spring 2020

For decades after World War I devastated Scotland's population and culture, much of Scottish traditional music was swept into local shadows. The bagpipes held sway as the primary international image of Scotland, a high art proudly developed and maintained in Scotland, and promoted by the British military and media. After World War II, however, Scottish traditional music experienced a folk revival, and gained traction in the 1970s and 80s as musicians eagerly explored their roots. In the 1980s and 90s, a whole generation of fine young musicians and singers was trained via educational efforts such as the Fèis movement, which started in 1981 in the far western isle of Barra and has grown into a national network of instruction and performance.

By the time the Scottish Parliament reopened in 1999, Scottish traditional music was a vibrant and growing phenomenon. That same year, the first graduates of the UK's only bachelor's program in traditional music received their degrees at the RSAMD (now the Royal Conservatoire) in Glasgow.

Soon, the new Scottish government began nurturing Scotland's strong musical culture by providing funds, coordination and networking to support the work of independent organizations such as Hands Up for Trad, the Celtic Connections Festival, the Fèis movement and many others. A great deal of effort has gone into teaching the skills of performance and career development for musicians, and creating more venues and appreciation for the music.

One of the organizations set up to promote and advocate for Scottish traditional music is the Traditional Music Forum (TMF). It began in 2003 as an advisory group for the Scottish Arts Council, and by 2009 had developed into an independent organization dedicated to advising and coordinating policy makers, musicians, educators, festivals, and businesses about what is happening and what should happen to nurture the music.

For the past decade, TMF has been supported by Traditional Arts and Culture of Scotland (TRACS), which helps coordinate Scottish traditional music, storytelling and dance. TRACS is financially supported by Creative Scotland (formerly the Scottish Arts Council), which in turn is funded by the Scottish Parliament. These layers of bureaucracy, established not to control but to nurture, are in themselves a testament to the vibrancy and complexity of the traditional arts industry in Scotland.

The goal of TRACS is to showcase Scotland's heritage and shape the political, cultural and economic environment in which these native arts flourish. The chair of TRACS, piper Gary West, used to write the piping column for *Scottish Life* magazine. West says, "There's a huge amount going on all the time here in Scotland in the traditional arts in general, and the TMF is one cog in that wheel."

The reason TMF is just a cog in the wheel is that, as the name "Traditional Music Forum" suggests, it is not creating music or making policy decisions, but serving as a forum to bring together the movers and shakers of the traditional music scene. As West puts it, TMF has given all parties in the trad music industry "the chance to get together to talk about all manner of issues, and to give a strong voice to traditional music within what is a very wide and diverse cultural scene here in Scotland."

The TMF's monthly newsletters feature events and announcements of new programs, and its blog invites musicians to share insights into how they approach their careers. The director of TMF, David Francis, explains that "a key pillar of our work is support for non-formal educational organizations and the musicians who work for them," offering workshops, formulating a code of quality practice, and managing an active mentoring project. Francis is a guitarist, singer, songwriter and has organized various educational projects. One of his claims to fame is the beautiful recording he made with his wife, Mairi Campbell, of the original version of Robert Burns's "Auld Lang Syne," which was used in a Hollywood movie.

In addition to being TMF's director, David Francis has also worked hard to help found the European Folk Network in 2016, and is now its chair. Some 20 countries are working together in the new group; at its first conference last fall, about 15% of the attendees came from Scotland.

Membership in TMF includes around 40 organizations from all parts of Scotland who bring their ideas to the table or use TMF for networking and information. These include agents, producers, venues, music industry companies, performing groups, festivals, the musicians' union, town representatives, and educational organizations such as Fèis groups, the National Piping Centre, and University of Edinburgh's School of Scottish Studies. Recently, the constitution was amended to allow individuals to join, and there are already about 20 who have.

Some members, such as Ceòlas in South Uist, or the Hebridean Celtic Festival in Lewis, are too far away to travel to meetings but appreciate TMF's newsletters and feedback, and its role as an advocate for the trad music industry.

Others, such as Live Music Now, are more locally involved. Live Music Now's vice-chair, Carol Main, serves on TMF's board and appreciates the bigger picture that TMF provides about the traditional music industry. A recent research report sponsored by TMF, for example, gathered data about traditional musicians' incomes, geographical distribution, frequency and location of performances, information about touring, recording, marketing, and some of the barriers to success for various ages, genders, and genres. Such a report helps groups like Live Music Now to better target their work where it is needed most.

Live Music Now, which helps emerging musicians reach new audiences, was founded by violinist Yehudi Menuhin, and originally focused on classical music. Today, about half of its musicians are traditional musicians, due to the growth in strength and quality of traditional music in Scotland. This transition from a fully classical focus to having a strong traditional component reflects major changes in Scottish culture over the past 50 years.

A window into the outdated attitudes about Scottish culture that prevailed 50 years ago can be glimpsed in the first report of the Scottish Arts Council, which was established in 1967. This report, part of the annual report of the Arts Council of Great Britain, began with a very strange observation: "There is an old saying that you can give a dog a bad name and hang him. Perhaps, too, if you give him a good one you can expect great things of him." After detailing its support of the arts in Scotland, the report complained that Scotland has "often looked backwards at lost battles and... a dimly remembered golden age of makars and musicians and dancing in the streets." Was this a hint of hope that this "golden age" might be revived, or a dismissive comment about such hopes? Unfortunately, it was probably the latter, given that the music supported by the Council at that time was exclusively classical. This British report then concluded the section on Scottish arts with a decidedly patronizing comment referring to the lion, historically a symbol of Scotland: "A living dog, with a good name, is better than a dead lion."

Within three decades of that report, the "dimly remembered golden age" of Scotland's traditional music had already been revived, and it has only grown stronger since then. Scottish music is an increasingly integral part of the culture, and an important export as well. This fall, the University of Edinburgh launches a Masters in Traditional Arts Performance, apparently the first such degree in the world. Thanks to major efforts by musicians and organizations, supported by Scotland's own Parliament, and the advocacy of groups such as the Traditional Music Forum, the lion is now very much alive and well.

91 ~ Young Musicians
winter 2002-03

"Where did they come from? Out of the blue?" That's part of the buzz when young musicians wow an audience with versatility, sheer energy, and sometimes a good deal of musical maturity as well.

After all, some of those 20-year-olds have been performing for half their lives. But where? Perhaps in musical families, community ceilidhs, jam sessions, and competitions. Scotland hasn't always made it easy for young people to learn their native music. Nowadays, however, the opportunities are growing, and the corresponding impact of Scottish musicians in Celtic-based music around the world is noticeable.

A 2002 compilation CD called *The Future Sound of Gaeldom* purports to be "the essential selection of contemporary Celtic music" but the contents are almost exclusively Scottish. Veterans such as Capercaillie are featured along with young, restless bands such as Croft No. Five. Martyn Bennett, Paul Mounsey, Big Sky, and the Peatbog Faeries specialize in pushing the traditional envelope using electric effects; meanwhile, under the name "Keltik Elektrik," several stalwarts of the Edinburgh folk scene let loose, reshaping traditional tunes with contemporary dance beats.

Gaelic songs on this album are given a contemporary atmosphere, not only by members of Capercaillie, who are well known for this, but also by Mouth Music, Nusa, and Alyth McCormack. In other tracks, traditional tunes or parts of tunes are played in a new context. For example, Angus R. Grant, the son of the great Highland fiddler of the same name (though different middle name!), plays fiddle tunes that swim in the dance grooves of the band Shooglenifty, and the Scottish band Salsa Celtica incorporates a bagpiper playing a traditional pipe tune as if it was meant to be accompanied by a salsa beat.

The Future Sound of Gaeldom describes these artists quite well as "a new breed of young musicians, steeped in the musical roots of their land, pioneering an innovative fusion of traditional songs and instrumentals with contemporary sounds and beats."

Perhaps the key phrase there is that they are "steeped in the musical roots of their land." This is what makes them part of "Gaeldom."

While some choose to use traditional music as a launching pad, others pour their fresh energy into music within traditional boundaries. Either way, knowledge of the tradition is the foundation that identifies the music as Scottish.

These days, young musicians in Scotland are finding it a little easier, and more respectable, to learn and perform the music of their own land. Some primary and secondary schools are beginning to offer traditional music lessons, and others are making room for it through after-school activities. The Gaelic College in Skye has been offering music classes since the 1980s. A summer music and dance program in Uist called Ceòlas began in 1996. The Royal Academy of Music and Drama in Glasgow now offers a BA in Scottish traditional music, after a long period of slowly warming to a respect for Scotland's own music. An associated program at the National Piping Centre offers a BA in piping. In 2000, a center for Scottish traditional music was established at Plockton High School, supported by the Scottish Parliament, the first of several such projects.

One of the most active groups promoting traditional music in Scotland is the Fèis (pronounced "faysh") movement. Begun as an educational festival and presentation in 1981 on the Isle of Barra, this organization has expanded to offer some 37 Fèisean this past year, about half of them in the Highlands and half throughout the rest of Scotland, including the cities of Edinburgh, Glasgow, and Aberdeen.

The Fèisean, geared towards kids aged 8-18, offer workshops and performance opportunities in traditional instruments such as fiddle, clarsach (harp), accordion, bagpipes, and whistle, as well as instruction in Gaelic song, language, dance, drama and Gaelic sports. Most of the 4,000 participants are involved in the music and song workshops. Supported by the Scottish Arts Council and the Highland Council, many of the Fèisean present year-round programs in their communities, drawing on the talent of local instructors.

Among the more than 200 Fèisean teachers can be found many top performing musicians, busy "backstage" working with the youth of Scotland. The director of the national organization of Fèisean is a great Gaelic singer, Arthur Cormack, and Fèis employees include some names to look for, such as clarsach player Ingrid Henderson and Gaelic singer Rachel Walker.

In Edinburgh, the brilliant concertina player, Simon Thoumire, created his own program to encourage young musicians, which culminates in the annual BBC Young Traditional Musician Award. The award competition is for musicians aged 16-25 and is clearly intended to be as educational for all the competitors as it is rewarding for the winner. The process includes a weekend for twelve semifinalists playing music together and taking workshops in how to find gigs, write bios, develop stage presence, and handle rehearsals and sound checks. At their performance, six finalists are selected, who go on to play at a sold-out concert in Glasgow at the Celtic Connections Festival.

The winner of the award gets to record an album on Thoumire's Foot Stompin' Records label, is given career advice and materials for a year, and receives bookings, including a followup concert at the next year's Celtic Connections Festival.

The first two winners of the award were singer and fiddler Gillian Frame of Arran, whose band recorded *Back of the Moon* last year, and singer and accordionist Emily Smith of Dumfrieshire, whose album, *A Day Like Today*, will feature music reflecting the traditions of her home area. The new winner will be announced at the Festival in January 2003.

Supportive organizations and programs make it easier for young people to get involved in the music. Through the years, of course, the passing along of tradition has depended on great individuals who served as teachers and mentors in song, pipes, fiddle, and so on. A fine tribute to one such teacher, Donald Riddell, recently took the form of a CD called *A Highland Fiddler*. Riddell was a piper and fiddler who taught hundreds of young people in the Highlands. The album features his compositions performed by three of his fiddle students, Iain MacFarlane, Duncan Chisholm and Bruce MacGregor, who are now professional soloists, and band members of Blazin' Fiddles, Wolfstone, and Cliar. In their turn, they also teach at Fèisean, passing the music to a new generation.

It is exciting to think of how many talented teens are learning traditional music in Scotland today. I wish I could list all the names to watch for. Many of them will join their elders (the ones in their 20s!) whose talents are now bearing fruit in Scotland's thriving music scene.

One is fiddler Alasdair White of the Isle of Lewis, who at 13 was already being called a "maestro" in *The Scotsman* newspaper. Now 18, White has earned a spot in one of Scotland's longest running bands, the Battlefield Band, renewing the band's mix of musical maturity and youthful vigor. The band's new album, *Time and Tide*, even features some of White's compositions. White replaced John McCusker, who, at the ripe age of 29, left the band after touring with them for 11 years.

Where do musicians like White come from? We could simply call them talented, but talent is only potential. The growing support in Scotland for traditional music is certainly encouraging, for it takes dedicated teachers, playing opportunities, and great performances to inspire young people to work hard and turn their talent into a living reality.

We get to sit back and enjoy the results.

92 ~ *Young Trad Winners*
winter 2012-13

Only a few decades ago, a youngster in Scotland had to be pretty dedicated to traditional music in order to withstand the pressures against taking this music seriously. Many kids shied away from it entirely, and there was little, if any, support for it in the educational system.

But after the disruptions of World War I, musical traditions continued within families, in communities that valued them, and in post-World War II folk clubs and festivals. Starting in the 1980s, mini-festivals and workshops for traditional arts called Fèisean grew from a single event in the Western Isles to hundreds of events sponsored by more than 40 Fèisean a year, inspiring and training young people throughout Scotland.

School programs began to support traditional music, recognizing it as an important part of Scottish culture. In 1996, the Royal Conservatoire of Scotland (until September 2011 known as the RSAMD, or Royal Scottish Academy of Music and Dance) started offering a full-time, four-year undergraduate degree program in Scottish music. In 2000, a high school program called the National Centre of Excellence in Traditional Music began in Plockton.

Since then, award programs such as the BBC Scotland Young Traditional Musician of the Year and the MG Alba Scots Awards have given young people high-profile recognition for their talents, and the Celtic Connections Festival has established youth showcases and commissions for new compositions.

A new generation of Scottish musicians has been equipped with skill, confidence, and knowledge. Their virtuosity and adventurous spirit, strongly rooted in tradition, has made them fearless exponents of Scottish music.

One such bold young Scottish musician is the accomplished harper and singer Maeve Gilchrist of Edinburgh. A few years ago, I had the opportunity to play Scottish music on a small tour with her and my son, pianist Neil Pearlman. Inspired by working with these young people, I wrote a tune called "Fearless," expressing my awe at their virtuosic handling of their instruments in the service of traditional Scottish music. Maeve has settled in the Boston Celtic scene, as has Neil. Both bring their knowledge of jazz and other genres into music that is strongly connected to Scottish tradition. Still in her mid-twenties, Maeve has performed at many major events, including the opening of the Scottish Parliament, Celtic Connections, and with major artists such as Esperanza Spalding, Alasdair Fraser, Unusual Suspects, and Martyn Bennett.

Fearless is the word that often comes to mind when I hear today's young Scottish musicians. It is a contrast to the reserve and even self-doubt that seemed more prevalent in past decades. Brian McNeill, a founder member of the Battlefield Band, recalled the freshness of hearing Cape Breton bands in the 1990s. Their unabashedly powerful renditions of Scottish tunes and songs cut through the caution and, as he put it, "prettiness" that Scottish musicians often seemed to feel was required of them at the time.

Last summer, I attended an Edinburgh house concert to hear two of Scotland's top young award-winning musicians in a converted storefront. On stage were Anna Massie and Mairearad (rhymes with "pirate") Green. Interspersed with jolly commentary by Anna, and mild, unassuming smiles and wry quips from Mairearad, their music sparkled with energy, creativity, and fun. Mairearad, from Wester Ross, plays the accordion and pipes, and Anna, from Kinlochbervie in the northwest Highlands, plays guitar, fiddle, mandolin, and tenor banjo.

Mairearad plays accordion and pipes with ease and grace. She is also a composer, winning the 2009 MG Alba Scots Composer of the Year. She wrote a film score, and a work for the Celtic Connections Festival. This festival's New Voices program commissions young composers to create new works based on traditional idiom, and then to pull together a band of contemporary Scottish musicians to perform their pieces. Mairearad's composition, called "Passing Places," was presented to a sold-out audience at the festival, and was subsequently recorded and published. Mairearad has toured with Karine Polwart, Eddi Reader, and the Poozies, in addition to working with Anna.

Anna Massie also composed a work for Celtic Connections, and won the 2003 BBC Radio Scotland Young Traditional Musician of the Year award. She has been nominated several times for Best Instrumentalist at the Scots Trad Music Awards. Netrhythms, an online site reviewing traditional music, called Anna "another wonderful example of how youth embraces and refreshes traditional culture." In her duo with Mairearad, and sometimes adding guitarist and singer Jenn Butterworth, Anna has toured Europe and Canada as well as the UK. She has recorded with top whistle player Michael McGoldrick, with Phil Cunningham and Aly Bain, and with Cape Breton fiddler and pianist Troy MacGillivray.

In recent years, Anna was tapped to join the band Blazin' Fiddles, along with another young musician, fiddler Jenna Reid of Shetland. Jenna won the 2005 Best Up and Coming Artist award at the Scots Trad Music Awards, and has played with Dochas, Unusual Suspects, and in Aly Bain's televised Transatlantic Sessions, now on DVD.

In the audience at Anna and Mairearad's house concert last summer was a great young fiddler named Mike Vass, who is also a multi-instrumentalist and composer. He, Anna, and Mairearad performed at the London Olympics, representing Scottish music. Like Anna and Mairearad, Mike has composed and recorded a Celtic Connections New Voices commission, which he called "String Theory." He was a BBC Young Trad Musician finalist, and has played with a number of bands, including Malinky, and as the Scottish fiddler with Fiddle Rendezvous, a band which showcased five different traditions. When he can, Mike plays (and has a CD) with his twin sister, Ali, on piano and vocals.

Scotland need look no further than its own youth to enjoy some of the best talent in today's traditional music scene.

93 ~ *Pandemic*
summer 2020

In the second week of March, I contacted some folks on our summer music and walking tours in Scotland to tell them that out of 5 million people, Scotland only had 18 cases of coronavirus, had an excellent and free health care system that everyone could avail themselves of, and had been doing a fair amount of testing in order to have accurate numbers. We thought at the time things might possibly be in pretty good shape for travel by June. How fast things changed!

Two days after that, one Edinburgh musician was playing at a midweek session when he got an email that his gig at a church ceilidh that weekend was canceled due to the spread of the virus. Within 48 hours, the rest of his gigs for the month were gone. Since then, the remaining gigs for the year have been canceled and with it much of his income. He's reluctantly gone into teaching online and has presented some live performances on Facebook with a link for donations.

A Gaelic singer from Glasgow was on a ten-date tour at the time. His tour was cut short after two shows. No more performances, but he is able to continue teaching his university Gaelic courses online.

A well-established touring musician based outside of Glasgow took the initiative of canceling his Canadian tour because he was not convinced that the audiences would be comfortable coming out to see him, and was not even sure he and his wife could get back home. He lost the tour income plus his travel expenses, and is crossing his fingers that tours planned later in the year to Germany and Australia will be able to run.

The meetings of strathspey and reel societies, pipe bands, fiddle and accordion clubs, and traditional music schools in Glasgow, Edinburgh and Aberdeen, as well as all music sessions at pubs (often led by a paid musician) have all been suspended. One fiddler, Duncan Chisholm, started a #CovidCeilidh hashtag on Twitter, where many musicians have posted tunes each day to entertain each other and build a musical online community. Bruce MacGregor, leader of the band Blazin' Fiddles, and owner of MacGregor's Pub in Inverness, started a daily live Facebook session at the pub for all to watch and play along with in the safety of the internet.

One Scottish fiddler from the Borders lost his gigs but has taken this opportunity to focus on completing his Masters in Folklore through the University of Aberdeen via internet.

In Orkney, The Reel in Kirkwall had to close, depriving Orkney of a busy social and musical center with its cafe, shop, concerts, sessions, and music lessons. The Reel's music classes and lessons, taught and coordinated by the well-known fiddle and guitar duo, the Wrigley Sisters, are going strong online, however. Another Orkney musician was scheduled with his band to play at large upcoming music festivals, such as Cambridge Folk Festival, Hebridean Celtic Festival, Shetland Folk Festival, Orkney Folk Festival, and the St Magnus International Festival. All have been canceled. The band is no longer sure whether or when they can release their new album. Fortunately, this musician is able to make and email videos to his fiddle students to keep them going, and has a job with the local council for additional income.

Up in Shetland, music gigs have evaporated, but some musicians have additional jobs and teaching that can be done from home. It's been especially tough there. A couple brought the virus back with them from Italy and in a short time, there were 24 cases, a toll well out of proportion to the rest of the UK. Shetland acted quickly, however, taking the initiative before the UK government did, by canceling two Up Helly Aa celebrations, closing the schools, and promoting a strict social distancing policy, which slowed the spread of the coronavirus.

In the Outer Hebrides, music programs at Benbecula College, the University of the Highlands and Islands music program, and Ceòlas in South Uist are all continuing online, keeping musicians employed, and students busy and progressing.

Musicians who were teaching traditional music in Scottish primary schools had to stop several weeks early, but some sponsors of these programs, such as Fèis Ross, have been able to continue paying instructors for the missed sessions.

Fèisean nan Gàidheal has also been able to pay musicians for lost work. Based in Skye, this organization manages cultural programs throughout Scotland, particularly in the Highlands and western islands. Fortunately, Creative Scotland and Bòrd na Gàidhlig have continued their funding, so Fèisean nan Gàidheal is able to offer good will payments to their music tutors, equivalent to full pay through the end of the school year for 95 full-time-equivalent (FTE) positions.

Arthur Cormack, director of Fèisean nan Gàidheal, said that all their instructional programs and other activities have been canceled. "We take seriously our responsibility to look after employees and contractors at all times," said Cormack, "but more so during this difficult period." Some local Fèis committees are postponing their events to later in the year, hoping things will be under control by then, and others are moving their activities online.

Various charities and governmental programs have stepped up to help musicians. Creative Scotland, which is funded by the Scottish government, established a "Bridging Bursary Fund" with an initial investment of £2 million to help freelance artists who have lost significant income due to the Covid virus. Help Musicians, an independent charity for professional musicians, created a £5 million emergency fund, with additional donations from Spotify, Amazon, the Royal Society of Musicians, and Arts Council England.

The Musicians' Union set up a £1 million hardship fund for its members, and PRS (Performing Rights Society), which licenses compositions and pays royalties to support musicians, established an emergency relief fund for members who are suffering a loss of income due to the pandemic. Many Scottish traditional musicians, particularly bagpipe composers, work with PRS for their recordings.

The UK government is reaching out with a "Covid-19 Self-Employment Income Support Scheme" which seeks to provide self-employed workers such as freelance musicians with income equivalent to 80% of their average income from the last three years. There is also a government effort to provide a form of sick pay to these self-employed workers, equivalent to the statutory sick pay required of regular employers.

It is heartening to see the support and appreciation, and yet the fact remains that in Scotland, as elsewhere, musicians have been hit hard with a significant loss of income from canceled gigs, without knowing when these events will return. Many have adapted by teaching online and performing online in scheduled performances that provide listeners an opportunity to donate to the performers. This not only helps the musicians, but lifts the spirits of their house-bound listeners.

Our music and walking trips were postponed until after the pandemic, but our travelers will enjoy a chance to meet and hear our music guests online this summer. As with so many efforts to find silver linings to the isolation, this solution gives the musicians a chance to share their music and still earn a fee, while transporting listeners to a world beyond the isolation many are experiencing.

"As ever in a crisis, music is keeping people going," said Arthur Cormack. "It would be great if, at the end of this, people remember how their spirits were lifted by the music and they continue to support those musicians into the future."

94 ~ *Internet Music*
spring 2013

Wherever you live, you can enjoy Scottish music via the internet. Listen to radio programs 24/7, or read about great clarsach players, Gaelic singers, fiddlers and pipers while you hear them perform. Download podcasts to enjoy personal radio programs on your computer or mp3 player, or look up audio samples of an artist before buying an album or attending a concert.

These offerings represent a major shift in the way people create, distribute, and listen to music. It's certainly exciting but also a bit confusing, not least to the industry itself. The ease of recording and sharing music digitally has shaken the foundations of physical products like CDs and the businesses that have depended on them. Artists are experimenting with streaming, downloads, auctioning or even giving away CDs and downloads so as to bring people to performances. Many musicians are reaching out to fans in new ways with social media, including services such as KickStarter or Artistshare, to create music funded by their fans.

But while musicians and music businesses struggle to adapt to a new world, listeners can enjoy hearing and learning music in ever-changing ways. Let's take a look at some ways to find Scottish music online. We won't clutter up the text with URLs, though – it's best to search for the most current addresses to find them.

The Scottish government created an informative website with concise descriptions of many aspects of Scottish music, along with recorded tracks. This site was organized by Education Scotland, which was formed in 2011 through the merger of several government organizations in support of Scottish curricula and education technology.

Music is just one of the many subjects addressed by this site for educational purposes. Information and excellent audio tracks drawn from CDs were made available to illustrate a broad variety of topics about Scottish music. One section discussed the instruments popular in Scotland, with recordings of great musicians playing the pipes, fiddle, clarsach (harp), bellows pipes, accordion, and dance band music. A section on Gaelic songs presented nearly 70 songs sung for various purposes, each with words and a recording. Other links explored different styles of tunes, how songs have traveled, songs and tunes for kids, and multiple versions of the same tune. For example, one discussion included five different recordings of the tune "Mrs MacLeod of Raasay" along with an explanation of where the tune came from.

If you'd like to just listen to Scottish music without stopping to read about context, you can try any of several internet radio stations and podcasts. BBC Radio Scotland allows you to listen to its programs online any time until the next edition of the program airs. It's easiest to find a BBC program if you know the exact title. There are three weekly programs devoted particularly to Scottish music: *Pipeline* is hosted by Gary West (*Scottish Life's* piping columnist); *Travelling Folk* (don't forget the two Ls!) hosted by Bruce MacGregor who airs a variety of music and interviews top Scottish musicians; and *Take the Floor*, Robbie Shepherd's show featuring dance bands as well as other styles of Scottish music.

Celtic Music Radio, based in Glasgow, is available online, and calls itself "Scotland's first listener supported music station." Its goal is to broadcast and promote an appreciation for a full range of Celtic music, but with a particular focus on artists living in the Glasgow area. Scottish traditional music, as well as various other genres, are aired on this station.

Simon Thoumire, the brilliant concertina player and tireless promoter of Scottish music, produces free weekly podcasts which anyone can download from his Footstompin Records site. These can be heard on a computer or put on an mp3 player. Each podcast includes about six tracks, or a half hour of great music, with brief commentary by Simon to introduce each selection. The only slight bit of advertising is the occasional reminder that if you like the music, you can buy it from Footstompin Records. In May, Simon produced his hundredth podcast, choosing music from legendary folk bands Easy Club, Battlefield Band, and Silly Wizard, a Gaelic song by Julie Fowlis, and an old Scots song sung by Rod Paterson. All the Footstompin podcasts, dating back to 2007, are still available.

One popular way to hear Scottish music online is on YouTube, which has an astonishing collection of videos, giving you a chance to watch performances by great Scottish musicians over the past century. For example, all the performers featured in Simon Thoumire's hundredth podcast listed above can be viewed in performance on YouTube. There are also amazing older clips, such as one showing Harry Lauder teaming up with Charlie Chaplin in a 1917 film made to benefit wounded soldiers during World War I.

Another way to hear Scottish music without necessarily seeking out a particular artist is through a streaming service such as Spotify, Rhapsody or Pandora. These sites do not allow you to download the music to keep, but do give access to a large selection, though it's good to keep in mind that there are many artists not represented on these sites. Musicians appreciate your listening to their music, but unfortunately they only earn about a thousandth of a penny each time a recording of theirs is played on these services!

MusicScotland allows people to find Scottish CDs or DVDs. Each album is presented with audio samples taken from various parts of the recording. You can learn about many artists on this site that you otherwise might not have heard of, and can gain enough of a sense of their music to decide whether to buy it.

Other online resources are available if you have a particular artist in mind, such as artist websites, Facebook pages, and stores such as Amazon, where individual tracks as well as CDs can be purchased. CDBaby is similar, and though it doesn't contain as much Scottish music as Amazon, it does allow you to search by region. Bandcamp has a wide selection, including free streaming and fees favorable to musicians. All these services will inevitably change as technology requires.

It's hard to guess where all this availability of music will end up for Scotland and for music in general, but it's worth exploring while you can. It's a great way to become acquainted with some of the great Scottish musicians, whether they've been around for decades, or just made a splash in the scene last month.

The availability of free digital music, and the ease of copying music rather than buying it, raises the question as to whether there will continue to be enough people purchasing recordings, funding creative projects, and attending live concerts, that the musicians can afford to keep on making their music. There's no substitute for the spirit and energy of a live musical performance, so hopefully concertgoers will be in no short supply. But enthusiastic fans who try too hard to get free digital music risk killing the golden goose.

Overall, technology is expanding our opportunities to explore music. When we want to explore the latest fiddle band, or hear what Gaelic psalm singing is like, or listen to a favorite song recorded by a new artist, we can turn to the internet for access to great Scottish music, any time, and just about anywhere.

95 ~ *Scottish Music Rising*
winter 2014-15

The recent independence campaign in Scotland reverberated throughout Scotland, England, and even around the world. September 18 revealed a confident Scotland, with nearly universal voter registration, a vigorous debate, and support for independence surging to 45% by the time of the vote.

It was gratifying to see Scottish self-confidence on display, after having watched it grow on the music scene over the course of 35 years, as an observer, performer, teacher, and promoter of Scottish music. For more than half that time, of course, I've also been writing about Scotland's music. Taking a look at a few of our previous chapters, we can trace the amazing development of Scottish musical confidence in recent decades.

On the heels of the 1979 devolution referendum, the 1980s were a time of exploration for Scottish music. Temple Records had just started up in 1978 in response to a lack of interest in Scottish traditional music by Topic, the English folk label (see Chapter 83). Ian Green started Greentrax recordings in 1986 to spotlight Scotland's music, also with the sense that many of Scotland's musicians had been neglected by the British music industry. Green felt there had been a stereotyping of Scottish music which had "caused untold damage to Scotland's real traditional music" (see Chapter 84).

In 1982, Fiona Ritchie began her *Thistle & Shamrock* radio program in the U.S., which, despite initial fears about her Scottish accent, turned into one of National Public Radio's longest running programs. Ritchie grew up near Greenock, and recalls television programs showing a "very prettified version of our heritage. Let's be honest – that was some programmer in London deciding how to represent Scottish culture." In the past 30 years, Ritchie says, "I have seen such a change in the Scottish cultural climate. There is confidence, a fluency in expression, and a real sense of cultural identity which is both contemporary and deeply rooted in our history and heritage" (see Chapter 89).

Fiddler Alasdair Fraser used to speak of the "cultural cringe," a sense that many Scots were somewhat embarrassed by their own culture. In his youth, despite winning the National Mod for fiddling, he could hardly find session musicians familiar with Scottish tunes. The stifling of Gaelic and Scots added to Fraser's feeling of being tongue-tied about his own culture (see Chapters 20 and 28). But through his relentless performing, teaching, and encouraging musicians to find their own voice, and in the context of the growing vitality of Scottish music, Alasdair feels the "cultural cringe" is virtually gone, like old baggage tied up and left on a shelf (see Chapter 49).

I began to notice this "cringe" in the first decade or so of directing the Boston Scottish Fiddle Club. In contrast to the unabashed pride of Irish musicians in Boston, many Scots that I brought in for workshops and concerts seemed not only reserved but curiously conflicted. At times I wondered if they feared that overplaying their Scottishness might cross over into undermining their Britishness. The director of a teen Scottish fiddle orchestra once told me that his group not only played Scottish music "but also the good stuff – Handel and Haydn." To his credit, he got the kids playing Scottish music, but he did not seem to respect it very much. That same group now has a director who has his own ceilidh band, and a degree in traditional Scottish music from the Royal Scottish Academy of Music and Drama (RSAMD, now the Royal Conservatoire).

The decision in 1996 by the RSAMD to institute full-time degree programs in traditional Scottish music added legitimacy to traditional music, building on developments of the previous decade. The Fèis (pronounced "faysh") movement, starting with a single event on Barra in 1981, grew to engage thousands of students aged 8-18 in learning traditional arts throughout much of Scotland, employing hundreds of instructors. Other supportive institutions have been developed, such as those led by Simon Thoumire's Hands Up for Trad, including a summer school and various awards aimed at encouraging and honoring both young musicians and professionals (see Chapter 88).

When the Scottish Parliament arrived in 1999, it moved quickly to implement Scottish Arts Council recommendations. Within a year, the first high school music program began, at the National Centre of Excellence in Traditional Music at Plockton.

David Francis of The Cast, who has worked with the Scottish Arts Council and many other high-profile projects aimed at students as well as professionals, said recently that "the biggest change over the last twenty years or so is the sheer number of young people now playing traditional music, and the astonishingly high standard at which they do so." (See Chapter 90.) Much of this is thanks to skill and confidence developed at schools, camps and other programs — "the infrastructure which supports the younger player," as harper, teacher and bandleader Corrina Hewat put it. It is an infrastructure "which was not around when I was younger," she adds. "I have an increase in confidence, too. The music I play is not a minority music anymore, but a vibrant music connecting all facets of the community together."

Another source of inspiration and understanding came from the creation in the 1990s of the Celtic Connections Festival in Glasgow, with its annual three weeks of top-notch traditional and new music (see Chapters 72 and 78), and across the Atlantic, the cross-fertilization of Scots and Cape Bretoners at the Celtic Colours International Festival in Cape Breton (see Chapter 73).

Musicians from Cape Breton, Nova Scotia had a strong impact in Scotland, especially in the 1990s. Not only did they present an exciting old style of playing Scottish music, but they also inspired many Scottish musicians to let go of their "cultural cringe." Brian McNeill, a founding member of the Battlefield Band, described a time when "the Scottish folk club bands took for granted that what we were going to do was this gentler thing." When the Cape Breton musicians arrived in Scotland with "this burst of energy," it made him want to see Scots play their music for all it was worth (Chapter 17). Singer and fiddler Mairi Campbell helped reintroduce Scottish (Cape Breton) stepdancing (see Chapter 33), and piper and pipemaker Hamish Moore brought back ideas about old-style bagpipe playing (see Chapter 58).

In my phase as a distributor of Scottish recordings to US stores, I found at first a great skepticism about Scottish music early in the 1990s, but by the end of the decade, even the primarily Irish record label Green Linnet was releasing more and more Scottish music. "Scottish music sells," they told me. When Compass Records bought Green Linnet, its director, Garry West, pointed out that the Scottish music scene is "incredibly vibrant, really creative," fostering a lot of the changes coming about in Celtic music today (see Chapter 86).

Accordionist and composer Phil Cunningham, Artistic Director of Scottish Music at the Royal Conservatoire, summed up the cultural changes in this way: "I do a lot of work with children and adults who are just learning to play, and the current climate in Scotland is just great. I'm not worried about being an old person any more, because I know there's going to be music for me to listen to" (see Chapter 73).

Has the vitality of the Scottish music scene contributed to Scotland's political self-confidence, or has it just been a reflection of it? Alasdair Fraser tells me he is "in the middle of making a documentary about the power of music and its ability to cause change socially and politically as we have seen in Scotland over the past 30 years."

The vibrant effort to explore Scottish music over the past 30 years has created a healthy new generation of Scottish musicians (see Chapter 92), equipped with virtuosity and adventurous spirit, and yet strongly rooted in tradition. Perhaps they will bring a nation along with them.

INDEX

H

I

J

K

U

V

W

Y